P9-CBV-340

THE COLLECTOR'S ENCYCLOPEDIA OF

SECOND EDITION

A Reference and Value Guide

David Edwin Gifford

COLLECTOR BOOKS
A Division of Schroeder Publishing Co., Inc.

The current values in this book should be used only as a guide. They are not intended to set prices, which vary from one section of the country to another. Auction prices as well as dealer prices vary greatly and are affected by condition as well as demand. Neither the author nor the publisher assumes responsibility for any losses that might be incurred as a result of consulting this guide.

On the Cover:
Clockwise from center:

Missionware vase, 8", Early Niloak, $275.00 – 325.00 (+/-).

Hywood by Niloak, hand-thrown vase with applied handles, 9½", Ozark Dawn II, unmarked, $125.00 – 175.00.

Castware pitcher, 6", Art Deco/streamline design, George Peterson designs in *Ozark Blue,* Niloak block letters, $150.00 – 200.00 (+/-).

Hand-thrown vase with three applied handles, 5½", *Sea Green,* Hywood Art Pottery, Stoin glaze, $300.00 – 400.00 (+/-).

Castware ashtray, 4¼" x 3½", "Arkansas" with Pegasus, diamond (recessed) is a symbol of Arkansas, Niloak low relief, $75.00 – 100.00 (+/-).

Searching For A Publisher?

We are always looking for knowledgeable people considered to be experts within their fields. If you feel that there is a real need for a book on your collectible subject and have a large comprehensive collection, contact Collector Books.

Cover design by Beth Summers
Book layout by Karen Smith

COLLECTOR BOOKS
P.O. Box 3009
Paducah, Kentucky 42002-3009
www.collectorbooks.com

CONTENTS

Dedication

I gratefully dedicate this second edition to the late Lee Joe Alley and his family for their extreme generosity in sharing their family history with us; and last but not least, to Susanne R. Williams

Acknowledgments

I am indebted to many wonderful people and grateful for the help that enabled me to compile this first comprehensive book on Arkansas's famous Niloak pottery. As a historian, I have researched the manufacture of Arkansas art pottery. Now it's time to thank all those who have made this book possible.

First and foremost, I thank Jimmie W. Garner of Gadsden, Alabama, for changing my life in a positive way. Jimmie gave me direction and hope when I had none. He inspired me to be more than just average; to make something of myself. He encouraged me, a high school dropout, to earn my GED and enter college. Through a series of seemingly unrelated events, my first step ultimately became a life's work with purpose, fulfillment, and enjoyment. I can never repay you. Thank you Bos'n!

While attending the University of Central Arkansas (UCA) at Conway, Arkansas, I was fortunate to have Maurice C. Webb as my world history professor. He taught me to love history, what it meant, and why it is important to us all. It is to his credit that I chose to pursue a degree in history rather than medicine as originally planned.

During my days at UCA, I had the fortunate opportunity, thanks to Mrs. Bertha Jordan, to work under Tom W. Dillard, director of the University of Central Arkansas Archives and Special Collections. After becoming interested in my research on the Arkansas clay industry (from a seminar paper I wrote on Niloak Pottery for Dr. Waddy Moore) and reading my research, he offered to publish the Arkansas Art Pottery Bibliography through the UCA Archives in April 1989. Offering guidance and constructive criticism, he encouraged me to continue my research as well as my education in the public history field.

Niloak collectors Gary and Carrol Smith successfully argued for me to seek a contract with Collector Books to author a Niloak pottery price guide. At first I resisted the very notion, but their persuasion won me over, and I looked forward to correcting often misleading and contradicting information about Niloak pottery. Gary and Carrol introduced me to Bill Courter who coached me through. Thanks Mr. Courter! And thanks to Gary and Carrol for their continuous support, access to the ultimate castware collection, and most of all, their patience. I hope you two like "your" book!

Once things began to move, I contacted collectors and began locating Niloak pottery collections. Above all I thank Doyle Webb II who provided immediate permission to use his vast Missionware collection. Also to Virginia Lewis for sharing with me her extensive castware collection and helping me prepare for the huge pottery shoot. (Thanks as well to Cleta Gullion who convinced Mrs. Lewis to participate in the first place!) I am also grateful to many who agreed to loan items with no hesitation: Nellie Stucky Noble Blizzard and the late Grady Noble; Tom and Mary Dillard; both the late Dixie Drye and the late Hal Drye; Ed and June Freeman; Gretchen Freeman and Alan Silverman; Cleta W. Gullion; Bob Harris; Margaret and Seth Kinney; Arlene Hyten Rainey; Doyle and Ethel Tull; Walter Wright, Sr.; and Walter Wright, Jr. I learned of new collections and received permission to borrow pottery from Nita Alexander; Mr. and Mrs. Mike Bevins; Mr. and Mrs. Horace Boyld; Robert and Marilyn Chowning; Curtis Cox; Kenny and Stephannie Culpepper; Nettie Dacus; Leola Dove; Mrs. V.C. Elms; Jeff and Sonya Gerwin; Bob Gundoff; Norm and Barbara Haas; Bill and Tish Henslee; Linda Howard; Ken Hughes; Marilyn and the late Buck Jones; Laura Kaspar; Alice Moore LaPlant; Lori Lazar; Debbie Ledford; Tom Mathius; Susan McClendon; Esther Mitchell; the late Joe Otto; the late Dr. A. D. Parsons; Lynn Price; Al Treadway;

John and Linda Vile; Maurey Miller; Candy Webb; Mrs. Pat Wilbanks; the late Hardy L. Winburn IV; Perry and Darlene Yohe; and Billie and the late Bob Young.

I am truly indebted to many institutions, their staffs, historians, and other persons who helped me in my research: Tom W. Dillard, director, University of Central Arkansas Archives and Special Collections; Dr. John L. Ferguson, state historian, Arkansas History Commission; Dr. Bobby Roberts, director, Central Arkansas Library System; Valarie Thwing, former head of Interlibrary Loan, Central Arkansas Library System; Linda Pine, director, University of Arkansas at Little Rock Special Collections; William H. Long, former curator, Old State House; Dr. Michael Dabrishus, director, University of Arkansas Archives and Special Collections; Melba Laird and Billie Sharp of the Gann Museum; Joda Marano, Arkansas's Secretary of State Office; Martha Irby, Interlibrary Loan, Mitchell Memorial Library, Mississippi State University; Paul Evans, author of *Art Pottery of the United States*; Dr. Marion Nelson, author of *Art Pottery of the Midwest*; Deb and Gini Johnson, authors of *Beginner's Guide to American Art Pottery*; Ralph and Terry Kovel, authors of *Kovels' Collector's Guide to American Art Pottery*; Dr. James Houdeshell, author of *Houghton and Dalton Pottery* (and to Sara Barnes who referred me to Dr. Houdeshell); Harvey Duke, author of *Pottery and Porcelain*; Thomas G. Turnquist, author of *Denver's White Pottery*; the late Hardy L Winburn IV, former president, Winburn Tile Company; Virginia Heiss; Norman Haas; Nicol Knappen; the late George H. Wittenberg; the late Mrs. Anges Grant; Calvin Brown; Burdell and Doris Hall; Bette Bogart; Wes Garton; John Martin (who located the wonderful Niloak Pottery letterhead); Kenneth Mauney; James and Darlene Dommel; Tim Wells; and Bryon and Tamara Gunderson.

Over the past years, I have been fortunate in locating many persons (or their immediate family or descendants) who worked for or were associated with the Niloak Pottery Company. Their interest and graciousness in granting interviews and lending historically valuable materials is acknowledged wholeheartedly: Leola Dove and the late Charles Dove; Arlene Rainey and Norma Bush, daughters of Charles Hyten; Alice Moore Laplant; the late Howard S. Lewis; the late William F. Long (son of Frank Long); Mrs. Lydia Stoin; the late Hardy L. Winburn IV; the late Sinclair Winburn; A.V. Hutcheson; the late Mrs. Beatrice Sanders; and Mrs. Elsa Sanders Shannon.

I also want to thank Bob and Sharon Huxford for their encouragement and advice in helping me do this book; Doyle Beatty, who took vague oral instructions and made the shelves on which the pottery was photographed; and to Mrs. Sue Bryson for locating adequate facilities for the photographic session.

I am grateful to Cindy Momchilov of Camera Work and Gene Taylor, Old State House staff photographer, for the quality color and black and white photography. Both went beyond the call of duty.

I am most grateful to the following persons, knowledgeable about Niloak Pottery values, who helped me do the value guide: Gary and Carrol Smith, Jim Messineo, the late Dr. A. D. Parsons, John Edwards, Paul and Marla Frawner; Ann Greer, and Fred and Lila Schrader.

In addition, I am indebted to the late Hardy L. Winburn IV, former president of Winburn Tile Company, for allowing me access to the Niloak Pottery and Tile Corporation records, its directors/stockholders minutes, and scrapbooks. His kindness and help are most appreciated.

I want to thank my "editorial staff" who helped finalize the manuscript. I am appreciative of each perspective which substantially improved the text's integrity: Tom and Mary Dillard, Cheryl Gall, Sara Gifford, William "Bill" Long, Anne Nash, and Judy Rich. Moreover, I am indebted to Billy Schroeder, publisher of Collector Books, and my editor, Lisa Stroup, for their patience and for allowing this book to become a reality.

Also, I thank my former employer of over six years, Ruebel Funeral Home, which allowed me time to do tremendous amounts of research on the Arkansas clay industry and pursue my master's degree: Thanks to the late Jack Reed, the late George H. Wittenberg, Tom C. Wittenberg, Kenneth R. Culpepper, and staff.

Special appreciation goes to my mother, Sara Raymond Gifford, who has encouraged and supported my work, typed many pages, proofread drafts, and worked hard on this book in many ways. She once said she was only helping so that the book would get finished. She actually thought things would end with this publication. However, I am sorry to say Mother, I think this is just the beginning.

Last but certainly not least, my very special thanks go to Judy Rich. More than the support, advice, and encouragement she gave, she is just as responsible for getting this book finished as I am. Often working as hard as I have, she has had a hand in virtually every stage of production toward getting this book to Collector Books. From the initial work in locating pottery examples, to helping set up the plates and noting descriptions, recording my research, to typing and proofreading the manuscript, to loaning significant, key pieces from her impressive collection, and to making sure things were done right, she has been there for me all the way. Thank you Judy, I could not have done it without you.

PREFACE

Welcome to the second edition of the *Collector's Encyclopedia of Niloak Pottery*. Since its publication in 1993, while collectors nationwide have had a source to find information on Niloak Pottery, new and unusual pieces and more historical information have come to light. As a result, this second edition has been rewritten and revamped to bring collectors the most complete book on Niloak Pottery possible. Collectors will find hundreds of new or unusual pieces that have surfaced. Best estimates indicate that 99% of Niloak's castware production has been identified. This, of course, excludes Missionware production since its uniqueness will never allow every pattern or shape to be cataloged.

While much of the historical record is known, a vast amount is unknown. As readers have observed, there were gaps in the history simply due to the lack of historical data. This has been remedied to some extent as a great amount of new information has been introduced. Though the complete story will probably never be known, a better understanding of Niloak Pottery history is provided. The most important additions to the history of Niloak Pottery comes from the late Lee Joe Alley and his involvement at Niloak Pottery as a designer.

Mr. Alley, then living in California, but with family residing in Benton, received as a present the first edition of this book upon its publication. Surely much to his chagrin (and subsequently mine), his involvement was not even noted! While attempts were made to reach him prior to the first edition's publication, they proved unsuccessful. Thankfully, Joe Alley was a gentleman and would raise his hand and ask to beg the difference, so to speak, on Niloak Pottery's history of production during the later years. As a result of correspondence, telephone interviews, and a personal visit to his home, there is a better, more complete history of Niloak Pottery. For this reason, I first want to acknowledge and thank him for allowing me once again to enjoy the benefits of learning first hand the history of Niloak Pottery.

This publication, like the first, would not have been possible without the generous help and continued support of so many people. First I want to thank Billy Schroeder for agreeing to publish *Collector's Encyclopedia of Niloak Pottery* as a revised, second edition. I also want to thank my editor, Lisa Stroup, and her assistant, Amy Hopper, for their support. Through two serious disasters that threatened completion, Lisa's and Amy's support (and more importantly their patience) allowed this publication to become a reality. For additions and clarifications to historical record, I want to thank again the late Joe Alley as well as Mrs. Joe Alley, Ronald and Ella Ruth Alley, Ida Mae Milot (granddaughter of the late Arthur Dovey), Kathy and Rita Lewis (daughters of the late Howard Lewis), Dale Stoin (son of the late Stoin W. Stoin), Charles Tucker (Evans family), Brenda Johnson Escoto (granddaughter of late Fred Johnson), Mark Bassett, Joey Brackner, Harvey Duke, Paul Evans, Lance Gardner, Brenda F. Keech, Nicol Knappen, Melvin and Pat Minton, Dr. Marion John Nelson, Al Pilch, Laura Kasper, Shirley and Ira Slover, Nancy Williams, and Sarah F. Weston. I also want to thank and apologize to the Benton couple (I've lost their names) who loaned and allowed me to photocopy a file folder of historical documentation pertaining to Niloak Pottery!

Niloak Pottery collectors, again, played an important role in making this a more complete *Collector's Encyclopedia of Niloak Pottery.* I want to acknowledge Ronald and Ella Ruth Alley, Robert Berry, Cleta W. Gullion, Mom and Dad Haas, Bill and Kathy Henderson, Pat Hillis, Glenda Hooks, Kathleen Jackson, Virginia Lewis, Melvin and Pat Minton, L. Randall Mourning, Lynn Price, Bud, Katie, Bruce, and Beth Roberts, Molly Satterfield, Doyle and Ethel Tull, Doyle Webb, Roy and Dorothy Wright, and Walter Wright, Jr. I also want to thank the following institutions and their personnel who provided valuable assistance: Gail Moore and Dale Walters of the Old State House Museum; Tom Dillard and Tim Nutt of the Butler Center for Arkansas Studies at the Central Arkansas Library System; Roger Saft of the Fort Smith Public Library; and Swannee Bennett and Mr. Ebay Traitor (BW) of the Arkansas Territorial Restoration.

For good reasons, I want to thank the following persons to whom we all owe a great deal of appreciation. Without them, this book would have never been finished! First of all I want to thank Henryetta Vanaman (and Sister) for her help getting me past the problems with photography (disaster #1). Second, I want to thank Melvin and Pat Minton as well as Kathleen Jackson for going above and beyond the call of duty with help on photographing (I'll let Pat tell you the story). Third, a heartfelt appreciation goes to Stacy Brod for her voluminous help. Ms. Brod graciously volunteered to, for the lack of a better word, re-format my computer files on Niloak Pottery after my computer crashed (disaster #2). I am also thankful to her for her tedious and meticulous work on the computer graphic enhancements on a Eagle Pottery and Niloak Pottery advertisement as well as other images. Later, and on a last moment notice, Stacy Brod and my mother, Saralou R. Gifford, literally re-typed the entire text chapters so as to facilitate the updating of information in this second edition. Fourth, I want to thank Rita Andrews of the Old State House Museum for her generous help with providing last minute images for this book.

I am appreciative of the support of Rhonda Camp, James and Judy Rich-Clements, Rex Decker, Tony Freyaldenhoven, Saralou R. Gifford, Norm and Barbara Haas, Virginia Heiss, Ida Herrin, Bill and Donna Hodge, and not to forget, Miss eb, Miss SS, Big Al, and Holly Jo. I want to apologize for leaving out Dr. Shastri and Ken Hughes's name in the first edition's acknowledgments and misspelling the names of contributors Lydia Stoin and Jim Messineo.

Finally, I must thank my mother and Susanne for helping me finish this book. I could not have done it without them.

INTRODUCTION

For nearly 30 years, Niloak Pottery has been collected nationally. This revised edition continues to be based on intensive and exhaustive research into primary sources. Although Missionware and now the industrial castware have been the collectors' focus for many years, Eagle and Niloak's stoneware have become more and more collectible. Niloak's Hywood Art Pottery had been relatively unknown since few collectors knew of its connection to the Niloak Pottery Company. Hywood Art Pottery remains, however, relatively scarce, if not rare. As widely known and appreciated as the pottery has been, Niloak's history had never been researched extensively or published until Collector Books published the first edition in 1993. Virtually all of the previously published accounts relied only on secondary sources and thus perpetuated considerable misinformation based on local traditions and an uncritical acceptance of early accounts of Niloak as well as the company's own promotional hype.

I am still a revisionist in my approach to the history of the Niloak Pottery Company. This research is a work in progress as I continue to search for new information. Even as I re-write this introduction (February 2000), I am hopeful of securing new data that might lead to changing a major conclusion about just who is responsible for the swirl concept in Arkansas. My efforts of the past 14 years have uncovered vast amounts of new data as well as never-before-seen photographs, catalogs, memorabilia, and other literature. The ceramics industry in Arkansas is a rich area for research, and I will continue to seek answers to many of the questions that remain. They include issues such as Charles Hyten's connection to Ouachita Pottery, Arthur Dovey's relationship with Hyten, and what led them to form a pottery company in Benton by 1909. Who is responsible for the commercially viable swirl concept at Niloak Pottery and what roles did other Eagle Pottery employees play? What was Niloak's production in the early years with respect to decorated wares? Last, what was the extent and validity of Niloak's connection with the Arts and Crafts Movement?

All the factors that led to the development of Niloak Pottery will probably never be fully ascertained. But some interesting circumstances, beginning in 1904, are noteworthy. The 1904 St. Louis World's Fair, celebrating the centennial of the purchase of the Louisiana Territory in 1803, brought together the possibilities for the eventual establishment of Niloak Pottery's Missionware production in 1910. These possibilities involve the fair's many pottery exhibitions, the Arkansas visitors, and the inevitable discussions resulting from a concentration of like-minded potters, ceramists, and clay-capitalists. It is probable that Hyten attended the 1904 St. Louis World's Fair (Fred Johnson is said to have been there). Hyten and/or Johnson may have begun relationships with other pottery companies' employees as well as the owners or employees of the Ouachita Pottery of St. Louis at that time. Or if Arthur Dovey attended, as a part of the team from fair exhibitor Rookwood Pottery, his employer at that time, he and possibly Hyten/Johnson may have had a glimpse of a new type of pottery thrown by a potter named George Ohr.

George Ohr of Biloxi, Mississippi, the self-proclaimed "Mad Potter of Biloxi," was a master at pottery throwing and glazing. With hand-thrown vessels, egg-shell thin, and glazes of unconventional coloration, he established by himself an impressive art pottery operation by the turn of the century. Ohr's operation, furthermore, may be an important connection to a part of the development of the Arkansas art pottery industry since he produced a swirl product called "scroddled" pottery. Research indicates that it was in production sometime during the years 1902 and 1907. Possibly in production for the 1904 World's Fair at St. Louis, it could have been seen by individuals who later established the Ouachita Pottery in Hot Springs and the Niloak Pottery operation in Benton, Arkansas, a few years later. If a clay industry were to develop in Arkansas, a better understanding of quantity, location, and quality was needed, and Dr. John C. Branner, the State Geologist for Arkansas, undertook an exhaustive study to locate and describe clays found throughout the state.

Published in 1908, Professor Branner's *The Clays of Arkansas* was the first in-depth analysis of Arkansas clays that included a comprehensive look at the various types and quantities and qualities of these clays. In Saline County, the existence of pottery clays had been known and utilized for many years. "That Benton is well supplied with excellent clays for the manufacture of the common grades of stoneware and pottery," Branner wrote, "is a fact established by the experience of many years." Many Benton potters opened "pits" to furnish clays for their potteries. For one particular pit, "Woosley," which undoubtedly furnished clays for the Eagle Pottery (predecessor to Niloak Pottery), Branner noted that the clays ran 5 to 6 feet thick, covered about 1⅓ acres, was located on "'the old military road leading northeastward from Benton," and was "the finest clay in the district." While claims might have been exaggerated and hopes set too high, the fact that Arkansas had workable clays is true. It just needed the combination of capital, personnel, and a desire to create an industry.

Arkansas's mineral wealth, including clays in the central area of the state, also received much publicity for the promotion of Arkansas's potential as it related to the state's industrial progress. Much of the responsibility, perhaps, for the beginning of a different pottery industry is the result of the promotional efforts of newspapers in general and individuals like Professor W. S. Thomas of Alexander in particular. Back in 1904, the *Arkansas Democrat* wrote an extensive article on the "prosperous and progressive" city of Benton. Among other things, the paper stated: "Within the past few years the underground wealth of the county has attracted the attention of the miner and capitalist at home and aboard...[and that] beds of kaolin of unusual quantity are found only a short distance North of Benton." Professor Thomas, who reported on Saline County's clay deposits in 1908 and advocated a clay industry for Arkansas, held great hope that the Benton area could become a southern ceramics center. As reported in the *Arkansas Gazette,* Thomas discovered deposits of kaolin in abundance "that seem adapted to the higher ceramic uses."

Hyten seemed to acknowledge these comments in 1911 when he noted that "not many years ago" kaolin clay was discovered in the area. Did the *Arkansas Democrat* and Professor Thomas's statements infect Hyten with "clay fever" and cause him to contact his "friend" Dovey in Missouri and begin efforts toward art pottery manufacture? Or did Dovey, who possibly still had contacts in Arkansas, become aware of this information and eventually connect with Hyten? Arkansas ranked 28th in the nation in the production of clay products during this time. There were 58 Arkansas establishments, the majority engaged in manufacturing bricks and tiles. There were only three potteries making stoneware and other miscellaneous clay products, and they employed less than twenty people. With clay deposits being investigated and developed statewide, a modern ceramic industry seemed inevitable.

Fortunately for American art pottery collectors, the activities of the Ouachita Pottery Company in nearby Hot Springs soon changed forever the emphasis and identity of Benton's Eagle Pottery operation. Perhaps inspired by the nationwide American art pottery movement and the neighboring Ouachita Pottery, there was, in 1909, a shift in the emphasis of Eagle Pottery from utilitarian ware to art pottery. And eventually a name for the new product, Niloak — the word kaolin spelled backward. Disregarding the misinformation, what is known is that Dovey threw swirl pottery for the Ouachita Pottery and arrived in Benton in 1909 to help set the direction for Arkansas's second art pottery company.

This book examines Niloak's history without reliance on secondary sources, numerous articles in modern, popular media, and traditional lore. Long thought to be the creative genius of Charles Hyten, Missionware may have actually come from the knowledge and skills possessed by Arthur Dovey, Fred Johnson, Frank Ira Long, Matt Carlton, and/or the McNeil family. As at Ouachita, the combination of clay, capital, and personnel mixed well in the beginning to set the foundation for the first of two successful potteries in Arkansas during the early twentieth century. The employment of Arthur Dovey from Rookwood not only enabled Ouachita Pottery to make art pottery, but set the foundation for Niloak's eventual success in Missionware manufacture. Ouachita Pottery in an attempt to "build a million dollar plant," wanted to create an industry (just as Camark Pottery wanted to do years later) to compete and, more importantly, rival the potteries in Ohio. The Hot Springs venture ultimately failed, yet to its credit, the Ouachita Pottery brought Arkansas into the American art pottery mainstream.

In 1908, after three years at Ouachita Pottery, Dovey went to work for Ouachita's sister operation in St. Louis. After a year in Missouri, Dovey returned to Arkansas to work with Hyten on the development of an art pottery operation at Benton. Dovey undoubtedly played a major role, as he possessed both the knowledge of pottery making and the specifics of the swirl technique. Dovey purchased property from Hyten, which might have been Dovey's investment in the venture, and worked with Hyten at the yet-to-be-named Niloak Pottery Company. It was a marriage of necessity. While Dovey contributed technical and artistic abilities, Hyten owned the plant, employed experienced potters, and possessed the clays. More importantly, Hyten had connections in Benton's business circles and thus was able to raise needed capital (primarily from prominent Benton families to whom he was related). From this partnership, the Eagle Pottery and Niloak Pottery of Benton would realize for Arkansas a unique and special place in American material culture.

For nearly a year, the potters at Eagle Pottery experimented to make the swirl pottery concept a viable, commercial reality. Hyten then turned to Frederick W. Sanders, a long-time family friend and Little Rock businessman, to help promote Niloak Pottery, one of the major reasons for Niloak's success in the early years. Although Dovey subsequently left Arkansas, Hyten persevered in the effort to make Niloak Pottery a viable business. Niloak was Arkansas's only pottery concern, for more than fifteen years, until the Camark Pottery was formed in Camden, Arkansas, in 1926.

Niloak Pottery grew out of a small utilitarian pottery using the creative experiences of Arthur Dovey and others, and the ambitions of Charles Hyten. Without a doubt, Hyten sought to do more than continue a family business that faced a slow but certain death in the face of industrialism. Exactly how Dovey and Hyten came to know each other may never be known. Regardless, the teaming of Dovey's knowledge, Hyten's physical assets, and the experiences of other Eagle Pottery's employees led to the creation of the Niloak Pottery and the production of a totally different and unique American art pottery. While not the first to make swirl pottery, Eagle's commercial venture with production based primarily on swirl pottery deserves recognition.

More importantly, recognition for developing the swirl technique at Niloak Pottery should not go to Hyten, in spite of the fact that family lore and promotional hyperbole states Hyten as the creative genius of the swirl pottery concept. If anything, Hyten can only be credited with helping to perfect, popularize, and patent the technique and ironically, in a move away from art pottery, he was most probably responsible for the standardization of Missionware. Possibly the creative product of Dovey or other local potters like Fred Johnson, the concept was unique in its technique of mixing and throwing artificially colored clay into shapes with one-of-a-kind swirl patterns.

In the many promotional efforts by Arkansas boosters, this Arkansas-based product, Niloak Pottery, was used as an example of the possibilities Arkansas possessed. The first commercially viable product of its kind, Niloak Missionware quickly became popular for its uniqueness, as the aesthetics of other American art pottery came from either applied exterior decorations or from applications of glaze. Thus the potential for promoting Benton's art pottery industry (and the city of Benton itself) was tapped in the beginning by the manner in which the pottery was marked. Eagle's Niloak line was first marked "Niloak Pottery, Benton, Ark." (See Marks #1 and 2.) James F. Lee, cashier of the People's Bank and president of the Benton's Business Men League (in addition to being an early capitalist in the Niloak Company), sought this promotion of Benton through manufacturing efforts as early as 1906 when Benton secured the Owosso Manufacturing Company (makers of screen doors and windows). He stated: "The products of the [Owosso] plant with the name 'Benton, Ark.' on every piece will go into thousands of homes in the South, Southwest, and West and the town becomes a household word throughout the country."

Benton was also ideally suited for the tourist trade, and Niloak certainly benefited from it. As Benton was situated on the railroad midway between Little Rock and Malvern (the railway connection for travelers to and from the Hot Springs spa resort), many tourists over the years frequented the pottery. The railroad as well facilitated Niloak's marketing outside the region. Niloak and later Camark Pottery were the only active pottery industries in Arkansas during the mid to late twentieth century although many state geologists, businessmen, and interested parties sought to develop a statewide clay industry. Despite all the promotion, no major center for clay manufacturing ever developed in Arkansas or the South. Nonetheless, Niloak Pottery held on for over

40 years and produced huge amounts of ceramics as the company struggled through World War I, the Depression, and World War II.

Niloak's Missionware and castware were not local developments. Although they used local clays and for the most part local clay-workers (this is not to say the local potters were not invaluable), Niloak Pottery had to rely on experienced potters, ceramists, designers, and artisans from outside the state, especially from Ohio. While all their efforts brought both artistic expression and commercial viability, this network of itinerant potters provided a national connection to the American art pottery movement. Arkansas had an abundance of clay, but the lack of educated personnel in certain production areas was a major issue. This made the hiring of ceramists like Stoin M. Stoin (creator of the Hywood Art Pottery line), Howard S. Lewis (creator of the Hywood by Niloak line), as well as designers like Rudy Ganz and George Peterson essential. Lee Joe Alley, the last known designer on the Niloak staff, seems to be the only local to rise to this particular level. It is all too probable that without these experienced, out-of-state clay-workers, Arkansas's potters might never have been more than suppliers of utilitarian ware for local and regional markets. Without a doubt, Niloak Pottery benefited from their experience that brought some of its wares into the mainstream of the American art pottery movement. Niloak needed these experienced out-of-state workers to provide the technical skills and the artistic ability needed to produce art pottery and their previous work experiences contributed to what we may call an Arkansas art pottery movement.

Finally, Eagle's introduction of Missionware with its swirling pattern effect, was, however, not new in any sense. In fact, it was ancient! Interestingly enough, swirl production in the twentieth century is only the latest chapter of an old story. Since ancient times, swirl wares or wares with a marbleized effect have been known. Supposedly originating in Egypt, the technique moved into Crete, over to Rome, then China, and finally into Europe by the sixteenth century. Often utilizing mixed slips, glazes, and colored clays, virtually every country made a "marbled ware since it was first devised to imitate stone...." Marbled, swirl-like patterns have been made by many groups and date back perhaps 1,500 years. A Chinese technique of making marble ware dates back to at least 600 – 700 AD with the Tang Dynasty.

Niloak's Missionware is distinguished by an upwardly, clockwise spiraling design motif, and its early production can be differentiated by soft colors and sometimes blurred lines. Apparent from Niloak's later production, the early pieces accurately portray the beginnings of another Arkansas art pottery manufacturing concern within the scope of the American art pottery movement.

George Ohr's "scroddled" pottery, c. 1905.

History of Eagle Pottery

The documented story of Arkansas pottery manufacture began in 1843 with the Bird Pottery of Clark County, but it was only after the Civil War that the pottery industry in Central Arkansas began in earnest. Lafayette Glass, a potter from Dallas County, who apparently learned the pottery trade from a black slave about the time of the Civil War, "established the industry" in Saline County by 1870. Shortly thereafter, "Saline County actually dominated pottery production in the state...." The utilitarian producing potteries existed in the area which became known as the old pottery shop hill. During the 1880s and 1890s, there were several pottery and brick operations in or near Benton.

In the 1880s, there were at least five potteries which made the stoneware business the chief industry in Benton at that time. These included the Alfred Wilbur Pottery and the Dixie Stoneware Company. By the early 1890s, there were potteries operated by Lee Davis, Samuel Henderson, and David Womack. There may also have been plans for utilizing the local clays for a tile company as there were various announcements that machinery for a tiling factory had arrived in Benton. However, to date, no tiles known to have been made in Benton have surfaced.

Charles Dean "Bullet" Hyten grew up in the world of jug and crockery manufacturing. Charles, since childhood, had the nickname "Bullet," and throughout his life, he was known personally, socially, and professionally as Bullet Hyten. Born in 1877, shortly after the Hyten family relocated to Arkansas from Missouri, Charles Hyten spent his childhood days in and around Benton's pottery shops. Bullet Hyten was a second generation potter. His father, John Hyten, had worked at a pottery back in Missouri and worked at a pottery in Benton until his death. John Hyten began work at a business that may have started back in 1868. After John Hyten's death in 1881, Frank Woosley took charge of the pottery and eventually married Charles's widowed

Eagle Pottery postcard, c. 1915. ***Courtesy of Steven Hanley.***

mother. Afterwards, Charles Hyten would work with his stepfather, Frank Woosley and later with his brothers Lee and Paul before having complete control of the works around 1900.

In 1895, the Woosleys moved back to Frank's Ohio homeplace. Hyten and his two brothers, however, elected to remain in Benton and take charge of the pottery. By 1897, the business was known as the Hyten Bros. Pottery. As with the majority of pottery production in Arkansas, few potters took the time to mark their wares. Hyten Bros. Pottery was no exception and to date only a couple of pieces have surfaced with the Hyten Bros. Pottery signature. Its production consisted of jugs, crocks, and churns for the local, state, and (possibly) regional markets. According to Bullet Hyten's daughter, Arlene Rainey, the pottery, either Hyten Bros. or Eagle, was shipped into eastern Arkansas on board the steamer A. R. Bragg by the Black and Current River Packet Company.

During the late nineteenth century, Charles Dean Hyten developed the skills necessary to continue the family business and, as fate would have it, to own and operate the famous Niloak Pottery Company of Benton, Arkansas. Charles Hyten would soon be the last family member in the pottery business. For unknown reasons, his brothers Paul and Lee would leave this family pottery for other work. For the historical record, conflicting statements put Charles Hyten's sole ownership of the family business between 1900 and 1901. Hyten Bros. Pottery is listed in Arkansas gazetteers for the years 1898 and 1900 along with at least five other potteries, including the Smith & Warren Pottery. Family tradition put Hyten in partnership with Alfred Warren and the company was named Eagle Pottery by 1901. It is definite, though, that the company was named Eagle Pottery by 1904.

The *Arkansas Democrat* wrote about the pottery during 1904, stating Eagle Pottery was the "largest pottery ware business" as well as the "leading stoneware business" in or near Benton, adding that there had been a recent expansion with new infusion of capital and equipment. Furthermore, according to the article, Hyten had just burned 5,300 gallons (production of stoneware is measured in how many gallons the number of pieces collectively hold) in his new down draft "Stewart patent kiln" with little breakage, and he was preparing another firing of 6,000 gallons (the kiln's stated capacity). The *Arkansas Democrat* identified the company as the "Eagle Pottery Works" with employees numbering about 20. The clay came from a source "lying conveniently" near Hyten's shop. Its products included "all kinds of crockery wares, churns, jugs, milk pans, jars, and flower pots" with more equipment soon to be added for the manufacture of "white ware." Hyten is listed in another Arkansas state gazetteer (a paid entry) as the only pottery in Benton. Although the early business history of the Hyten family is very sketchy, Eagle Pottery was one of the few, if not the last, fully operational pottery in Benton after about 1905.

Dr. John C. Branner, Arkansas State Geologist, compiled for the U.S. government the first major publication on Arkansas clays. Entitled *The Clays of Arkansas,* research had taken place over many years before its publication in 1908. Branner's entry for the Eagle Pottery stated it was located about one and a half miles from Benton, had a wood-burning kiln and had the capacity to make between 800 and 900 gallons of crockery per day. It took six and one half pounds of clay to make a one-gallon vessel, and its clay came from two different pits. One clay pit had a "chocolate color," and the other source was a "dark-blue stratified clay." A mixture of equal amounts of each clay burned to a "beautiful buff color." This is another major fact that leads to the conclusion that Missionware was indeed produced with artificial colored clays. Continuing the making of traditional utilitarian wares started by his father, Hyten's Eagle Pottery was one of, if not the most, successful stoneware pottery operations in Benton.

By now Hyten was the sole owner of the Eagle Pottery Company which had a fine "reputation [for] white and brown glazed ware." This shiny "brown" glazed ware, one of the most common glazes of the "Albany" slips, was one of the most popular colors among potters. The company had new equipment and had increased production a full 65 percent. Eagle's daily capacity was 1000 gallons with products including jugs, churns, flower pots, pitchers, and jars ranging from a quart to 25 gallons. This new equipment was undoubt-

The Eagle Pottery

C. D. HYTEN, Proprietor.

Manufacturer of High Grade

Commercial Stoneware

Such as

Jugs, Jars, Churns, Flower Pots, Etc.

We have also an Art Pottery Department, which is the only one south of Ohio. In this department is made the most beautiful and artistic pottery.

Office and Plant at Benton, Ark.

Eagle Pottery advertisement, 1909. ***Courtesy of the Butler Center for Arkansas Studies, Central Arkansas Library System.***

Rare Eagle Pottery butter crock, c. 1905.
Courtesy of the Gann Museum, Benton, Arkansas.

edly part of the equipment that was readying Eagle to begin work on Missionware.

The Hot Springs paper, the *Sentinel Record,* stated in 1910 that the Eagle Pottery Company was an exhibitor at the annual Arkansas state fair in Hot Springs during October. Moreover, the *Arkansas Gazette* reported that "the Benton Pottery Works of Benton presented Roosevelt with a costly souvenir" when he opened the fair. Confusion arises in that there is no historical record for the name Benton Pottery Works. Since Missionware was in production, it is probable that a piece of this new American art pottery was given to the former President as it is seems improbable that any piece of Arkansas stoneware could be described as a "costly souvenir" in 1910.

By 1913, Charles Hyten owned and operated Eagle Pottery (he was only manager of the Niloak Pottery) with employees numbering 10 to 18, depending on both seasonal factors and supply and demand. Its products included a "class of jugs [that] command the patronage of the largest jug consumers in Arkansas and other states." Throughout the teens and the rest of the history of the Niloak Pottery Company, utilitarian ware remained a part of the company's production. At times, in the late teens and early 1920s as well as the early years of the Depression, utilitarian production was very important, if not vital to the company's survival.

Whenever Missionware manufacture was limited due to demand, Hyten repeatedly turned to stoneware production. In 1918, toward the end of World War I, the Eagle Pottery company had its first known advertisement since 1909, asking consumers and neighbors to do "a patriotic service" by buying stoneware so as to conserve "tin for more important purposes." Furthermore, it encouraged buyers to order stoneware together to get reduced prices. If neighbors together placed an order for 100 gallons or more, their price would be 12½ cents per gallon; otherwise, an order of less than 100 gallons would cost 15 cents per gallon. By the mid 1920s, stoneware manufacture was more active than in previous years with production at capacity requiring massive amounts of overtime to meet demands.

Unfortunately, after the mid 1920s, very little has been uncovered about the utilitarian production of Eagle Pottery, then Niloak Pottery. By late 1928, products like "sewer pipe well curbing" became a part of the production. In 1931, Art Wilbur, whose family had been associated with many pottery operations in Arkansas since at least the 1880s, was manager of the Eagle plant with nine employees. The Eagle Pottery remained a separate business entity, at least in the marking of pottery, until after 1934 when the Eagle name (and the Hywood name) were dropped. Joe Alley, a designer for Niloak, remembered that stoneware was made by Josh and Romine McNeil (also long time Niloak employees) in the late 1930s and early 1940s. Thus it would appear that stoneware manufacture continued until Niloak's conversion to the Winburn Tile Company. The contributions of these utilitarian works are immeasurable and one point is clear: It provided work for locals citizens and utilized local resources for the economic advantage and growth of both Benton and Saline County.

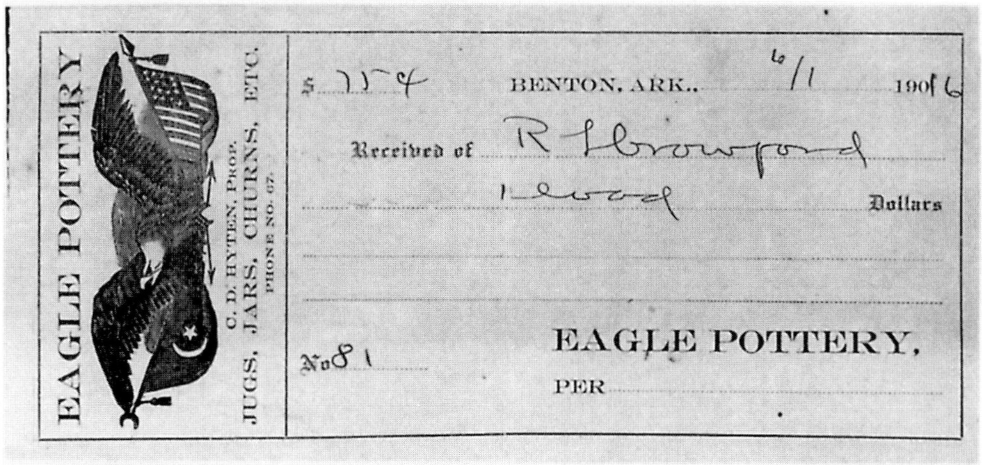
EAGLE POTTERY

C. D. HYTEN, PROP.
JUGS, JARS, CHURNS, ETC.
PHONE NO. 67.

$ BENTON, ARK., 6/1 1916

Received of

Dollars

No 81

EAGLE POTTERY,
PER

Eagle Pottery receipt, 1916. ***Author's collection.***

History of Niloak

It's been over 90 years since Eagle Pottery introduced its radically new and different art pottery. With extensive research, many questions have been answered, some questions have been left unanswered, and too many new, sometimes difficult, questions have surfaced. These new questions demand a complete review of the historical record. The two most important questions left unanswered are interrelated: First, what was the relationship between the employees of the Ouachita Pottery and the Eagle Pottery Companies? Second, who was responsible for the commercially viable swirl concept in Arkansas? Circumstantial evidence does exist that Charles Hyten was aware of Arkansas's first art pottery company. Although no direct relationship has been established between the two companies, the proximity of the two cities (less than 30 miles apart with regular railroad transportation between them) and the fact that Ouachita Pottery exhibited at Arkansas's first and second state fairs in 1906 and 1907, and advertised regularly, leads one to speculate that Charles Hyten had to have ventured over to Hot Springs to learn about a related business.

Hyten did establish a relationship with two Ouachita employees, Arthur Dovey, former Rookwood potter, and Paul E. Cox. The important unanswered question is when these relationships started. In 1908 Dovey went to work in Missouri but returned to Arkansas the following year to help Hyten with the development of an art pottery operation at Benton. Cox, who left for Newcomb College at New Orleans and later headed the ceramic department at Iowa State College in Ames, had an association with Hyten which lasted into the 1930s. Dovey undoubtedly played the more important role, as he possessed general knowledge of pottery making and knew at least the specifics of throwing the swirl technique.

During Dovey's brief stay in Benton, several occurrences are noteworthy. In late July 1910, Arthur Dovey purchased a plot of land from Charles Hyten and this purchase may have been Dovey's investment in their venture. During the latter half of 1910, it is evident (i.e. existence of the patent pend'g mark) that someone undertook an attempt to patent the Missionware line. By late December 1910, Dovey had sold his property and departed Arkansas in February 1911. These series of events (the quick land transactions, the failed patent attempt, and Dovey's departure) seem to point to a conclusion that either someone maligned Dovey's efforts and he left under bad terms, or that Dovey simply had a better offer (he went to work for the Valentien Pottery in California after leaving Arkansas). Yet confusing facts dealing with the company's history are not uncommon in researching Niloak Pottery, as will be shown in the case of just who invented Niloak's Missionware.

Left: Ouachita Pottery plant interior, Pleasant Street, Hot Springs, 1906; Arthur Dovey, left foreground. Right: Close up of swirl pottery. *Courtesy of Dovey's granddaughter, Ida Mae Milot, and Paul Evans, author of Art Pottery of the United States.*

Charles Dean "Bullet" Hyten, circa 1911. ***Courtesy of University of the Arkansas Archives and Special Collections.***

Unbeknownst to everyone until Paul Evans, the eminent historian of American art pottery and author of *Art Pottery of the United States,* located photographic documentation in the Dovey family's possession, Ouachita Pottery (in 1906) produced a swirl pottery! While no examples of Ouachita swirl have surfaced, the existence of photographic evidence is enough to make one certain point: Dovey was more than a potter; he was undoubtedly a skilled ceramist and his experiences helped launch Eagle Pottery's Niloak Missionware line in February 1909. It is possible that Dovey, knowing about the clays in Saline County, sought work with Hyten in manufacturing swirl pottery that he knew how to produce. A new and developing twist to just who developed the swirl concept comes from the family of Fred Johnson, a long-time potter at Niloak Pottery.

Although not substantiated with historical documentation, the Johnson family history contends that it was Fred Johnson who, having supposedly worked for Ouachita Pottery before moving over to Eagle Pottery, invented the commercially viable swirl product! Moreover, it was Johnson who toiled over the swirl technique for many years to get the process to the point of having a patent issued, not in Fred Johnson's name, however, but in Hyten's name alone. Unfortunately no substantial evidence has been uncovered yet to explain how and why things occurred as they did. Nonetheless, some facts speak for themselves. Inspired to create artistic wares, or just desiring to keep his business open in the face of slowly decreasing demands for his jugs, crocks, and the like, Charles Hyten, along with Arthur Dovey, Fred Johnson, and perhaps others planned and initiated the necessary steps to create a new type of art pottery which had no rival in the world.

Setting the responsibility of the swirl concept aside, it was a marriage of necessity as both these men needed one another. While Dovey contributed technical and artistic abilities, Hyten had connections in the business circles of Benton and was able to raise needed capital. Prominent local businessmen headed the 1909 list of organizers, including Arthur Dovey, Charles Hyten, Elijah Y. Stinson, John J. Beavers, James F. Lee, George Brown, W. H. Lawer, A. W. Warren, and Dr. Dewell Gann. The capital stock was $10,000 with $2,000 invested. Utilizing this capital, Dovey and Hyten spent February 1, 1909, in Little Rock, purchasing equipment to supplement what already existed in Benton "to establish a plant for the manufacture of art pottery." Potters like the Johnsons, Carltons, Rowlands, and others no doubt provided, at the very least, their particular ceramic skills at the plant, located on Pearl Street at the end of South Market Street. The equipment for the plant included a new kiln "exclusively for the burning of the finest Bric-a-Brac ware." "Bric-a-Brac ware" did not have the same connotation back then as it does today. It is a keyword for the better ceramics including art pottery. The new line "is certain to be a winner, as nowhere is this line made that will compare with [the Niloak] ware, except at the works of the art potteries at Zanesville, and the famous Rookwood Pottery of Cincinnati, Ohio...." It is possible that this new line was going to be marketed as Eagle Pottery, as one early piece has surfaced with an Eagle Pottery circle ink stamp commonly found on the utilitarian wares. This known example may indicate that production was achieved during late 1909, but the name changed by early 1910.

Building of kiln in Benton under the supervision of Tom Glass, c. 1930s. ***Courtesy of the late Hardy L. Winburn IV.***

Eagle Pottery plant, Hyten to the right of large Missionware vase, 1911. This vase is in the possession of the Dovey family. ***Author's collection.***

The optimistic organizers hoped to begin production in early 1909. However, production did not begin until at least January 1910. Many difficulties and delays were obviously encountered in perfecting the swirl process, but the technique was refined to the extent that a salable product was achieved by March 1910 — this product now called Niloak and manufactured by The Eagle Pottery Company. The pottery's production during the early years was limited. Dovey threw many of the pieces before his departure. In addition to being at least partly responsible for bringing the swirl pottery concept to a commercial reality, Dovey is obviously responsible for producing some glazed, decorated wares of which none to date have surfaced.

While Hyten did not own a part of the corporation at this time, he was the company's manager. It is apparent that while Hyten managed the Niloak Pottery, he still owned and operated his Eagle Pottery. It's probable that the Niloak incorporators and Hyten made an agreement to let Hyten keep his Eagle Pottery while operating Niloak Pottery. This seems reasonable as none of the financial backers had much experience running a pottery plant, much less making art pottery. By the end of 1911, however, Hyten became financially involved in the Niloak company. The "Financial Report of The Niloak Pottery" filed February 3, 1912, shows that most of the Niloak directors had increased their share holdings with Hyten now owning 40 shares.

The origin of the name Niloak (kaolin spelled backward) is unknown. It is likely that the idea of how the name was derived came from Arthur Dovey. It had been a common practice for pottery companies to create names for their companies and/or the individual lines they produced. For example, Weller Pottery had a line called Louwelsa that combined the first three letters of Sam A. Weller's daughter's name (Louise), the first three letter of his last name (Weller) and his initials (S. A.). Teco Pottery is derived from the first two letters of the first two words in the company's name, Terra Cotta Tile Works. Finally, many years later, Hardy or his brother Sinclair Winburn used this old trick to spin off a comical spelling of porcelain. They combined "por" (from porcelain) with saline (Saline county is where Benton is located) to coin "Porsaline" as their name for the clay mixture Niloak Pottery developed for castware production during World War II. Knowing or probably familiar with these plays on words, Dovey may have at least jump started the idea to create an unique name for the pottery.

As local tradition has it, Niloak was first offered for sale at the Bush Drug and Jewelry Company of Benton. Niloak Pottery caught the attention of many in and around Benton and Little Rock. Moreover, tradition has it that Bush's display resulted in immediate sales to tourists who, waiting for their trains to depart, wandered uptown and purchased pieces as souvenirs of their visit to Arkansas. Within a couple of years, Niloak Pottery was a well-known Benton business. A key factor in Niloak's initial success was the family relationship between the Hytens and F. W. Sanders of Little Rock. Frederick W. Sanders operated Sanders & Company on Main Street and was a dealer in glassware, china, and pottery.

Beginning in 1910, Sanders & Company was the sole distributor of Niloak pottery outside of Benton. A well-known jobber to many companies in the South and East, Sanders promoted Niloak pottery through his many contacts with merchants, retailers, and wholesalers. The earliest known Sanders advertisement, in a March 1910 issue of the *Arkansas Gazette,* announced: "Beautiful Art Pottery from Benton, Ark.," with "[r]ich glazed effects [and] soft matt finishes." Existing early pieces indicate that production centered on dull-finishing of the clay swirl. On the other hand, a few surviving examples of exterior clear glazed pieces suggest that efforts were made to produce a glazed ware (similar to the Rookwood "Standard glaze") as potteries were doing in Ohio. This technique, used infrequently, was dropped by 1911 because either the line was not selling or the clear glaze often darkened to such an extent that the swirls were obscured.

The first exhibition of Niloak pottery (and most likely its national debut) came in March 1910 at the Marion Hotel in Little Rock during a land congress convention boosting Arkansas economic advantages and development. Apparently a big hit among the public, a selection of the pottery, "beautifully striped with colored earths," was incorporated into the Missouri Pacific Railway's exhibit at the United States Land and Irrigation Exhibition in Chicago later that year. From all indications, 1910 was a successful first year for the Eagle Pottery Company's manufacture of Niloak with increased attention and sales of this "wholly natural" and unique Arkansas product. Niloak Pottery's initial successes led to the inclusion of its own exhibit in the "Arkansas on Wheels" tour, a state-wide advertising campaign for economic development that toured the Northeast in 1911. The *Arkansas Democrat* reported that the "Niloak pottery of Benton has a choice display" on the train. Falsely advertised as "wholly natural" (its colors were actually produced with oxides; cobalt for blue, ferric for red, etc.), Niloak sold thousands of dollars worth of this unique Arkansas product to several large northern retail houses.

In May 1911, after months of preparation, the United Confederate Veterans converged on Little Rock for its annual reunion. In response to the grand event, the *Arkansas Democrat* published an oversize commemorative issue that contained the first extensive history of Niloak Pottery with two unique photographs. One general characteristic of promotional literature by Niloak was unabashed hyperbole. One statement revealed that "experts...claimed the Niloak far superior to the famous Rookwood ware in every way...." The article commented further that the "freakish" designs caused a brisk national sale, that popular acceptance by the public resulted in enormous demands, and that "over the past two years" as many as 25 potters were employed. Moreover, this immense success led the company to make plans to "manufacture this magnificent ware on a more elaborate scale." From all indications, Niloak enjoyed an initial popularity as it caught the eye of the public as the first successful art pottery devoid of the typical decorations and glaze manipulations associated with other United States potteries.

The success of Niloak Pottery can also be contributed to the work force at Benton. In the 1910 United State Census, over 20 persons are identified with unnamed potteries as either laborers, throwers, or owners. Long ignored by local researchers (including myself), these potters undoubtedly contributed greatly to the development of the swirl concept early on, but more importantly, they set the foundation that Niloak built upon for the next 40 years. Persons included on this census, and are known to or likely to have worked at Eagle/Niloak Pottery, include George. E. Wilbur, Alfred E. Wilbur, J. E. Johnson, J. Rowland, Colonel McNeil and his sons Romine and Joshua, Charles Glass, Matt C. Carlton, Alvin Carlton, Fred Johnson, Paul Hyten, and Frank Ira Long. Some of these potters had been "potting" for over 30 years in the Benton area. Arthur Dovey is listed as well and it's interesting to note that while these potters listed their occupations as "throwers," Dovey stated his as a "turner." They mean the same thing.

Long-time Niloak potters, who show up in historical materials later on, include Fred Johnson, the McNeil family, the Rowland family, the Glass family, and Frank Ira Long. Fred Johnson worked with every facet of Niloak production up to the early 1930s at least. He left Niloak Pottery and eventually joined his uncle Matt Carlton at the Bauer Pottery in California. While much is not known about the McNeils and Glasses, they too spent years working for Niloak. Frank Long left Niloak briefly in the late teens. He returned by the mid 1920s, he was working in northern Alabama to make Hy-Long pottery as well as swirl pottery marketed as Muscle Shoals and Marie (see Not Necessarily Niloak). Long returned to Arkansas in 1927 to work as Camark Pottery's only thrower, a job he held until retirement. These potters were Niloak's most skilled employees during their tenure and while their contributions may never be fully known, their impact nonetheless was extremely important and noteworthy.

Optimism blossomed as Benton businessmen, including members of the prominent Bush and Caldwell families, incorporated the Niloak Pottery company in July 1911. Active in administrative duties of the new company were Ernest J. and Fred C. Bush, owners of the Bush Drug and Jewelry Company which first displayed Niloak pottery in their front window. Other financiers were E. R. Norton, as president of Niloak, A. G. Wheeler (owners of the Norton Wheeler Stave Company), and James M. Caldwell, the vice-president (and co-owner of the Caldwell and Kelly General Store) who was Charles's in-law (he married Cora Zella Caldwell in 1901). Corporate records show that Norton, Wheeler, Caldwell, and the Bush brothers collectively subscribed to 240 of the 400 outstanding shares at $25 per share, totaling $6000 of the $10,000 company capital. Hyten's duty was to see that the company manufactured, promoted, and sold a wide range of art pottery, earthenware, brick, and tile. Much of the early financial history of the pottery will never be known, and we will never know if the $6000 injected into the corporation allowed for further expansion and manufacture or just covered existing debt accumulated since 1909.

Moreover, the lack of company records will allow only conclusions based either on indirect evidence and/or local tradition. It is impossible to know exactly what went on in the pottery between 1911 and 1913. References are often made to a fire at the plant and to the creation of a national sales force by a "connoisseur" from Chicago around 1912. Although reasonable and possible on both accounts, no evidence has surfaced to substantiate either claim. The differences between the May 1911 photograph of the Eagle pottery showroom (single floor) and a 1915 layout of the Niloak Pottery plant in Sanborn Insurance Maps show an expanded plant with two floors. Therefore, there must have been sufficient business to necessitate either an expansion or rebuilding, if indeed there had been a fire. More importantly, there has been no confirmation as to who the "connoisseur" was and whether or not a "national sales force" was ever established.

Another confusing point concerning Niloak Pottery was its labeling as "Mission Art Pottery," implying a connection to the Arts and Crafts Movement of the early 1900s. Some people discounted this as advertising hype, yet a Niloak cover story appeared in *The Clay-Worker* in May 1913 raises questions about the validity of the "mission" designation. The extensive article, written by an unnamed Niloak employee or local promoter, uses the term "mission." However, we do not know if Hyten (or anyone else at Niloak, for that matter) had any opinions of or inclinations toward the philosophy of the Arts and Crafts Movement. Of the extensive research undertaken on the local level, only one reference, from the *Benton Courier* (1913), used the word "mission" in describing Niloak pottery.

The Hyten family, on the other hand, knows of no association and never remembered Charles Hyten referring to or advertising Niloak Pottery as Missionware. While some Little Rock retail businesses and their advertisements provided commercial exposure to the movement as early as 1900, the extent of Hyten's commitment to any philosophical

A Group of Niloak Mission Art Pottery—The Coloring is Wholly Natural.

Left: Cover of the May 1913 *Clay-Worker*.
Above: Interior photograph noting "Niloak Mission Art Pottery."
Both photos courtesy of the Mitchell Memorial Library, Mississippi State University.

aspects of the Arts and Crafts Movement is difficult to ascertain. Perhaps Niloak pottery manufacture had "simplicity" in design, and maybe the "mission" designation seemed reasonable within the stylistic framework of the American Arts and Crafts Movement. Its recognition, however, was deserving whether Hyten consciously sought such an affiliation or not. Nonetheless, with the introduction of Missionware pottery back in 1910, Dovey and Hyten brought radically different art pottery to the market. Hand thrown, with classical shapes, the pieces typically consisted of two to three earthtone colors with a matte, satin finish. Niloak's dull swirling patterns of colored clays, with an inherent notion of simplicity in design, further and firmly placed itself within the context of the American Arts and Crafts Movement. Therefore, the designation of Niloak swirl as Missionware is not only noteworthy, it is absolutely valid.

The uniqueness of the Missionware concept allowed Hyten to issue a challenge as well as allow the company to secure distributors. Hyten offered a $1000 reward to anyone who could find two pieces of Niloak with identical swirl patterns. Hyten never lost this bet as he knew this was an impossibility due to the random patterns created by the centrifugal force of the potter's wheel. As for early distributors, local tradition has it that a Chicagoan became Niloak sales representative. In addition, it is known from the 1913 catalog that Brown-Robertson Company of New York represented Niloak. Moreover, it is apparent from this catalog that Niloak Pottery Company possibly took back control of its sales operation. Did this Fifth Avenue company quit business? What happened to the sales representative from Chicago? Or did Missionware sales fail to materialize causing the Niloak Pottery Company to be dropped as a client? In spite of these initial distributors and the national coverage provided by the cover and feature article in *The Clay-Worker,* it appears that Niloak's business began failing during the general economic woes of the mid-1910s and did not recover until the early 1920s. Moreover, if a survey of the size of Sander's Niloak advertisements in the *Arkansas Gazette* from 1910 to 1917 are any indication, the business peaked in 1913 and declined thereafter.

Sander's first advertisement for Niloak's Missionware appeared in the March 13, 1910, issue of the *Arkansas Gazette.* At 1/16 page, the display advertisements were the same size until 1912 when the size for the December Christmas advertisements increased to almost 1/4 page. In 1914 there were no Christmas advertisements; afterwards the Christmas advertisements began to decrease in size. Moreover, after 1914, Niloak advertisements were incorporated into the regular Sanders Christmas advertisements for toys. By 1917, the advertisements decreased from 1/32 page to single sentences mentioning Niloak pottery. Between Christmas 1918 and 1920, there were no Christmas advertisements by Sanders. A final Christmas ad featuring Niloak pottery appeared shortly before Sanders sold out to the Gus Blass Company, a large department store in Little Rock (Dillard's Department Store is the modern successor to Blass). Finally, between 1914 and 1921, no articles were written and few advertisements appeared in the local or state newspapers or other publications. The Sanborn maps of 1915 and 1921 show little difference in the Niloak plant. The major change was the removal of Hyten's experimental kiln during this period. With Hyten focusing on a standardized ware, it is possible that this kiln was no longer needed as shapes and the process of using red, white, blue, gray, and brown colored clays became the norm.

From 1915 to 1922, Niloak Pottery's activity is, to a great extent, unknown but two occurrences deserve mentioning. Hyten apparently wanted to produce glazed, decorated ware. From the earliest known photograph of Niloak pottery, published in 1911, we see an example of art pottery other than Missionware. This attempt, by Dovey, to create a line of decorated artware undoubtedly failed. However, during a visit in 1918, the Little Rock artist Pansy McLaughlin, a student of the Cincinnati Academy of Art, the Cincinnati Institute, and the Chicago Art Institute, was approached by Niloak to "undertake the management of their designing department...." Although she declined, this event, combined with Paul E. Cox's first known visit back in 1917, suggests that preparations were underway to do more than Missionware. Therefore, it seems efforts were undertaken to compete with the Ohio art pottery establishment. Finally, it is possible that production and marketing sagged after 1915 due to Hyten's desire to produce more than Missionware. When this failed, Hyten turned his attention back to Missionware production. Another circumstance which puts the company's viability in question is the surrender of the Niloak Pottery Company's charter in 1918.

On January 21, 1918, President Norton and Secretary F. C. Bush signed documents resolving "that the assets of the Niloak Pottery, a corporation of Benton, Arkansas, be distributed among the stockholders thereof, and the charter of said corporation be surrendered." If business had been good, why would stockholders surrender the charter? Whatever the cause, stockholders relinquished control to Hyten. Interestingly enough, the *Benton Courier* made no mention of the transaction. From all indications, Niloak pottery production and sales were minimal from the mid-1910s to the early 1920s. During the second half of

1917, advertising appeared in the *Benton Courier* pertaining to the sale of Eagle Pottery's molasses jugs (due to wartime shortages of tin for containers). With the first regularly published Eagle Pottery advertisements appearing right before the corporation's surrender, they must have been Hyten's only hope of staying in the pottery business. In addition, by the first part of 1919, he turned to another business, with hopes of making a living. From January to May 1919, Hyten advertised weekly in the *Benton Courier* his "Truck Service and Moving Company." Hyten's delivery service promised: "Special attention given to hauling of household goods, and best care given to all kinds of hauling. Careful drivers and prompt service."

It is apparent that Eagle Pottery's production of utilitarian ware was Hyten's only pottery concern into the very early part of the 1920s. More importantly, the *Benton Courier* provided little news about the pottery from 1914 to 1922. With the surrender of the Niloak charter and non-Missionware ads, it is probable that Hyten's art pottery business was declining. When his attempt to hire a decorator failed, Hyten turned his attention back to Missionware production. This time with standardized clay colors and shapes. At this point, Niloak's Missionware in concept and design becomes less art pottery and more utilitarian, florist, and giftware in nature. Although most Missionware was hand thrown, Hyten was able to achieve a mass production level with his experienced potters including Frank Long, Reagan Rowland, Romine and Joshua McNeil, and Fred Johnson. By the 1920s, the Niloak Pottery facilities included a building measuring 40' x 140', three kilns, and 15 – 20 employees. Fortunately, the best years were just ahead.

The 1920s became Niloak's best years as Hyten, Fred Johnson, and Frank Long soon traveled extensively to sell and demonstrate the swirl technique for retailers' customers. If a particular store purchased a certain amount of Missionware, a Niloak employee would travel to the store and give a personal demonstration. Throughout the twenties, Niloak concentrated on the retail markets in larger cities, in department stores and art shops, with sales distributors from coast to coast, in the Midwest and Southwest, and in Arkansas, especially in resorts such as Hot Springs and Eureka Springs. Clubs and organizations purchased and used this home product of Arkansas, such as the Masonic Lodge. The Albert Pike Lodge in Little Rock purchased about a dozen Missionware cuspidors for outdoor use by its members. Along with Niloak's success during the 1920s, other accomplishments were achieved including the patenting of the unique swirl process.

Truck Service and Moving

Special attention given to hauling of household goods, and best of care given to all kinds of hauling. Careful drivers and prompt service.

PHONES 285 or 29

C. D. HYTEN

Hyten's advertisement for his Truck Service and Moving Company. ***Benton Courier*, 1918. *Courtesy Arkansas History Commission.***

Molasses Jugs

The government is advocating the use of jugs in putting up molasses, owing to the scarcity and high price of tin. We have a large stock of jugs on hand, but the supply may be exhausted before the unusually large crop of sorghum cane is made up, so would advise that you order them now.

EAGLE POTTERY

Order Jugs Now!

Those who expect to put up sorghum in jugs this year are urged to get their orders in early as labor conditions are such as to make it necessary that we begin now if we are to supply our trade.

Tin buckets will be very high and in many instances not obtainable, but by anticipating at least part of your wants, jugs can be supplied when you need them.

Let us know about how many jugs you will need this year so we can begin making preparations now to take care of your wants later.

EAGLE POTTERY

Benton, Arkansas

Left: Eagle Pottery advertisement, *Benton Courier*, 1918.
Courtesy Arkansas History Commission.
Above:* Eagle Pottery advertisement, *Benton Courier*, 1918. *Courtesy of the Arkansas History Commission. Graphic enhancements courtesy of Stacy Brod.

Demonstration trips and linkage with the state boosterism movement and other promotions were important to the success of Niloak Pottery in the 1920s. Hyten took to the road in response to business interests wanting to use demonstrations of making Missionware as a promotional technique. Over the course of five years, Hyten or his close, long-time associates like Long and Johnson, made numerous automobile trips to southern, midwestern, and eastern states to visit department stores. These included Wanamaker's in Philadelphia, the May Company in both New York and Los Angeles, and Marshall Field's in Chicago. The greatest promotion of Niloak Pottery came in the early 1920s when the American Federation of Women's Clubs decided to launch a nationwide tour for American art pottery. The Arkansas Federation of Women's Clubs secured the participation of Niloak Pottery in this traveling exhibition that lasted for several years. Seeking to "bring art to the people," the Federation included in its exhibit a pottery section which featured Niloak Missionware among examples of Marblehead, Newcomb, Rookwood, and Van Briggle.

The American Federation of Women's Clubs had long promoted the value of art, regardless of the medium. The exhibition and Niloak's inclusion were noted in an article in the September 1922 issue of *International Studio* magazine. Beyond just displaying the many different types of American art pottery for its artistic appreciation, the Federation also promoted the sale of the pottery. As a result, a new, more informed audience began purchasing Niloak's Missionware. Finally, Niloak advertised itself in the annuals of the Arkansas Division of the United Daughters of the Confederacy. Published in connection with Arkansas's UDC annual convention, display ads appear in consecutive issues between 1923 and 1926 and that undoubtedly promoted Niloak as a home product worthy of loyal patronage by Arkansans.

Another reason for Niloak's renewed success involved the company's strong connection to boosterism in Arkansas. Attempting to counter the negative attitudes directed towards Arkansas, Niloak Pottery helped respond, in their promotional literature, with statements like Arkansas was the "home of the Niloak Pottery" or Niloak was an "Arkansas Wonder." Organizations such as the Arkansas Advancement Association, which was responsible for changing Arkansas's motto from the "Bear State" to "The Wonder State," frequently promoted Arkansas products as testaments of Arkansas's economic advantages. The fast growing economy and the resulting increase in buying power by the middle class also benefited Niloak as more and more people were purchasing goods described as luxury items. As a result, these reasons undoubtedly brought increased sales to Niloak. Therefore, Niloak had to increase its production to keep up with sales by standardizing its Missionware line.

In January 1922, Hyten visited Colorado Springs, Colorado, and Salt Lake City, Utah. This western trip received notice, like many others to follow, in the *Benton Courier* and started an odyssey which took Hyten and others from one coast to the other to demonstrate the swirl technique. In a series of trips, Hyten alone visited Missouri, Ohio, Pennsylvania, Washington D. C., New Jersey, New York, Illinois, and then headed west to Colorado Springs and Salt Lake City. This time, with the family in tow, the group visited Los Angeles for two weeks, Long Beach for a month, and then skipped down to Tijuana, Mexico, for a brief respite before heading home. During this trip Hyten had secured at least one sales outlet — the Pussy Willow shop near Santa Barbara, California. The touring by Hyten and others probably helped Niloak attract new distributors. By 1923, Niloak Pottery secured Geo. Borgfeldt and Company of New York with its outlets from coast to coast. Borgfeldt soon advertised Missionware as "Mother Earth's art...fashioned by the hand and eye of man."

One of the most unusual demonstration trips was made by Frank Long to Lancaster, Pennsylvania. On the night of April 22, 1924, the local Lancaster radio station announced the pending Missionware demonstration at a local store, describing it as one of "the wonders of the Wonder State." This example of boosterism, came during the time when Arkansans worked vigorously to promote their state as an industrialized, progressive place with opportunities for all. Although similar trips were made through 1927, the peak of activities occurred during 1923 – 1924. Connections to Arkansas's boosterism resulted in Niloak Pottery becoming a highly visible and "valuable advertisement medium for Arkansas." In November 1923, the Niloak Pottery Company was invited to include a display in the first annual Arkansas Traveling Exposition train which visited the East Coast presenting examples of the resources of Arkansas. Missionware examples were given to many dignitaries including President Coolidge and his wife.

Former Arkansas Governor Charles Brough, in attendance, gave an account of the visit with President Coolidge: The President "expressed almost boyish delight" in receiving the Niloak Pottery smoking set and asked if the clay was "artificially colored or whether it [was] natural." While Brough did not elaborate on what answer was given, he did comment on the sales displays he had seen: "Just here may I say that I was delighted to see so many first-class pottery establishments in the East carrying Niloak among their sales exhibits, and to know at first hand that the famous store of Sterling, Welch & Co., of Cleveland, installed Niloak as one of its holiday attractions." Gifts of Missionware became customary for visiting officials and for other grand occasions. With its commis-

Niloak plant, Pearl Street, "Niloak Pottery Class, Benton, Ark., 10-27-24, Hendrix Studio, Benton, Ark." Fred Johnson, standing, far left. Hyten is to the left of the Missionware vase. ***Courtesy of the late Hardy L. Winburn IV.***

sioning in 1923, the third Arkansas battleship was presented a Niloak Pottery smoking set by the Little Rock/Pine Bluff Shriners during a ceremony at Annapolis, Maryland.

By the mid-1920s Niloak was one of the "wonders" of Arkansas. As attempts continued to boost Arkansas as the "Wonder State," Niloak Pottery became one of Arkansas's marvels due to its uniqueness as a product pointing to the unlimited possibilities of Arkansas's natural resources. Missionware became an attraction at local, state, and regional fairs. Between 1925 and 1928, Niloak Pottery displayed Missionware and demonstrated the swirl technique at Morrilton, during its Centennial Exposition, at the Arkansas State Fair in Little Rock, and at the Tri-State Fair in Memphis, Tennessee. Fred Johnson is known to have participated in at least one demonstration trip, going to Savannah, Georgia, in 1926. Other trips involving Fred Johnson occurred as well. Virginia Heiss, the historian of Indiana's Muncie Pottery states that a Niloak potter came to Muncie about once a year and threw Missionware. Brenda Escoto, Fred Johnson's granddaughter, revealed that it was her grandfather who took these trips (each lasting three months) to Muncie Pottery, and they spanned a time period of about five years (although when these trips were taken is not known). These varied activities gained Niloak Pottery much publicity which no doubt contributed to its rising popularity and success.

The Niloak Pottery, like Camark Pottery just a few years later, was the site of numerous tour stops, family visits, and school children's field trips. Mary D. Hudgins was a party to one such visit on July 13, 1925: "We stopped at the old pottery down on the railroad track. Mr. Hyten asked only that visitors pay $1.00 each for the privilege of being given a gob of clay (several colors). With a little instruction each 'potter' was left in front of the wheel and told to control the wheel's turning by a foot pedal. The result of his 'crafting' was properly fired and sent on to him by mail. I accepted the clay, and began to pedal, curving my hands as I had been told, the thumbs in control. By a small miracle I achieved a symetrical [sic] urn in short order. If only I had had sense enough to take my foot off the [pedal] at once, all would have been well. My foot shook. My hand trembled. 'Let it go down to a blob,' said Mr. Hyten, standing by, 'and start over.' Never again could I do anything with that blob. My 'ash tray' is a cherished possession; but poor in workmanship." (This item is in the collection of the University of Arkansas Museum.) Niloak continued to welcome guests and even promoted tours of its facility. According to some reports, at least 1,000 visitors annually toured the plant site by the late 1920s.

Niloak Pottery was also busy trying to secure exclusive rights to the Missionware technique. In March 1925, the company secured Niloak as a trademark, and later the same year set in motion an application for a patent. It seems possible, and rightly so, that other established potteries recognized the swirl pattern's appeal and were capitalizing on it with their versions. In order to protect his market, Hyten sought to prevent others in Arkansas and elsewhere from making a similar product (see Not Necessarily Niloak). The need for protection rose from two possible competitors, one in Arkansas and the other in Colorado. From early 1923, Niloak Pottery sold well in and around Colorado Springs. Although there is no proof yet, it is probable that Denver's White Pottery manufactured its swirl as a result of the popularity of Niloak. According to Tom Turnquist, author of *Denver's White Pottery,* swirl production started in Denver during the early 1920s. Was it just a coincidence or did White capitalize on Niloak's Missionware technique? There was concern in Arkansas since some advocated passing a law to force Colorado to accept marked pieces of Niloak.

Although virtually all Missionware was marked, it was noted that "The name (Niloak) is stamped on the bottom of each piece — save that manufactured and sold in that state [Colorado] as a native product." This mysterious statement is compounded by the fact that the Niloak mark is sometimes covered up by Colorado shop stickers. Finally, the mystery of the definitely Niloak but marked "mineralized" pieces has been uncovered. Company literature by the Van Briggle Pottery of Colorado has surfaced that connects Niloak's "mineralized" pieces to Colorado and back to Niloak Pottery. This 1920s literature states: "Van Briggle truly reflects the spirit of Colorado, just as the striped pottery (sometimes called mineralized pottery), made at Benton, Ark., reflects the spirit of Arkansas." What is not known at this time is when Niloak Pottery made these wares for retail in Colorado.

The Arkansas challenger was Charlie Stehm's Ozark Pottery of Eureka Springs. Although his swirl production did not begin until after Niloak Pottery had filed for a patent in 1925, Stehm's work undoubtedly provided added impetus for the company to obtain his patent. Tradition has it that Hyten threatened to sue Stehm if he continued making swirl. From all indications, Ozark Pottery production ceased by the end of 1927 — just before Niloak Pottery was granted a U.S. patent on its swirl process. Swirl pottery was made in the 1920s by other companies though it is not known whether former Niloak employees were involved. The most active production came from the Evans Pottery of Missouri. In addition, Frank Long, long-time potter at Niloak, worked for the Spruce Pines Pottery of Alabama and made swirl pottery, most in the shapes he threw for Niloak. Later Howard Lewis, after leaving Niloak in 1934, made the Badlands pottery for Dickota Pottery of North Dakota (see Not Necessarily Niloak). Since other swirl pottery never achieved the "complicated or delicately adjusted character" of Niloak, it is possible that no significant swirl production resulted from the involvement of former Niloak employees. For whatever reasons, Niloak Pottery began final efforts to secure rights to the Niloak name and product.

On November 6, 1924, the Niloak Pottery Company filed for a registered trademark for Niloak. It submitted "five specimens showing the trade-mark as actually used by applicant upon the goods, and requests that the same be registered in the United States Patent Office." Trademark 195,889 was registered on March 3, 1925. As Niloak Pottery enjoyed increased sales and publicity, the company desired to keep its product from being copied elsewhere by other potteries. As a result Niloak Pottery filed "5 claims" for a patent on July 24, 1924. Nearly four years later, on January 31, 1928, Niloak Pottery was granted patent number 1,657,997. As noted in the *Official Gazette of the United States Patent Office* for 1928, the "present invention relates broadly to the art of ceramic, and particularly to a novel clay product and the process of manufacturing the same. The invention, more specifically, has to do with the production of clay pottery of a decorative character by virtue of the use of clay of different colors.... A cylindrical shaped ceramic product composed of a plurality of different colored clays, each different clay containing a shrinkage controlling substance so proportioned relative to the color base as to impart to such clay approximately the same shrinkage characteristic as the other clays, said clays being displaced circumferentially as an incident to manipulation during rotation of the composite clays while in plastic condition so as to produce a blended and variegated striae of irregular form." Though this must have been a high point for the Niloak Pottery Company, it is very odd that no mention was made in the *Benton Courier.* In addition, neither the 1925 issuance of the trademark nor the incorporation of Niloak Pottery and Tile Company on September 6, 1928, was acknowledged. Niloak Pottery did receive notice that it had "won preferred honors" during its exhibit at the 1928 national convention of the American Mining Congress in Washington, D. C.

A year before, *The Clay-Worker* announced that Niloak planned an addition and that other improvements were "under consideration" by Hyten. By March 1928, plans were revealed for a new Benton showroom to be built (and housed with modern equipment) at a cost of $20,000 on the Hot Springs-Little Rock Highway (now known as Military Road). In early September, the ground was broken for a grand, one-story showroom with a Spanish facade. To further the debate on (if not help prove) whether Hyten was aware of the missionware connotation, the author of *Art Pottery of the United States,* upon publication of the first Niloak edition, made an interesting observation. Paul Evans wrote: "The 1929 Military Road [showroom, photograph of the building,] is as 'mission' as anything I have ever seen: the architecture California Mission and...the interior fireplace... is very Arts & Crafts Mission." This new showroom became the exclusive manufacturing site for Missionware. Shipped to the original plant on Pearl Street, the wares were fired and then returned to Military Road for shipment and retail sales. Five months later, on February 16, 1929, the new showroom formally opened. The front room was adorned with red roses in Niloak pottery vases. Guests drank punch served from a Niloak Missionware punch bowl and danced to the music of the Corn Huskers, a Little Rock orchestra. The showroom must have been a grand sight as dancers stepped lively over the large swirl-tiled floor and set their glasses of punch on the fireplace mantle adorned with similar, smaller tiles. None of the revelers could know at this stage that Niloak Pottery had already reached its zenith and that a slow decline lay ahead.

The years 1929 through 1931 are not well documented. Except for a time of regrouping and adjusting to the hard times brought on by the Depression, little else is known until the introduction of Hywood Art Pottery in December 1931. What is known is that the early 1930s included hard times for Benton, like everyone else. As with many other industries around the nation, Niloak suffered from a lack of sales. In addition to the expense of the showroom, the company printed a new catalog (Indian girl on the cover) and spent an extraordinary amount on new four-color letterhead and promotional memorabilia, including mechanical pencils. Combined, these expenses added to Niloak's existing debt. This, coupled with heavy debt from financing the new showroom and pre-existing debt, bankrupted the company. The Depression has been blamed for the woes of Niloak Pottery; however, financial problems existed at the time that plans for the showroom were announced.

Corporate records in 1928 reveal "recent indebtedness" to the Benton Bank and Trust Company (Hyten was once one of its directors) as well as an approved motion to seek more that $25,000 in funds to finance the new construction and pay off the current debt. The Depression had led to the accep-

This magnificent Niloak showroom built on Military Road in 1929 has not survived. The Niloak Pottery/Winburn Tile Company turned the showroom over to be used as a plastics school by the summer of 1948. Backed by the Young Business Men's Organization of Benton, the School of Arts and Plastics was one of four such schools in the United States at the time. According to the *Benton Courier,* the school offered a "complete course in plastic fabrication" and its 71 students (mostly GIs and some disabled) learned both theory and the practical manufacturing of plastics. In the mid 1970s, after having been used as apartments and later lain vacant, the building was torn down. The remaining tiles in the building (some had been pried off and removed by collectors and souvenir hunters), were taken by the present owner of the property, Calvin Brown, and installed in his Benton area home. The site today has a historical marker, and the Niloak name is commemorated along with its use in commercial development and historical activities. Note large monumental Missionware vases, planters, and bird baths. *Courtesy of the late Hardy L. Winburn IV.*

Stoin M. Stoin, 1930.
Courtesy of Dale Stoin.

Gus Blass advertisement introducing Hywood Art Pottery, *Arkansas Gazette*, December 1931. *Courtesy of the Butler Center for Arkansas Studies, Central Arkansas Library System.*

tance of a loan from K. K. Bell of Chicago to cover the existing $20,000 indebtedness. To survive, the directors (Hyten, his wife Cora, and Wilbur J. "Red" Whitthorne) mortgaged all the company's property. Wilbur Whitthorne, from a long-time Benton family, was hired back in February 1928 as Niloak bookkeeper and soon rose to the position of secretary-treasurer. With sales still not materializing by September 1930, employees were laid off, and the salaries of those who remained were slashed. Hyten, nevertheless, persevered and plotted the company's future. Believing Missionware sales to be an expensive luxury item to most and that these sales would not recover immediately, Hyten decided to manufacture glazed ware.

Although no evidence exists as to what Hyten desired to make, he hired a former Weller employee, Stoin M. Stoin, suggesting that he was familiar with the "Weller Art Pottery" sold at the Bush Brothers Store since the mid-twenties alongside Missionware. Stoin, who was born in Troyan, Bulgaria, on March 28, 1895, would also worked for the Houghton and Dalton Pottery of Dalton, Ohio. Stoin brought to Niloak both his knowledge of glazes and the shapes he used at Weller Pottery. No doubt Stoin is responsible conceptually for the Hywood Art Pottery line, as Hyten, after more than 20 years of Missionware production, had limited knowledge about the methods in making traditional art pottery, its clay bodies, and glaze preparation. Finally the physical results of new shapes and glazes (both shapes and glazes were similar to other potteries' products) point to Stoin being the mastermind behind Hywood Art Pottery. The lasting result was a change in ceramic production away from Missionware and ultimately to industrial castware.

Arriving in the summer of 1931, Stoin, a ceramics engineer, worked on Niloak's newest creation-Hywood Art Pottery (a relatively unknown Niloak line until the late 1980s). This line was introduced to maintain the income needed to sustain the pottery's production when Missionware sales dropped. It represented Hyten's attempt to produce pottery with artistic merit and remain operational during the Depression. Based on traditional methods for making pottery, Hywood Art Pottery differed from Missionware in the way it was made and priced, as there were more costly and skilled steps involved with Missionware, from mixing the clay body, coloring the clays, mixing the color types for throwing, throwing the objects, removing them to the lathe for finishing, and finally firing them in the kiln.

Unveiled during the Christmas season of 1931 at the Gus Blass Company with a "first time, exclusive" 400-plus exhibit, traditional glazed ware manufacturing began. The *Arkansas Gazette* reported that demonstrations would be performed by Hyten on an "old-fashioned cake wheel." Although most items were thrown, some were molded. By early 1932, Hywood Art Pottery was being handled by George Rumrill's Arkansas Products Company (which also handled Camark) along with other distributors in the Midwest and New England. Another known distributor was J. W. Bakster of Chicago. This progressive step, however, failed to bring Niloak back from the brink of bankruptcy as times became increasingly difficult. With a disastrous $3,000 fire in March of 1932, Hyten again faced a serious dilemma. Then Stoin left in the spring of 1932. This created another major setback for Hyten, since Stoin, who controlled the Hywood Art Pottery production, took his glaze formulas with him. This left Hyten not only without a skilled ceramist, but also with no way to continue on his own.

Undaunted, in May 1932, Hyten visited his long-time friend, Paul E. Cox, now head of the ceramic engineering department at Iowa State College in Ames. Arriving during the annual spring festival (Veishea), Hyten hired the soon-to-be ceramic engineering graduate Howard S. Lewis. (Hyten also demonstrated his skills on the potter's wheel during the festival.) Lewis arrived in Benton the next month and redeveloped the chemical process for glazes, worked out a new firing schedule for the kilns, and produced a new clay mixture for the Hywood by Niloak line (the successor to the Hywood Art Pottery line). Per Hyten's instructions, Lewis tried to copy as near as possible the glazes made by Stoin. Experimenting through the summer of 1932, Lewis developed a number of glazes utilizing mottling, air brush, and drip techniques. This new glazed ware was now marketed as Hywood by Niloak in hopes that better sales would result from linking the Hywood name to the readily recognized Niloak name. For nearly two years, Lewis, along with sculptor and mold maker Rudy Ganz, worked with Hyten on both the hand-thrown and the earliest castware.

The introduction of mold production and its technical aspects at Niloak mirrored the introduction of traditional glazes used on Hywood Art Pottery. The manufacture of molded pieces required personnel skilled in the area of modeling, block and case work, and mold production. While some crockery was produced at Eagle Pottery by means of a jigger, a revolving mold-like apparatus, its design and operation were nothing like the procedures needed for molding. For this experience Hyten hired Rudolph Ganz, a "well known designer." Although little is known of Ganz's life and career before his arrival in Benton in September 1931, Ganz was a skilled sculptor and mold maker from Baden, Germany. He came to America in 1929 and studied art at the National Art Academy in Chicago. For about a year and a half, Ganz worked for the Indiana Limestone Company in Bloomington. He reportedly received some education at the University of Indiana and may have worked for Frankhoma Pottery. Ganz told the *Arkansas Gazette* in 1932 that he decided to take a vacation and traveled through Arkansas. As a result, he spent two months at "Camp Rudy" near Fort Smith teaching Boys Scouts how to model in soap. The story goes on that Hyten visited the camp one day when Ganz was making a clay bust of a Boy Scout official. Hyten "decided his plant needed him."

Hyten hired Ganz who produced molds for the few Hywood Art Pottery pieces which were not hand thrown. By September 1932, Ganz had produced 30 molds and completed designs for nearly 200 more molds for the new Hywood by Niloak line. One mold, a yet-to-be-seen crow, had five different pieces to its mold. In October, the *Benton Courier* announced Ganz's acceptance of a part-time teaching position in modeling "at the Brewer School of Art in Little Rock." With Stoin's departure and Hyten's apparent decision to limit hand-thrown wares, Ganz responsibilities were expanded as castware production increased. He designed, modeled, and produced molds for the Hywood by Niloak line, many of which were molded. Sometime in late 1933, Ganz moved to Fort Smith and worked for the Daly Monument Works. In 1936, Ganz became the foreman at Daly Monument Works and married (his wife's name was Willene). He was no longer living in Ft. Smith by 1938, but by 1940 he was working as a designer and mold maker for the Shawnee Pottery of Zanesville, Ohio. At Shawnee, Ganz was the co-creator of Shawnee's "first figural cookie jars" and would hold 17 design patents. He left in 1942, and his employment after Shawnee Pottery is not known.

Rudy Ganz, c. 1940s. ***Courtesy of the Ohio Historical Society.***

In 1934, after two years, Howard Lewis left and would work for a variety of pottery companies including Dickota Pottery (Dickinson, North Dakota); Broadmore Pottery (Denver, Colorado); Mason Brick and Tile (Mason City, Iowa); W. I. Tycer Pottery (Roseville, Ohio); and finally the Rosemeade Pottery of Wahpeton, North Dakota. In an interview, Lewis reminisced about his first days as a ceramist: "I just remember that times were hard while we were there and at times we hardly got enough to live on. It just depended on how much stoneware they sold each week. The conditions were bad when I came to Niloak Pottery. The men working in the stoneware plant were being paid 10 cents per hour. The main income was from the sale of stoneware. I started making pottery and in a few weeks Mr. Hyten raised the pay to 25 cents an hour. Stoneware production and pottery production increased, but there was a shortage of money for a long time. I was to get $25.00 a week, but many times I never got that much. Things were that way when I left, but there was some improvement." Lewis related that the stoneware truck often came back half full and whatever proceeds were left, Hyten split among the employees. In 1956, Lewis went into teaching and never again worked with ceramics.

If there was a highlight for the Niloak Pottery Company in the early 1930s, it came in 1933 when the pottery was included in the Chicago Century of Progress Exposition. Hyten spent a month demonstrating the pottery technique (presumably swirl) and Niloak (along with Camark) had an exhibit in the Arkansas Building of the Hall of States. Unfortunately, whatever positive publicity came with this was offset by what some called an "unfinished" exhibit which would "shame any native Arkansan." In a letter to A. W. Parks, Secretary of the Arkansas Commission for the Century of Progress Exposition, George C. Merkel of the Pine Bluff Chamber of Commerce refused further cooperation as both the Camark and Niloak exhibits were in "haphazard form" and the attendant had "soiled clothing and about two days' growth of beard." Moreover, Merkel suggested that the exhibit be removed and that Arkansas withdraw from the Exposition altogether.

The situation at Niloak continued to worsen, and Hyten turned to other means for survival. In 1934, a group of Little Rock businessmen, led by Hardy Lathan Winburn III and his grandfather C. L. Durrett, purchased the Niloak Pottery and Tile Company, reportedly in receivership. Although the particulars of the transaction are not known, they brought in another Little Rock businessman, Ben Searcy, and along with Hyten formed an alliance. The company, with each man possessing an equal share of stock, now had the capital to continue in business. Historically speaking, much about Winburn's entry into the Niloak Pottery Company is obscure. Winburn, a chemistry graduate from Ouachita Baptist University in Arkadelphia, Arkansas, ran the Hope Brick Company out of Little Rock in the late 1920s. By the early 1930s, before coming to Niloak, Winburn sold roofing materials in Tulsa, Oklahoma. Little else, however, is known during this period since corporation records do not restart until September 1934. Hyten had quit keeping minutes in September 1930, resulting in a four-year gap. Nonetheless, Winburn, his grandfather Durrett, and Searcy brought both capital and business acumen to Niloak when it needed it the most.

Although it would take several years to regain financial stability, the company's concentration on industrial castware facilitated recovery. Winburn and his associates no doubt brought to Niloak pottery the necessary business skills that Hyten lacked. Winburn, in particular, implemented better business practices in both production and marketing as he sought to streamline business procedures and increase efficiency. With this introduction of organizational skills and the active pursual of their selected duties, these four men (all directors) revived the company's ability to do business as production and sales were up by late 1935. Troubles were by no means over, unfortunately, as there still existed an over $15,000 debt from the 1920s.

Hardy Winburn's general manager's report of February 1936 was not a cause for rejoicing at the stockholder's meeting. Despite sales all over Arkansas, in every bordering state, to individuals (one purchase from Fairbanks, Alaska, totaled $3.68 worth of goods), and to drug stores and gift shops, bakeries and cafes, and hardware and furniture stores (also including a vinegar jar for the Gregory-Robinson-Speas Company), the company still operated at a loss. From September 1935 to February 1936, the company operated "normally" for only four weeks. Even though distinct business divisions (management, production, and sales) were created, "enforced idleness" resulted from ineffective operations among these three departments. Measures were promised to assure better business operations and a "harmony of action between sales and production departments." Specifics included piecework and percentage pay, new equipment such as a kiln, and the transfer of the offices back to Benton (they had been moved to Little Rock in August 1935). If attainable, in Winburn's view, Niloak would achieve "uninterrupted normal operation."

During 1936 and 1937, Niloak Pottery strove to continue in the ceramic business. Most importantly, the directors wanted to make Missionware a "salable line" again. Even though overall sales were a little better, the company adopted a retrenchment stance and curtailed production since debts needed retiring. Confusion abounded as internal reorganization continued and by June 1937, the sales office had been moved to Little Rock for the second time and then back to Benton. While sales and production departments had yet to attain "harmony," the company decided to build a new kiln and hire an experienced general superintendent to increase production. This new employee, George M. Peterson, another Iowa State College graduate, became both the company's mold designer and its ceramic engineer.

Lee Joe Alley, c. 1930s.
Courtesy of Ronald and Ella Ruth Alley.

This photograph of the Niloak Pottery showroom located at 4115 Asher Avenue in Little Rock (circa 1940) was taken by Charles Dove, a Benton photographer, who worked for Niloak Pottery in the late 1930s. He also took pictures at the Niloak plant in Benton. His complete photograph collection is housed at the University of Central Arkansas Archives and Special Collections.

George Peterson was hired back in mid 1936 and was responsible for many production aspects at Niloak. Peterson created many wonderful shapes, some identified by Joe Alley, for Niloak and spent considerable time "trying to perfect glazes against crazing." Niloak Pottery finally decided to invest in a new kiln, and Winburn visited Camark Pottery to inspect its kilns. For what orders Niloak did receive, there were problems meeting those demands, and the company decided look into the possibility of a tunnel kiln to reduce manufacturing time from 6 weeks to several days. While Niloak did install a new kiln, it decided instead to build a round periodic kiln. The kiln was built by the end of 1937 and placed under the supervision of Peterson and Tom Glass (Glass and his family were long-time Benton potters). According to corporation minutes, Peterson resigned from Niloak in June 1940 (eventually he went to work for the Haeger Pottery of Illinois) and was replaced by Lee Joe Alley.

Alley, employed in the castware production department since June 1937, stated it was Niloak's secretary Austelle Lloyd who got him appointed Niloak's new designer and master mold maker. It is apparent that Alley worked as a part-time designer along with Peterson before he quit. Alley remembered that all his skills were learned as a result of on-the-job-training. Alley, working next to Peterson, constantly observed Peterson and all that he did to created molds. Alley wrote: "My friend, George Peterson, unknowingly taught me a lot about master mold making as he worked within ten feet of my work station." As for designing, Alley said that came naturally. Alley in addition worked with Hyten on throwing Missionware and did free-lance work for the Camark Pottery making about a dozen pieces.

During his full-time employment, Alley created over 150 original castware designs, worked with Hyten on the limited Missionware production, as well as designed the stoneware kitchenware line (consisting of mixing bowls, canisters, crocks, and flower pots with "vertically indented decorations"). Alley also created the two lines of planters called "Bright Whimsies" and "Stars of the Big Top." Alley remained with Niloak until September 1943. Alley's departure from Niloak was purely patriotic. Sinclair Winburn, vice president of Niloak Pottery, wrote: "Separation from this company was brought about by Mr. Alley's desire to be employed in an industry where his peculiar abilities would be more beneficial to this nation's war effort. For his past work and his present patriotic motives, we are happy to recommend him." Alley also worked for the Frankoma. Pottery and the Texas Pottery Company.

In 1938, however, with the new kiln built and the castware department enlarged, nothing was accomplished toward attaining a "vigorous sales program." There appeared to be a split in opinion between Hyten and Hardy Winburn as to how the company should operate. Winburn continued to obtain more and more shares and by March 1939, he owned nearly 459 shares to Hyten's 140 shares. By July, more business management practices were introduced, a warehouse and retail store opened on

Asher Avenue in Little Rock, and advertising was expanded. As old debts were paid and with production (stoneware, castware, and limited Missionware) at capacity, better times for the Niloak Pottery Company were ahead.

The 1930s closed with Winburn controlling the entire company (now with 575¼ shares) and Hyten selling his stock to Austelle Lloyd, the secretary-treasurer. Hyten did not leave Niloak Pottery but became the traveling castware salesman in August 1939. Suddenly, after 31 years with Niloak Pottery, Hyten resigned. Although local tradition holds that there was ill-will between Hyten, a potter and co-founder of Niloak Pottery, and Winburn, a businessman and savior of Niloak Pottery, historical records reveal nothing as to why C.D. Hyten tendered his resignation as the castware salesman on January 31, 1940. Hyten might have felt that he had no real control over production. Missionware production was limited; its sales had been $1,174.55 to the castware sales of $31,154.17 during the past year. While economics dictated the manufacture of non-descriptive industrial castware, the lack of artistic individualism and loss of control over a family business he had nurtured since the turn-of-the-century must have bothered him.

Charles Dean "Bullet" Hyten, it must be said, became an artisan, who, along with Arthur Dovey, Fred Johnson, and others, created a unique American art pottery. However, Hyten's lack of professional business skills was probably one cause of Niloak Pottery's financial instability throughout the years. Yet, Hyten did not give up an interest in pottery. He opened and operated (with his daughter Arlene) the Hyten's Pottery and Gift Shop on the Little Rock Highway near Benton. He even became a traveling salesmen for the Camark Pottery Company and handled its pottery line as well as Fenton Glass in his shop. Unfortunately, fate did not allow Hyten to build upon his new business. While at a church function on September 6, 1944, Hyten, at the age of 67, drowned while wading in the Saline River.

The 1940s were times of diversity at Niloak Pottery. Businesses across America were benefiting from Roosevelt's New Deal, and World War II soon would bring prosperity to Niloak. While its primary production centered on castware, Niloak produced stoneware, flower pots, novelties, and a limited amount of "natural" Niloak (i.e. Missionware). By mid 1940, optimism ran high among officers as the Asher Avenue store was remodeled with shelving built into each of the plate glass windows. James Larrison, who previously worked as a traveling salesman, became the store's manager. A West Memphis store opened in July and Larrison was transferred there as its manager. The store's sales, however, were poor and it was closed by September.

As previously noted, Niloak Pottery's castware business boomed. By late 1940, the stoneware kiln was converted for castware use, the glaze room enlarged, and more importantly, a decision was made to "conservatively build up" jobbing lines (selling other companies' pottery). The company hoped to handle lines of hotel china, glassware, and dinnerware so that those profits could pay the expenses of Niloak production. Initially, Niloak Pottery brokered the wares of the Shawnee Pottery Company and Robinson-Ransbottom Pottery of Zanesville and Roseville, Ohio, respectively. By summer, results were impressive enough to perma-

Charles Dean "Bullet" Hyten, c. 1920s. *Courtesy of the Butler Center for Arkansas Studies, Central Arkansas Library System.*

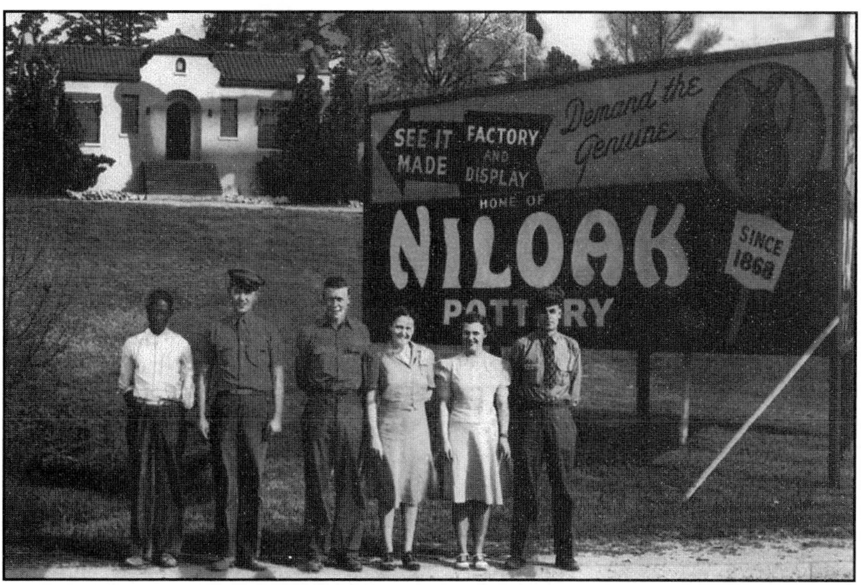

Niloak Pottery showroom on Military Ave., c. 1940. Left to right: Pinkey Franklin, Joe Alley, Vernon Brown, Rose Edwards, Louise Lockridge, and Jim Ellis. *Courtesy of Ronald and Ella Ruth Alley.*

nently continue jobbing. Also good sales led to the building of another kiln. Although business was vastly better than during the depths of the Depression, the coming years would seesaw between good and bad for Niloak.

A new chapter began when war erupted in Europe. During 1941, Winburn and other officers initiated actions to participate in the national defense program. Since the war's effects on the company's operations included sales by correspondence (lack of tires, etc. for the salesmen's automobiles) and other changes, Niloak Pottery sought to supplant the increasingly limited retail trade with war work under the supervision of Sinclair Winburn. Sinclair was Hardy's brother and a chemistry graduate from Louisiana State University. The year 1941 was the best year under Winburn's management. Sales were at a record high as the war started. When the general trade slackened, Niloak competed and won government contracts for the manufacture of metal substitutes (mostly containers of various sorts) and war supplies. Mid-1941 saw the first production of porcelain electrical insulators. Soon Niloak was producing ceramic jars for the Lone Star Ordinance Plant of Texas and the Maumelle and Arkansas Ordinance Plants in central Little Rock.

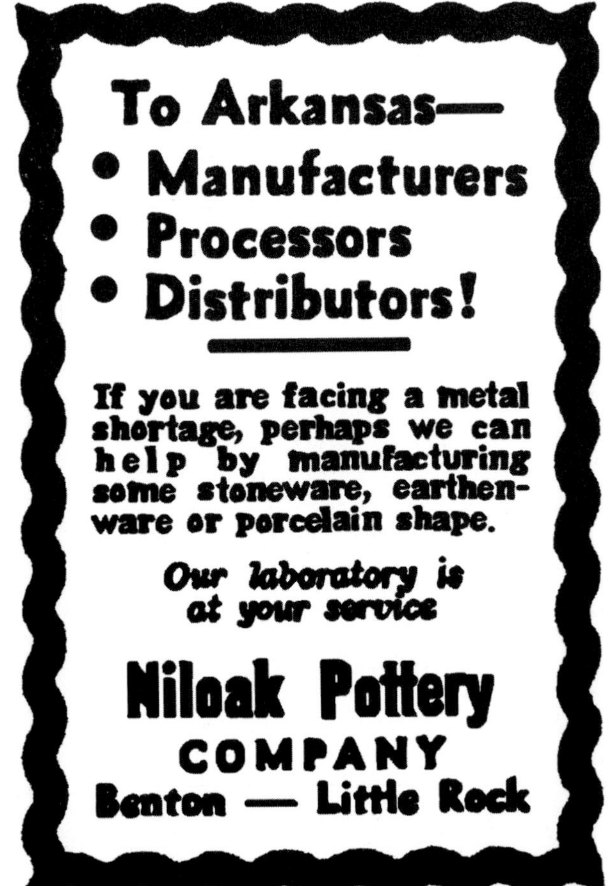

Niloak Pottery advertisement during World War II, *Arkansas Gazette*, March 1942. *Courtesy of the Butler Center for Arkansas Studies, Central Arkansas Library System. Graphic enhancement, courtesy of Stacy Brod.*

By the summer of 1942, Niloak Pottery was largely converted to war work, and its officers actively sought more war work. New contracts included sand jars for Fort Sill in Oklahoma, both chemical jars and porcelain flasks for industrial use, and electric insulators for the Arkansas Power and Light Company. In addition, Niloak on a daily basis made containers and other equipment for the military, as well as the manufacturing, agricultural, and dairy industries. Sinclair Winburn, working as Niloak's ceramist and superintendent, announced the company's involvement in ceramic made equipment for research and development of man-made rubber since, in the Pacific Theater, Japan successfully blocked the United States' supply of rubber from plantations in southern Asia. A critical element for war production, equipment made of ceramic to facilitate work to supplant the rubber shortage became a priority at Niloak Pottery.

The first major contract came in October 1942 when Niloak won its bid to produce coffee mugs for the Navy. The most significant and longest running contract concerned the production of clay pigeons for anti-aircraft practice. With this clay pigeon contract came the necessity for a larger plant. During the autumn and winter of 1942–1943, the Asher Avenue location became the warehouse and shipping center. The offices and retail sales departments were moved to 1213 Broadway, formerly the offices of the RumRill Pottery Company, which had recently closed after Rumrill's death. The Benton salesroom on Military Road was closed due to diminishing sales, but the original plant on Pearl Street remained in operation. After a renewed U. S. Army contract in late 1943, the new Broadway offices and the Asher warehouse were closed and a large tract of east Little Rock property was purchased for a complete, one-site location for the Niloak Pottery and Tile Company.

The new site was 1709 East Ninth Street in Little Rock. If there were uncertainties as to Niloak's future, they centered on problems with internal operations. While pay was at its highest, production faltered as the company faced difficulties in holding "an experienced crew." The new aluminum processing plant in Saline County took many of Niloak's most valuable male employees. Moreover, manufacturing costs climbed steadily as the cost for employee training increased with the high turnover. The manpower shortage was relieved when women were hired to replace the departing male employees. Combined with the unavailability of new parts and equipment, the company's net profit totaled only a little over $300.00 for 1943. Nonetheless, Niloak persevered with jobbing

World War II paper label. ***Courtesy of the late Hardy L. Winburn IV.***

orders and limited castware production, concentrating on fulfilling war contracts.

The majority of jobbing orders during the war were received from Robinson-Ransbottom Company, Shawnee Pottery, Louisville Pottery Company, Hall China Company, Western Stoneware Company, the George Brogfeldt Corporation, and other northern potteries. In addition, what little castware Niloak produced went to retailers like the McLellan Stores of New York, William R. Moore Dry Goods Company of Memphis, Sears and Roebuck, Walgreens, and the Sterling Stores of Little Rock. The wartime shortage of gas and tires placed many restrictions on salesmen's travels. While traveling on trains and buses, Niloak salesmen concentrated on orders for defense work, agriculture, and dairy needs. Production levels varied while Niloak Pottery had trouble getting needed parts, keeping skilled laborers, and securing raw materials. Wartime difficulty did not hinder expectations for hopeful post-war production. Beginning in mid-1943, Hardy Winburn planned for the future with the intention of catering to better class department stores.

The Niloak Pottery Company, reportedly in business in one form or fashion since 1868, celebrated its Diamond Jubilee in 1943. Although the war tempered festive occasions, Winburn dreamed of bigger, better plans for his company. Winburn saw production centering on decorated porcelain and enamel ware with hopes of producing the "finest line of painted china." During 1943, Hardy and Sinclair Winburn attended the American Ceramic Society meeting in Pittsburgh, Pennsylvania. Afterward they toured the Homer Laughlin, Newell, Robinson-Ransbottom, Roseville, and Shawnee Pottery companies, studying the competition in hopes of improving their manufacturing process.

A new direction came in 1944. After months of study and preparation, Niloak opened its chemical division under the guidance of William E. Crockett, a clay technologist from the University of Missouri. He was assisted by E. S. Amos, a ceramic engineer from Ohio State University. Promoting the economic development of Arkansas clays, Niloak announced the opening of a laboratory for "research and development of clay and other non-metallic raw materials." Working with the Arkansas State Geological Survey, plans included testing and classifying clays and locating markets for them. Lawrence N. Rapp, a designer and mold maker, made his first known trip to Niloak in August and worked through September on, as yet, unidentified work. By late 1944, future plans centered on vitreous cooking ware, serving ware, fancy ware, and specialties. These postwar plans, however, never materialized. By year's end, Niloak Pottery employed about 30 persons. However a disastrous fire at the Benton plant in early 1945, led the company to focus on filling voluminous backorders of castware with production from the Little Rock plant. Rapp made another visit and made molds in July while plans were implemented for building a tunnel kiln at the Little Rock plant. Under the supervision of Crockett, the kiln was finished in October 1945.

With the end of the war, Niloak started its re-conversion back to normal production. The Niloak Pottery, under Hardy and Sinclair Winburn's direction, acted within 24 hours after its war contracts were canceled. It received attention for its efforts with the *Arkansas Democrat* stating Niloak had set a record for re-conversion. Niloak Pottery had made 1,000,000 clay pigeons a month for the past two and a half years. With around 50 employees, the company ran a 24 hour production schedule to produce targets for the Army Air Force (forerunner to the U. S. Air Force) as well as America's allies (through the lend-lease program). The completion of Niloak's re-conversion took about 90 days as the Little Rock plant was enlarged and new equipment purchased and installed. While the number of post-war employees is unknown, Niloak Pottery had in its employ six war veterans.

Meanwhile, new sales were minimal. Hoping to jump start its sales, the company introduced a "Buyers Guide" to Niloak Pottery. Advertising itself as "Arkansas's oldest and most dependable source of pottery and house wares," Niloak Pottery asked retailers to participate in a month-to-month purchasing program where by they would receive

Hardy Lathan Winburn III, circa 1960s.
Courtesy of the late Hardy L. Winburn IV.

monthly, updated catalog sheets informing them on the up-to-date trends. Jobbing with the previous northern wholesalers (now including the Homer Laughlin Company) continued, with their sales outperforming those of Niloak's own "disappointing" sales. When the backlog of orders were finally filled in 1946, production was curtailed on many of Niloak's items and the plants' personnel reduced accordingly. Niloak Pottery then attempted to get into the dinnerware business itself. Niloak Pottery turned to its former designer Joe Alley for this new dinnerware line call "Bouquet." Under contract, Alley designed this dinnerware pattern with "French modern decorations" with some block and case work and molds made by Lawrence Rapp. The line was introduced in January 1947.

In June 1947, Rapp made another trip to Niloak Pottery, and the *Benton Courier* announced that a new metal pre-fab building and the Military Road showroom were opened. More importantly, the newspaper article stated that the "original, natural Niloak will be made." By September, the *Benton Courier* reported that the Niloak Pottery had announced the erection of a new Benton warehouse since the shipping department was being moved back from Little Rock. Employees numbered 24 with four full-time and six part-time salesmen. These salesmen included C. E. Hootman, J. S. Slovall, C. R. Lappin, W. H. Winburn, J. W. Adams, and E. Thomas. Immediate plans were to handle a dinnerware line (presumably its own Bouquet) as well as garden pottery. Unfortunately sales sagged, and the officials of Niloak knew that time was running out for the Niloak Pottery. But from the Niloak Pottery ruins rose the Winburn Tile Company. Avoiding business myopia, the Winburn brothers sought a new direction by bringing to an end the production of castware.

Opting not to continue this ceramic line, Hardy Winburn and his brother Sinclair began searching for new avenues for the Little Rock based business. The Winburns realized the need to either sell the business or form a different type of clay company. Back in early February, the Niloak Pottery and Tile Company was changed to H. L. Winburn and Company. In March, moreover, a Niloak Pottery Company was incorporated (only to be dissolved in late 1952). Although details are sketchy, they purchased tile making machinery in September 1947. About this time, the "assets [of the new Niloak Pottery Company] were traded for the equity in a new company that manufactured tile." Shortly thereafter, the Winburn Tile Company was formed as a branch of the Mosaic Tile Company of Zanesville, Ohio. Winburn management seemed resistant to give up castware production. Up to July 1950, management still sought to produce castware, but stated it was having "big kiln problems." Into the early 1950s, the Winburn Tile Company continued jobbing and extremely limited castware production while concentrating on beginning tile manufacture. Jobbed items centered on many dinnerware lines including Dixie Rose, Haviland Spray, Needlepoint, Poppy Spray, and Yellow Rose. For all practical purposes, however, the late 1940s were the death years for castware production. Sporadic sales and production continued, but steadily dwindled until production ended sometime in the early to mid 1950s.

The Winburn Tile Company would remain a part of the Mosaic Tile Company until 1970. For over 50 years, Winburn Tile Manufacturing Company has produced ceramic mosaic tile at the East 9th Street location. It manufactures tiles suitable for all surfaces. In addition, the company has executed many murals and produced specialty tile for the restoration of historical landmarks. They include San Francisco's old Court of Appeals building (one of the few structures to survive the 1906 earthquake) and Mississippi's State Capitol. Today the Winburn Tile Company, with a history of over 110 years in ceramic manufacturing, continues as a viable business in Little Rock and Maumelle, Arkansas.

Patented Jan. 31, 1928. **1,657,997**

UNITED STATES PATENT OFFICE.

CHARLES DEAN HYTEN, OF BENTON, ARKANSAS.

POTTERY.

No Drawing. Application filed July 24, 1924. Serial No. 727,999.

The present invention relates broadly to the art of ceramics, and particularly to a novel clay product and the process of manufacturing the same. The invention, more specifically speaking, has to do with the production of clay pottery of a decorative character by virtue of the use of clay of different colors.

It is quite common in the art of pottery making to produce clay products in colors, that is, each article is made from a homogeneous mass of a particular color of clay, either from naturally or artificially colored clay, but the art which has been founded by me involves the use of multi-colored clay in each manufacture, the varying colors in the composite formation of the particular article being caused to blend or the layers of the different colors to be displaced relatively to each other in such a manner as to produce a beautiful, distinctive, and highly artistic decoration.

It is a well known fact in the art to which this invention relates that clays of different colors shrink in drying or in firing in different degrees, depending more or less upon the silicate content or the character of the color base, so that before my contribution to the art it was impracticable to use different colors of clay in a single or composite article of manufacture with any degree of success without encountering difficulties of distortion, fracture or breakage.

My invention therefore resides primarily in the preparation of the clays preliminary to the forming and firing of the product so as to enable the use of various colors for decorative purposes and to obtain a uniform shrinkage of the clays under firing, this being incident to the use of either natural or artificially colored clays.

In carrying out my invention the natural or white clay is mined in the usual way and is then introduced into a blunger mill along with water where it is thoroughly mixed into a solution or suspension of the consistency of cream, substantially speaking. While in the mill and in this state of consistency, the coloring mixture is added, prior to which step, however, the proper proportioned ingredients controlling the degree of shrinkage of the clay are incorporated. This coloring mixture varies according to the particular color which is involved, but the proportions only and not the ingredients are all that require modification to produce a composite clay mass in which the shrinkage characteristics of each of the clays is designed to be uniform throughout. Naturally the chemical constituents of the particular clay's base used are taken into consideration. A desirable composition is composed of 90 per cent clay and an admixture of approximately 10 per cent coloring matter, whiting and ground flint.

As an exemplification of the preparation of the coloring mixture, the following formulae may be used for the respective colors in the approximate proportions specified, it being understood that the white colored clay does not require a coloring pigment, but does ordinarily require a shrinkage controlling factor or ingredient.

	Whiting.	Ground Flint.	Color pigment.
	Grams.	*Grams.*	
Blue	350	350	300 grams cobolt oxide.
Red	350	350	475 grams ferric oxide.
Gray	350	350	350 chromic oxide.
White	4	4	92 white clay

Specifically, to the dry ingredients of any one of these formulae a sufficient amount of water is added to make a solution of cream consistency, and this is then introduced into a ball grinder for pulverizing. When thoroughly ground and mixed the solution is then added to the clay solution in the blunger mill where further thorough mixing of the ingredients is accomplished. It is notable that in the blue coloring mixture, the clay in plastic condition is black, but this, when fired, will turn into a shade of blue, the particular shade of which depends upon the degree of heat as its controlling factor. In like manner, the gray color mixture changes from a green plastic to gray when fired, so that it will be understood that I am able to produce clays of a wide range of shades from the formulae which are herein given, by simply controlling the degree of heat.

Other coloring bases than those specified may be used when desired and they are given merely as examples of the manner in which I obtain the artificially colored clays, if the natural colored clays are not employed.

Proceeding with the process followed, after the introduction of the coloring mixture into the blunger mill as above specified, and its thorough admixture, it is run through a screen while in solution of approximately 140 mesh, after which it is put into plaster bottomed vats to extract the surplus water; the pasty mass is then allowed to dry for a period running from a week to ten days depending upon atmospheric conditions.

At this time the colored clay is in plastic condition about the consistency of putty but somewhat more plastic. Each separate colored clay prepared in accordance with the foregoing process is then kneaded well and a lump of each clay desired is taken. These lumps are placed one upon another and the whole cut into the proper sized mass for forming the particular object to be manufactured. This cut composite mass is then placed upon a potter's wheel and manipulated in the usual well known manner to form the particular shaped vessel or article. In this form a very great range of variations in decorative effect may be produced by the potter so that the different colors which are displaced with relation to each other form beautiful surface designs.

When shaped as desired they are removed from the wheel and allowed to partly dry, whereupon they are put on a turning lathe and polished until they have a smooth, fine finish.

After thorough drying, a glaze solution such as used in the ordinary pottery manufacture is pumped inside the dry article which adhering to the piece somewhat as a coating like whitewash produces under fire a glaze which makes the vessel waterproof.

After the glaze is applied the pottery is put in a kiln and fired approximately forty-eight hours at a temperature of approximately two thousand degrees Fahrenheit.

It will be apparent from the foregoing that an article made in the foregoing manner may possess any combination of colors desired and will vary in the shade of colors according to the degree of heating which is applied to the formed article.

Having thus described my invention, what I claim as new and desire to secure by Letters Patent is:

1. The process of preparing a clay for the manufacture of ceramic objects which consists in reducing the clay to a consistency of cream, separately admixing and grinding a color base material, and a shrinkage controlling material, combining the color mixture with the clay and mixing the same, extracting the excess moisture until in plastic condition and finally rotating said plastic material and shaping an object therefrom during such rotation.

2. The process of forming composite ceramic products which consists in reducing separate batches of clay to a substantially liquid consistency, adding to each batch a color base, and a shrinkage controlling material, each batch being proportioned relative to the color base used to produce a uniform shrinkage in subsequent firing of an article formed of the combined batches, extracting the surplus moisture from the batches, rotating said combined batches and forming an object therefrom during such rotation, and subjecting the formed article to a substantially high degree of heat.

3. The process of producing a ceramic object which consists in superposing a plurality of batches of different colored clays in plastic condition, and rotating the superposed batches during the shaping formation of the object to blend said batches.

4. The process of producing a ceramic object which consists in superposing a plurality of batches of different colored clays in plastic condition, and rotating the superposed batches during the shaping formation of the object to blend said batches, each of said batches having an ingredient to effect uniform shrinkage of the several batches when fired.

5. A cylindrical shaped ceramic product composed of a plurality of different colored clays, each different clay containing a shrinkage controlling substance so proportioned relative to the color base as to impart to such clay approximately the same shrinkage characteristic as the other clays, said clays being displaced circumferentially as an incident to manipulation during rotation of the composite clays while in plastic condition so as to produce a blended and variegated striae of irregular form.

In testimony whereof I affix my signature.

CHARLES DEAN HYTEN

NILOAK PRODUCTION: 1910 – 1947

The introduction of Missionware was remarkable for many reasons. First, the concept was a radical departure from the known art pottery production by all other American art pottery producers. Second, its introduction by a small, unknown pottery proved to be a formidable task. Third, there was the problem of obtaining the investment capital and other resources necessary to begin production on a great enough scale to correctly manufacture, market, and distribute a salable but new product. Although many factors remain unknown, the Niloak Pottery prevailed as a manufacturer of "something different" for collectors of art objects. After nearly a year of preparation, Niloak production was inaugurated by January 1910 with the first products displayed in Benton and Little Rock stores by March of that year.

The Niloak Pottery Company claimed that its product contained naturally colored clays. This is not exactly true, however, as the use of naturally colored clays was probably very limited and may never have even occurred. Colored clays were found in the Benton area, but if they were used, this only happened in Missionware's earliest years and with the use of cream, gray, and brown colors. Heinrich Ries wrote an article for *The Clay-Worker* on kaolin in 1900. Ries stated "kaolin is usually applied to those deposits of **white-burning clays**... [and] there are many deposits of white clay in the far South, that are sometimes erroneously called kaolin.... Such deposits are not true kaolins." (Bold letterings those of the author.) Although often printed in company literature and stated in interviews with Hyten (and repeated in countless secondary sources ever since then), statements about the use of naturally colored clays were simply an advertising ploy. Most of the clays in Missionware, if not all, used artificial dyes. A 1911 revelation that the "process of coloring and mixing the clay [was] the secret of the manufacturer," combined with Niloak Pottery's 1928 patent stating that cobalt, ferric, and chromic oxides were introduced to create the blue, red, and gray colors, respectively, made the "natural colors" claimed by Niloak simply not true. Moreover, the Missionware patent revealed that "the natural or white clay is mined in the usual way." Howard S. Lewis, the ceramist who developed the glazes for Niloak's Hywood by Niloak line in the early 1930s, also disputed claims that Missionware contained naturally colored clays.

Clay deposits were scattered throughout Saline County. These deposits varied in both quantity and quality but always needed additives to make the clay acceptable for use. The point that the clays were not naturally colored becomes clear when one reviews the 1928 patent. While some of the early pieces may well have some natural colors (such as cream, browns, and grays), most do not. Years later, it was written that the Saline County clays' "greatest uniformity [was] in fired colors that for the majority of the clays range from nearly white to buff." Geological surveys of the time stated that clays in Saline County often turned pink or gray after firing. Finally, if Niloak's clay was indeed kaolin (supposedly a fine white clay), the color certainly had to be added. The notion that the clays were of natural colors was advertising hype but became accepted as fact over the years. The retailer's promotion of Missionware, with its unique swirl effect, which resulted from the natural forces of the potter's wheel,

Howard S. Lewis, 1932.
Courtesy of James and Darlene Dommel.

Niloak Pottery advertisement, March 1910.
Courtesy of Arkansas History Commission.

included many far-fetched references to its origins. Some dealers sold it as Japanese pottery or the works of other Orientals, while others sought to promote it as a product of skilled Egyptian potters or the handiwork of Native Americans. The simple fact is that this most unusual, natural-looking pottery was the product of an Arkansas company.

The production of 1910 and 1911 consisted primarily of vases, and these early pieces exhibit three characteristics — sharp edge on bottom, interior clear glaze to rim, and soft looking, sometimes indistinct, blurred swirl patterns. These early pieces, typically rougher in texture, had the clear interior glaze to make them waterproof. This early clear interior glaze has a green tint that indicates a presence of vanadium efflorescence in the mixture. Collector's should note that the presence of this green tint on pieces with the First art mark indicate production during 1911 and perhaps 1912 before a new interior glaze was instituted. Few pieces exist with both an interior and an exterior glaze. It is probable that these exterior glazed Niloak pieces were Niloak's tip-of-the-hat to the successful production of what is known as the Standard glaze created by the Rookwood Pottery of Cincinnati, Ohio.

Rookwood had popularized Standard glaze with its decorative, slip-painted effects covered with a glossy exterior glaze. Creating almost an art painting effect, Standard glaze pieces had decorations of many subjects including motifs of flower arrangements, wildlife and animals, American Indians, and related subjects. Potteries across Ohio, particularly in Zanesville, then began producing their own copies of

Eagle/Niloak showroom, Hyten on steps, Benton, 1911. ***Author's collection.***

Rookwood's Standard glaze, once it was recognized as a salable line. Here in Arkansas, Ouachita Pottery even made items similar to Rookwood's Standard glaze as Ouachita attempted to work in the "Rookwood style." Niloak's Standard glaze-like Missionware, therefore, was typical of the art pottery commercially produced at Rookwood Pottery. It is probable that Dovey, definitely knowledgeable of the Standard glaze, sought to create a similar look and thus a salable product.

With Dovey's presence in Benton, therefore, it is all too probable that the exterior glazed Missionware was an attempt by Niloak Pottery to compete with Rookwood. This competition may also explain Niloak Pottery's references boasting its employment of former Rookwood employees. For years it was thought that these exterior glazed pieces were experimental and thus the earliest, but this is not the case. Although production of the glossy exterior glazed Missionware was limited, its production expands to at least the first year of production, a fact made clear with the discovery of a piece marked "Pat. Pend'g." With less than a dozen pieces known to exist, their rarity is established; but what is not known is whether their demise in production was a result of the product being unmarketable or that the exterior glaze often darkened and obscured the color swirls, thus leaving no aesthetic value. On the other hand it could be that Niloak Pottery saw the unglazed satin-like exterior as a more salable line since matte finishes had been the rage among the public since the turn-of-the-century.

Missionware artistic effects included the use of varying shades of one color, like blue, the use of two colored clays such as blue and white, or the use of a single color. The use of varying shades of a single color can have an unusual and most pleasing effect. Very rarely seen examples of this technique, like the candlestick in plate 3, represent experimentation, special commission, or an aesthetic intent on the potter's part. On the other hand, a few examples of bi-color Niloak pottery have surfaced, primarily in blue and white (see vases in plates 11, 14, and 21). The simplification of the surface, through the use of two colors, rather than the common four or five, provides a grace and simplicity to these classically shaped vessels. The proportions of height to width is reinforced by the two-color swirls rendering truly elegant examples of Niloak pottery. The use of a monochromatic or single color has artistic value. The bulbous vase (plate 34) is the most dramatic, largest, and most pleasing example found to date. Formed of a single color clay, its coloration extends through the body of the piece as in the Missionware. A truly simple, clean, and classically designed piece, it is perhaps one of the finest and most unusual examples of Niloak pottery extant. These variant uses of one color allow these pieces to be a significant cornerstone in the study and appreciation of Niloak Pottery as they represent a rare and successful variant to the more widely accepted notions of Niloak's Missionware production. Surely definable as works of art, these examples assist in the study of what constitutes Arkansas art pottery due to their unique use of color.

The early wares are varied with respect to coloration and shape. In general, the early pieces are dull looking and rough feeling compared to later Missionware. Some have scratches made during the finishing process. Early Niloak Pottery Missionware has been described as those with earthen colors. By the late 1910s the standardization of shapes slowly caused Niloak Pottery to move away from individual artistic expression in its art pottery. Moreover, the use of brown, gray, blue, red, and white together over and over became the norm, leaving little attention to coloration as an aspect of artistic expression. The company essentially began mass production to meet the increasing demands of the 1920s, similar to what Rookwood Pottery did during the 1920s with its heavy commercial glazed ware production.

As for the merit of the designation "art" pottery, the 1913 *Clay-Worker* article described the works as "real art, according to the laws of nature." Moreover, it stated that Niloak pottery had "lasting merit" as its "decorative ornaments are ingrain[ed] through the entire thickness of the article...while other art potteries obtain their decorations only in surface form, usually by glaze process." Much of Niloak's production after the late 1910s is not art pottery since little individual creativity was allowed because of the standardization of shapes and colored clays as the company focused on mass producing Missionware, but exceptions exist. This standardization is further magnified by the use of tools such as a jigger, whereby the "smaller... pieces are molded by machinery." Finally, the use of natural gas from the mid-teens on puts the company further into an industrial mode.

Earliest known photograph of Missionware, 1911. Note decorated piece in lower left-hand corner. *Author's collection.*

The process for clay took from one to two weeks. After the initial mud-grinding and mixing (with the removal of grit and other trash), the clay was placed into a mill for the final grinding process and then soaked in vats of water. It was then screened through 1550 mesh of wire cloth and dried to a state which permitted handling (i.e. throwing). Niloak employees acknowledge that there were many important variables in the production of Missionware. The blending of colors required time. The mixing process involved lopping off chunks of the different colored clays, stacking them up, and cutting them across a stretched wire. Sometimes this manipulation resulted in unusual color schemes for some pieces. Once thrown, the pieces underwent a difficult, delicate finishing process where each piece was trimmed and smoothed on a horizontal lathe. Last, the firing was itself important, and this aspect has frequently been described as the "secret" to making Missionware. As particular skills within the Missionware process were needed for perfecting each piece, this fact is an important reason why potters like Long, Rowland, Johnson, the McNeils, and others should be recognized for their efforts.

A major contribution lies in the standardization of Missionware which incorporated the use of multicolored clays into a single piece, a most difficult task due to the different shrinking, drying, and firing rates of the individual clays. Using a mixture of 90% clay and 10% additives consisting of coloring and shrinkage control agents — blue (cobalt oxide), red (ferric oxide), gray (chromic oxide), and white (white clay), these potters mastered this most difficult aspect, and as stated in the 1928 patent, they were "able to produce clays of a wide range of shades...by simply controlling the degree of heat." Some of the early color variations may be accounted for because of the difficulty associated with maintaining a precise and consistent temperature in a wood-fired kiln. The use of natural gas as a kiln fuel insured better temperature control and a more consistent color rendering. Unfortunately, taken together, these steps toward standardization were moving Missionware away from the concept of "art pottery."

Niloak plant interior; Pearl Street, Benton, Arkansas, 1912.
Hyten right foreground; Frank Ira Long, second from right, background (facing straight ahead). ***Courtesy of Arlene Hyten Rainey.***

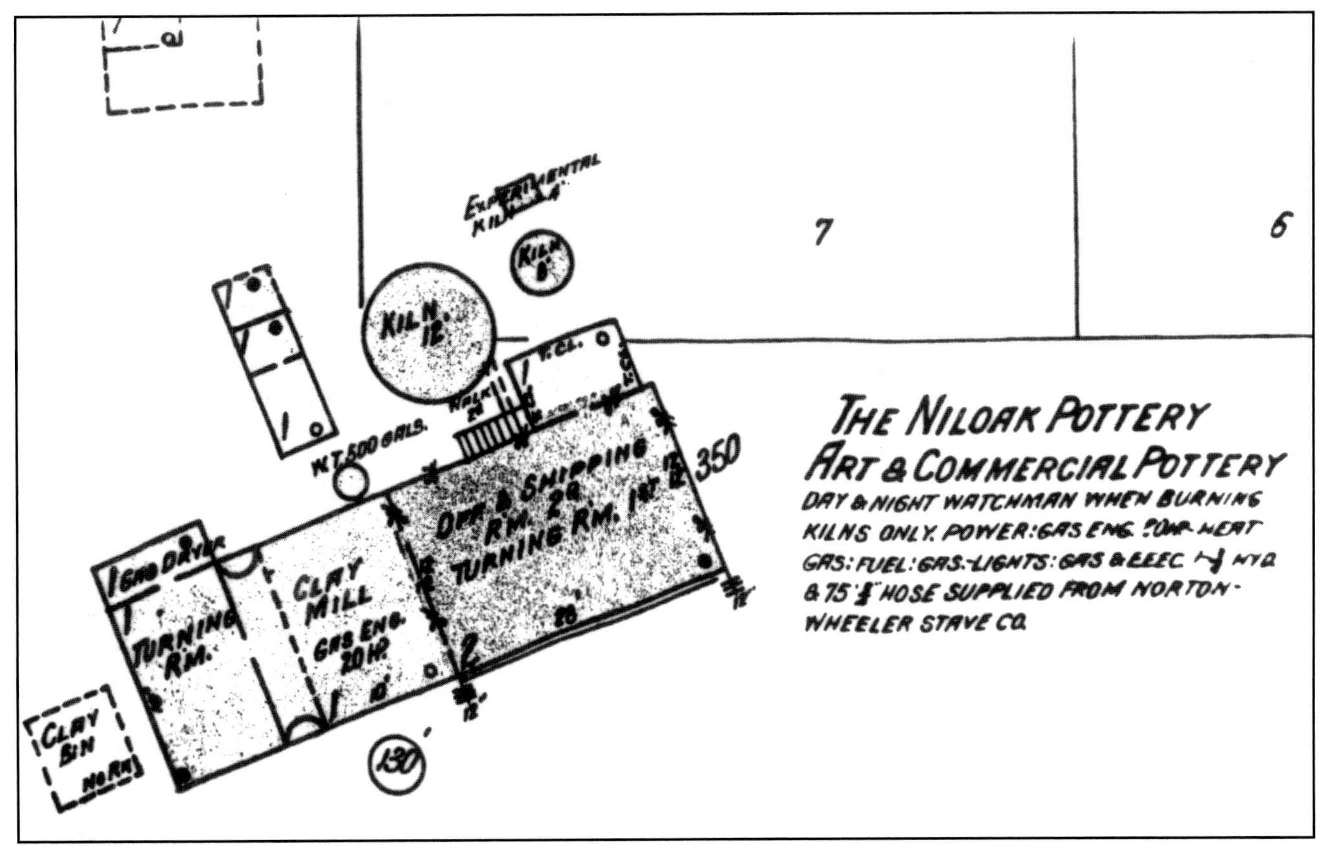

Niloak Pottery plant, Pearl Street, Benton. 1915 Sanborn Insurance Map. ***Courtesy of Arkansas History Commission.***

The mid and late 1910s were times of transition at Niloak. Few sales occurred during World War I and business advertising was minimal. However, it was the time when standardization took its biggest leap. Work was implemented on the swirl process which ultimately led to a patent. By the early 1920s the shapes were standardized. The color schemes were limited, if not restricted, to red, white, blue, brown, and gray. Thus a mass-produced mode existed at Niloak as production increased to match its growing popularity across the country. With its unique variegated coloring, Niloak production purportedly reached between 50,000 and 75,000 pieces annually. However, no records exist which can confirm or deny this statement. Bob Doherty, in the *American Clay Exchange,* convincingly argued that this often repeated production estimate was too high. Combined with claims that Charles Hyten threw all the Missionware, it is hard to believe production ever reached this number. However, Hyten (although he claimed sometimes that he threw every Missionware piece) had other experienced potters like Frank Long, Reagan Rowland, Romine and Joshua McNeil, and Fred Johnson. All were skilled throwers and Niloak employees as early as 1910.

Records do exist, however, on the production of raw clay used by Niloak Pottery (measured in short tons) starting in 1923. These raw clay measurements included both the production of Missionware and Eagle's utilitarian wares. During 1923 – 1925, the average was about 1,500 tons with a sharp drop to about half the previous average for 1926 and 1927. Over 1,000 tons were mined in 1928, with a tremendous increase, close to over 5,800 tons, in 1929. This precipitously dropped to just over 300 tons for 1930. Since no extensive business records exist prior to 1934, little can be said as to why production varied so much throughout the 1920s. Niloak Pottery, in a 1925 report to the *Crockery and Glass Journal* stated "interest is just fair" in the Niloak art line, but orders were increasing and a "strong fall and holiday business [was] expected." Nonetheless, the business apparently fared well through the 1920s with a dramatic production increase in the late 1920s just before the Great Depression.

For years, local lore and many secondary sources claimed that Niloak Pottery's Missionware was sold in Cuba. While this has yet to be proven, it is known that Niloak received an order and shipped to Cuba a train carload of water filters. It may be that the facts over the years were forgotten and/or embellished. In addition to Missionware production, Niloak in the mid-1920s began the production of "plaster plaques, baby dolls, candlesticks, and other items too numerous to mention for hand-painting and decorating." Hyten

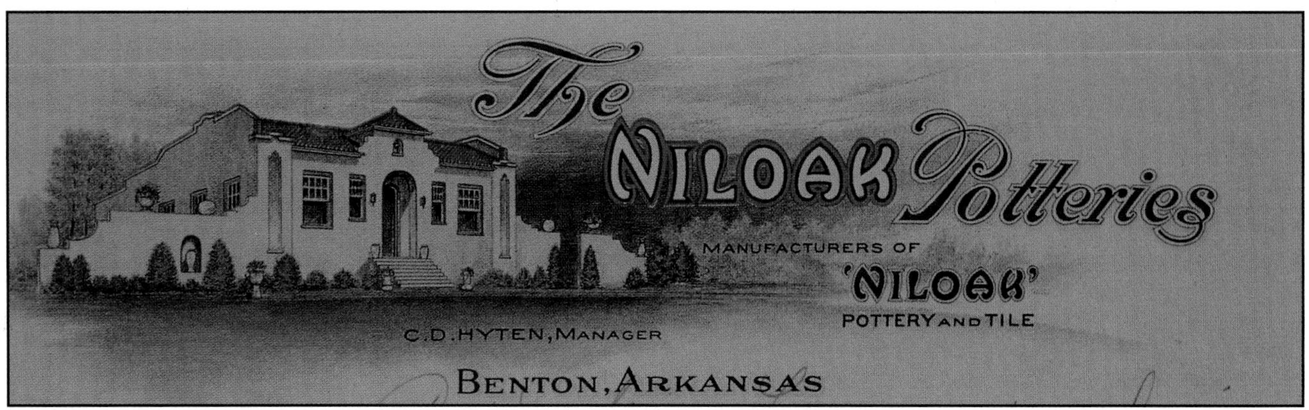

Original four-color lithograph Niloak Pottery and Tile Company letterhead, circa 1930. A costly item and a rarity among Arkansas businesses. This expensive letterhead undoubtedly was an additional factor, combined with the 1929 showroom construction and catalog publication, in Niloak's financial woes during the onset of the Depression. Author's collection.

explained further: we "put out plain white vases for hand decoration ...as many women and girls have become interested in decorating their own vases." Two signed vases, solid cream in color, have surfaced with hand-painted decorations (see one in plate 52). They remain some of the more unusual and interesting items known to exist. Collectors should be on the lookout for these unique, uncommon pieces; watch for Niloak shapes.

Another development was to have a designer create items with colored clays for possible production and marketing by Niloak Pottery. In 1970, Mary D. Hudgins, local historian of Hot Springs, wrote to Paul Evans (then editor of the *Spinning Wheel,* Western Division), as follows: "F. D. Basore was a woman, interested in crafts even before they moved to Hot Springs area in the early 1920s. She visited the Niloak plant and was excited. Mr. Hyten agreed to give her all the clay she wanted to work with (All specimen [sic] I've seen of her modeling are in putty grey[sic].) Her daughter says that the agreement was that her mother was to be furnished clay, and her works fired. If any of her designs proved the sort to warrant Niloak issuance, they would automatically become the property of the firm. She sold her wares from her home; and they were purveyed at Arbordale, a fashionable swimming and dancing resort near Hot Springs. She modeled busts of members of her own family, and even attempted to duplicate specimen [sic] of Caddoan Indian pottery. She crafted many small items of interest. One in particular was popular — a log with stumpy branches — hollowed out for a match holder. Which of her designs were tapped for commercial Niloak production her daughter doesn't know." One of these rare items, a bookend, can be seen on plate 84.

Throughout the 1920s, Niloak concentrated on the retail market in larger cities in department stores and art shops and, with sales distributors from coast to coast, in the Midwest and Southwest and in Arkansas to resorts such as Hot Springs (the Biggs Art Store) and Eureka Springs. Yet, nothing could prevent the Great Depression and the dramatic changes Niloak Pottery Company would undergo during this unfortunate time in America. Hyten apparently had the utmost faith in the Niloak product when he mortgaged nearly all of his assets to build the new showroom on Military Road in early 1929. When the Depression hit, this debt became disastrous for the company. During 1929 and 1930, retrenchment occurred with emphasis given to selling Eagle Pottery's utilitarian ware. It was probably at this time that Hyten sought renewed financial help as well as administrative assistance from others. As sales for Missionware fell, Hyten sought to produce much cheaper ceramics as did other pottery manufacturers of this time. To produce art pottery and survive, Hyten secured the services of Stoin M. Stoin from the Weller Pottery Company of Zanesville, Ohio, to create the Hywood Art Pottery line. The result was a complete change in ceramic production away from Missionware to traditional glazed ware and ultimately to industrial castware.

Stoin brought to Niloak both his knowledge of glazes and shapes he used at Weller. No doubt Stoin is responsible conceptually for the Hywood Art Pottery line as Hyten, after over 20 years of Missionware production, had little knowledge of traditional ceramics, its clay bodies, and glaze preparation. Hywood Art Pottery, Hy from Hyten and wood from the re-instatement of wood as kiln fuel, was introduced in December 1931 after several months of experimentation and development. The clay was the same as that used in making Missionware, the shapes were mostly hand thrown, and some had applied handles. Glaze descriptions of the new line included "mottled greens and blues, shades of tan, yellow, red, and russett" with "mat and glossed finishes." From comparisons of the Hywood Art Pottery catalog to photographs and catalog pages of Weller Pottery's Nile, it is obvious that at

Niloak Pottery Stoin introduced several identical shapes from his previous employer. Some Hywood Art Pottery glazes, as well, were similar to those at Weller including Fruitone and Frosted Matt (but with less dramatic glaze curl). Hywood Art Pottery glaze names included Ozark Dawn, Peacock Blue, and Sea Green. The glazes were primarily matte, but some glossy finishes were produced as well. Hywood Art Pottery production lasted only until early 1932 when Stoin left for employment in Zanesville, Ohio. Again, not being knowledgeable of typical ceramic manufacture, Hyten unexpectedly dropped in to see his friend, Paul E. Cox, at Iowa State College. Cox had visited Hyten in 1917 and in 1925.

While it is not certain as to what Cox was doing at Niloak Pottery back in 1917 (other than a personal visit), it is known that Cox's visit in 1925 related to ceramic manufacture. Cox was "engaged by the Niloak Co. to do research work...[as the] company is working out several new lines that will later be shown in addition to its present line of art ware." It is not known whether any "new lines" were developed and marketed, but since the only known Niloak production of the 1920s was Missionware, it seems unlikely anything came about due to Cox's visit. While we may never know the extent of their professional relationship, Cox may have helped Niloak Pottery write the patent application during his 1925 visit. It is possible, moreover, that this "research work" later became the groundwork for the Niloak Hywood Art Pottery line. During his trip to Arkansas, Cox even wrote, for his "good friend," a couple of articles for an Arkansas publication called *Dixie Magazine.* "Arkansas," he wrote, " has in C.D. Hyten and his corps of experts a group of amateurs 'who have the taste, the penchant' for working clay into beautiful forms and even though they earn their living thereby, they are amateurs, because they love every minute of the day's work," Cox's description of the Niloak Pottery employees as "corps of experts" further underlines the importance of the work by the other potters.

Hyten's visit to Iowa resulted in his employing Howard S. Lewis, a recent ceramic engineering graduate. Arriving in June 1932, Lewis began to develop new glazes and a new clay body for a new line called Hywood by Niloak. Although some names were retained such as Ozark Dawn and Peacock Blue, their appearances were different: therefore, Stoin's Ozark Dawn is labeled as I and Lewis's as II. This applies as well to Peacock Blue I (Stoin's) and Peacock Blue II (Lewis's). Lewis developed other glazes including Ozark Blue, Maroon, Ivory, and Green and Tan Matt which Niloak used until around the beginning of World War II. These Lewis glazes became extremely popular with the buying public since they were used by the company for nearly ten years, long after Lewis's departure from Niloak Pottery. Meanwhile, the company discontinued the Hywood Art Pottery name and replaced it with Hywood by Niloak. Clearly the objective was to connect the Hywood line with the already well-known Niloak name.

However, shortly thereafter, Niloak began using primarily molds in its production due to the ease of manufacture and low production cost per unit. Therefore, the earliest of Howard Lewis's Hywood by Niloak line consisted primarily of hand-thrown vases, bowls, and candlesticks. But by the end of 1932, Niloak began using more and more molds designed by Rudy Ganz. It is probable that the designs of the marked castware examples of Hywood Art Pottery and Hywood by Niloak lines are those of Ganz. By now, three different clays were mixed with other chemicals and blended into a cream-like consistency. During the ensuing year, castware production became the dominant production method due to the ease of manufacture and the low production cost per unit.

Niloak Pottery simply realized its need to change its manufacturing process to increase production even more to ensure more sales while at the same time cutting costs further. This allowed the company to increase its daily output significantly over what past Missionware and Hywood Art Pottery production had allowed. Niloak Pottery's new task in mold production centered on re-adjusting and experimenting in making pottery with standard methodologies which castware production brought. With this modernization, art pottery was not necessarily lost. The Modernistic (Art Moderne) movement, beginning in the 1920s, brought Art Deco and Streamline influences (designs attributed either to Rudy Ganz or George Peterson) to the company by the early to mid 1930s. Niloak Pottery's other endeavors involved artistic pottery of monochromatic and bi-chromatic glaze manipulations including mottles, stipples, drips, but primarily oversprays.

Although Missionware production continued into the 1930s (known throwers included Howard Lewis and Fred Johnson) and into the early 1940s (by designer Joe Alley), it was very limited. Fred Johnson, Niloak's long-time potter, threw a great deal of Missionware. As remembered by Niloak Pottery employee Albert V. Hutcheson, Johnson threw most of what little Missionware (mainly miniatures) was made, especially out at Niloak's Military Road showroom for tourists wanting to see how Missionware was made. Hutcheson also remembered that the Missionware process took two weeks (ideally) from raw "gray" clay to the salesroom, and that the process involved great skills, particularly in the finishing process of each piece on the lathe. Hutcheson also remembered Clyde Bridges, Mrs. Van Wright, and Jim Durrett being Niloak employees from the late 1930s and early 1940s. It is also known that Howard "Barney" Irwin, another student of Iowa State College, was a Niloak Pottery

Photo of early Hywood production, c. 1933. ***Courtesy of the late Hardy L. Winburn IV.***

Navy mug by Niloak, designed by Joe Alley.
Courtesy of Perry and Darlene Yohe.

employee; however, it is not known what were his responsibilities.

Fortunately, Lewis's two year employment after his arrival in the summer of 1932 set the foundation for Niloak's successful operations for the next decade. Lewis came to Niloak to redevelop the Hywood Art Pottery glazes but ended up formulating new glazes for the Hywood by Niloak line. In an interview before his death, Lewis said: "I have fond memories of the two years I spent there [at Niloak]. I have made a lot of glazes, but the Peacock Blue and the Ozark Dawn were two of my favorites. I named the Peacock Blue and Mr. Hyten named the Ozark Dawn." According to Lewis, the most popular glaze in Niloak sales and a favorite of Hyten was Ozark Dawn II. It was Niloak's most produced color combination, as it is the most common glaze found today on pieces available in secondary markets.

In 1935, debt ridden and in need of more accurate controls and simplified procedures, Niloak, under Winburn's direction, attempted to increase both production and sales. Throughout the latter half of 1935 and the first half of 1936, the Hywood by Niloak line became standardized with fewer thrown shapes and more castware. George Peterson, Niloak's designer, continued work, like Lewis before him, on correcting the problem with crazing, especially with the Ivory (white matte) glaze. New sales offices were established in Dallas, St. Louis, New York, and Los Angeles. As a result, sales began to increase as Niloak Pottery secured new places in the ceramic retail market.

Of noted interest (not only to Niloak collectors) is the production vinegar jars for the Gregory-Robinson-Speas Company (see plate 129) between 1935 and 1936. Douglas G. Hollandsworth's publication, *Speas Vinegar II,* revealed this discovery in company literature and photographs. And in fact, the Niloak Pottery and Tile Corporation records revealed sales totaling $433.21 to Gregory-Robinson-Speas sometime between August 1935 and September 1936. Based on an estimated per piece cost of $1.50, nearly 300 vinegar jars were made (at least). While this vinegar jar is found unmarked most of the time, it has been seen with either the second Hywood by Niloak stamp or the Second art mark. By early 1937, the Winburns sought to further modernize the plant and simplify the business. By the end of 1937, the Hywood by Niloak name was discontinued and all castware was simply marked "Niloak." This applied to the stoneware (Eagle Pottery) as well.

The late 1930s were unpredictable times with periodic expansion followed by retrenchment. Despite continuous efforts to coordinate departments, Niloak Pottery's production remained between 30% and 50% of normal. Moreover, glazes and clay bodies were performing below expectation. These problems resulted in an above normal increase in "seconds." Many of the poor quality pieces on the market today result from Niloak's sales of second quality items. The company sold these seconds in lots of $80.00 worth for $30.00. Among the problems was leakage. Since Niloak produced many assorted vases and planters, the composition of the clay (and in some instances, the glazes) was changed to improve adherence to the clay. Collectors should pretest any vessel before using since some Niloak castware pieces do leak (as my mother will testify). Beginning with 1939, molds contained recessed bottoms (hence the beginning of marks in the molds themselves) which allowed the bottoms to be glazed as well.

By mid-1939, corporate records reflect better results in production, sales, and distribution, including new firing schedules, systematized sales efforts, regular, improved sales routes, and better shipping schedules. With the closing of the 1930s, new ventures were undertaken to increase Niloak's market share and to diversify its production. Niloak Pottery even started a special orders department. The four-inch castware creamer in Lewis's Fox Red has been seen with "J. C. Harbin's Good Milk, Memphis" on the side in low relief. Another special order was for the Hotel Will Rogers. Using a "sprig" technique, a thin layer of clay in the shape of a shield or crest-like emblem was applied to the surface of the pottery piece (in this case a pitcher). At this time, Alley designed 21 new shapes, in addition to the current 60 available shapes, and also created a new novelty line for the 1939 Christmas trade. These items, fired in Benton and hand painted in Little Rock, consisted of three bells of different sizes and one angelic candleholder (see plate 146). Another interesting item was introduced about this time in what are now referred to as State pitchers, also designed by Alley.

These pitchers had the state's name and related emblem in low relief on one side and the American eagle and U. S. A. in relief on the other side. An undocumented story surrounding their creation is that they were ordered by a particular railroad company that had railways through Arkansas and the surrounding states. The State pitchers include Arkansas (diamond/flag emblem), Kansas (wheat bushel emblem), Missouri (mule/donkey emblem), Texas (Lone Star emblem), Louisiana (pelican emblem), and Mississippi (rebel flag emblem). To date, neither an Oklahoma nor Tennessee state pitcher has been seen. However, a Memphis pitcher with a tugboat symbol has surfaced. Last, a pitcher with just the eagle/U.S.A. on both sides was found. The State pitchers have been seen in most of Howard Lewis's glazes.

Alley also created a new line known in-house as "Eagle Novelties." These novelties consisted of a small line of figurines (10 items) and miniatures (10 items). Since catalogs do not exist, the figurine shapes are unknown (probably the small animals), but the miniatures were undoubtedly the many small molded pitchers. Alley was also responsible for Niloak's utilitarian Kitchenware line with Art Deco influences. Finally, Alley's Niloak employment resulted in several designs which became good sellers. These include the squirrel planter and the elephant on trunk planter which were produced and reproduced in various and similar forms into the late 1940s.

The squirrel planter represents a mass production shift in ceramic manufacture at Niloak and probably at many other clay companies. When first introduced in the late 1930s, this planter's design was quite detailed with distinct features such as the eyes, the lines in the body, and the open arms holding a nut. The mold design required lengthy and expensive construction, but when the first molds wore out, their replacements often had fewer details. Over time, some details were left out. The overall result was a lesser quality item but with an easier and less costly manufacture. This trend happened with many other popular items such as vases, novelties, and planters as mold quality dropped to maximize profits.

The winters at Niloak traditionally meant new design development, new catalog preparation, and an overall gearing up for spring/summer/fall production

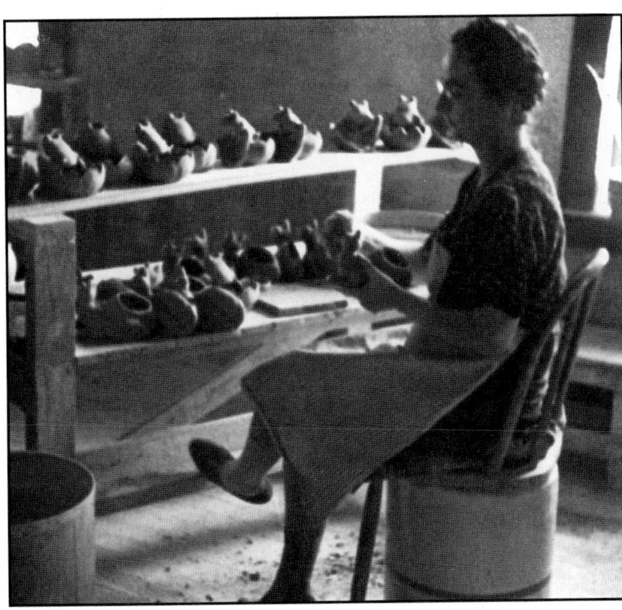

Finishing room with Mrs. Westbrook working on fox planter, c. 1940. ***Courtesy of the late Hardy L. Winburn IV.***

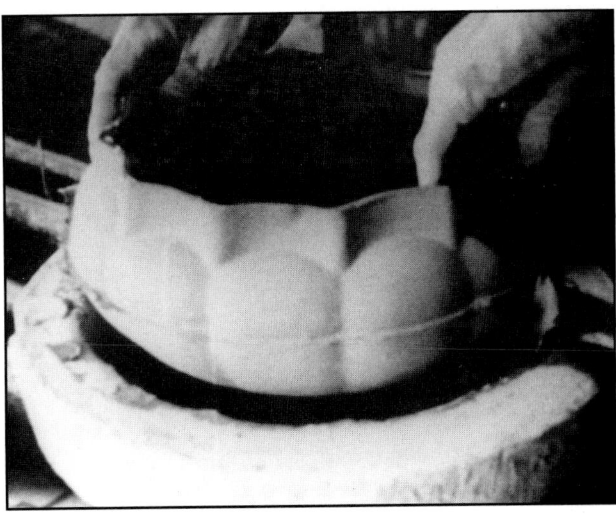

Mold room close-up of greenware being removed from mold, c. 1940. ***Courtesy of the late Hardy L. Winburn IV.***

Worker loading/unloading stoneware in kiln, c. 1940.
Courtesy of the late Hardy L. Winburn IV.

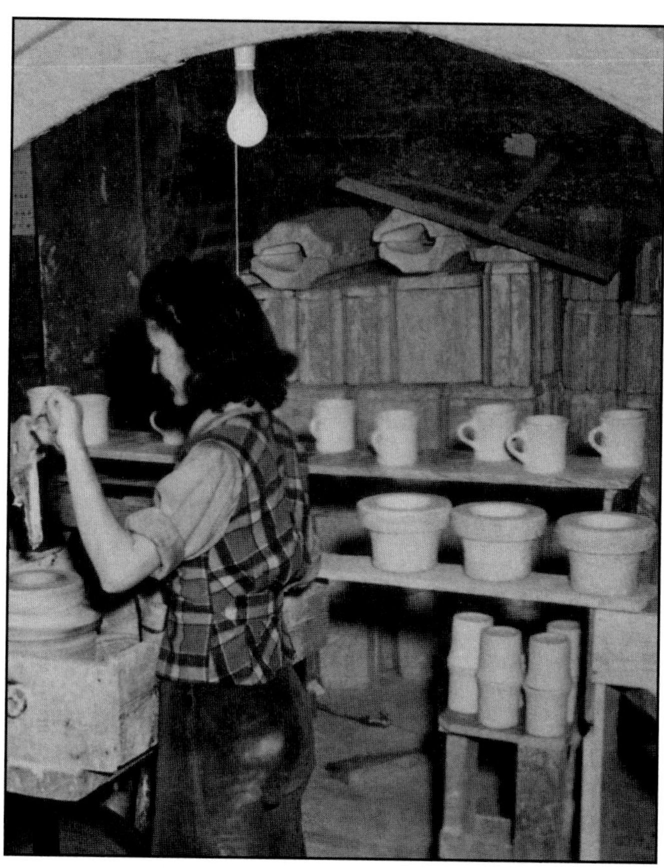

Niloak Pottery plant, Pearl Street, Benton, early 1940s, Miss Bardwell making mugs for the Navy.
Courtesy of the late Hardy L. Winburn IV.

Mold room with workers removing Winged Victory vases from molds, c. 1943. ***Courtesy of the late Hardy L. Winburn IV.***

and sales. For April 1940, 48 shapes, including 18 new shapes, were in production. Niloak's sales continued very well up until World War II, and production reached capacity. At this point utilitarian production was minimal, and its kiln converted to castware manufacture. Corporate records reveal record-breaking production and sales, greater than at any other time during the history of the company. It is not known, however, whether this meant back to 1934 when Hardy Winburn took over or 1911 when the Niloak Company was established. As in the past, the company was always looking for new products. Since early 1940, Hardy Winburn had been interested in manufacturing glassware, but this never materialized. Nonetheless, the figurines and miniatures introduced back in January proved to be a salable line and were in production until at least World War II.

By the end of 1941, America entered World War II. During 1942, this presented new challenges for Niloak. Government restrictions began with tin and cobalt oxides in January 1942. Sinclair Winburn began experiments for color replacements and by late 1942, worked to replace all glaze mixes with non-essential materials. Hardy Winburn lamented that "very little of the colors by which our artware has been recognized for so many years is now being used." Because of limited clay supplies and problems with past clay bodies, Sinclair developed a new clay body. More watertight, this clay was in production by the summer of 1943 and called "porsaline," a comical combination of porcelain and Saline County. This clay had a denser composition and was gray in color. Also started at this time was the use of hand decorations highlighting certain products. They are commonly found on Alley's parrot and kangaroo design from the Pacific Planters group. Alley also designed during this time his patriotic Winged Victory vases, and they became popular sellers for Niloak Pottery.

Niloak underwent yet another transformation during 1943. Castware production became more and more restricted with most work being done by women. Utilitarian production ceased when Niloak began purchasing the stoneware output of Hope Pottery of Hope, Arkansas. War work became the priority at Niloak when it secured the first of several U.S. contracts in the summer of 1943. The major contract involved the production of clay pigeons for training anti-aircraft gunners. Made of asphalt from the Lion Oil Company of El Dorado, these targets would duplicate the approximate speed of enemy planes. Since the shortage of metal limited the production of containers, Niloak produced stoneware mercury containers and covered crocks for the Army. For domestic consumption, Niloak made stoneware pie pans, porcelain electrical insulators, and bushings for generators. Only one line of Niloak Pottery's war production has surfaced on the collector's market. During 1943, Niloak secured a contract to produce ceramic mugs for the Navy. With a jiggered body and applied handles, it is probable that existing examples were seconds. Although castware production was reduced considerably, the business remained viable due to the manufacturing of non-metallic supplies for the armed forces, as well as chicken waterers for agricultural use, filters for industrial use, bushings, and other technical wares.

In 1944 and 1945, preparations were made for the resumption of normal production of castware. With many changes locally, nationally, and internationally, Niloak found itself attempting to change its scope completely. It aimed for better ceramic lines for the upper class trade market in the better department stores. However these hopes never materialized, and Niloak Pottery continued to manufacture castware. The biggest difference after the war lies in the type of glazes used with the porsaline clay. While prewar glazes were predominantly matte or dull finishes, the postwar finishes were primarily glossy or shiny. The new light-colored glazes were single-fired, and some pieces had decoration. The colors included light blue, pink, green, and white. With postwar production at capacity because of huge existing back orders, Niloak shipped castware as fast as it was produced. With high sales and shipments steady, weekly production soared to 24,000 pieces with 30 different shapes, and sales rose to $146,423.71 for 1945.

General production during 1946 – 1947 at the Little Rock plant consisted of 30 different items of the "medium price range" including hand-painted decorations. Attempts were made at both underglaze and overglaze decorations, but these experiments proved unsuccessful in active production. Moreover, concerns existed for improved quality which never quite materialized. Yet the company plugged on and introduced several new designs by Joe Alley. Alley, now employed by the Texas Pottery Company of Houston, was contacted by Hardy Winburn during the summer of 1946 to come back to Arkansas and work. Alley agreed by September, but only that he would work under sub-contract (while still employed at Texas Pottery). Alley would create new designs, and working with Lawrence N. Rapp, a founder of the Cliffwood Art Potteries (later known as Midwest Potteries) of Illinois, help with block and case and mold work. Rapp came once a year to Niloak (since 1944) to undertake block and case work and make molds as the designer could not do all the work involved in mold making and fulfill his designer duties and other responsibilities. Rapp probably made some designs and the molds for new and existing pieces after Alley's departure since it is unknown as to whether or not Niloak Pottery ever hired a permanent designer.

It was Joe Alley (not Rapp) who designed two groups of planters known as the C135 Assortment. The first group was called the "Stars of the Big Top" and consisted of the Clown Drummer, Circus Elephant, and Clown and Donkey (similar to the Keystone cops). These were described in promotional literature as "light" and "gay" and "colorful as a parade." Alley remembered hand decorating (in detail) about five or six of the Clown Drummer and Clown and Donkey planters that were placed on the market. This test marketing failed to attract buyers and Niloak Pottery instead manufactured the "Stars of the Big Top" with regular glazes and applied simple cold-water decorations. The second grouping was called "Bright Whimsies" and included the Fish Plant Bowl (swimming fish), Deer & Fawn, and Peter Pan Bowl. The colors for these planters were white, blue, pink, fox red, and green, and the planters sold for $9.00 per dozen. They were introduced around October and production of these items continued to about 1950.

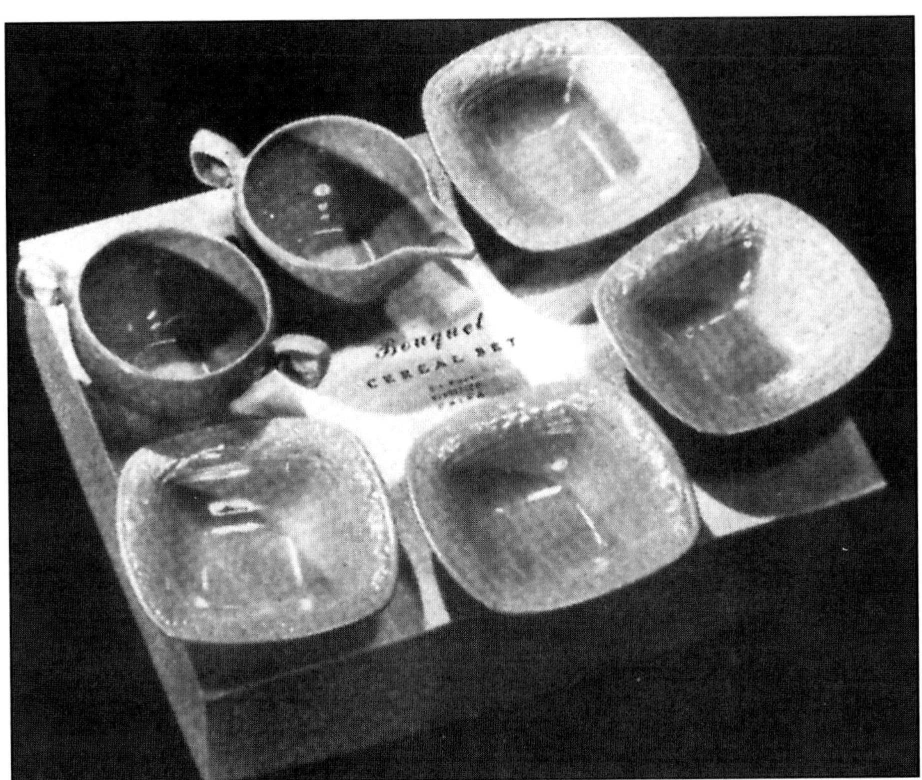

Bouquet Cereal Bowl photograph, 1947. *Author's collection.*

Sales faltered toward the end of 1946. One last production innovation involved a dinnerware line called Bouquet, starting in January 1947. Joe Alley agreed to design the line, do the block and case work, and make the molds for 10 to 15 pieces. Alley spent three months on this dinnerware line, his last creation for Niloak Pottery. Bouquet included a variety of tableware including an 8" vegetable bowl, 10" platters, 8" plates, salt and pepper shakers, cereal bowls, salad plates, creamers, beverage pitchers, cups, and saucers. Three different "sets" were marketed consisting of the Hostess Set (a pitcher and four cups and saucers), the Ice Tea Set (a pitcher and six mugs), and the Cereal Set and Berry Set (identical set of four bowls and an opened sugar bowl and creamer each). Collectors should note that most, if not all, of Niloak's sugar bowls were sold as open. "Open" in that no lids were sold with the bowls. Therefore, a sugar bowl without a lid is not incomplete. Having a lid, however, is a rarity!

All Bouquet sets were sold in mixed or solid colors, and perhaps the Hostess Set, the Ice Tea Set, and the Berry Set came in marked boxes as did the Cereal Set. There was also a vase with handles called a Rose Jar. Examples marked Bouquet do exist but are rarely seen. The most common examples are the pitcher and four matching mugs or cups with saucers. Unfortunately, the large plates/platters and bowls warped during drying and firing. What limited sales that did occur were handled by the Newton Sales Company of Chicago. Unfortunately for Niloak Pottery, most of the line ceased production by the end of 1947 after continued warpage problems, and more importantly, sales failed to materialize. In September 1948, the W. S. Dickey Clay Company re-ordered the promotional frog ashtray that the Niloak Pottery made "several years ago." It is not known, however, whether Niloak Pottery was able to fulfill the re-order. Yet some production of Alley's Bouquet line did continue in the 1950s with the manufacturing of pitchers, mugs, and cups and saucers. Although converted to the Winburn Tile Company, castware production continued into early 1950s. It may be that the castware production ceased after the failure of the Bouquet line. All that is known is that tile production supplanted castware production by the mid 1950s and its manufacture continues today.

NILOAK MARKS

1. Benton, Ark. Mark: Impressed die-stamp mark (block letters) first used when Niloak was introduced in 1910.

2. Benton, Ark. Stamp: Applied black ink stamp used during early 1910.

3. Early Niloak: Impressed die stamp mark (block letters) used before September 1910. Note that this mark is not the same size mark as the block letter marks used in the mid to late 1930s on beginning castware production or the hand-tooled animals. (See marks numbers 21 and 22.)

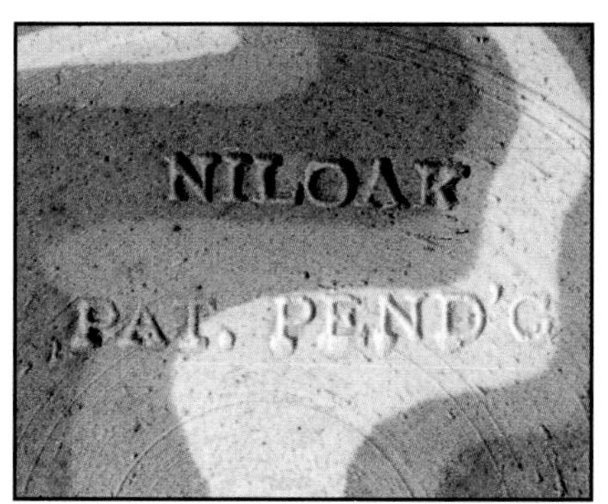

4. Patent Pend'G: Impressed die-stamp mark (block letters) used before September 1910. This mark is the result of two separate impressions, the Early Niloak (#3) and the addition of "pat. pend'g."

5. Round Niloak Blue Sticker: Common blue and white paper label used periodically from 1910s throughout the 1920s.

6. Round Niloak Red Sticker: Identical, but rarely seen, red and white label found on early pieces, typically in the mid to late teens.

7. First Art Mark: Impressed die stamp (art letters) used from September 1910 to 1924. Further break down on dates can be determined by the examination of the swirl's colors and the shapes used. Generally speaking the following statements can be made: First, pieces in plates numbers 20 – 31 can be dated between September 1910 until about 1915. Second, pottery from plate numbers 32 – 38 are datable between 1915 until the late teens. Third items in plate numbers 39 – 40, and 43 are from the late teens up until the 1924. Note differences of design to Second art mark, particularly the noticable difference in the letter "N."

Above left: Niloak First art mark. Above right: Niloak Second art mark. Note the differences between these two marks.

8. Second Art Mark: Impressed die stamp (art letters) used from 1925 to the end of all Missionware production. This Second art mark can be found with the Patent No. 1,657,997 (black ink stamp), after patent was granted in January 1928, and it was used just briefly thereafter. Unlike Niloak's First art mark, it is more difficult to break down the dates for this mark. With the standardization of shapes and swirl colors used by Niloak, it is harder to narrow down a timespan for when a piece was made. One exception involves the use of bold colors. In general, pottery in plates 41 – 42 and 44 – 47 are datable to when Niloak began its production of castware with the use commercial oxides. The results were remarkably enhanced swirl colors. These pieces can be dated to the mid to late 1930s. This mark was made in two sizes.

9. Mineralized. Black ink stamp used in the 1920s and possibly into the 1930s. At this point, generally found on pieces that are definitely Niloak but unmarked and made for the tourist trade in Colorado. One pottery piece has surfaced with both a Second art mark and this stamp. With the publication of this mark, collectors should now be aware of the use of a modern ink stamp copying this mark on unmarked swirl pieces that are probably Evans Pottery or others. (See Not Necessarily Niloak.)

10. Hywood Art Pottery: Black (common) or green (uncommon) ink stamp used between fall 1931 and spring 1932. There are at least two different sizes to this mark. The largest is 1¼" high (the measurement of the line connecting the H, A, and P), and the smallest is ¾."

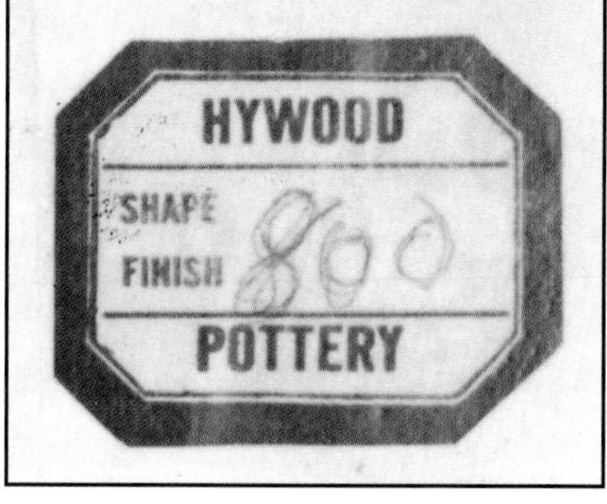

11. Hywood Paper Label: Fall 1931 through 1934. Rarely seen.

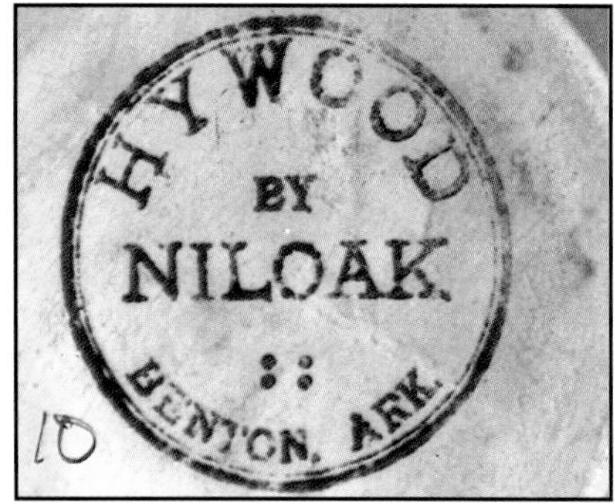

12. First Hywood by Niloak: Black ink stamp used from the summer of 1932 to 1934.

13. Hywood Mold Mark: Used in mid 1930s.

14. Hywood Block Letters: Black ink stamp used from 1935 to 1936.

15. A & B. Hywood Incised: Print or cursive letters, summer 1932 to 1936.

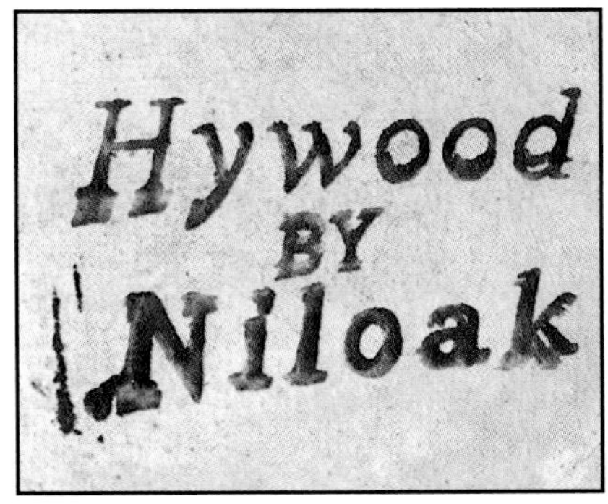

16. Second Hywood by Niloak: Black ink stamp used from 1935 to 1936. Collectors should be aware that a fake black ink stamp, using a modern ink stamp with simple block letters, has been seen.

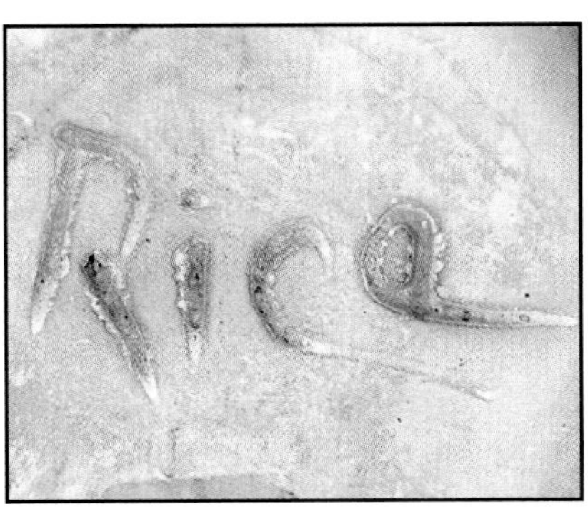

17. Incised Rice: Mark on carved pieces made during the mid 1930s (see plates 115 – 116).

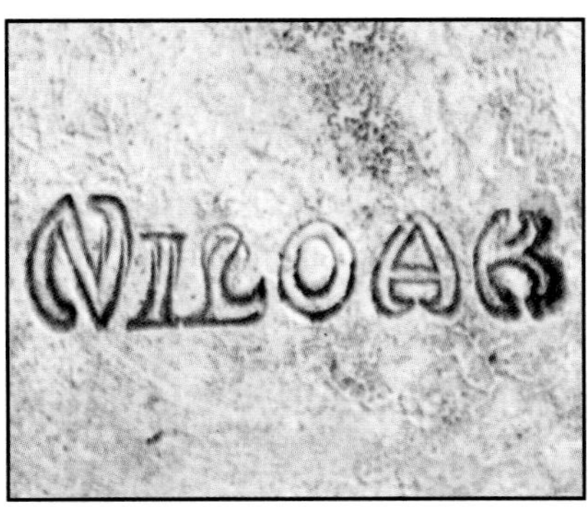

18. Second Art Mark: Same as #8, used randomly in the mid to late 1930s during the transition period as the Hywood name was phased out.

19. Potteries Sticker: Metallic or paper sticker used from the early 1930s (unusually on swirl/Missionware) to late 1930s (usually on artware).

20. Niloak 71: Black ink stamp used in mid-1930s (meaning of 71 unknown).

21. Smallest Niloak Block Letters: Impressed die stamp (similar to the Early Niloak mark but they are not the same), late 1930s and early 1940s. To date, found only on Peterson/Alley's hand-tooled animals as well as the turtle flower frog.

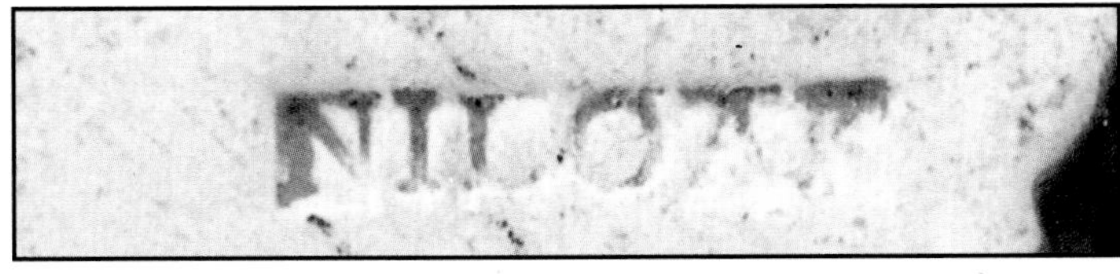

22. Niloak Block Letters: Impressed die stamp (similar to the Early Niloak mark but larger), 1937 to 1939.

23. Niloak Low Relief: Raised mold mark found either as print or curved letters and in varying sizes depending on size of items, 1939 to 1947.

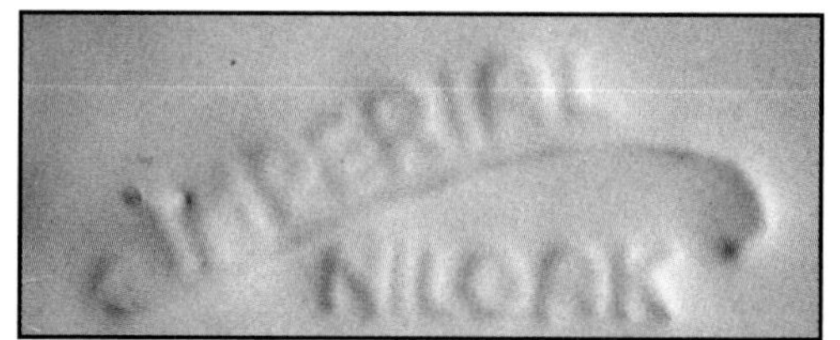

24. Imperial Mold Mark: Raised mold mark from the late 1930s, ultra rare.

25. A & B. Niloak Incised: In mold mark found either as print or curved letters and in varying sizes depending on size of items, 1939 to 1947.

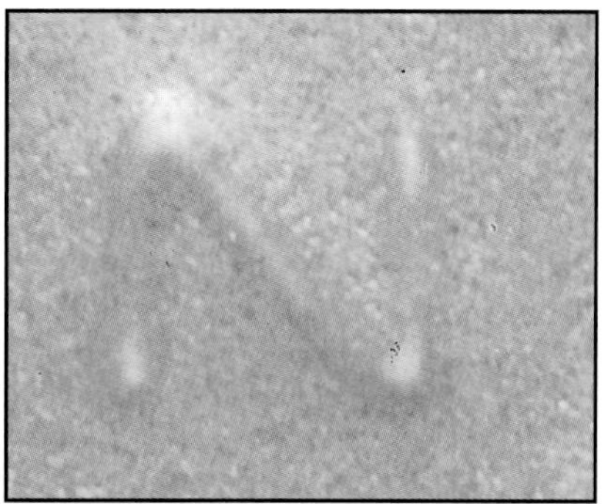

26. "N" Low Relief: Raised mold mark of "N," usually found on small castware items, 1940s.

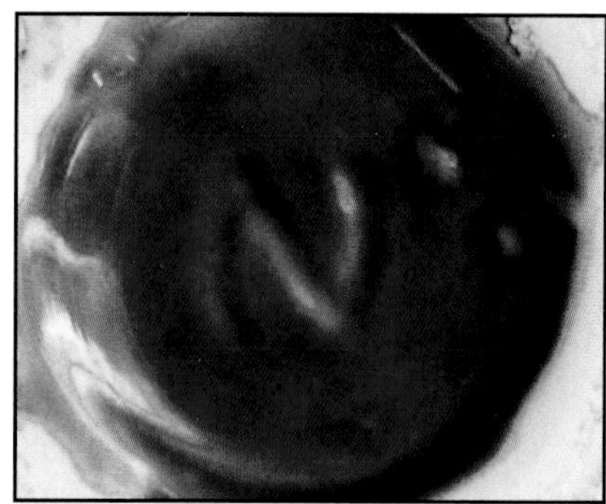

27. "N" Incised: Mold mark of "N," and is uncommon, 1940s.

28. Niloak for Victory: Raised mold mark used during World War II, rarely seen.

29. Niloak...–: Niloak for Victory, raised mold mark used during World War II.

30. 1868 Sticker: Used from the late 1930s to 1947 on glazed artware.

31. Bouquet: Uncommon blue ink stamp found on Niloak's dinnerware line, design by Joe Alley, from the late 1940s.

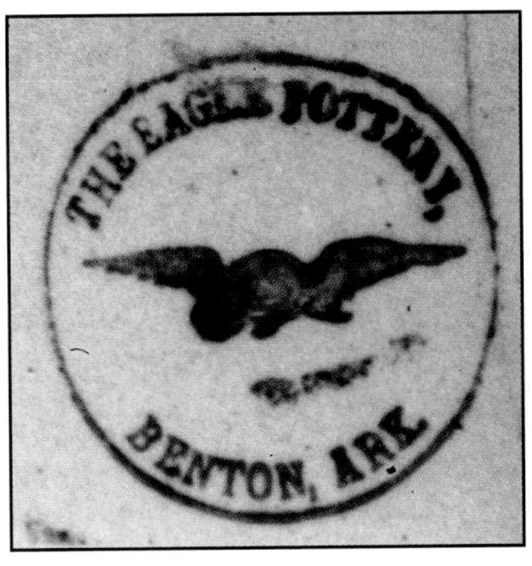

32. Eagle ink stamp. Ultra rare circular black ink stamp, dates back to the very early 1900s.

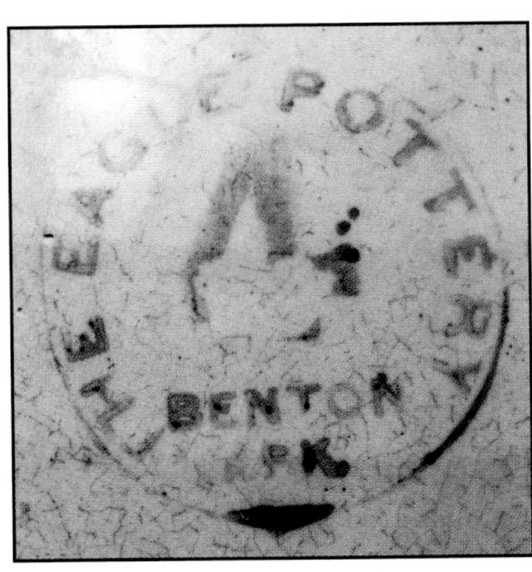

33. Eagle circle ink stamp: Common blue ink stamp found on Eagle's utilitarian ware up to the mid 1930s. There is also an uncommon Eagle rectangle ink stamp (not shown) that may have been used after the Eagle ink stamp and before the Eagle circle ink stamp.

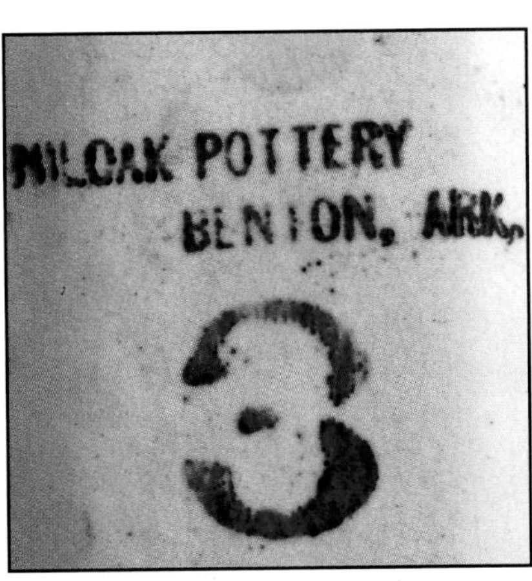

34. Niloak block ink stamp: Blue ink stamp used on all utilitarian ware after the Eagle name was discarded during the mid 1930s.

35. Niloak Circular Mold Mark: This particular mark is found on Niloak's WWII Navy mug, similar looking mold marks will be found on Niloak's kitchenware line.

Notes to Collectors and Dealers

1. Virtually all Missionware is marked with an impressed die-stamp mark (either the block or art letters). However, some pieces escaped marking either on purpose or perhaps accidentally. The pieces marked "mineralized" are a case in point. While it was known that these items were indeed Niloak due to certain characteristics, the story behind them remains totally unclear (see plate 58). These characteristics, such as shape, coloration, interior glaze, and finished bottom (virtually all Missionware bottoms are recessed), often allow for identification of the maker (of an unmarked piece) whether it is Niloak Pottery, Evans Pottery, or another producer (see Not Necessarily Niloak). In a few instances, some Missionware pieces are rarely marked (such as fan vases, whiskey jugs, wall pockets, and lamp bases). It is very important that collectors know that most swirl lamps (and unmarked vases) on the market today are not Niloak Pottery but are Evans Pottery of Missouri! In addition, Niloak Pottery's interior glazes are glossy with either a clear glaze with a green tint, a transparent brown or blue coloration, or brownish or bluish dull white looking finish (still glossy though) with dark speckles. Many unmarked swirl pieces found on the market today have either no interior glaze or a dark or chocolate brown matte interior glaze. These are not Niloak but are Evans Pottery pieces.

2. The issue of unmarked swirl with either an exterior glossy glaze or a waxed looking exterior surface has caused confusion. With the advent of online auctions, such as e-Bay, swirl pottery, with wild unsubstantiated claims as to what a particular unmarked swirl pottery piece actually is, has been sold. One important case in point is an unmarked swirl with an exterior glossy glaze. This piece, obviously either an unmarked Desert Sands or a piece from one of the Evans family, was sold as a rare exterior glaze piece of Missionware. Collectors should be wary of such claims because Missionware with an exterior glaze is a rarity! While they do surface, every once in a while, they will have at least one or two, if not all, of the characteristics of the production of 1910 and 1911. They exhibit three characteristics — sharp edge on bottom, interior clear (sometimes with a greenish tint) glaze to rim, and soft looking, sometimes indistinct, blurred swirl patterns. Finally, they should, but not necessarily will, be cataloged shapes from the 1910 catalog (see pages 298 – 307). Waxed items have long been found on the market and some have been marketed as an exterior glaze piece of Missionware (which they are not). Several stories are known to explain the waxing, including that it was a technique used by Niloak Pottery itself, or it was a signature of a particular potter. While either, both, or a combination of the two might have happened, no historical records to date have ever mentioned a wax technique. However, one story is true: A Niloak Missionware collector is known to personally "wax" his pieces with mayonnaise! What is not known is the permanency of mayonnaise as a wax. Therefore, waxing, while possibly done at Niloak, could have been done by anyone with a can of wax and a desire for a glossy finish.

3. When Niloak-looking castware and swirl are marked with a sticker only, beware of unscrupulous persons trying to pass off similar pottery as Niloak Pottery. Quite often, Niloak stickers are removed from already permanently marked Niloak pieces and placed on look-alike swirl and glazed wares. However, when this is done, the sticker is often mutilated in the process. Therefore be wary of unmarked pieces with damaged Niloak stickers. Although Niloak pieces are found with stickers only, the stickers are usually in very good condition or have normal wear. As for Niloak Missionware identification, remember although rarely unmarked, Niloak pieces have certain distinctive characteristics which every buyer needs to learn. The regular use by Niloak of ink stamp markings began with the introduction of Hywood Art Pottery in 1931. Unfortunately, some unmarked Niloak castware as well as other types of pottery similar to Niloak, have been located with simple black ink stamps. Using modern rubber stamp kits found in business supply stores, some persons have made the Second Hywood by Niloak ink stamp and a Niloak ink stamp and placed these on the bottoms of unmarked pieces. If the mark is not shown in this book, just be careful.

4. With rising demands and prices for Niloak Missionware, many chipped or broken pieces are

being ground down and sold without a notation of the modification. The finishing process that Niloak underwent was unique and an important part of the overall quality and look. When purchasing an unusual looking piece, be careful to note the top rim or edge of the piece. If it looks like it has been ground down, it probably has. With the exceptions of the early pieces (having a clear interior glaze to the rim) and some bowls made throughout Niloak Pottery's production history, most Missionware pieces have the interior glaze stopping short, usually ½" to 1 inch, from the rim or lip. Moreover, the rims/lips of vases, bowls, or other pieces should appear natural and smooth. Therefore, if the shape looks odd and the glaze extends to the rim/lip, it may be a ground down piece. Although some cylinder pieces have sharp edges, they will not appear to be ground as they were cut with a wire before firing.

5. Glazed wares similar to Niloak's were produced by other clay companies such as Dickota Pottery, Rosemeade Pottery, Camark Pottery, and Carillon Ware. Although most of the companies used marks, collectors need to be able to identify any similar unmarked pieces by maker. One company or product, Carillon Ware, produced glazes similar to Howard Lewis's Ozark Blue and Ozark Dawn II. This pottery has a dark tan/brown-colored clay bottom as compared to Niloak's light or cream-colored clay. It is usually marked with a small circle ink stamp but is often illegible. A piece is included on page 128. This piece of Carillon Ware is hand thrown with applied handles, and therefore, collectors should note the shapes, particularly when they are hand thrown, to help identify whether a piece is Niloak Pottery or not. Interestingly, this piece has a mutilated Niloak pottery sticker on it. Collectors should also note that several pottery pieces with seemingly identical glazes and/or shapes to Niloak Pottery are marked "Hand Made Original Kentucky Pottery" have surfaced. The two known shapes (see on plates 119 and 148) are definite Niloak shapes, however, the story behind these pieces is not known. Unfortunately, no information has been located on either the Carillon Ware or the Kentucky pottery. Other potteries with similarities to Niloak glazes are Dickota Pottery and Rosemeade Pottery. The responsibility of Howard Lewis, Niloak Pottery's ceramist in the early 1930s, pieces of Dickota Pottery and Rosemeade are identical and/or similar to both Niloak Pottery shapes and glazes.

6. With the popularity of collectible American pottery, including Arkansas's Niloak and Camark pottery companies, some are trying to capitalize on this market with fakes and misrepresentations. In addition to the fake shown in plate 179, the small bunny rabbit planter designed by George Peterson has been reproduced (see plate 149). It is poorly glazed in glossy black, has a bright white clay bottom, and is super lightweight. None of these characteristics is that of Niloak castware production! As for misrepresentation, a majolica looking planter marked Eagle has been represented as a rare product of the Eagle Pottery Company. It is not true as Eagle Pottery never had the capabilities to manufacture such an item. Moreover, it has to be a product of one of several other companies named Eagle.

7. Confusion has arisen over the dates of manufacture and claims of rarity of Niloak Pottery marked with block letter die stamps. There are three, distinctly different horizontal Niloak marks using block letters: Early Niloak (#3), Smallest Niloak Block Letters (#21), and Niloak Block Letters (#22). For whatever reasons, some dealers and collectors are not noting that there are distinct differences with these marks, different sizes of these three marks, and different time periods of use. Therefore both sellers and collectors are mis-identifying glazed pieces marked with Niloak Block Letters (#22) and to a lesser extent the Smallest Niloak Block Letters (#21) as being the rare, early exterior glazed examples. An early and rare exterior glazed piece is a clear glaze, not a colored glaze like Ozark Blue or Ozark Dawn II. This confusion has also been seen with ink stamps of Benton, Ark., Stamp (on Missionware) and the first Hywood by Niloak stamp (on glazed pottery) because of their incorporation of the locale, Benton, Ark.

8. The prices in this book reflect those pieces that are in mint condition. With particular respect to Missionware, sellers are noting mint examples as having no chips (and chigger or flea bites), cracks, repairs, etc. Furthermore, mint claims are made with an additional note that a piece has stains of various sorts. If an item is stained, however, it is not mint! The reason Missionware is glazed on the interior is because the clay body is porous, and the interior glaze rendered the piece waterproof. Yet since there is no exterior glaze (with the exception of Niloak Pottery's rare and early exterior pieces), there is nothing to keep substances like oil from one's hand (repeated handling), hamburger grease (just ask LRM), or soot (many pieces were kept on mantles above fireplaces), etc. from penetrating from the outside inwards and permanently staining the piece. While one can clean Missionware (but only to a certain extent), one is advised to be very cautious. Finally, the best way to see what an example of a stained piece of Missionware might have originally looked like straight from the showroom, is to look at the protected bottom of the piece. One will be amazed!

GUIDE TO NILOAK POTTERY VALUES

The prices in this book represent approximate national averages. Even though there are exceptions to the rules, the lower prices reflect national averages and the higher ones reflect more local and regional markets. Prices in Arkansas may be even higher due to local demand and appreciation. Yet, the actual selling price is determined by the sellers and buyers themselves. Many factors are considered before arriving at a price on a specific piece of Niloak. These include quality, availability or rarity (shapes/sizes/coloration), demand, locality, and markings. Together they determine why one pot is more or less valuable than another.

Quality can refer to early art pieces versus later mass-produced examples. As stated elsewhere, art examples of Missionware were generally made during the first 10 years of production. The rare exterior glaze examples (where color swirls are seen) as well as the bi- and monochromatic Missionware pieces generally have better monetary (not to forget artistic) value compared to the later standardized, three to five colors and commonly found examples. Therefore, rarely seen color patterns will bring exceedingly high prices when they come on the market. Also, many pieces marked Hywood Art Pottery (most representing artistic intent) are accorded higher values. Stoin created wonderful glaze treatments for these unique, mostly handthrown vases (even better when they have applied handles). First thought to be uncommon, Niloak Pottery's Hywood Art Pottery line is now considered quite scarce, if not rare.

Values are higher on pieces with artistic influences as seen in some of the pieces in the Hywood by Niloak line as well as some industrial castware. Early Hywood by Niloak pieces with the greatest value (monetary as well as aesthetic) include those with Ozark Dawn II and especially Peacock Blue II. The production of Ozark Blue eventually replaced Peacock Blue II. Production pieces with either Ozark Blue or Ozark Dawn II have great artistic appearance, and therefore value, among collector's today. With designers like Ganz, Peterson, and Alley, a number of castware items have greater value like those with Art Deco/Streamline effects.

Quality in manufacturing is also important. Very few Missionware pieces were poorly made, marked, and sold. Of the 15,000 plus examples reviewed, only a handful had manufacturing flaws. The bulk of these were lathe scratches on early pieces (circa 1910) and a very few with clay separations (usually on the bottoms). Manufacturing flaws in Hywood lines and castware influence price more. Hywood Art Pottery had very good quality in both throwing and glazing. Hywood by Niloak and later glazed ware, of which most were mass produced in molds, varied tremendously in quality; seconds were sold, and as a result, many poor Niloak examples are on the market today. There is a definite visual distinction between first quality versus second quality. Flaws include cracks, glazed over chips, and defects such as exposed mold lines, glaze misses, uneven glaze application, warpage, and extensive crazing (especially in Ivory).

Repaired pieces are worth less, especially if not done by a professional. Thence a broken nonrepaired piece is worth more than one repaired. A professionally repaired piece is worth less than a mint example. As for castware, the same rule applies. As mentioned elsewhere, Missionware examples with either broken off pieces or chips near the top have been ground and offered as originals. The interior glaze generally should not come to the rim of the piece unless it is an early piece (and most of the time these pieces have a green tint to the glaze), a large bowl (e.g. punch bowl), or drinking vessel. Buyers should look closely for obvious grinding and any unnatural look to a piece (see plate 43). The factors mentioned above must be taken into account in determining a piece's value.

Availability or rarity is another factor. Obviously, early Missionware had limited production and is quite scarce. Uncommon shapes and unusual swirl colorations or aberrations are more valuable than the common shapes and pieces with the standard red/blue/brown/cream colors. Size is important, too. For vases, sizes 4" to 10" are the most common while a 3" piece is slightly less common. Vases less than 3" and taller than 10" are scarce and more valuable. In addition, swirl novelties, unusual items, and extremely large pieces are hard to find. For certain pieces, I have placed a (+/-) to indicate uncertainty as to exact value. As with all collectibles, locality and demand influence selling price. For glazed pieces (Hywood Art Pottery to castware), availability is important for both shapes and colors. In general, higher prices reflect rarity. For example, the castware rocking horse is rarer and thus more valuable than the common large deer planter. The deer planter, like the "closed" handed squirrel, was a popular item and was produced continually (with varying quality) throughout Niloak Pottery's later years. Yet the "open" handed squirrel is much harder to find than the large deer planter and therefore has greater value.

Common pieces (and this applies to Missionware as well) are obviously less valuable. In recent years, common pieces (Missionware included) have flooded the market and prices remain stagnant. The glaze on a piece is important. For Hywood Art Pottery, its scarcity (due to limited production) make the issue of glaze not as important; and besides, it was very good in the first place. Ozark Dawn I is an uncommon color and Peacock Blue I is very hard to find. On the other hand, Peacock Blue II continues to be less common than Ozark Dawn II in the Hywood by Niloak line. Of these early glaze colorations, Ozark Dawn II and the Ozark Blue were popular and therefore common colors through the 1930s and the early 1940s. Uncommon colors are matte and glossy black, Sea Green, Delft Blue, burgundy, and pink with blue overspray. Blue and Tan Matt is uncommon compared to Green and Tan Matt with the Green and Tan Bright being the hardest to find. Common colors are Ozark Dawn II, Ozark Blue, Ivory, Fox Red, matte green, matte white with green overspray, as well as the light-colored glossy finishes of the mid to late 1940s.

A marked piece is worth more than an unmarked piece, even though it is unmistakably Niloak. Fortunately, Missionware was permanently marked 99% of the time; therefore, collectors must be careful when buying unmarked swirl pottery (see Not Necessarily Niloak). From my own experience Missionware jugs, fan vases, wall pockets, and true lamp bases are rarely marked. In regard to swirl lamps, see Evans Pottery in Not Necessarily Niloak. While a majority of castware was permanently marked, many glazed pieces may have had only paper labels which have been removed through time and use. For castware, some persons have resorted to either making fake marks (in this case one known second Hywood by Niloak ink stamp) or removing paper labels (these usually become mutilated) off otherwise marked Niloak Pottery and placing them on unmarked pieces (see Notes to Collectors). Unfortunately for Niloak Pottery collectors, several other companies made similar type glazes and shapes to Niloak or possibly sold Niloak as their own product. This may be the case with pieces marked "Hand Made Original Kentucky Pottery (see plate 148 and Notes to Collectors).

Another important factor involves locality. In general, rare and unique pieces bring greater prices, especially among collectors in Arkansas and, to some extent, the South. Another big influence on price is demand. The ultimate determination for value is what a buyer is willing to pay. Regardless of whether it is an extremely rare or ultra common item, value is dependent upon a piece's worth to the collector. Finally, one must always remember that this price guide is only that — a guide. Happy collecting!

Color Plates

Missionware

Vases

Plate 1

(Left to right)

Top Row:

1. 7½", Patent Pend'g. .... $275.00 – 325.00
2. 8", First art mark .... $275.00 – 325.00

Bottom Row:

1. 8½", First art mark .... $275.00 – 325.00
2. 7½", Second art mark .... $275.00 – 325.00

Beginning in 1910, Niloak production of Missionware spanned over three decades. These vases represent various attempts by Niloak potters to create artistic wares. The first vase is unique with strikingly fine swirl stradations and unusual colors. The second vase is unusual due to the accidental swirl patterns while the third is uncommon in shape and coloration. The fourth vase made in the mid to late 1930s is unique in form and bold colors and represents a final effort to create Missionware as an art object.

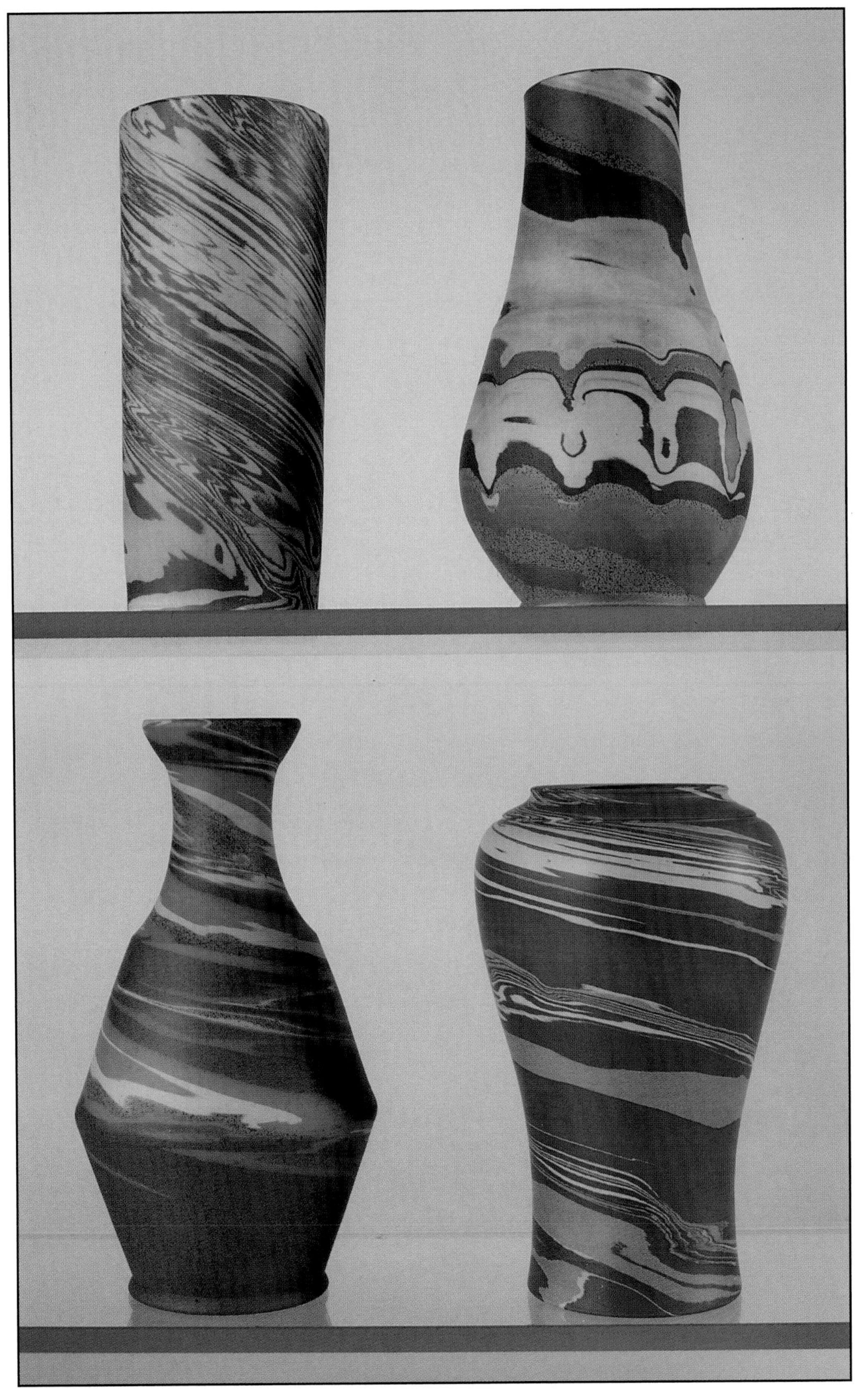

Plate 1

Missionware
Early Vases and Pieces

Plate 2

(Left to right)

1. 10¾", Early Niloak ....$375.00 – 425.00
2. 10¼", Patent Pend'g ....$400.00 – 500.00 (+/-)
3. 8¾", Patent Pend'g ....$350.00 – 400.00

Plate 3

(Left to right)

1. Vase, 10½", Patent Pend'g ....$400.00 – 500.00
2. Candlestick, 9¾", Patent Pend'g ....$400.00 – 500.00 (+/-)
3. Vase, 11¼", Early Niloak ....$500.00 – 600.00

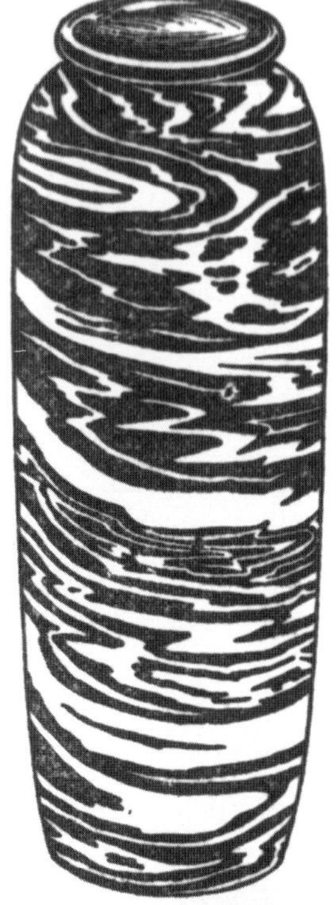

Niloak Pottery

MADE IN ARKANSAS.

A product of art, beautiful in its oddity, original in its manufacture. Niloak Pottery is in a class to itself.

The soft and soothing blends of a bit of Niloak Pottery are readily appreciated by people of refinement and taste, and is in direct contrast to the gaudy and high colored imported wares with which the market has recently been flooded. Furthermore, it is unique, inexpensive and cannot be duplicated. As a souvenir from Arkansas, a wedding gift or anniversary gift, can you think of anything that would be more acceptable? A new shipment just received, including Vases, Jardinieres, Jugs, Candlesticks, etc.

Prices range from 25c to $20.00.

Illustrated catalog sent upon request.

F. W. SANDERS & CO
CHINA, GLASS, QUEENSWARE
408 MAIN STREET.

Niloak Pottery Advertisement, October 1910. ***Courtesy of Arkansas History Commission.***

PLATE 2

PLATE 3

EARLY VASES AND PIECES

PLATE 4

Vase, 13", Early Niloak....................$600.00 – 700.00 (+/-)

PLATE 5

(Left to right)

1. Vase, 10½", Early Niloak ....$400.00 – 500.00
2. Vase, 9¼", Early Niloak ....$350.00 – 400.00
3. Vase, 8", Early Niloak ....$275.00 – 325.00

PLATE 6

(Left to right)

1. Vase, 9", Early Niloak....................$350.00 – 400.00
2. Vase, 9¼", Early Niloak ....$350.00 – 400.00
3. Vase, 8¼", Early Niloak ....$275.00 – 325.00

PLATE 4

Plate 5

Plate 6

EARLY VASES AND PIECES

PLATE 7

(Left to right)

1. Vase, 8½", Early Niloak ....$275.00 – 325.00
2. Pitcher, 10½", Patent Pend'g ....$1,000.00 – 1,200.00 (+/-)
3. Vase, 9¼", Patent Pend'g ....$350.00 – 400.00

PLATE 8

(Left to right)

1. Vase, 8", Benton, Ark. mark (die stamp) ....$275.00 – 325.00
2. Vase, 7¼", Patent Pend'g ....$225.00 – 275.00

PLATE 9

(Left to right)

1. Vase, 7", Benton, Ark. mark (die stamp) ....$225.00 – 275.00
2. Vase, 6½", Early Niloak..$200.00 – 250.00
3. Vase, 6½", Early Niloak ....$200.00 – 250.00

PLATE 7

PLATE 8

PLATE 9

EARLY VASES AND PIECES

PLATE 10

(Left to right)

Top Row:

1. Vase, 6½", Patent Pend'g ....$200.00 – 250.00
2. Mug, 5½", Patent Pend'g ....$300.00 – 400.00
3. Vase, 5¾", Early Niloak ....$150.00 – 200.00

(Left to right)

Bottom Row:

1. Bowl, 3¼", Early Niloak ....$125.00 – 175.00
2. Bowl, 4½", Patent Pend'g ....$150.00 – 200.00
3. Bowl, 3¼", Patent Pend'g ....$175.00 – 225.00

PLATE 11

Vase, 3¾", Benton, Ark. mark (die stamp) ....$200.00 – 300.00 (+/-)

PLATE 12

Vase, 7¾", Benton, Ark. mark (die stamp)..$275.00 – 325.00

PLATE 13

Jardiniere/pedestal (two pieces formed into one), approximately 24", Patent Pend'g...N/A

PLATE 10

PLATE 11

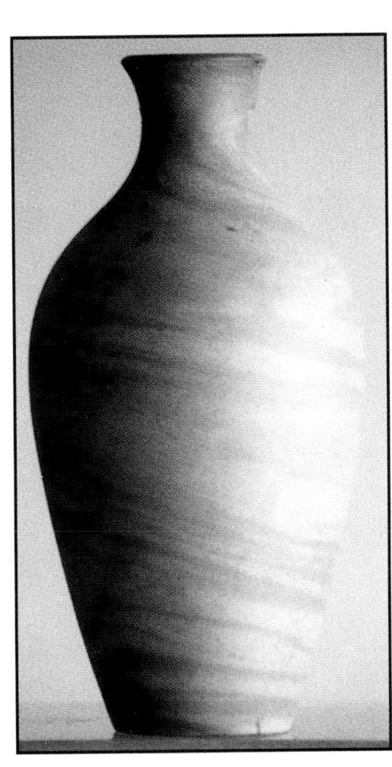

PLATE 12

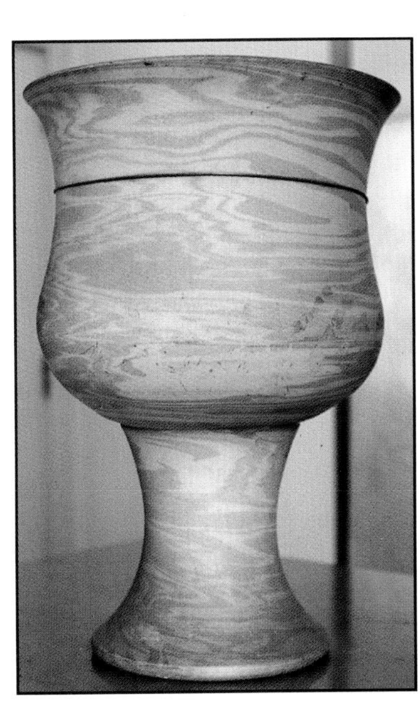

PLATE 13

EARLY VASES

PLATE 14

(Left to right)

Top Row:

1. Vase, 6¼", Patent Pend'g .... $200.00 – 250.00
2. Vase, 6½", Early Niloak .... $200.00 – 250.00
3. Vase, 8", Early Niloak .... $275.00 – 325.00 (+/-)
4. Vase, 7¼", Early Niloak .... $225.00 – 275.00

Middle Row:

1. Vase, 7¼", Early Niloak .... $225.00 – 275.00
2. Vase, 10½", Early Niloak .... $400.00 – 500.00
3. Vase, 9½", Patent Pend'g .... $400.00 – 500.00 (+/-)
4. Vase, 7¾", Early Niloak .... $225.00 – 275.00

Bottom Row:

1. Vase, 9", Benton, Ark. mark (die stamp), Round Red Niloak Sticker .... $400.00 – 500.00 (+/-)
2. Vase, 11", Early Niloak .... $500.00 – 600.00
3. Vase, 10¼", Early Niloak .... $400.00 – 500.00

PLATE 14

EARLY PIECES WITH EXTERIOR GLAZE

PLATE 15

Vase, 9¼", Patent Pend'g ....$1,000.00 – 1,500.00 (+/-)

PLATE 16

Cracker jar, 7" x 6½", Benton, Ark. mark (ink stamp)........$1,500.00 – 2,000.00 (+/-)

PLATE 17

Vase, 9", Benton Ark. mark (ink stamp)...............................$1,000.00 – 1,500.00 (+/-)

PLATE 18

Vase, 7¼", Benton, Ark. mark (ink stamp)................................$650.00 – 850.00 (+/-)

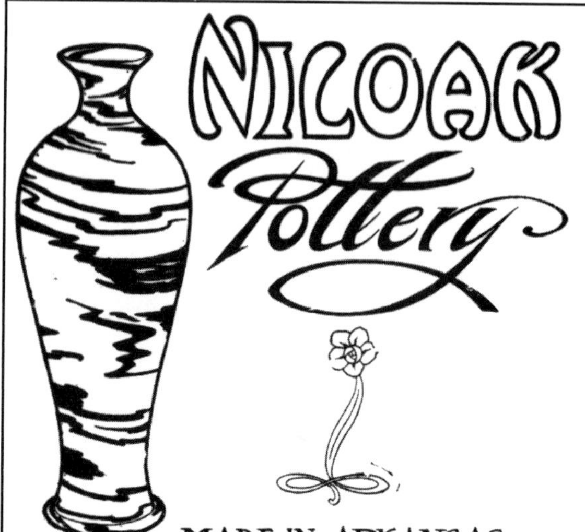

Why Not Send Your Friends A Piece of NILOAK Pottery

A home-made product; it makes an ideal souvenir and a beautiful and unique Christmas gift. One thousand pieces just received from the pottery. The colors and blendings are entirely new, and we invite your inspection. Nothing like it made anywhere and no two pieces alike.

THE LINE CONSISTS OF

VASES, from..................50c to $10
PITCHERS and TANKARDS..$2.50 to $5
PITCHERS and TANKARDS..$2.50 to $4
FERN DISHES, from............$2 to $3
TUMBLERS, from.............50c to 75c
TOBACCO JARS, from........$2 to $3.50
JARDINIERES, from..........50c to 75c
HAT PIN HOLDERS, from.....50c to 75c
ART TRAYS AND MATCH HOLDERS, from...............35c to 50c
STEINS AND CUPS, from....50c to $1.50

F. W. SANDERS & CO.
THE GIFT STORE OF LITTLE ROCK
408 Main Street

Niloak Pottery Advertisement, December 1912. *Courtesy of Arkansas History Commission.*

Plate 15

Plate 16

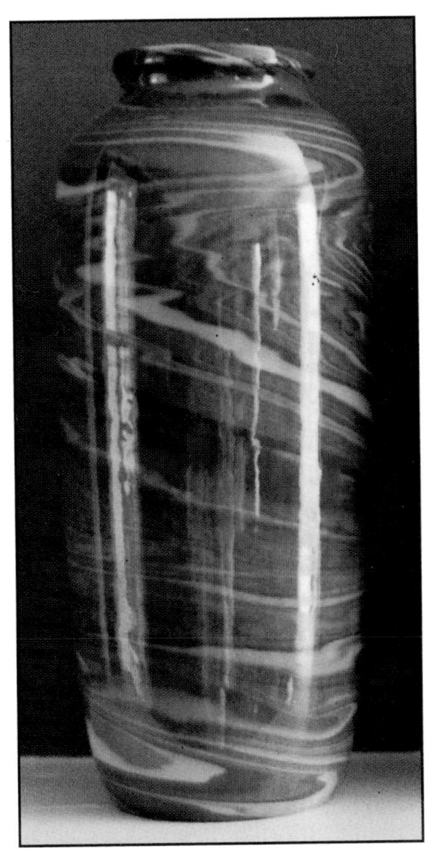

Plate 17

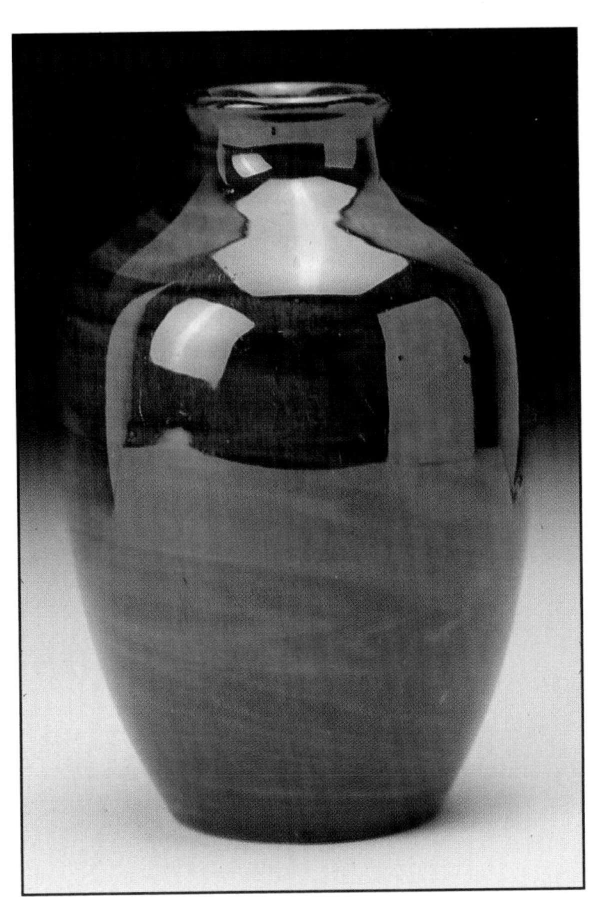

Plate 18

Early Pieces

Plate 19

(Left to right)

Top Row: All Patent Pend'g

1. Tumbler (?), 5" ....$200.00 – 250.00
2. Ink well, 2½" ....$250.00 – 350.00
3. Tumbler (?) with single groove motif at base, 4¼" ....$175.00 – 225.00
4. Tumbler (?) with single groove motif at base, 4¼" ....$175.00 – 225.00

Middle Row:

1. Vase, 6¾", Early Niloak ....$200.00 – 250.00
2. Candlestick, 7¼", Early Niloak ....$250.00 – 300.00
3. Vase, 7", Patent Pend'g above Niloak * ....$225.00 – 275.00

Bottom Row:

1. Vase, 5½", Patent Pend'g ....$150.00 – 200.00
2. Vase, 7¾", Benton, Ark. mark (die stamp) ....$225.00 – 275.00
3. Vase, 5¼", Patent Pend'g ....$150.00 – 200.00

* This piece revealed that the use of "Pat. Pend'g" was a separate die stamp mark from the Early Niloak mark.

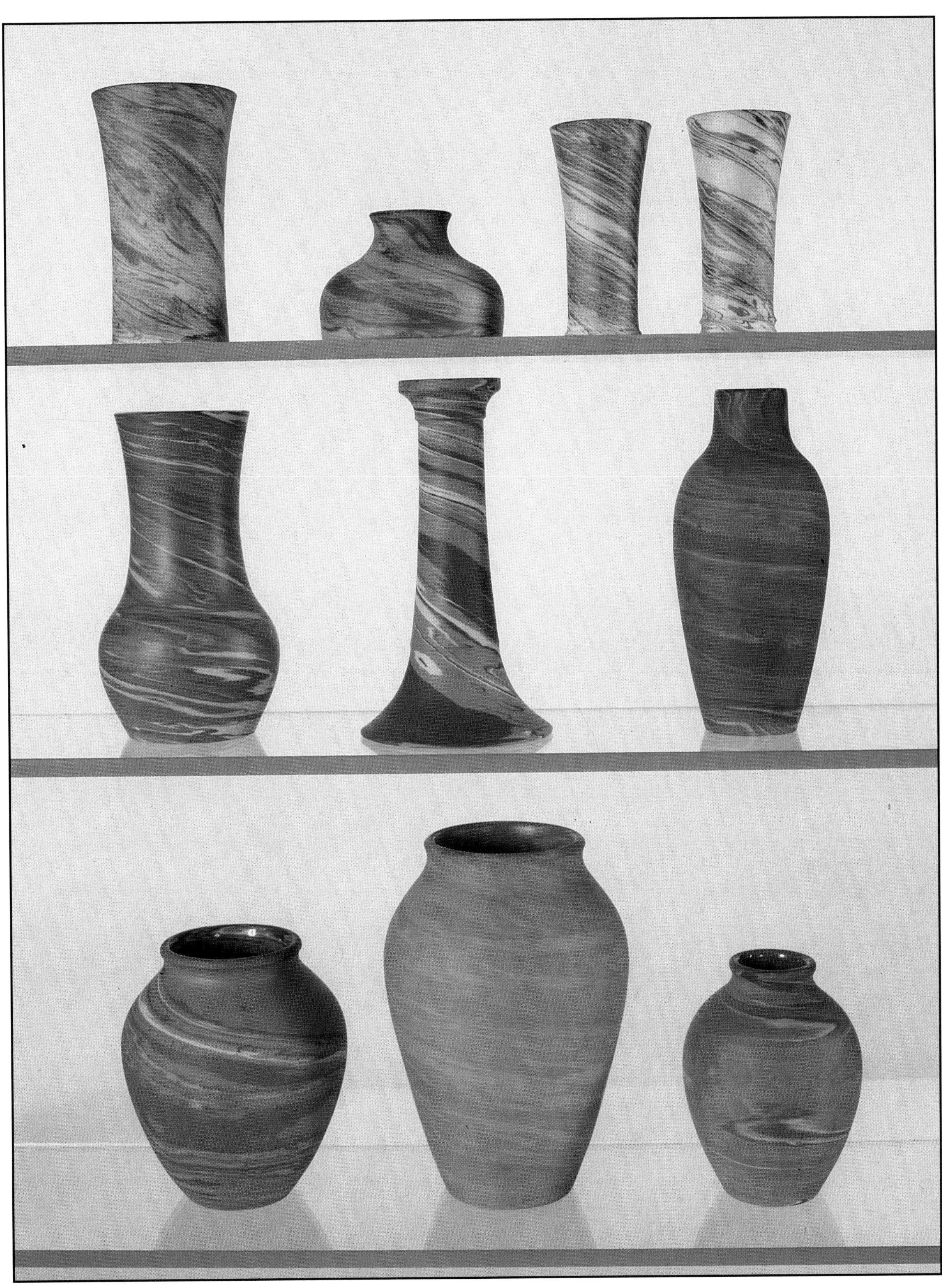

Plate 19

VASES WITH FIRST ART MARK

PLATE 20

Vase, 13½", First art mark .... $600.00 – 700.00 (+/-)

PLATE 21

Vase, 10½" .... $400.00 – 500.00

PLATE 22

Vase, 10" .... $400.00 – 500.00

PLATE 23

(Left to right)

Top Row:

1. Vase, 10" .... $400.00 – 500.00
2. Vase, 10½" .... $400.00 – 500.00

Bottom Row:

1. Vase, 9" .... $350.00 – 400.00
2. Vase, 10" .... $400.00 – 500.00

PLATE 20

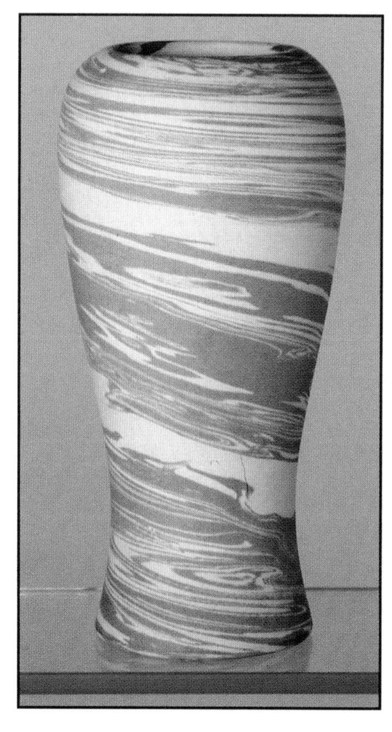

PLATE 21

PLATE 22

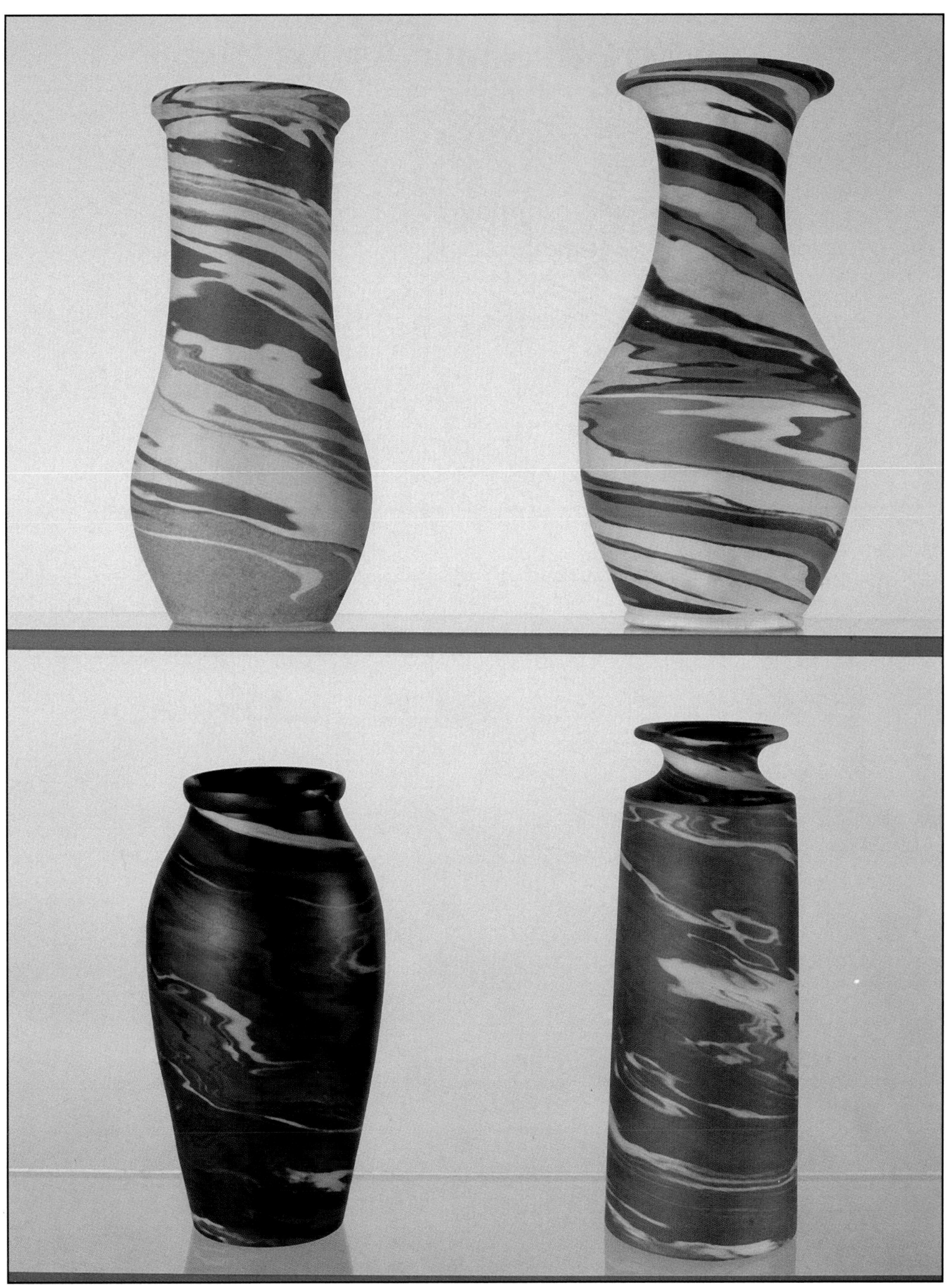

PLATE 23

VASES AND PITCHER WITH FIRST ART MARK

PLATE 24

Pitcher, 7⅛" x 6½", First art mark..$700.00 – 900.00 (+/-)

PLATE 25

(Left to right)

Top Row:

1. Vase, 8"..$225.00 – 275.00
2. Vase, 9¾"..$350.00 – 400.00
3. Vase, 8"..$225.00 – 275.00

Middle Row:

1. Vase, 7¾"..$175.00 – 225.00
2. Vase, 9¾"..$300.00 – 350.00
3. Vase, 8¼"..$225.00 – 275.00

Bottom Row:

1. Vase, 10"..$375.00 – 425.00
2. Vase, 10¼"..$375.00 – 425.00
3. Vase, 10"..$375.00 – 425.00

PLATE 24

Plate 25

VASES WITH FIRST ART MARK

PLATE 26

(Left to right)

Top Row:

1. Vase, 10" ....$375.00 – 425.00
2. Vase, 10½" ....$400.00 – 450.00
3. Vase, 9" ....$300.00 – 350.00
4. Vase, 11½" ....$450.00 – 500.00

Middle Row:

1. Vase, 9¼" ....$275.00 – 325.00
2. Vase, 10¼" ....$400.00 – 450.00
3. Vase, 10½" ....$400.00 – 450.00
4. Vase, 9½" ....$300.00 – 350.00

Bottom Row:

1. Vase, 10¼" ....$400.00 – 500.00
2. Vase, 10¼" ....$400.00 – 500.00
3. Vase, 9" ....$275.00 – 325.00
4. Vase, 9¼" ....$275.00 – 325.00

PLATE 26

VASES WITH FIRST ART MARK

PLATE 27

(Left to right)

Top Row:

1. Vase, 8¼" .... $225.00 – 275.00
2. Vase, 6¼" .... $225.00 – 275.00
3. Vase, 7" .... $175.00 – 225.00

Middle Row:

1. Vase, 8" .... $225.00 – 275.00
2. Vase, 9¼" .... $275.00 – 325.00
3. Vase, 8¼" .... $225.00 – 275.00

Bottom Row:

1. Vase, 8¼" .... $225.00 – 275.00
2. Vase, 8" .... $225.00 – 275.00
3. Vase, 8¾" .... $225.00 – 275.00

PLATE 27

VASES WITH FIRST ART MARK, UNLESS NOTED

PLATE 28

(Left to right)

1. Vase, 14" .... $700.00 – 900.00 (+/-)
2. Vase, 18½" .... $1,000.00 – 1,500.00 (+/-)
3. Vase, 16¼" .... $800.00 – 1,000.00 (+/-)

PLATE 29

(Left to right)

Top Row:

1. Vase, 8⅛" .... $225.00 – 275.00
2. Vase, 10¼", unmarked .... $375.00 – 425.00
3. Vase, 8" .... $225.00 – 275.00

Bottom Row:

1. Vase, 9⅛" .... $300.00 – 350.00
2. Vase, 9" .... $300.00 – 350.00
3. Vase, 9⅛", unmarked .... $350.00 – 450.00
   Unusual "candy cane" effect

PLATE 28

PLATE 29

Pieces with First and Second Art Marks

Plate 30

(Top to bottom)

1. Vase, 14", First art mark ....$700.00 – 800.00 (+/-)
2. Vase, 14¼", Second art mark, note brighter colors * ....$700.00 – 800.00 (+/-)
3. Vase, 14¼", unmarked ....$700.00 – 800.00 (+/-)

* This piece, with clays having better commercial dyes, shows the distinctive difference in colors of Missionware production from the 1930s. The two outer pieces were made in the mid to late teens.

Plate 31

(Left to right)

First Row:

1. Vase, 6¼", Early Niloak ....$200.00 – 250.00
2. Vase, 6¼", Benton, Ark. mark (die stamp) ....$225.00 – 275.00

Second Row:

1. Chamberstick, 4 x 4¾" dia., First art mark ....$200.00 – 250.00
2. Candlestick, 3½ x 4¾" dia., First art mark....................$150.00 – 200.00

Third Row:

1. Vase, 4½", First art mark ....$100.00 – 125.00
2. Mug, 4", First art mark ....$300.00 – 350.00
3. Vase, 4¼", First art mark ....$75.00 – 100.00

Fourth Row:

1. Bowl, 4¼" dia., Patent Pend'g....................$125.00 – 175.00
2. Bowl, 4" dia., Patent Pend'g....................$125.00 – 175.00

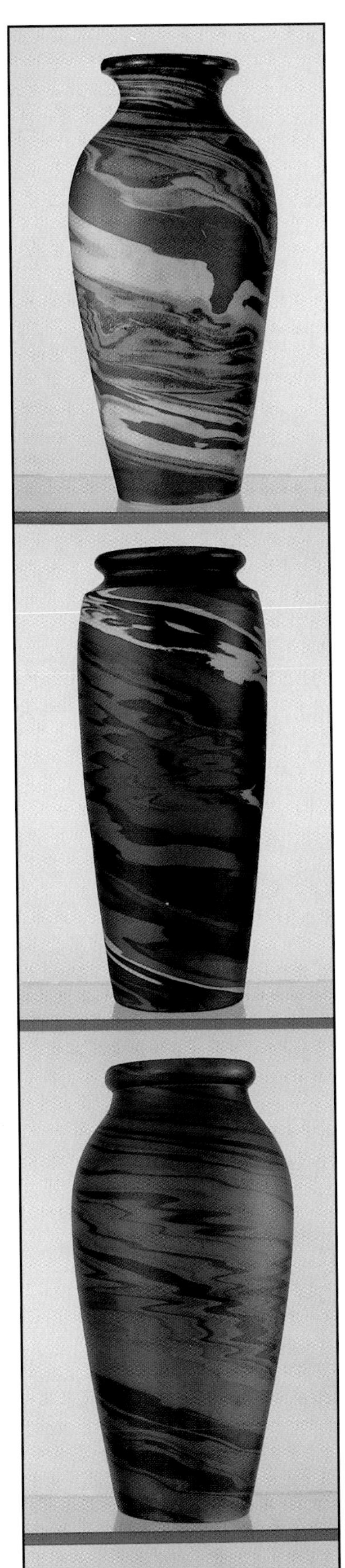

PLATE 30

PLATE 31

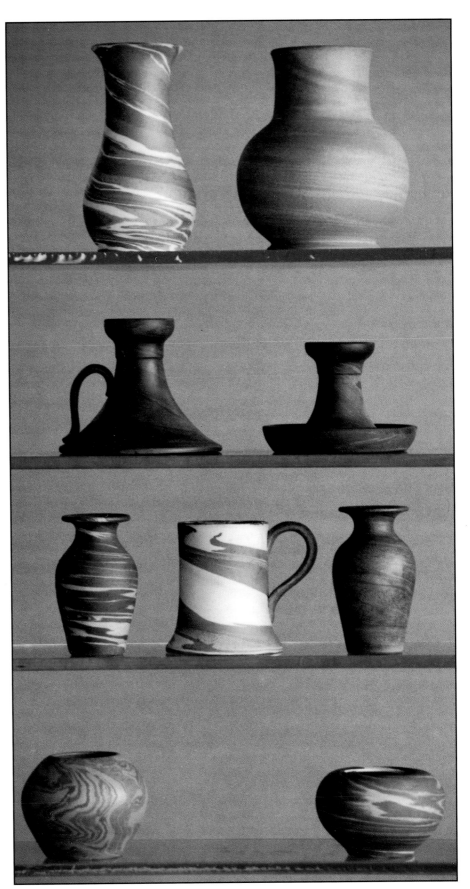

VASES WITH FIRST ART MARK

PLATE 32

(Left to right)

Top Row:

1. Vase, 9⅛" .... $275.00 – 325.00
2. Vase, 9⅛" * .... $300.00 – 350.00
   Red, black, and white sticker of "The Davis Jewelry Co., [?] E. Pikes Peak Ave. Colorado Springs, Colo. Mail Orders a Specialty."
3. Vase, 9⅞" .... $275.00 – 325.00
   Incised on the inside rim and on the bottom with "14 – 27 – scrap." Probably an experimental piece; actual meaning unknown.

Middle Row:

1. Vase, 8" .... $200.00 – 250.00
2. Vase, 8⅛" .... $200.00 – 250.00

Has two stickers on bottom. The first is a green and white oval shape with "Original Manitou Curio Shop, Photo Craft Views, Van Briggle Pottery, The Manitou Springs Bath House, Manitou, Colo." (with letters "ORX" penciled in). The second is a blue and white round sticker with "Mineralized Clay Pottery, Copper-Iron, Silver-Zinc, etc. R.S. Davis, Manitou, Colo." Penciled on pottery itself - "VLC."

3. Vase, 8" .... $200.00 – 250.00

Bottom Row:

1. Vase, 10¼" .... $300.00 – 350.00
2. Vase, 10¼" .... $375.00 – 425.00
3. Vase, 10¼" .... $375.00 – 425.00

* Niloak pottery was sold in and around southeast Colorado beginning in the early 1920s. Hyten visited Colorado Springs in January 1922 and his wares were sold in this tourist/resort town. It is quite probable that Denver White's production of swirl pottery resulted from a recognition that swirl pottery was marketable. From a 1913 *Clay-Worker* article: This latest design, the mission electrolier, had a "shade of mushroom shape, lined with silver on inside of shade for reflector. It is certainly swell, to say the least of it." (See page 312.)

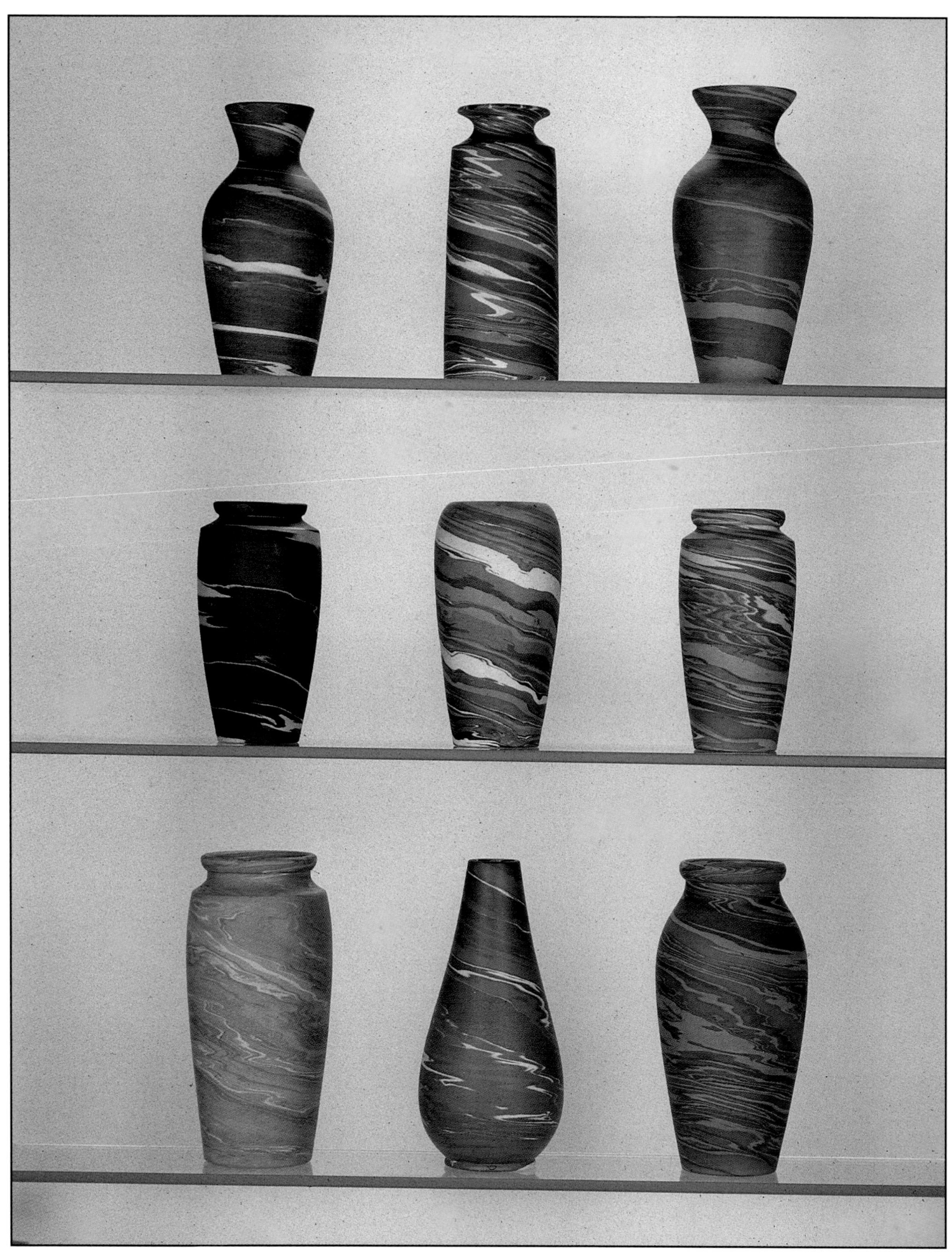

PLATE 32

VASES WITH FIRST ART MARK, UNLESS NOTED

PLATE 33

Vase, 7¾", solid blue, unmarked .... $225.00 – 275.00 (+/-)

Quintessential Niloak shape.

PLATE 34

Vase, 12¼", solid blue .... $600.00 – 800.00 (+/-)

PLATE 35

Vase, 6¼", solid white .... $200.00 – 250.00 (+/-)

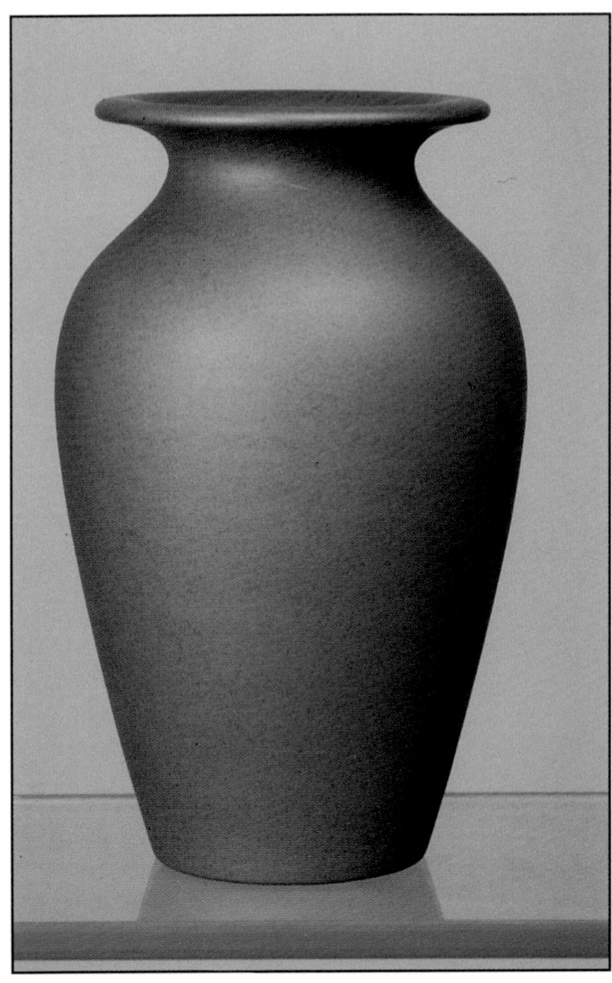

PLATE 33

Plate 34

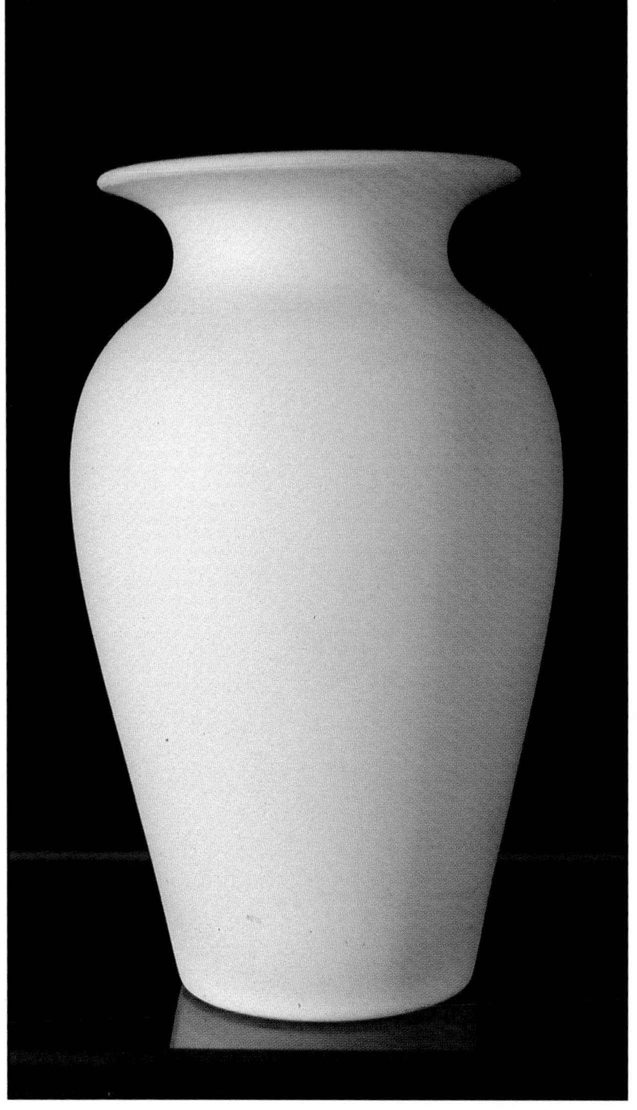

Plate 35

Vases with First Art Marks

Plate 36

(Left to right)

Top Row:

1. Vase, 10"........$300.00 – 350.00
2. Vase, 9"........$275.00 – 325.00
3. Vase, 9¾"........$275.00 – 325.00

Middle Row:

1. Vase, 9"........$275.00 – 325.00
   Roman numeral X scratched in bottom, significance unknown.
2. Vase, 9"........$275.00 – 325.00
3. Vase, 8"........$200.00 – 250.00

Bottom Row:

1. Vase, 10¼"........$300.00 – 350.00
2. Cone vase, 9½"........$325.00 – 375.00
3. Vase, 9¾"........$275.00 – 325.00

Plate 36

VASES AND PIECES WITH FIRST ART MARK*

PLATE 37

Vase, 8" .... $275.00 – 325.00

PLATE 38

(Left to right)

Top Row: Predominantly red

1. Cone vase, 9" .... $350.00 – 400.00
2. Vase, 6½" .... $150.00 – 175.00
3. Vase, 8" .... $225.00 – 275.00

Middle Row: Predominantly red

1. Vase, 5¼" .... $125.00 – 175.00
2. Humidor, 6" .... $400.00 – 500.00
3. Candlestick, 3¼" .... $200.00 – 250.00

Bottom Row: Predominantly brown

1. Vase, 8¾" .... $225.00 – 275.00
2. Vase, 8" .... $225.00 – 275.00
3. Vase, 9" .... $275.00 – 325.00

PLATE 37

* To date, no evidence has surfaced as to when these particular colors were made. However, the shapes featuring red indicate the mid-1910s while the shapes featuring brown indicate the late 1910s and early 1920s.

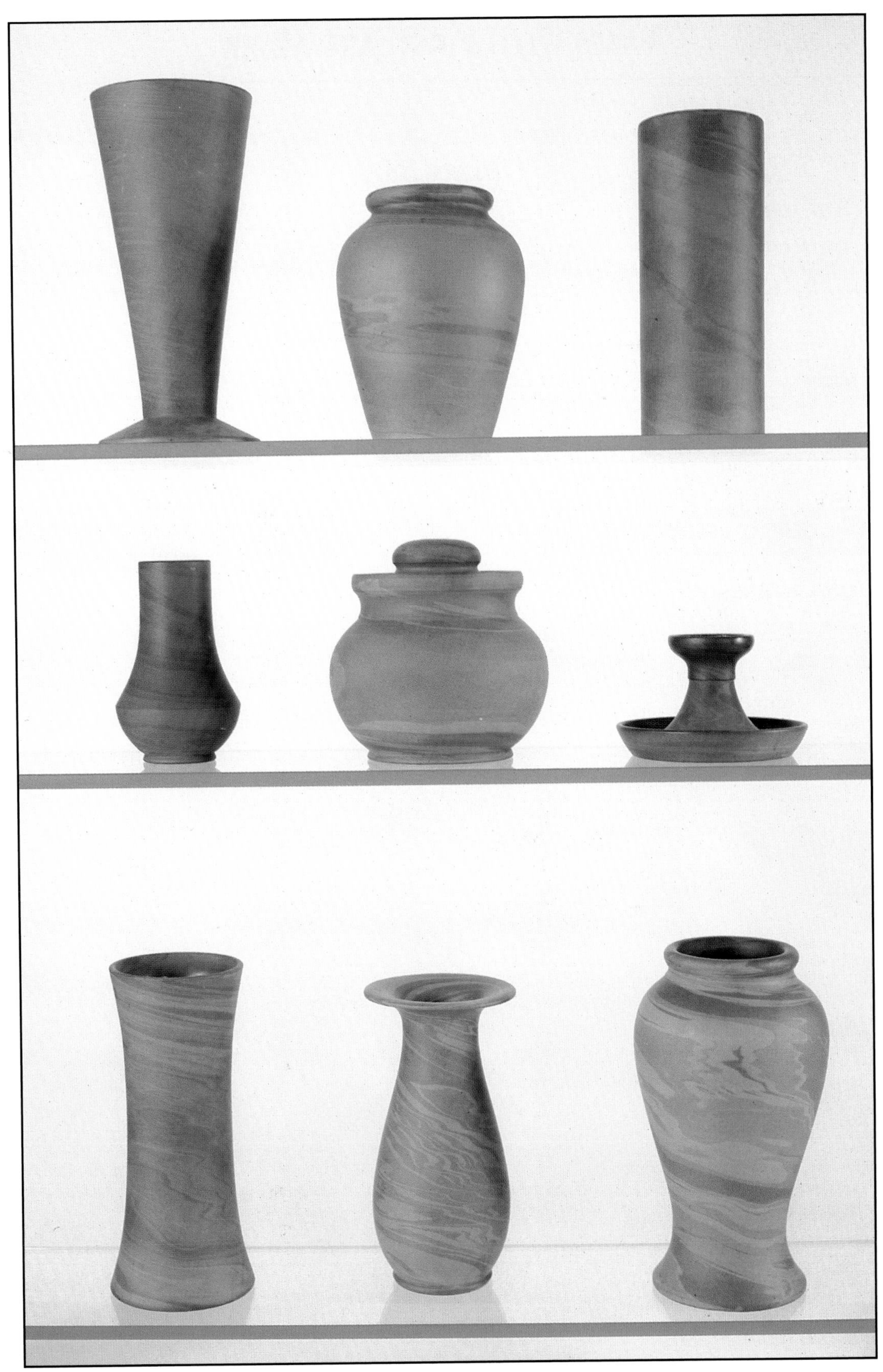

PLATE 38

VASES WITH FIRST ART MARK

PLATE 39

(Left to right)

Top Row:

1. Vase, 8¼" .... $200.00 – 250.00
2. Vase, 8¼" .... $200.00 – 250.00
3. Vase, 8" .... $200.00 – 250.00
   Has store sticker "E. Hertzberg Jewelry Co., San Antonio."

Middle Row:

1. Vase, 9" .... $275.00 – 325.00
2. Vase, 8¼" .... $275.00 – 325.00
3. Vase, 9¼" .... $275.00 – 325.00

Bottom Row:

1. Vase, 10" .... $300.00 – 350.00
2. Vase, 9¼" .... $300.00 – 350.00
   Highly unusual effect offering unique decorative design.
3. Vase, 10¼" .... $375.00 – 425.00

Plate 39

PIECES WITH FIRST AND SECOND ART MARK

PLATE 40

(Left to right)

Top Row:

1. Cone vase, 5½", Second art mark .... $150.00 – 200.00
2. Humidor, 4½", First art mark .... $400.00 – 500.00
3. Vase, 5½", First art mark .... $100.00 – 125.00

Middle Row:

1. Candlestick, 7", Second art mark .... $125.00 – 175.00
2. Vase, 11½", First art mark .... $550.00 – 650.00
3. Candlestick, 6½", First art mark .... $125.00 – 175.00

Bottom Row:

1. Cone vase, 8", Second art mark .... $275.00 – 325.00
2. Candlestick, 8", First art mark .... $150.00 – 200.00
3. Cone vase, 9¼", First art mark .... $325.00 – 375.00

PLATE 40

PIECES WITH FIRST AND SECOND ART MARK

PLATE 41

(Left to right)

Top Row:

1. Cone vase, 6¼", Second art mark ....$200.00 – 250.00
2. Bowl, 4 x 9½" dia., First art mark..........$400.00 – 500.00 (+/-)
3. Bowl, 6½ x 5½", Second art mark..........$200.00 – 250.00

Middle Row:

1. Whiskey jug w/stopper, 7¾", unmarked..........$800.00 – 1,000.00 (+/-)
2. Vase, 8¼", First art mark..........$200.00 – 250.00
3. Decanter, 9¼", Second art mark..........$800.00 – 1,000.00 (+/-)

Bottom Row:

1. Vase, 10", Second art mark, Second Hywood by Niloak..........$300.00 – 350.00
2. Candlestick, 10", First art mark..........$175.00 – 225.00
3. Tankard, 10¼", larger Second art mark..........$800.00 – 1,000.00 (+/-)

PLATE 41

PIECES WITH FIRST AND SECOND ART MARKS

PLATE 42

(Left to right)

First Row:

1. Ashtray, 1¾ x 4¾" dia., First art mark....................................$100.00 – 125.00
2. Bowl, 2¼ x 4¾" dia., First art mark..$125.00 – 150.00
3. Ashtray, 4¾ x ¾", Second art mark..$100.00 – 125.00

Second Row:

1. Wall pocket, 7¼", unmarked,
   inscribed "Starved Rock Hotel"......................................$275.00 – 375.00 (+/-)
2. Wall pocket, 8¾", unmarked...$300.00 – 400.00 (+/-)

Third Row:

1. Bowl, 5¾" dia., Second art mark,
   ink stamp of "Patent No. 1657997" ....$150.00 – 175.00
2. Fan vase, 5½", round blue Niloak sticker ....$275.00 – 325.00
3. Flower bowl, 2½ x 5¼" dia., larger Second art mark,
   with the black ink stamp "Mineralized"................................$175.00 – 225.00

Fourth Row:

1. Wallpocket, 6", round blue Niloak sticker,
   ink stamp of "Patent No. 1657997"................................$250.00 – 350.00 (+/-)
2. Plate, 8¾" dia., First art mark..$300.00 – 500.00 (+/-)
3. Wallpocket, 6¼", Niloak Potteries,
   round blue Niloak sticker...$250.00 – 350.00 (+/-)

* Starved Rock Hotel was in Illinois. This location was once known as a resort, but it is now an Illinois State Park.

PLATE 42

VASES WITH FIRST ART MARK, UNLESS NOTED

PLATE 43

(Left to right)

Top Row:

1. Vase, 8½" .... $275.00 – 325.00
2. Vase, 6½", swirl aberation, Second art mark * .... $100.00 – 125.00
3. Vase, 8", also has round Niloak sticker .... $200.00 – 250.00

Middle Row:

1. Vase, 7" .... $175.00 – 200.00
2. Vase, 6¼" .... $150.00 – 175.00 (+/-)
3. Vase, 6¼" .... $125.00 – 150.00

Bottom Row:

1. Vase, 8" .... $225.00 – 275.00
2. Vase, 8½", Second art mark .... $275.00 – 325.00
   Also has "Biggs Art Store" of Hot Springs sticker. **
3. Vase, 8¾" .... $200.00 – 250.00

* Note: This piece was identical to first shape on this row. Having been broken, it was ground down but sold as an original. Beware of pieces whose shapes seem unnatural and their edge sanded.

** Biggs Art Store of Hot Springs, Arkansas, was the sole distributor of Missionware in the area. It sold Niloak pottery from the mid-1920s until at least the early 1930s. In addition, it sold Camark's early ware from the late 1920s and early 1930s.

PLATE 43

LATE PERIOD VASES WITH SECOND ART MARK, UNLESS NOTED

PLATE 44

(Left to right)

Top Row:

1. Vase, 5½" .... $125.00 – 150.00
2. Vase, 6¼" .... $150.00 – 175.00
3. Vase, 5¾" .... $125.00 – 150.00

Middle Row:

1. Vase, 6¼" .... $150.00 – 175.00
2. Vase, 8½" .... $225.00 – 275.00
3. Vase, 5¼" .... $125.00 – 150.00

Bottom Row:

1. Vase, 10¼" .... $375.00 – 425.00
2. Vase, 8½" .... $225.00 – 275.00
3. Vase, 10¼", earlier piece, First art mark .... $300.00 – 350.00

In addition to the use of better dyes, some new shapes (by a different potter?) were introduced in the early 1930s for swirl production.

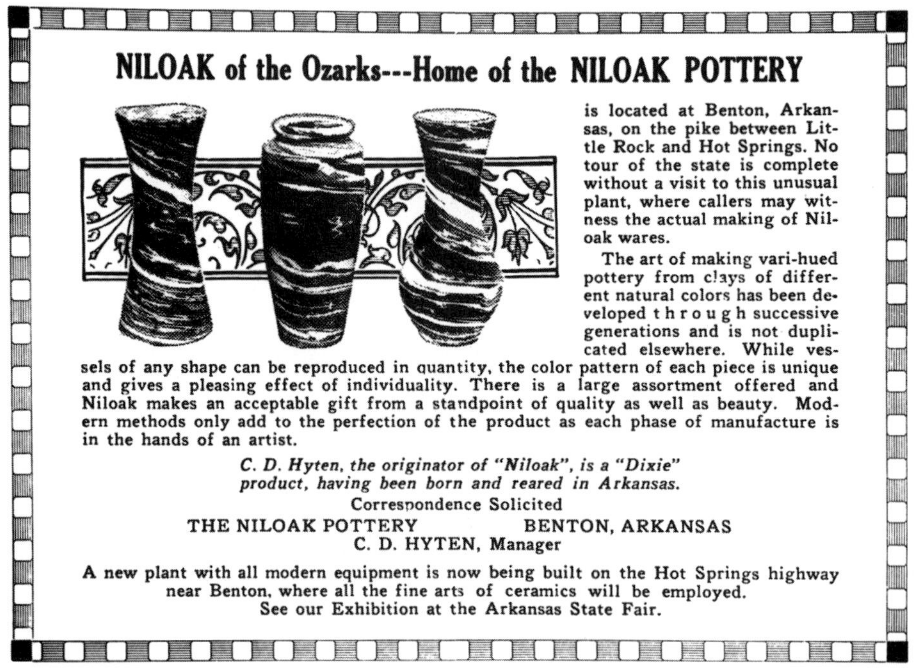

Niloak Pottery Advertisement, August/September 1928. ***Courtesy of Arkansas History Commission.***

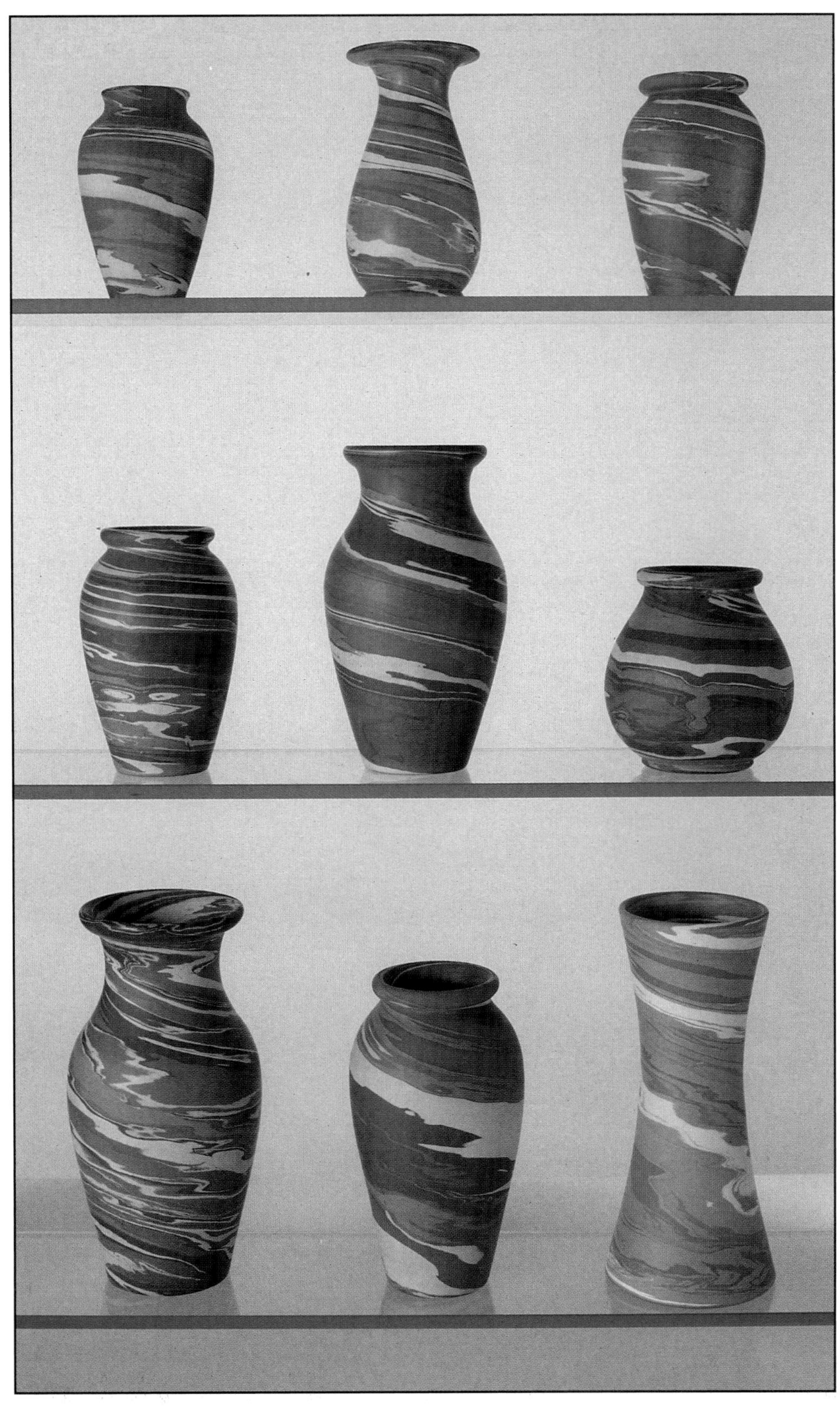

PLATE 44

LATE PERIOD PIECES WITH SECOND ART MARK

PLATE 45

Vase, 5", unusual with its predominance of green colored clay.....$150.00 – 200.00

PLATE 46

(Left to right)

Top Row:

1. Vase, 5¼" ....$150.00 – 175.00
2. Vase, 6¾" ....$150.00 – 175.00
3. Vase, 6¼" ....$150.00 – 175.00

Middle Row:

1. Vase, 6¾" ....$150.00 – 175.00
2. Vase, 7¼", Bigg's Art Store sticker ....$175.00 – 225.00
3. Vase, 8¼" ....$225.00 – 275.00

Bottom Row:

1. Vase, 8¼" ....$225.00 – 275.00
2. Bowl, 8¾" dia. ....$275.00 – 325.00
3. Vase, 9½", larger mark ....$300.00 – 350.00

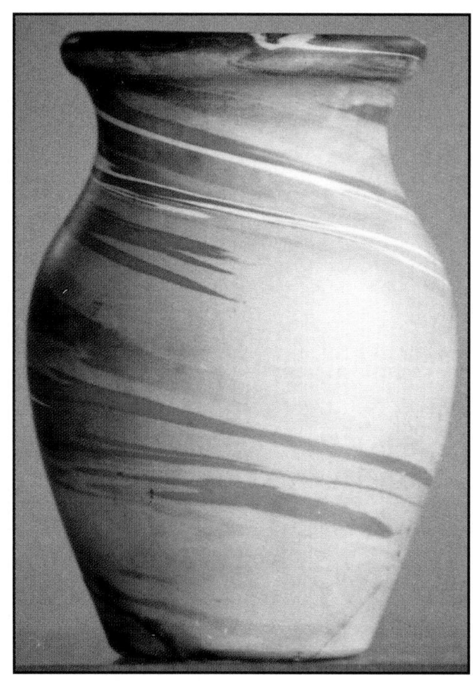

PLATE 45

PLATE 46

LATE PERIOD PIECES WITH SECOND ART MARK

PLATE 47

(Left to right)

Top Row:

1. Cone vase, 8" .... $275.00 – 325.00
   "Patent No. 1657997" black ink stamp.
2. Bean pot, 7¼" .... $800.00 – 1,000.00 (+/-)
3. Vase, 8⅝" .... $225.00 – 275.00

Middle Row:

1. Vase, 3¼" .... $75.00 – 100.00
2. Bowl, 5½" .... $125.00 – 150.00
3. Vase, 5½" .... $150.00 – 175.00
   "Grand Commandery of Arkansas, Detroit, 1928" black ink stamp.

Bottom Row:

1. Vase, 10¼", larger Second art mark .... $375.00 – 425.00
2. Vase, 9¾", round Niloak sticker .... $275.00 – 325.00
   "4.00, 12/30/33" in pencil.
3. Vase, 9¾" .... $275.00 – 325.00

PLATE 47

Missionware
Large Examples

Plate 48

Vase, 28", "Niloak" incised on bottom .... $2,000.00 – 2,500.00 (+/-)

Plate 49

Cuspidor, 19¼", larger Second art mark .... $1,500.00 – 2,000.00 (+/-)

Plate 50

Vase, 18", First art mark .... $1,000.00 – 1,500.00 (+/-)

Plate 51

Vase, 28", larger Second art mark .... $2,000.00 – 2,500.00 (+/-)

This is one of a pair of monumental vases commissioned by the Schudmak's Jewelry Store on Central Avenue in Hot Springs, Arkansas. Mr. Schudmak requested that Niloak pottery make a pair of large vases for display and/or sale in his business, and Mr. Hyten agreed to personally produce the pair. These vases were made from two pieces formed together. It is believed that most large examples are made this way. When completed, Hyten felt that they represented his best work and were the best matched pair he had made. Hyten tried unsuccessfully to repurchase them in subsequent years to no avail. After Hyten's death, Mr. Schudmak was again contacted about the vases. At this time he was considering retirement, and knowing Hyten's opinion of the pair, agreed to sell them back to the family.

Missionware
Solid White Vase, Decorated

Plate 52

Vase, 5¼", First art mark .... $150.00 – 200.00

Solid cream clay with painted-on decorations, signed "L. E. Adkins."

PLATE 48

PLATE 49

PLATE 50

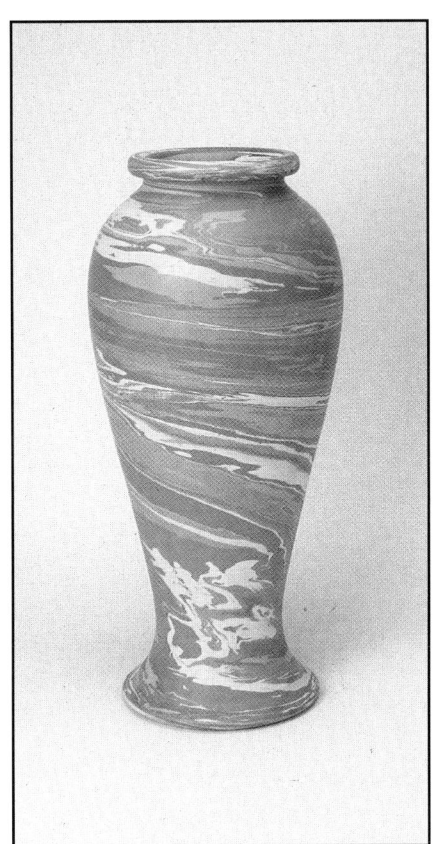

PLATE 51

PLATE 52

Vases with First Art Mark, unless noted

Plate 53

(Left to right)

First Row:

1. Vase, 6" .... $125.00 – 150.00
2. Vase, 4½", Second art mark .... $75.00 – 100.00
3. Vase, 5½" .... $100.00 – 125.00

Second Row:

1. Vase, 5½" .... $100.00 – 125.00
2. Vase, 5¼" .... $100.00 – 125.00
3. Vase, 4½", Second art mark .... $75.00 – 100.00
4. Vase, 5½" .... $100.00 – 125.00

Third Row:

1. Vase, 6" .... $125.00 – 150.00
2. Vase, 5½", Second art mark .... $75.00 – 100.00
3. Vase, 5½", Second art mark .... $75.00 – 100.00
4. Vase, 6½" .... $125.00 – 150.00

Fourth Row:

1. Vase, 6½", Niloak incised, art lettering .... $150.00 – 175.00
2. Vase, 6¼" .... $150.00 – 175.00
3. Vase, 6", unmarked * .... $150.00 – 175.00
4. Vase, 6¾", Second art mark .... $125.00 – 150.00

* Although this piece is an unmarked piece of Niloak, someone applied a sticker (mutilated) to the bottom of the piece to improve salability.

Plate 53

VASES WITH FIRST AND SECOND ART MARKS

PLATE 54

(Left to right)

Top Row:

1. Vase, 4", First art mark .... $75.00 – 100.00
2. Vase, 4½", First art mark .... $75.00 – 100.00
3. Vase, 3½", Second art mark .... $125.00 – 150.00
   Also oblong blue and silver metallic sticker of the emblem of the Chicago World's Fair with 1933 date.
4. Vase, 4", First art mark .... $75.00 – 100.00

Middle Row:

1. Vase, 4½", Second art mark .... $75.00 – 100.00
2. Vase, 4¾", Second art mark .... $75.00 – 100.00
3. Vase, 4", Second art mark .... $75.00 – 100.00
4. Vase, 4¼", Second art mark .... $75.00 – 100.00

Bottom Row:

1. Vase, 4½", Second art mark .... $75.00 – 100.00
2. Vase, 4½", round Niloak sticker .... $75.00 – 100.00
3. Vase, 4¾", larger Second art mark .... $75.00 – 100.00
   Incised "H.M.S., 7/7/36."
4. Vase, 4¼", Second art mark .... $75.00 – 100.00

PLATE 54

Cabinet Pieces with First and Second Art Marks

Plate 55

(Left to right)

Top Row:

1. Vase, 3½", First art mark..$125.00 – 150.00
2. Bowl, 2", Patent Pend'g..$200.00 – 300.00 (+/-)
3. Vase, 3¼", Second art mark...$150.00 – 175.00

Middle Row:

1. Vase, 3½", Second art mark...$150.00 – 175.00
2. Vase, 3½", Second art mark...$150.00 – 175.00
3. Vase, 3½", Second art mark...$125.00 – 150.00

Bottom Row:

1. Vase, 3¼", Second art mark...$150.00 – 175.00
2. Vase, 3", unmarked...$150.00 – 175.00
3. Vase, 3¼", Second art mark...$125.00 – 150.00

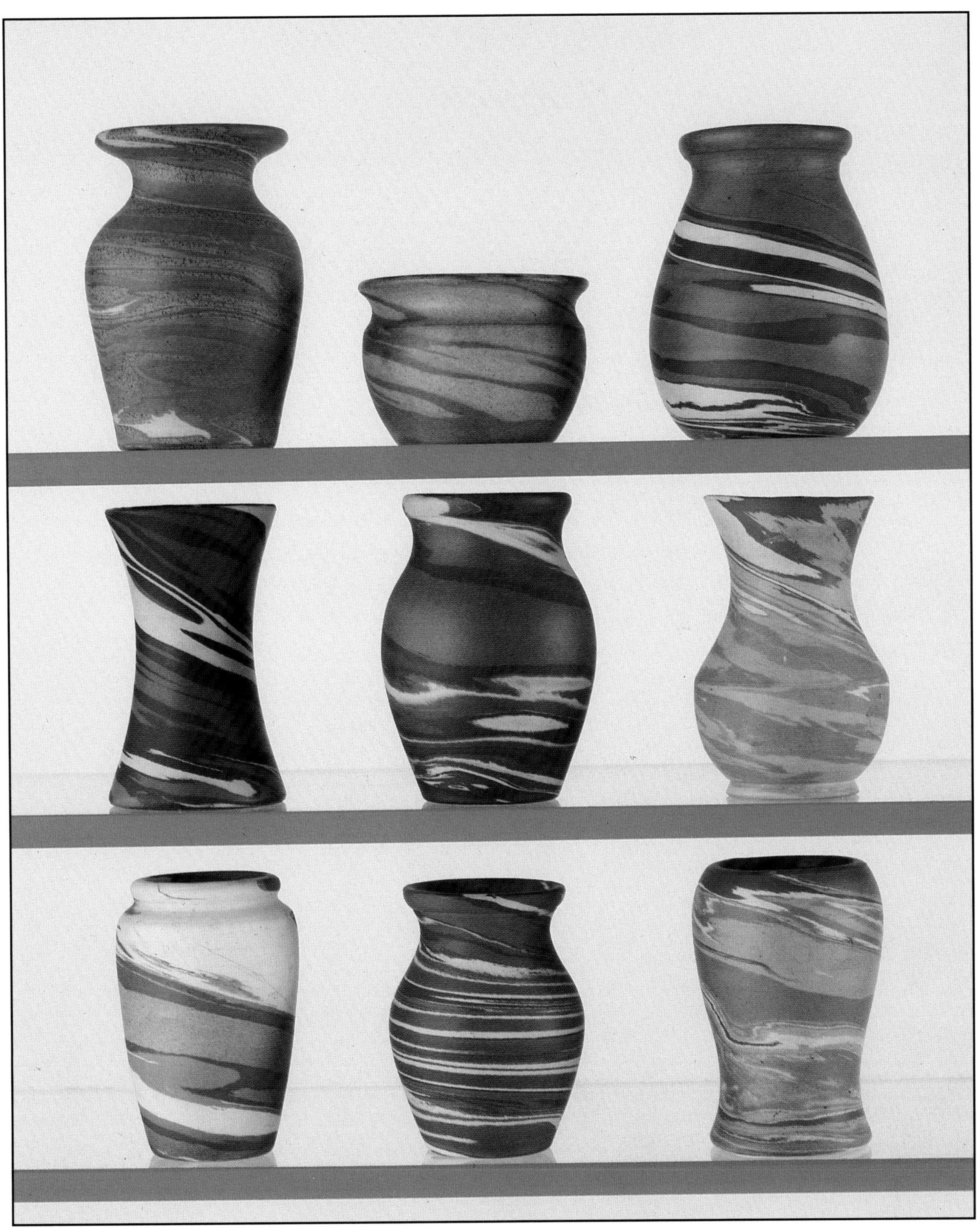

PLATE 55

MINIATURES

PLATE 56

(Left to right)

Top Row: Unmarked

1. Vase, 2" .... $175.00 – 200.00
2. Vase, 2" .... $150.00 – 175.00
3. Vase, 2" .... $175.00 – 200.00

Bottom Row:

1. Jug, 3½", unmarked .... $200.00 – 300.00
2. Match holder, 2", early Niloak .... $150.00 – 175.00
3. Jug, 3", First art mark, inscribed "Janie" * .... N/A

* This miniature jug was a cherished possession of the late Janie L. Crain. Mrs. Crain, an accomplished artist and teacher for over 50 years in the Little Rock area, acquired it on one of the numerous visits she made to the Niloak Pottery as a child.

Plate 56

UNMARKED MINIATURES, UNLESS NOTED

PLATE 57

(Left to right)

Top Row:

1. Bowl, 1" .... $250.00 – 300.00
2. Cone vase, 2" .... $250.00 – 300.00
3. Vase, 2¼" .... $200.00 – 250.00

Middle Row:

1. Bowl/vase, 1½", "Potteries" sticker * .... $150.00 – 175.00
2. Vase, 1½" .... $250.00 – 300.00
3. Vase, 1¾" .... $150.00 – 175.00
4. Vase, 2" .... $200.00 – 250.00

Bottom Row:

1. Vase, 2¾", incised "7 Falls Colorado" .... $150.00 – 175.00
2. Vase, 2½" .... $175.00 – 200.00
3. Vase, 2½" .... $175.00 – 200.00
4. Vase, 2" .... $150.00 – 175.00

* A.V. Hutcheson, who worked at Niloak Pottery in 1939, has an identical piece which he remembers being made. During the late 1930s and the early 1940s, Niloak pottery was produced only during demonstrations at the Benton plant on Military Avenue for tourists. He stated that other pieces were made as well, but the majority of items were these type of miniatures. Arlene Rainey, daughter of Charles Hyten, recalled the small pieces being made as party favors for her and her sister's birthday parties as well as other festive occasions. Another possibility is that these pieces were made at the end of the day with miscellaneous leftover clays. Last, it is probable that these small pieces were salesmen's samples. Therefore, if a vase is less than 3" (the smallest pieces made according to Niloak catalogs), it probably falls into one of these four categories.

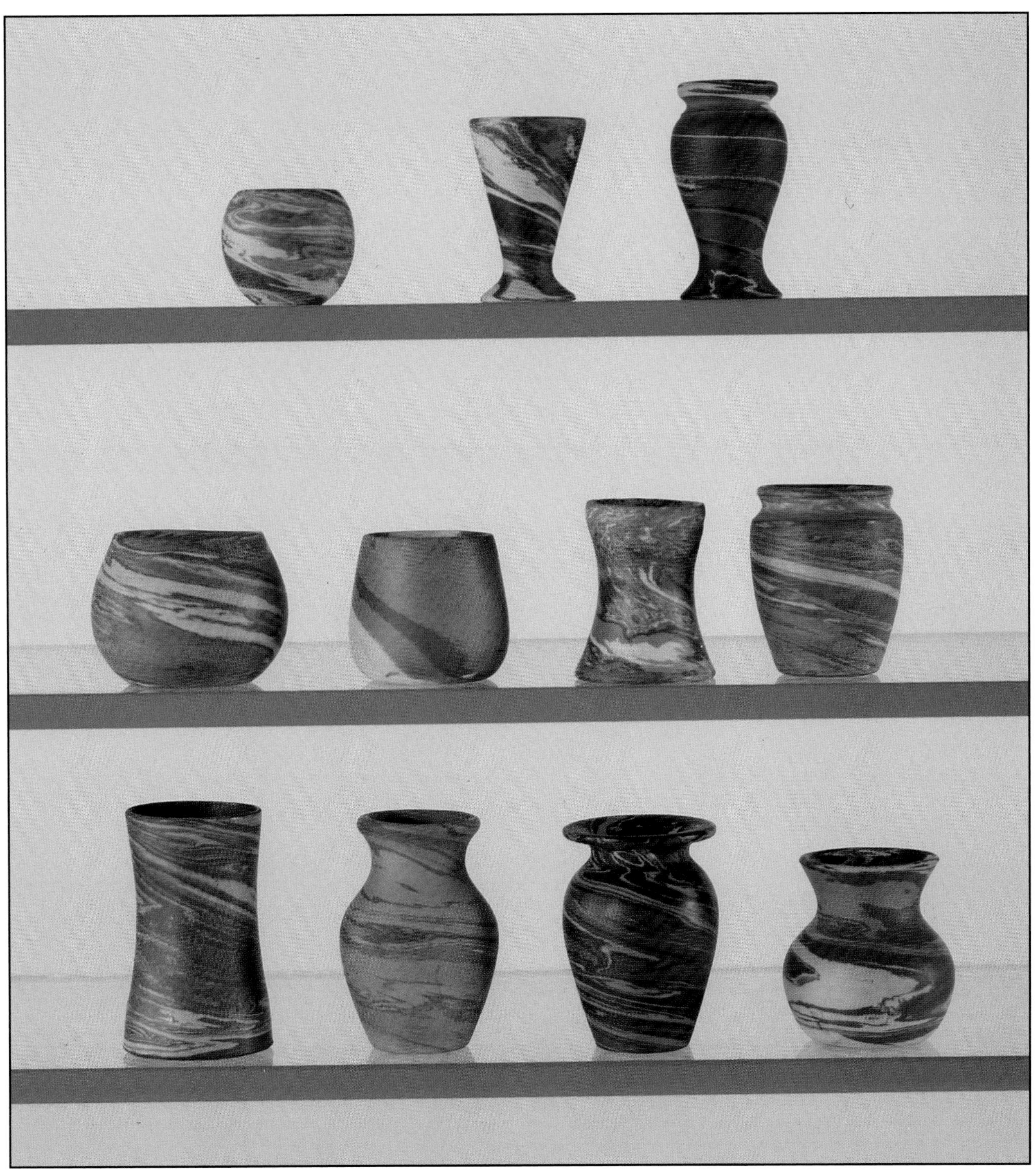

PLATE 57

PLATE 58

(Left to right)

Top Row:

1. Candlestick, 10" .... $175.00 – 225.00
2. Candlestick, 9" .... $175.00 – 225.00
3. Candlestick, 8" .... $150.00 – 200.00

Middle Row:

1. Chamber stick, 5" .... $200.00 – 250.00
2. Candlestick, 5½" .... $150.00 – 200.00
3. Candlestick, 4" .... $150.00 – 200.00
4. Chamber stick, 5½", unmarked .... $200.00 – 250.00

Bottom Row:

1. Candlestick, 9" .... $200.00 – 300.00
2. Candlestick, 10¼" .... $175.00 – 225.00
3. Candlestick, 10¼" .... $175.00 – 225.00

   Has blue and white sticker "Mineralized."

   (See page 84, middle row, item 2. Also see pages 23, 48, and 52.)

Niloak of the Ozarks
the Home of the Niloak Pottery

is located at Benton, Arkansas, on the pike between Little Rock and Hot Springs. No tour of the state is complete without a visit to this unusual plant where callers may witness the actual making of Niloak wares.

The art of making vari-hued pottery from clays of different natural colors has been developed through successive generations and is not duplicated elsewhere. While vessels of any shape can be reproduced in quantity, the color pattern of each piece is unique and gives a pleasing effect of individuality. There is a large assortment offered and Niloak makes an acceptable gift from a standpoint of utility as well as beauty. Modern methods only add to the perfection of the product as each phase of manufacture is in the hands of an artist.

C. D. Hyten, the originator of "NILOAK," is a "Dixie" product, having been born and reared in Arkansas.

Correspondence Solicited.

THE NILOAK POTTERY BENTON, ARKANSAS
C. D. HYTEN, Manager.

Niloak Pottery advertisement, December 1925. ***Courtesy of Arkansas History Commission.***

Plate 58

Vases with First Art Mark, unless noted

Plate 59

(Left to right)

Top Row:

1. Bud vase, 8¼"..$175.00 – 200.00
2. Bud vase, 8¼", single groove motif..$150.00 – 175.00
3. Bud vase, 8¾", double groove motif..$150.00 – 175.00

Middle Row:

1. Bud vase, 6½"..$125.00 – 150.00
2. Fan vase, 7¼", larger Second art mark..$350.00 – 400.00
3. Bud vase, 6", larger Second art mark, patent number (ink stamp)..$125.00 – 150.00

Bottom Row:

1. Vase, 8¼", unique "bull's-eye" effect..$200.00 – 250.00
2. Vase, 7¾"..$200.00 – 250.00
3. Vase, 7½", unusual "candy cane" effect..$200.00 – 300.00 (+/-)
4. Vase, 6½"..$175.00 – 200.00

Plate 59

Pieces with First and Second Art Marks

Plate 60

(Left to right)

Top Row:

1. Vase, 5½" x 3", Second art mark .... $200.00 – 250.00
2. Planter, 4½", First art mark .... $175.00 – 225.00
3. Vase, 6½" x 3½", Second art mark .... $250.00 – 300.00

Middle Row:

1. Fern dish:
   Insert — 6½" x 2", unmarked .... $175.00 – 200.00 (+/-)
   Planter — 7" x 3½", First art mark .... $200.00 – 250.00
2. Planter, 6", First art mark .... $250.00 – 300.00 (+/-)

Bottom Row:

1. Jardiniere, 7", First art mark .... $350.00 – 450.00 (+/-)
2. Jardiniere, 8¼", First art mark .... $450.00 – 550.00 (+/-)

Plate 60

WALL POCKETS AND FLOWER ARRANGERS

PLATE 61

(Left to right)

Top Row*: All unmarked

1. Wallpocket, 8¼" .... $300.00 – 400.00 (+/-)
2. Wallpocket, 6" .... $250.00 – 350.00 (+/-)

Middle Row: All unmarked

1. Flower frog, 4" x 1¼" .... $100.00 – 125.00
2. Flower frog, 3¼" x 1¼" .... $75.00 – 100.00
3. Flower frog, 3" x 1½" .... $75.00 – 100.00

Bottom Row:

1. Flower bowl, 4¾" x 4½", Second art mark .... $175.00 – 225.00
2. Flower bowl, 5¾" x 3", Second art mark .... $175.00 – 225.00
3. Flower bowl, 4¾" x 2", larger Second art mark .... $150.00 – 200.00

* Many wallpockets on the market are those made by Evans Pottery. (See Not Necessarily Niloak, pages 156 – 165.)

PLATE 61

BOWLS AND VASES WITH FIRST AND SECOND ART MARKS

PLATE 62

(Left to right)

Top Row:

1. Bowl, 4½", Second art mark....................$125.00 – 150.00
2. Bowl, 4", First art mark....................$125.00 – 150.00
3. Bowl, 3", Second art mark....................$100.00 – 125.00

Middle Row:

1. Vase, 7¼", First art mark....................$225.00 – 275.00
2. Vase, 6¼", "bull's-eye," First art mark....................$200.00 – 250.00

Bottom Row:

1. Bowl, 6½", First art mark....................$200.00 – 250.00
2. Vase, 6¾", First art mark....................$200.00 – 250.00

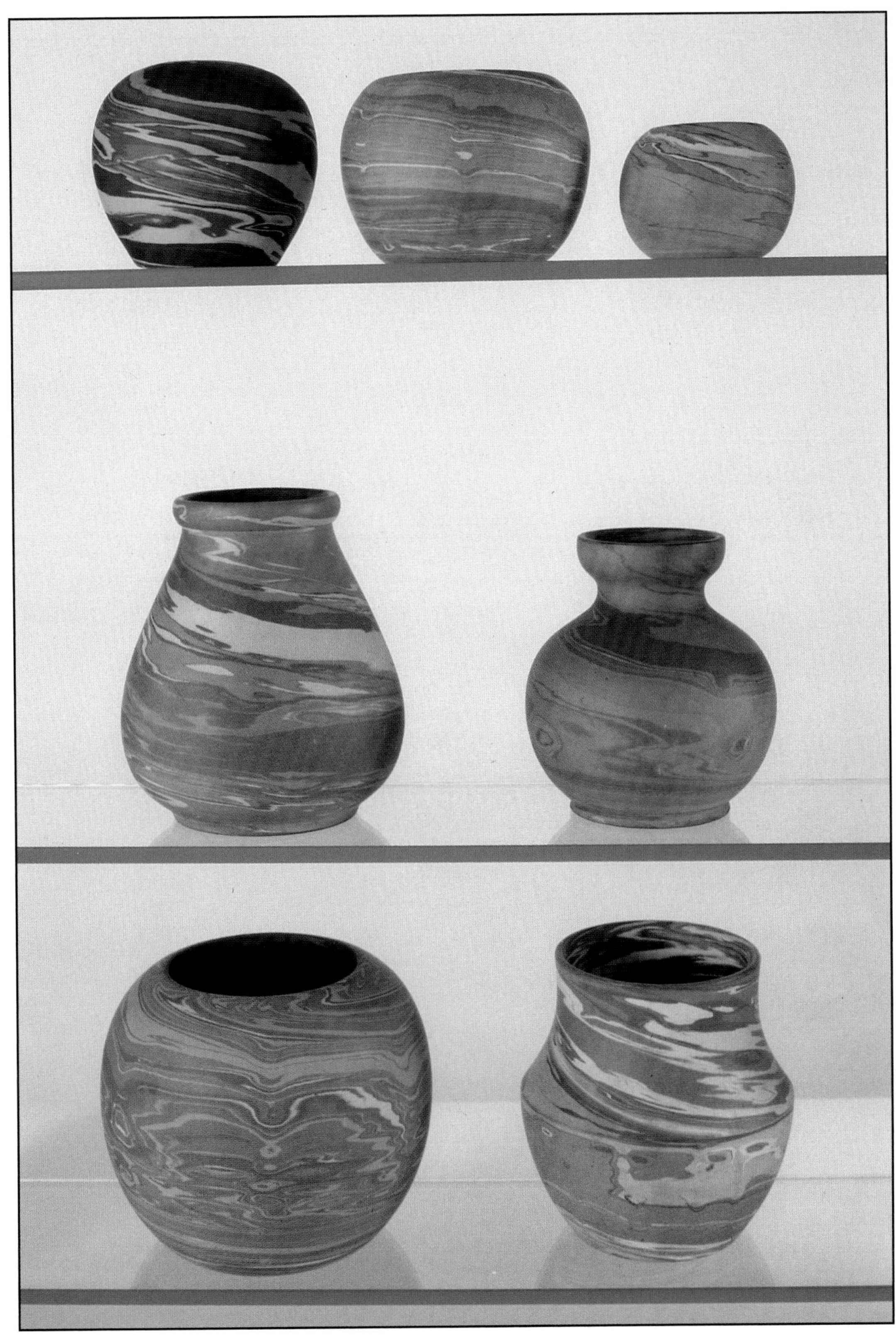

PLATE 62

Jardinieres with First and Second Art Marks

Plate 63

Jardiniere, 13" x 14", larger Second art mark ....$1,000.00 – 1,500.00 (+/-)

Plate 64

Combined height of 13½" ....$800.00 – 1,000.00 (+/-)

Plate 65

Both have First art mark.

Pedestal, 7¾" ....$400.00 – 500.00 (+/-)

Jardiniere, 5¾" ....$300.00 – 400.00 (+/-)

Plate 63

PLATE 64

PLATE 65

CABINET PIECES WITH FIRST AND SECOND ART MARKS

PLATE 66

(Left to right)

Top Row:

1. Cabinet vase, 3", First art mark .... $75.00 – 100.00
2. Cabinet vase, 3¾", First art mark, round Niloak sticker .... $75.00 – 100.00
   "#100" in pencil.
3. Cabinet vase, 3¼", Second art mark .... $75.00 – 100.00
   Ink stamp of "Patent No. 1657997."

Second Row:

1. Cabinet vase, 4", First art mark .... $75.00 – 100.00
2. Bowl/vase, 5" x 2½", First art mark .... $100.00 – 125.00
3. Vase, 3", First art mark .... $150.00 – 175.00

Third Row:

1. Cabinet vase, 3½", First art mark .... $75.00 – 100.00
2. Cabinet vase, 3", First art mark. .... $100.00 – 125.00
3. Cabinet vase, 3", Second art mark .... $75.00 – 100.00
4. Bowl, 2¼", Second art mark .... $75.00 – 100.00
   Incised "Helen Huchins, 11-29-30."

Fourth Row:

1. Cabinet vase, 3½", First art mark .... $75.00 – 100.00
2. Cabinet vase, 3", First art mark .... $75.00 – 100.00
3. Cabinet vase, 3", Second art mark .... $75.00 – 100.00
4. Cabinet vase, 3", unmarked * .... $75.00 – 100.00

* Possibly a late attempt at making swirl after an absence of production. Of the half dozen I have seen, only one was marked (Second art mark). Interior glaze is a milky white and blue. It is probable that these items are what were referred to as "natural" Niloak in the 1940s. (See page 29.)

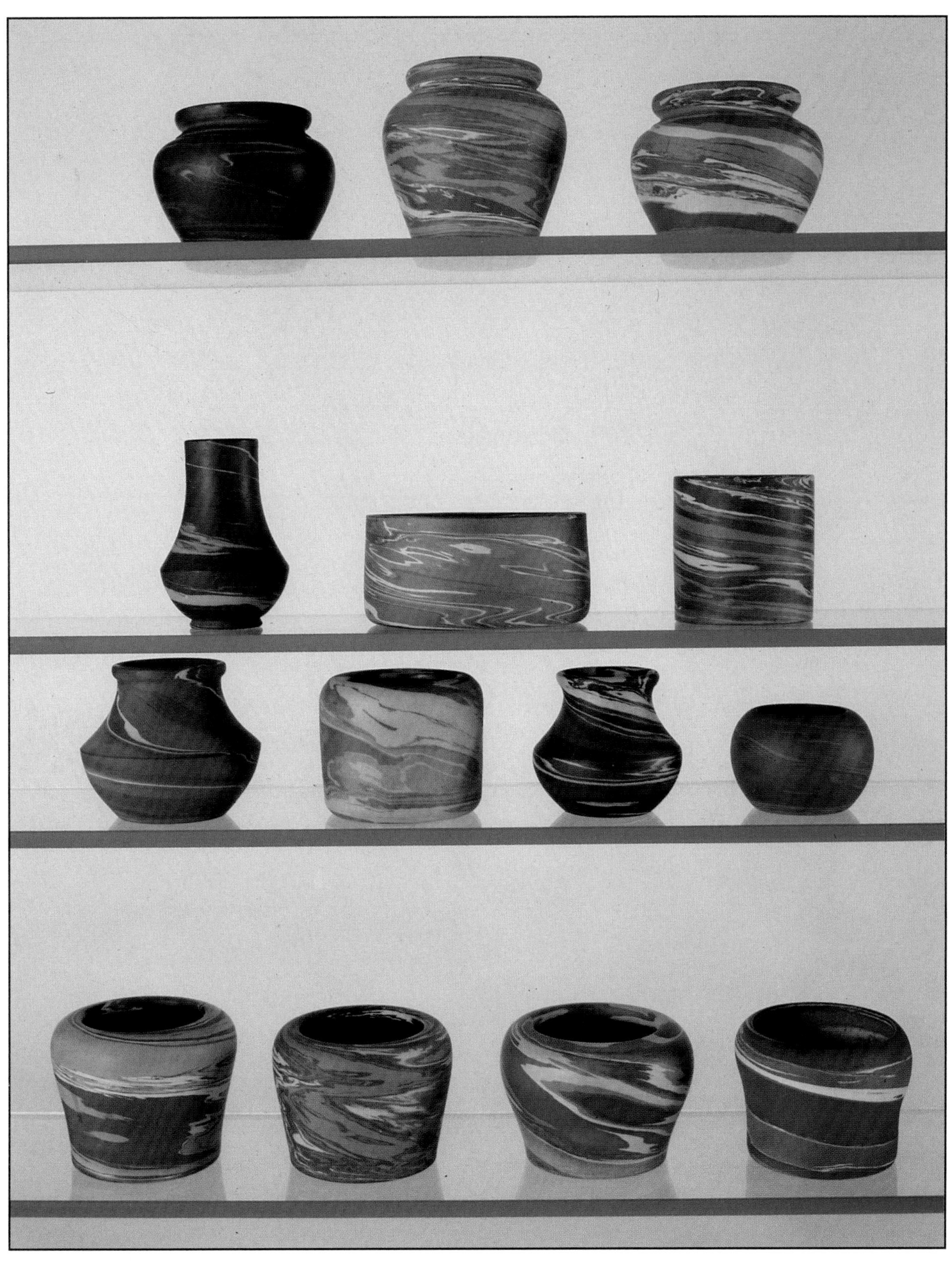

PLATE 66

PIECES WITH FIRST AND SECOND ART MARKS

PLATE 67

Bowl, $11\frac{1}{4}$" x $4\frac{1}{4}$", larger Second art mark..........................$800.00 – 1,000.00 (+/-)

PLATE 68

(Left to right)

Top Row:

1. Ashtray, $3\frac{1}{4}$" x $1\frac{1}{4}$", Second art mark......................................$75.00 – 100.00
2. Violet vase, $3\frac{1}{4}$", First art mark ....$200.00 – 300.00
3. Pin tray, $3\frac{3}{4}$" x $1\frac{1}{4}$", Second art mark ....$100.00 – 125.00
   "Starved Rock Hotel" incised on bottom.

Middle Row:

1. Bowl, 5" x $2\frac{3}{4}$", First art mark ....$125.00 – 150.00
2. Bowl, 5" x $2\frac{1}{2}$", First art mark ....$125.00 – 150.00
3. Bowl, $4\frac{1}{2}$" x $2\frac{1}{4}$", First art mark...$125.00 – 150.00

Bottom Row:

1. Bowl, 5" x 2", First art mark...$100.00 – 125.00
2. Bowl, $4\frac{3}{4}$" x $1\frac{1}{4}$", Second art mark...$100.00 – 125.00
3. Ashtray, 5" x $1\frac{1}{4}$", Second art mark.......................................$100.00 – 125.00

PLATE 67

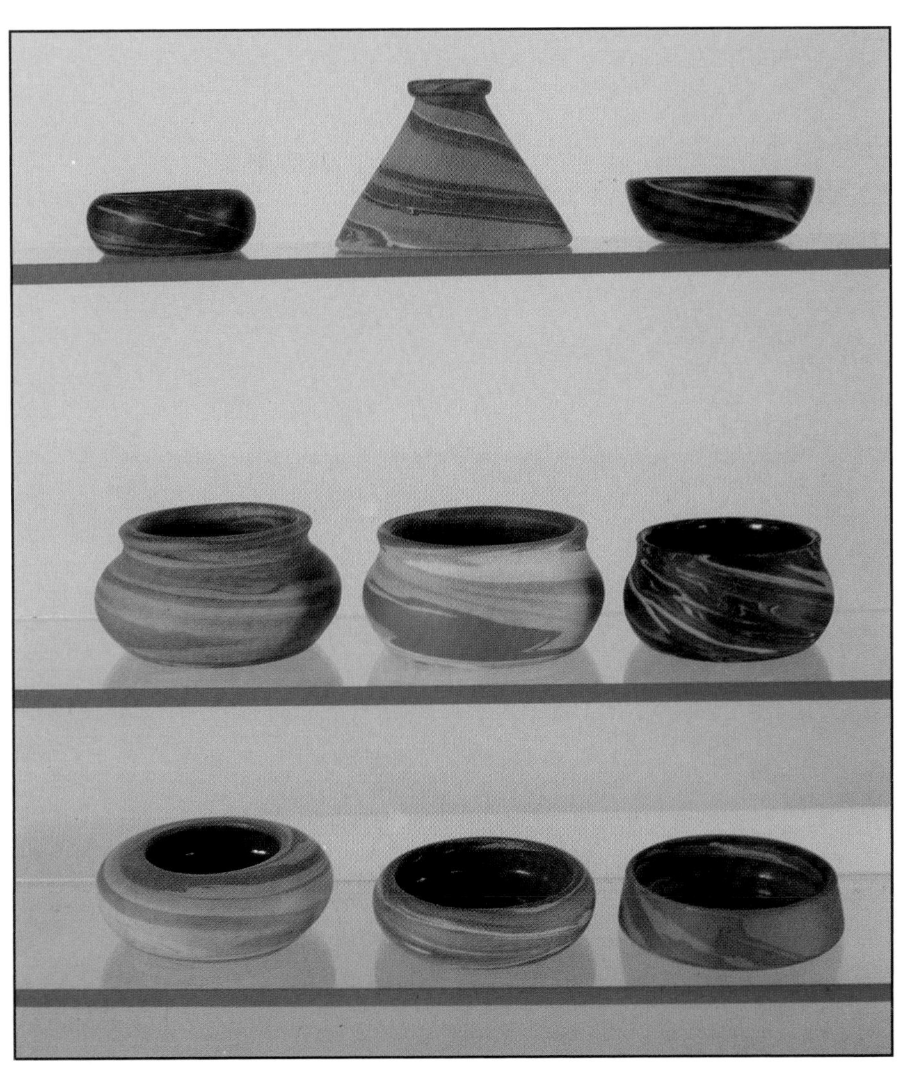

PLATE 68

Pieces with First and Second Art Marks

Plate 69

Bowl, 7½" x 3½", First art mark..........$400.00 – 600.00 (+/-)

Plate 70

(Left to right)

Top Row:

1. Bowl, 8" x 2", First art mark..........$150.00 – 175.00
2. Bowl, 6" x 3", First art mark..........$125.00 – 150.00

Middle Row:

1. Footed planter, 7½" x 2½", First art mark..........$275.00 – 325.00
2. Baby chamber pot, 6¼" x 2½",
   Second art mark..........$400.00 – 600.00 (+/-)

Bottom Row:

1. Bowl, 10" x 3", larger Second art mark..........$400.00 – 500.00 (+/-)
2. Compote, 8¼" x 6", round Niloak sticker..........$500.00 – 700.00 (+/-)
   Two pieces formed into one.

Plate 69

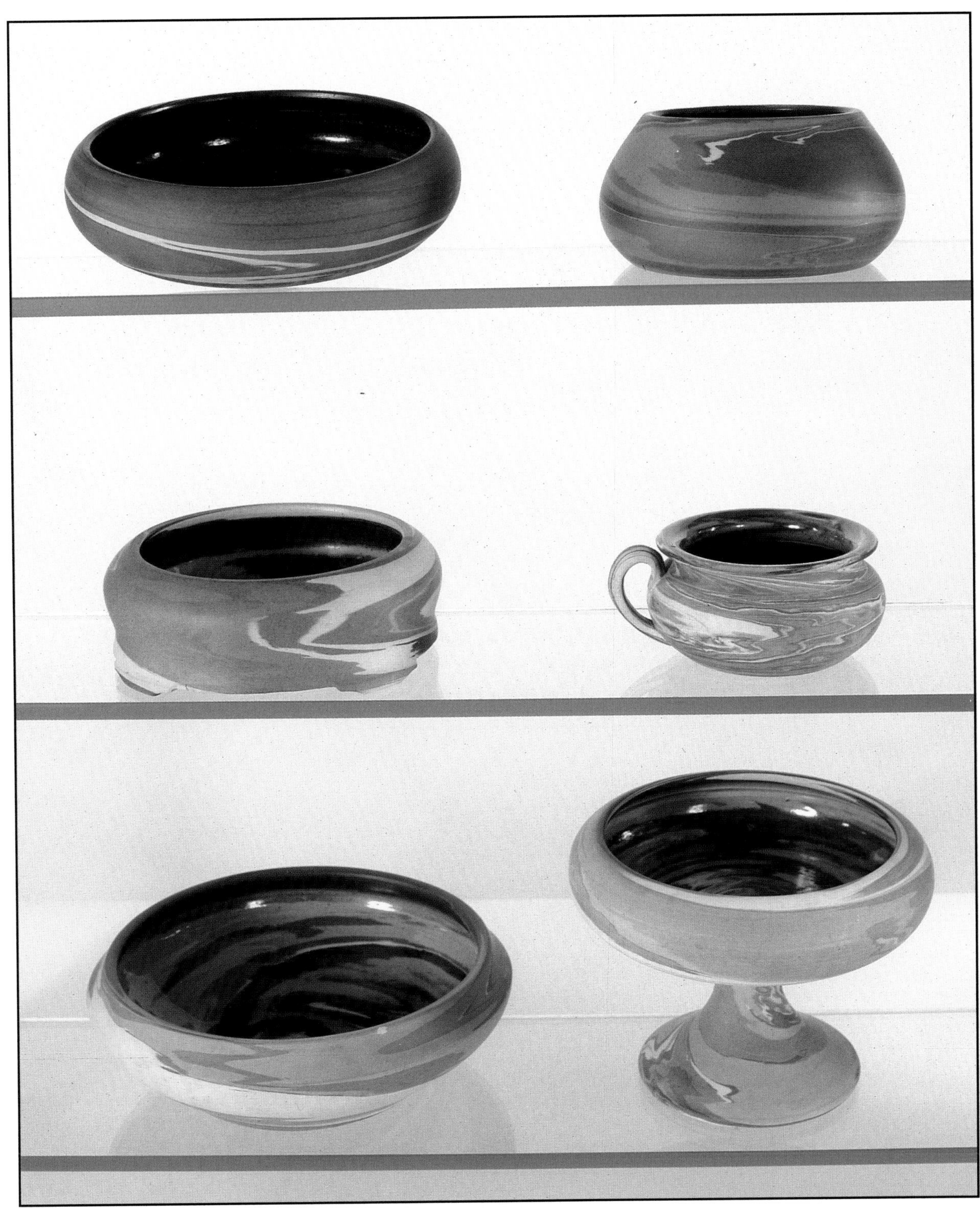

PLATE 70

COVERED PIECES WITH FIRST AND SECOND ART MARKS, UNLESS NOTED

PLATE 71

Covered rose jar .... $700.00 – 900.00

PLATE 72

(Left to right)

Top Row:

1. Powder bowl, 5" x 3", larger Second art mark........................ $350.00 – 450.00
2. Cigarette jar, 3¾" x 4½", Second art mark .... $275.00 – 325.00
3. Powder bowl, 6" x 3½", larger Second art mark..................... $400.00 – 500.00

Middle Row:

1. Humidor, 5" x 7", Second art mark... $600.00 – 800.00
2. Humidor, 5" x 7¼", Second art mark .... $600.00 – 800.00

Bottom Row:

1. Covered compote, 5¾" x 6", unmarked......................... $600.00 – 800.00 (+/-)
2. Rose jar, 5¾" x 8", First art mark *................................ $700.00 – 900.00 (+/-)

* One might assume that this shape was made only as the rose jar.

PLATE 71

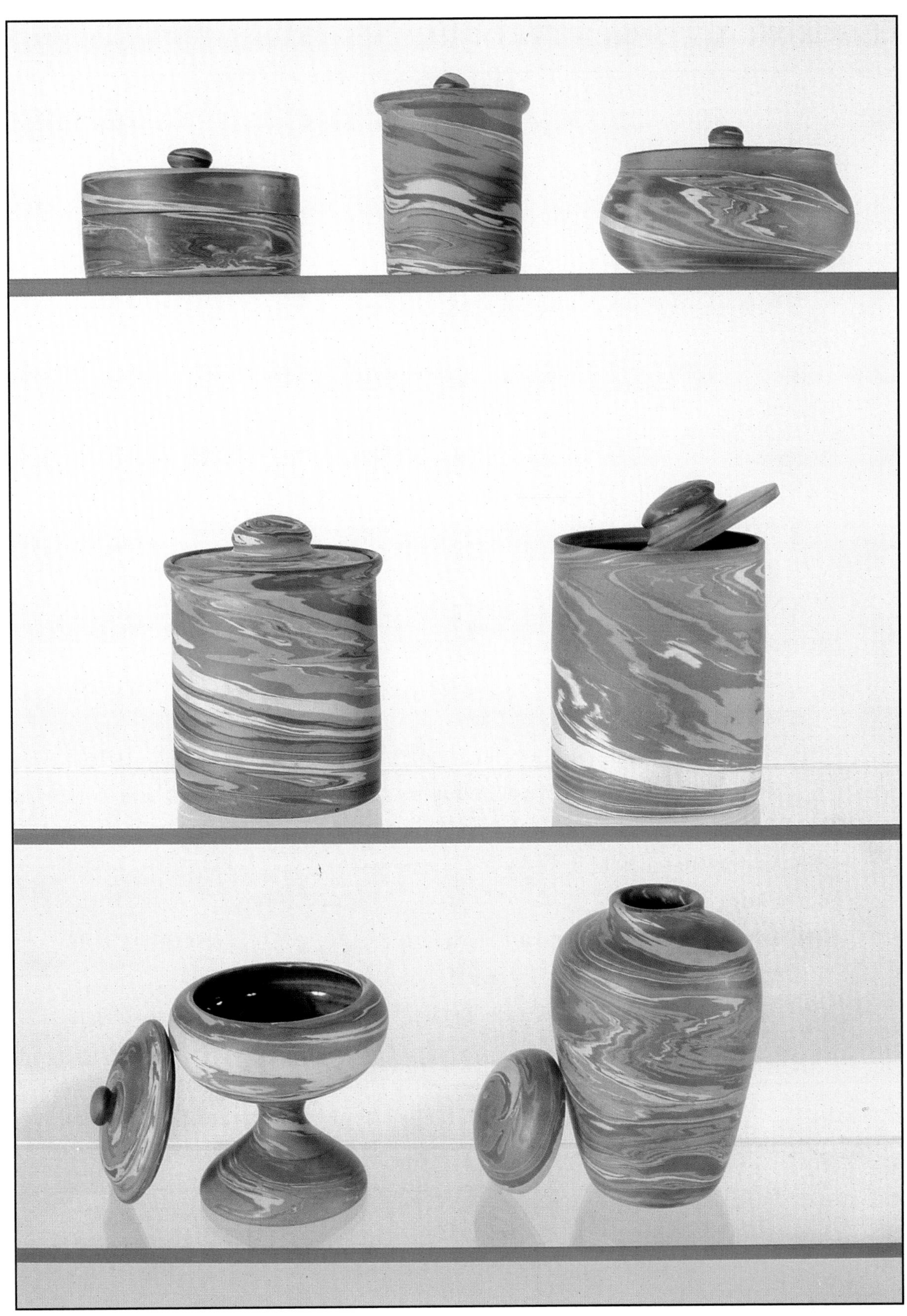

PLATE 72

SMOKING ACCESSORIES WITH VARIOUS MARKS, UNLESS NOTED

PLATE 73

(Left to right)

1. Cigarette jar, 4¾" x 3¼", First art mark .... $275.00 – 325.00
2. Humidor, 5½" x 6", Second art mark .... $600.00 – 800.00
3. Puff box, 3¼" x 4½", First art mark .... $350.00 – 450.00

PLATE 74

(Left to right)

First Row:

1. Matchstick holder, 2", Patent Pend'g .... $125.00 – 150.00
2. Matchstick holder, 1¾", double groove motif, Patent Pend'g .... $150.00 – 175.00
3. Matchstick holder, 1½", First art mark .... $125.00 – 150.00

Second Row:

1. Matchstick holder, 2½", First art mark .... $125.00 – 150.00
2. Matchstick holder, 2", Second art mark * .... $125.00 – 150.00
3. Matchstick holder, 1½", Second art mark .... $125.00 – 150.00
   This piece was received by one collector's father at a convention in Little Rock.

Third Row:

1. Ashtray/Match holder, 4¾" x 2¼", unmarked .... $175.00 – 200.00

Fourth Row:

1. Ashtray, 5" x 1½", Second art mark * .... $200.00 – 250.00
2. Ashtray, 5¼" x 1¾", First art mark, round Niloak sticker with "#119" penciled in .... $200.00 – 250.00

PLATE 73

* These three items appear to be pressed rather than thrown. In 1926, an article by Funk mentioned that a machine existed for the manufacture of smaller items.

Plate 74

DRINKING ITEMS WITH VARIOUS MARKS

PLATE 75

Covered water bottle .... $600.00 – 800.00

PLATE 76

(Left to right)

Top Row:

1. Handled stein/mug, 4¼", Patent Pend'g .... $300.00 – 400.00
2. Handled stein/mug, 4½", First art mark .... $300.00 – 350.00
3. Handled stein/mug, 4½", First art mark .... $350.00 – 400.00

Middle Row:

1. Drinking glass, 4", First art mark.. $150.00 – 175.00
2. Drinking glass, 3¾", Second art mark * .... $125.00 – 150.00
3. Drinking glass, 3½", First art mark.. $125.00 – 150.00
4. Shot glass, 2¼", Second art mark *................................ $100.00 – 125.00 (+/-)
5. Shot glass, 2¼", Second art mark.................................. $100.00 – 125.00 (+/-)

Bottom Row:**

1. Water bottle, 8½", First art mark.................................... $400.00 – 600.00 (+/-)
2. Water bottle, 7¾", with 4" drinking glass cover,
   Second art mark ** .... $600.00 – 800.00 (+/-)

PLATE 75

* Pressed, not thrown.

** Note the difference in the mouths of the water bottle and the water bottle with tumbler.

PLATE 76

DRINKING ACCESSORIES WITH FIRST ART MARK

PLATE 77

Stein, 4¼"..$400.00 – 500.00 (+/-)
Incised design with "Tarpon, Corpus Christi Bay."

PLATE 78

Whiskey jug, 6", squared..$1,400.00 – 1,600.00 (+/-)

PLATE 79

Decanter set..$1,800.00 – 2,400.00 (+/-)
All pieces have First art marks. Bottle – 10½", Tray – 12", Jiggers – 2¼".

PLATE 77

PLATE 78

PLATE 79

PUNCH BOWL SET AND PITCHERS WITH FIRST AND SECOND ART MARKS

PLATE 80

Punch bowl on base with cups, 10" x 14" ....$2,000.00 – 3,000.00 (+/-)

Punch bowl is two pieces fired into one; Cups 2½"; all pieces have First art mark.

PLATE 81

(Left to right)

1. Pitcher, 9", Second art mark,..$800.00 – 1,000.00 (+/-)
2. Tankard, 13½", First art mark..................................$1,000.00 – 1,200.00 (+/-)
3. Pitcher, 10½", First art mark..$700.00 – 900.00 (+/-)

ARKANSAS GAZETTE

New Home of Niloak Pottery

The Niloak Pottery
MANUFACTURERS OF
"NILOAK"
C D HYTEN Manager
BENTON, ARKANSAS
Visitors Always Welcome

This fireplace owes its charm to Niloak Pottery

A few of the many designs of beautiful Niloak Pottery

The Story of Niloak Pottery

When the natural forces made Arkansas a depository for raw materials of a thousand kinds, stored it up, they provided for future works of art as well as of general utility and service.

The several extensive deposits of Kaolin of superior quality found in Arkansas provide wonderful clay for an endless variety and supply of fine art ware.

In 1910, C. D. Hyten, President of the Niloak Pottery, conceived the idea of mingling the various colored clays and making the art pottery, employing a man at that time experienced in art pottery, and in about two years developed what is now known as Niloak pottery. These experiments were conducted at the old location of his father's plant, about 1½ miles north of Benton on the Military road. Today one of the largest and finest deposits of Kaolin is that of the Niloak Pottery of Benton, Arkansas, and the new plant which is pictured above, has just been completed on the Little Rock-Hot Springs Highway, one mile north of Benton, at a cost of $20,000.

The art pottery sent out by this company is widely celebrated for its beauty and coloring, the natural clay showing in cream, buff, brown, red, azure and deep blue and many grays. The fantasy of design is not less pleasing. No two pieces are ever alike, and the suggestion they make to the imagination varies as widely as do smoothly flowing sea rivers and scarfs of flying clouds.

President C. D. Hyten of the Niloak plant has developed the industry and is himself the master potter of the art shop.

Niloak Pottery Advertisement, 1929. ***Courtesy of the University of Central Arkansas Archives and Special Collections.***

PLATE 80

PLATE 81

LAMP BASES/VASES WITH FIRST AND SECOND ART MARKS, UNLESS NOTED

PLATE 82

All have open bottoms and are unmarked.

(Left to right)

1. Lamp base, 6½", "bull's-eye" ....$300.00 – 400.00 (+/-)
2. Lamp base, 7½" ....$350.00 – 450.00 (+/-)
3. Lamp base, 8½" ....$400.00 – 500.00 (+/-)

True manufactured lamps have openings at the top for the hardware and on the side for the cord. The company, as well as individuals, converted vases of various sizes into lamps by drilling a hole in the bottom or the side and adding the top parts. Collectors must be aware of swirl lamps that are not Niloak. Most swirl lamps on the market today were manufactured by Evans and later Desert Sands. Evan's pieces have either a semi-closed or closed bottom. See Not Necessarily Niloak.

PLATE 83

(Left to right)

1. Vase, 12", First art mark ....$400.00 – 450.00
2. Lamp base, 14¾", with drilled side, Second art mark (+/-) .$800.00 – 1,000.00
3. Hyacinth vase, 11¾", First art mark.......................................$450.00 – 500.00

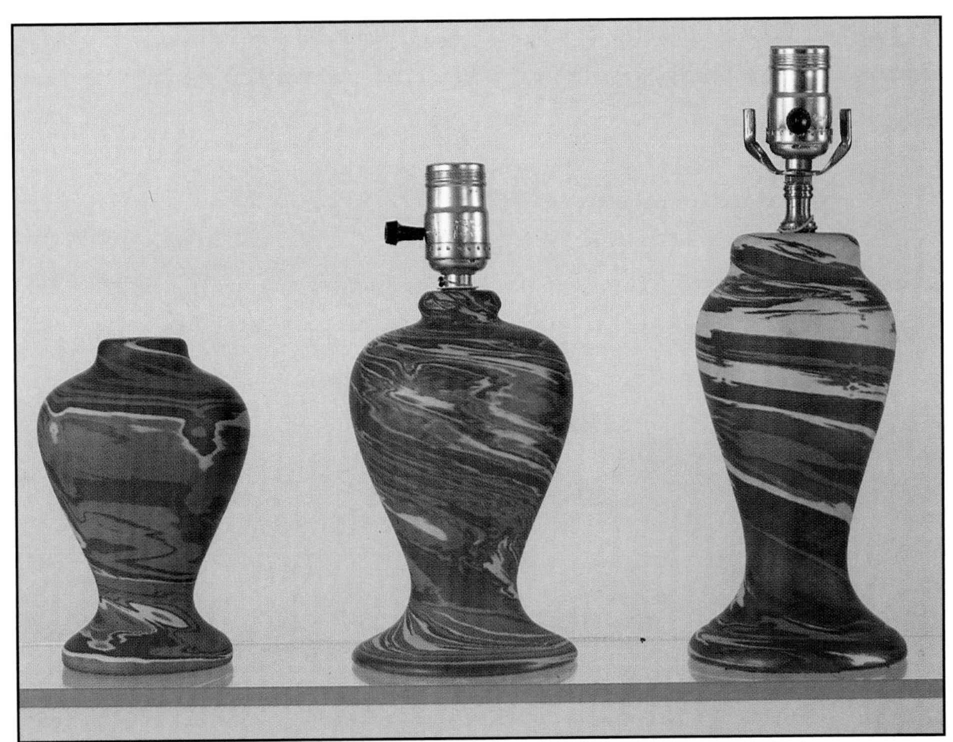

Plate 82

Plate 83

Novelties/Unique Pieces Unmarked, unless noted

Plate 84

Bookend, 4" x 4" x 4" .... $800.00 – 1,000.00 (+/-)

Formed from tiles. Incised on back "F.D. Basore – Handmade"; on front in the lower right-hand corner are the Greek symbols for Omega Sigma Phi.

Plate 85

(Left to right)

Top Row:

1. Candlestick, 5½" * .... $200.00 – 300.00
2. Clock, 4¼", First art mark .... $800.00 – 1,200.00 (+/-)
3. Candlestick, 5¼" .... $200.00 – 300.00

Middle Row:

1. Paperweight, 3" x 1½", Second art mark .... $175.00 – 200.00
2. Elephant, 2", molded ** .... $700.00 – 900.00 (+/-)
3. Gear shift knob, 2" .... $600.00 – 800.00 (+/-)
4. Paperweight, 3" x 1½", First art mark .... $175.00 – 200.00

Bottom Row:

1. Jug, 6" .... $600.00 – 800.00 (+/-)
2. Tile, 4½" x 4½" *** .... $500.00 – 700.00 (+/-)

Plate 84

* The candlesticks shown are thrown in the shape of an old-time crank telephone receiver. It has been said that these examples were made for attendees of a telephone convention in Little Rock.

** This swirl elephant was made from the mold of its castware counterpart.

*** This tile was probably appropriated in the early 1970s from the 1929 sales/showroom in Benton.

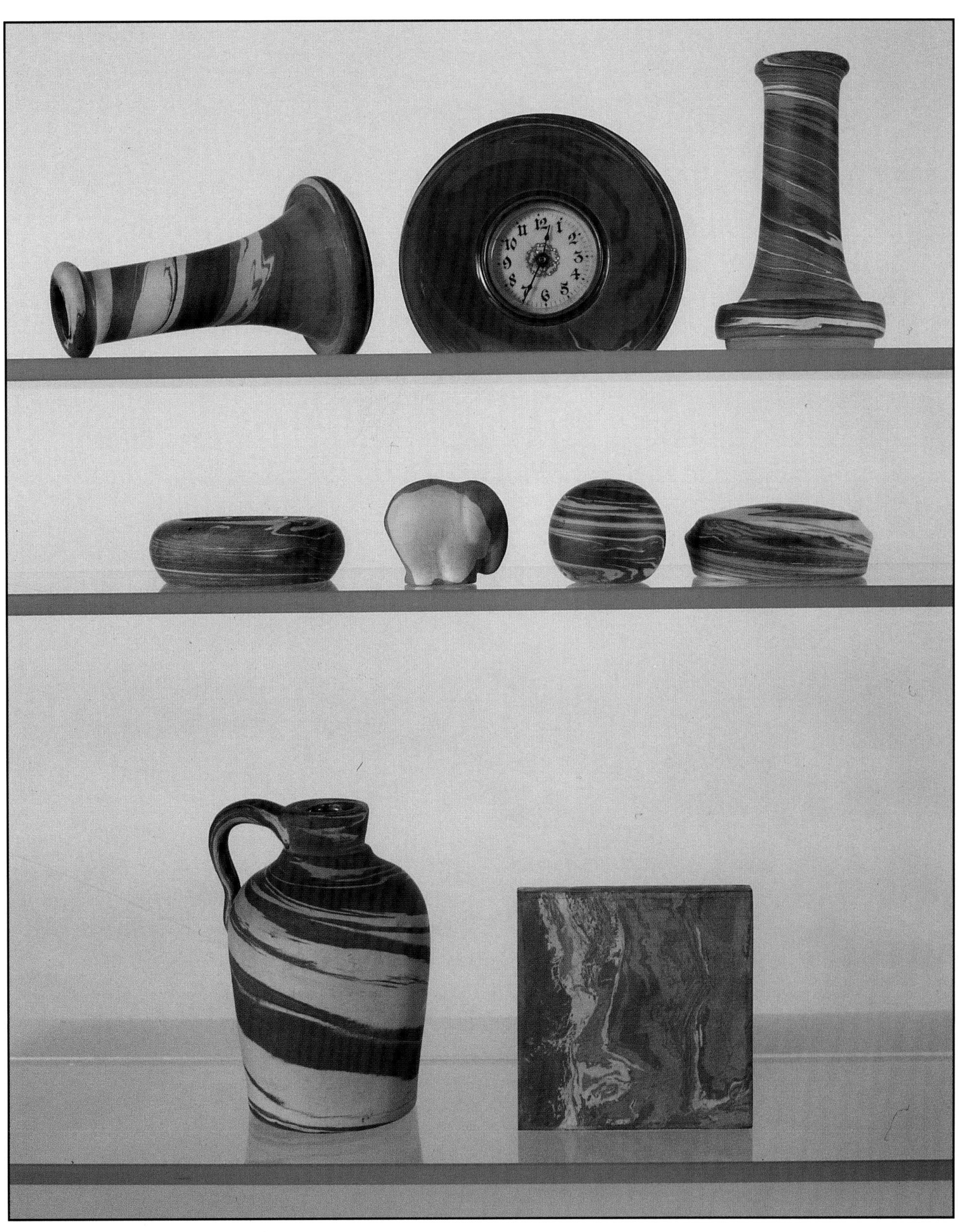

PLATE 85

MISCELLANEOUS PIECES WITH FIRST ART MARK, UNLESS NOTED

PLATE 86

(Left to right)

Top Row:

1. Whiskey jug, 3¼", unmarked ....$100.00 – 200.00 (+/-)
   "Pensacola Golden Corn" impressed on side. *
2. Vase, 2⅜" ....$150.00 – 200.00
3. Bowl/vase, 3" ....$100.00 – 125.00
4. Humidor, 4½" ....$400.00 – 500.00

Middle Row:

1. Bowl, 2¾" x 10⅞"..$175.00 – 200.00
2. Ashtray, 5⁄16" x 5½", round Niloak sticker.............................$175.00 – 200.00
3. Collection plate, 2" x 9¼" ** ....$400.00 – 600.00 (+/-)

Bottom Row:

1. Vase, 4¼" ....$75.00 – 100.00
   Also red & brown sticker with "Art Deluxe Quality Guaranteed,
   Tulsa Art Store, Tulsa, Okla."
2. Vase, 5⅛" ....$100.00 – 125.00
3. Vase, 6" ....$150.00 – 175.00
4. Candlestick, 9¾" ....$175.00 – 225.00
5. Vase, 7¾" *** ....$250.00 – 300.00

* Some collectors have questioned whether this miniature jug is Niloak or a product of the Muscle Shoals/Marie Pottery (see Not Necessarily Niloak, pg. 156). Having examined over 25 pieces of Muscle Shoals and Marie examples, I find they lack Niloak's technical and coloring expertise. This advertising jug, however, matches Niloak's characteristics. The market has recently been flooded with this item since an unknown quantity was dug up out of an old dump in Jacksonville, Florida, by bottle collectors.

** Thanks Mrs. Lewis for your insight.

*** This shape is similar to a jardiniere in Plate 63. The difference, however, is a ridge on the bottom of the planter which sets into the pedestal. This piece has no such ridge.

PLATE 86

VARIOUS HAND-FORMED AND/OR TOOLED PIECES

PLATE 87

Mantle clock, 8" x 4½" (approx.), swirl slabs, First art mark .... N/A

PLATE 88

(Left to right)

1. Ashtray/match holder, 1½ x 3¼", unmarked .... $75.00 – 100.00
2. Candlestick, 2¼" x 4¼", Second art mark, round blue Niloak sticker .... $100.00 – 125.00

PLATE 89

Planter, 13½" x 5½" x 6", swirl slabs, unmarked .... N/A

PLATE 90

Shoe, 2¾" x 6½", unmarked .... N/A

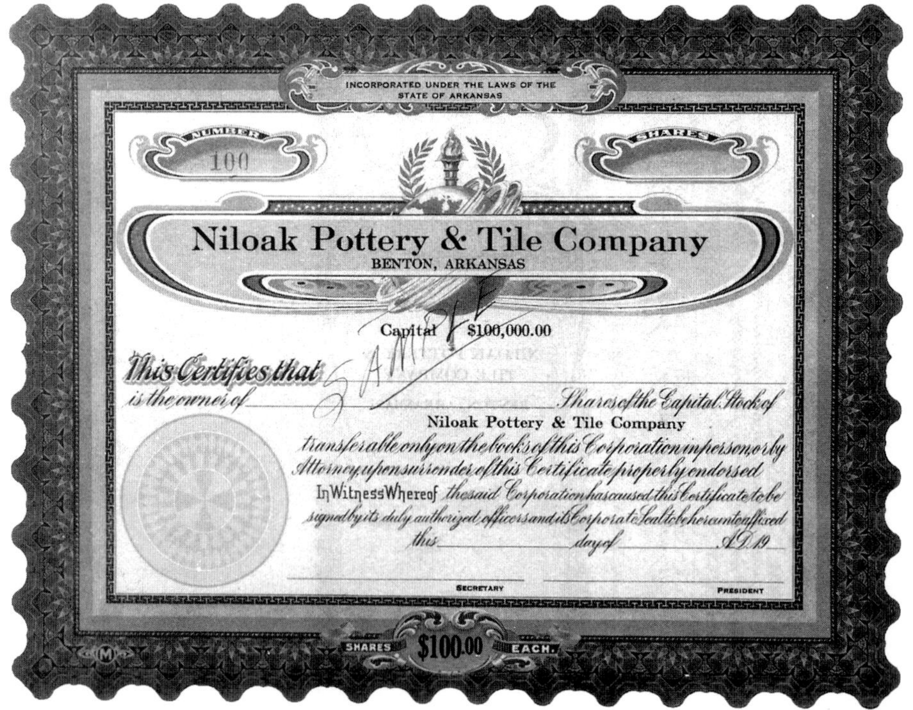

INCORPORATED UNDER THE LAWS OF THE STATE OF ARKANSAS

NUMBER 100 SHARES

Niloak Pottery & Tile Company
BENTON, ARKANSAS

Capital $100,000.00

This Certifies that ____ is the owner of ____ Shares of the Capital Stock of
Niloak Pottery & Tile Company
transferable only on the books of this Corporation in person or by Attorney upon surrender of this Certificate properly endorsed
In Witness Whereof the said Corporation has caused this Certificate to be signed by its duly authorized officers and its Corporate Seal to be hereunto affixed
this ____ day of ____ A.D. 19

SECRETARY PRESIDENT

SHARES $100.00 EACH.

Niloak Pottery & Tile Company Stock Certificate, 1928.
Courtesy of the Hardy L. Winburn IV.

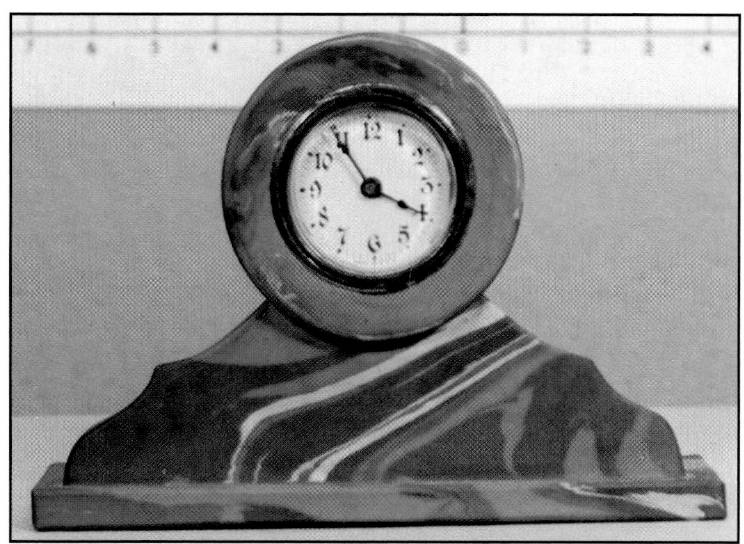

Plate 87

Plate 88

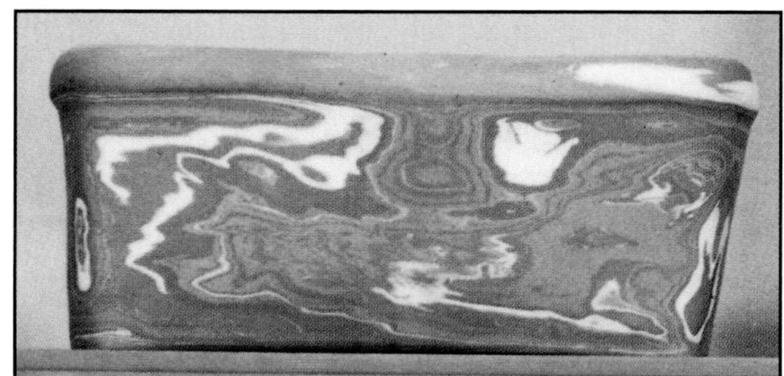

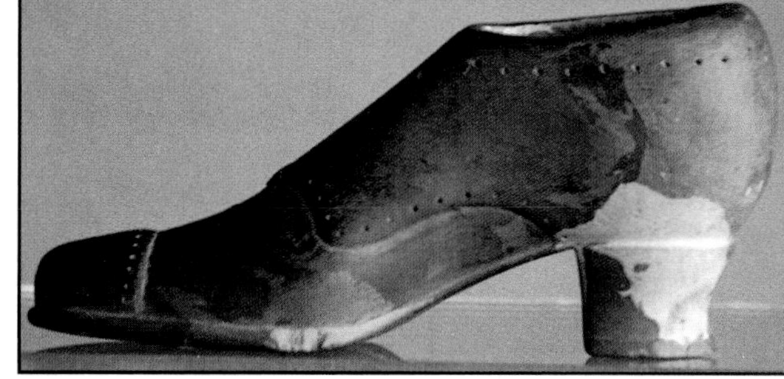

Plate 89

Plate 90

Not Necessarily Niloak

Missionware is collected nationally and demands good prices. Therefore the incidence of non-Niloak (unmarked) swirl being sold as Niloak pottery has increased. Either from lack of knowledge or at the hands of unscrupulous persons, unmarked swirl pottery, particularly Evans pottery, has been sold as Niloak. Paul Evans points out, however, that the novel idea by Niloak co-founders Arthur Dovey and Charles Hyten was not so new after all. In his *Art Pottery of the United States,* Evans mentions the Gay Head Pottery of Martha's Vineyard, Massachusetts, as a pre-Niloak producer of a sun-dried swirl pottery. There was also the scroddled pottery of George Ohr in Biloxi, Mississippi (with production circa 1905).

But it was Niloak Pottery, under the direction of Hyten and his close associates Frank Long and Fred Johnson, who by the early 1920s perfected, standardized, and streamlined Missionware. With Niloak concentrating on selling in the retail markets in larger cities, in department stores and art shops coast to coast, and in Arkansas at resorts such as Hot Springs and Eureka Springs, Hyten possibly did not initially see the downside to his company's success. With ever-increasing sales, other companies took notice and began to copy the Missionware product. In 1924, he secured Niloak as a trademark, yet a patent would be several years away.

As other established potteries recognized the swirl pattern's appeal, they began to capitalize on it with their versions. Only then did Hyten see a further need to protect his product and its market. His company needed protection from many competitors! While other companies made swirl pottery, none of them were able to match or exceed either the technical expertise or aesthetic quality of the Niloak Missionware. No other swirl pottery achieved a "complicated or delicately adjusted character" like Niloak. Years of experience and seasoned, skilled potters helped capture the natural looking qualities of different colored clays blended together which made Missionware one of the "Wonders of Arkansas."

Denver's White Pottery

From the early 1920s, Niloak pottery was selling in the resort town of Colorado Springs and elsewhere around southeast Colorado. Tom Turnquist, author of *Denver's White Pottery,* stated that swirl production began in Denver during the early 1920s. Therefore, it is probable that Denver's White Pottery manufactured its swirl as a result of the popularity of swirl pottery and the recognition that it was marketable. This swirl pottery is as good technically and aesthetically as Niloak but the swirls are typically narrower.

Ozark Pottery

Charlie Stehm's Ozark Pottery of Eureka Springs was at least one Arkansas challenger (see Ozark Skag Pottery). Although it was introduced during the 1925 Christmas season, the company was founded in 1926. A talented Ozark craftsman of German descent (long noted for his work with onyx), Stehm explained: "I probably never would have become a potter, however, if I could have gotten the agency for Niloak in my Eureka Springs shop. I found I needed pottery, so I went out, found my clays, and became a potter." Production was limited to about 150 pieces a month which included some decorated pieces featuring scenes of the Eureka Springs area. Although his swirl production began after Hyten had filed for a patent, Stehm's work undoubtedly reinforced Hyten's efforts to obtain the patent. With tradition having it that Hyten threatened to sue Stehm, all indications point to the fact that Ozark Pottery production ceased just before Hyten received a U. S. patent on the Missionware process. The significant difference, although both Ozark and Niloak potteries are somewhat comparable in color, technical, and aesthetic characteristics, is that the clay swirls on Ozark Pottery rotate counterclockwise. Missionware rotates clockwise. It is nearly always marked, incised in the clay, and sometimes dated as well. The pieces are either dated 1926 or 1927. Hyten received the Missionware patent in January 1928. Other than the fact that both produced swirl pottery, there is no known connection between Stehm and Niloak at the present time. The "Eureka" brick (see plate 93), one of several known to exist, has an applied swirl layer and is possibly a product of Ozark Pottery.

Evans/Desert Sands Pottery/Pinto Pottery

The most active post-Niloak patent production came from the Evans Pottery of Missouri. As a producer of "a great variety of utilitarian and ornamental ware" since 1859, it was located near the Arkansas/Missouri line in Stoddard County between Bloomfield and Dexter, Missouri. Started by Jacob Simmermon and continued by his son Thomas (Tom) and his family, it produced pottery from its inception until 1969 with only a couple interruptions. Tom Simmermon, interestingly enough, hired a potter out of Little Rock, Arkansas, named Hugh Evans. Evans eventually married Tom's daughter Lucinda, and they had two sons, Randall and Arthur. While information on Hugh Evans's activities in Arkansas has been researched extensively, to date there is no information connecting him with Niloak Pottery or any other potteries in Arkansas. Randall's son, Terrell, studied pottery at the Lewis Art Institute in Chicago and returned to Missouri to become partners with his father. The Evans Pottery began manufacturing swirl ware around 1928, and this production would continue until at least the late 1950s. Randall Evans would operate this pottery until it closed in 1969. Evans's swirl pottery is rarely marked but most pieces are distinguished by an unglazed interior or a matte "brown interior glaze." Production was heavy as many examples exist (some similar in shape to Niloak) on the market today — especially vases, bowls, and lamp bases (with semi-closed and closed bottoms). Terrell Evans moved to Boulder City, Nevada, in 1936. In the early 1940s, Arthur Evans and his family, including his son Ferrell moved to Boulder City, Nevada, and together with Terrell, started the Desert Sands Pottery. It is probable that this location was chosen because of the Hoover/Boulder Dam (completed in 1936 and fast becoming a tourist attraction) and the company's close proximity to Las Vegas (another tourist draw). Arthur and Ferrell made and sold swirl pottery (generally marked) with a high gloss interior and exterior glaze (although some pieces have a dull exterior glaze). Desert Sands Pottery was manufactured into the 1970s. Desert Sands Pottery is quite distinguishable from Niloak Pottery, although some have recently advertised unmarked Desert Sands pottery as the early and extremely rare exterior glazed Niloak Missionware. Finally, Pinto Pottery and the Mineral and Sands Pottery, both from Boulder City, Nevada, must have been a product of the Evans family but little else is known about them. At some point, some or all of the operations were moved to California.

Spruce Pines Pottery (Muscle Shoals/Marie)

Even former Niloak employees went on to produce swirl pottery elsewhere. Frank Long, a Niloak employee since at least 1910, departed for Spruce Pine, Alabama, in 1924. Long produced, in addition to the HyLong Pottery, two swirl pottery lines called Muscle Shoals and Marie for the Spruce Pines Pottery (in business by the early 1910s.) As a skilled potter, Long threw Missionware for Niloak, and was undoubtedly the driv-

Niloak Pottery plant on Pearl Street, ca. 1924. From left to right: Clisty Cason, Romine McNeil, Fred Johnson, Olin Call, Reagan Rowland, Gilbert Mason, Jule Palmer, Cecil Mason, Bob Crawford, Garland Bragg, Doris McNeil, Matilda McCoy, D. P. Boyd, Bullet Hyten, Emmett Mason, Roy Bumgardner, Clarence Mason, Alf Westbrook, Colonel McNeil, John Mason, Seborn Cotton, and Charlie McClue. ***Courtesy of the late Hardy L. Winburn IV.***

SINCE 1868
Home of
NILOAK
POTTERY
Interesting Native Industry
SEE IT MADE
at
BENTON, ARKANSAS

Postcard of the Niloak Pottery Company Showroom on Military Avenue in Benton. ***Author's Collection.***

ing force behind the Muscle Shoals and Marie lines (marks are impressed die stamps). Long made these swirl (as well as HyLong) pieces in classic Niloak shapes until late 1926 or early 1927. He left Alabama and returned to Arkansas to work for Jack Carnes at the newly founded Camark Pottery in Camden.

Dickota Pottery (Badlands)

A swirl pottery with another tie to Niloak Pottery is Badlands Pottery. Niloak Pottery employee, Howard S. Lewis, moved to North Dakota after developing Hywood by Niloak. Produced between 1934 and 1937, Lewis, a ceramic engineering graduate from Iowa State College, made swirl ware (called Badlands Pottery) for the Dickota Pottery Company (Dickinson Clay Products Company of Dickinson). Lewis's pieces tend to have a deeper and more brilliant color than typical Missionware examples. It is sometimes found with his initials (HL connected together). As for Dickota's castware, some pieces are similar to Niloak shapes, and Lewis even introduced a couple of his glazes at Dickota that he created while at Niloak Pottery.

Ozark Skag

Ozark Skag Pottery is a little-known pottery. Located either in northern Arkansas or southern Missouri, its production seems to have occurred sometime between the 1930s and 1950s. Its body is made up of different colored rocks, crushed and put into a clay-like consistency, and hand thrown. They were not fired, but rather shellacked and collectors should never put water in these vessels as they will self destruct due to a break-down of the clear finish (and I will attest to that). This pottery has no relation to either the Ozark Pottery of Eureka Springs or the Ozark/Zark Pottery of St. Louis, Missouri, of the early 1900s.

Houghton and Dalton Pottery

Another swirl ware was produced by the Houghton and Dalton Pottery of Ohio. This pottery was called Indian. Examples often have an interior blue glaze, and some pieces even have an exterior glossy glaze. Although little is known about any direct connections between the two companies, Stoin M. Stoin, developer of Niloak's Hywood Art Pottery, did work for this Ohio company. In addition to its swirl production, the pottery produced several shapes similar to Weller's Nile and Niloak's Hywood Art Pottery lines.

Leveritt Pottery

Arkansan Joe Leveritt's interest in pottery began as a child making clay marbles and "firing them in the [family] fireplace." After a Camark Pottery tour in the fifth grade (late 1920s), where he observed master potter Frank Long, Leveritt, with "thoughts of throwing his own clay," went home and salvaged a fly wheel and bearings from a Model T Ford and made his own potter's wheel. Throughout the rest of his school years, including his college studies in physical education, Leveritt dreamed of being a potter. Years later, during a visit to C.L. Emerson's Camark Pottery factory store in Little Rock, Leveritt told Mr. Emerson of his childhood visit, seeing Frank Long, and his desire to work with pottery. With encouragement, Leveritt, with no formal training, began practicing with clay purchased from the Acme plant in Malvern. By the early 1980s, Leveritt was residing in Conway and was manufacturing a swirl pottery with the Acme clay and commercially purchased dyes. Unlike Niloak's typical Missionware, Leveritt's swirl is glazed (clear) both inside and out. The bulk of Leveritt's swirl pottery was made in Conway during the 1980s. However, he occasionally makes swirl signed "Leveritt" (no location noted).

More Swirl Ware

Over the years, many other potteries and/or individuals made swirl pottery or marbleized (swirl-looking) pottery. Some of the wares are Silver Springs Pottery (Florida) and the related Ft. Ticonderoga (New York); North State Pottery (North Carolina); Royal Gorge (Colorado); Seven Falls (Colorado); Haeger Pottery (Illinois); Comanche Pottery (location unknown); Mt. Rushmore (South Dakota); Stangl Pottery (New Jersey); Loveland Art Pottery (Colorado); Dan Mercer Ware (West Virginia); Broadmoor Pottery (Colorado); Dunster Pottery (location unknown); Fleuron (New York); Garden of the Gods (Colorado); William Gordy (Greorgia); and Nemadji Pottery (Minnesota).

*Not Necessarily Niloak is the combination of new research by the author, the Swirl Imitators chapter from the first Niloak book, and two articles written by author, Nicol Knappen, and Carol Carlton in the January–February 1993 issue of the *Journal of the American Art Pottery Association* (Volume VII). Information on the Evans Pottery came from Fred Burnett's *The Evans Family Pottery of Southeast Missouri, 1858 – 1969* (Cape Girardeau, Missouri: Southeast Missouri State University, 1978).

* I wish to thank Nicol Knappen, former editor of the *Journal of the American Art Pottery Association,* for this wonderful title!

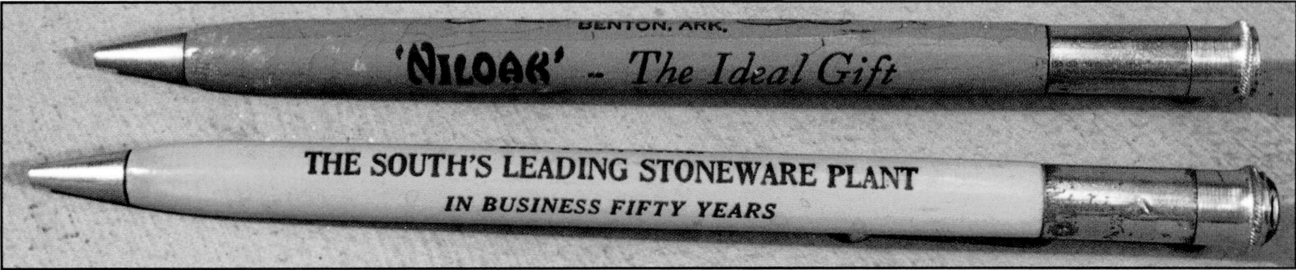

Mechanical pencils promoting Niloak Pottery, c. 1929. ***Author's Collection.***

Plate 91

(Left to right)

First Row:

1. Dickota Badlands, 4¼", initialled "HL" ....N/A
2. Evans Pottery, bottle, 9¾", unmarked ....N/A
3. Denver White (?), 4¼", incised "D" ....N/A

Second Row:

1. Ozark Pottery, 6¾", inscribed "Ozark Pottery, Eureka Springs, Ark. Stehm" with date ....N/A
2. Ozark Pottery, 5½", inscribed similar to above ....N/A
3. Ozark Pottery, 5", same as above with date "7-1-26" ....N/A
4. Silver Springs Pottery, 3", impressed "Silver Springs, Fla." ....N/A

Third Row:

1. Desert Sands, 5¼", unmarked ....N/A
2. Evans Pottery, 5¾", unmarked ....N/A
3. Evans Pottery, bowl, 3¼", unmarked ....N/A
4. Evans Pottery, 5½", unmarked ....N/A

Fourth Row:

1. Muscle Shoals/Spruce Pines Pottery/Marie, 8", impressed "Muscle Shoals" ....N/A
2. Evans Pottery, 7¾", unmarked ....N/A
3. Desert Sands, 6¾", ink stamped "Desert Sands" ....N/A
4. Evans Pottery, lamp base, 8¾", unmarked ....N/A

Plate 91

Not Necessarily Niloak
Swirl Wares Made by Other Manufacturers

Plate 92

(Left to right)

Top Row:

1. Silver Springs Pottery, 4¼", impressed "Silver Springs, Fla." .... N/A
2. Evans Pottery, 2½", unmarked .... N/A
3. Dryden Pottery, 2¾", incised "Dryden, 1983" .... N/A
4. Dickota Pottery, 3½", incised "Dakota Badlands" .... N/A
5. Nemadji Pottery, 2", ink stamp "Nemadji" .... N/A
6. Sherman Pottery, 4", gold metallic sticker — "Sherman's Handmade Pottery," made in Little Rock .... N/A

Middle Row:

1. Evans Pottery, 6", unmarked .... N/A
2. Silver Springs Pottery, 4¾", impressed "Silver Springs, Fla." .... N/A
3. Evans Pottery, 5¼", ink stamped "Lake of the Ozark" and "8-29 38" in pencil .... N/A
4. Muscle Shoals/Spruce Pines Pottery/Marie, 4½", impressed "Marie" .... N/A
5. Dickota Pottery, 5½", incised "Dakota Pottery, Badlands" .... N/A

Bottom Row:

1. Pinto Pottery, 6", ink stamped "Pinto Pottery, Handmade in Boulder City, Nevada" .... N/A
2. Evans Pottery, 7½", unmarked .... N/A
3. Desert Sands Pottery, 6¾", ink stamped "Desert Sands, Boulder City, Nevada" .... N/A
4. Muscle Shoals/Spruce Pines Pottery/Marie, 6½", impressed "Muscle Shoals" .... N/A
5. Ozark Pottery, 6¾", incised "Ozark Pottery, Eureka Springs, Ark, Stehm" .... N/A

PLATE 92

SWIRL WARES MADE BY OTHER MANUFACTURERS

PLATE 93

(Left to right)

Top Row:

1. Leveritt Pottery, 6¼", incised "Leveritt–Conway, Ar." ....N/A
2. Ozark Skag, 7¾", two ink stamps — "Ozark Skag U. S. A." and "Reg. 15488" ....N/A
3. Muscle Shoals/Spruce Pines Pottery/Marie, 8", impressed "Muscle Shoals" ....N/A

Bottom Row:

1. Ozark Skag Pottery, 4½", two ink stamps — "Ozark Skag U. S. A." and "Reg. 15488" ....N/A
2. Ozark Pottery (attribution), swirl faced brick, 8" x 2" x 4", incised "Eureka, 135" ....N/A
3. Ozark Skag, 5", two ink stamps — "Ozark Skag U. S. A." and "Reg. 15488" ....N/A

PLATE 94

Desert Sands Pottery, 6" (approx.), exterior glaze, circle ink stamp "Desert Sands Hand Made," with image of hand ....N/A

PLATE 95

Camark Pottery, 4½", unmarked * ....N/A

* Camark is just one of many companies, groups, and individuals across the United States that produced this marbleized ware resembling the swirl pattern on Niloak Missionware. The process is where colored oils are floated on water, swirled with a large comb-like tool, and the resulting pattern transferred to a bisque piece.

PLATE 93

PLATE 94

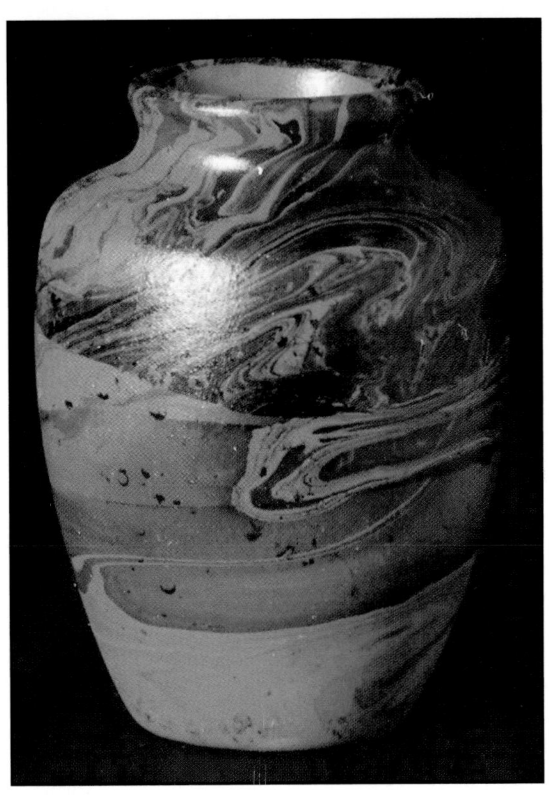

PLATE 95

Hand-thrown Vases with Stoin Glazes

Plate 96

(Left to right)

Top Row:

1. Vase with handles, 6", *Ozark Dawn I*, unmarked ....$150.00 – 200.00
2. Vase with three applied handles, 5½", *Sea Green*, Hywood Art Pottery ....$300.00 – 400.00 (+/-)
3. Vase with handles, 6¼", castware, *Ozark Dawn I*, first Hywood by Niloak..................................$150.00 – 200.00

Middle Row:

1. Vase, 9", castware, first Hywood by Niloak and "Potteries" sticker..$200.00 – 250.00
2. Vase with two applied handles, 8", *Peacock Blue I*, Hywood Art Pottery ....$400.00 – 500.00 (+/-)
3. Vase, 8½", castware, *Ozark Dawn I*, unmarked ....$200.00 – 250.00

Bottom Row:

1. Vase with two applied handles, 9½", *Pearled Green*, unmarked ....$500.00 – 600.00 (+/-)
2. Vase, 9", *Sea Green*, Hywood Art Pottery ....$450.00 – 550.00 (+/-)

PLATE 96

Hand-thrown Vases with Stoin or Lewis Glazes

Plate 97

(Left to right)

First Row:

1. Vase with applied handles, 5¾", *Peacock Blue II*, first Hywood by Niloak, Lewis glaze ....$100.00 – 125.00
2. Vase, 9", first Hywood by Niloak, *Blue and Tan Matt,* Lewis glaze, castware ....$150.00 – 200.00
   "BO" in grease pencil, shape similar to Weller Pottery's Nile and Houghton and Dalton Pottery's crimped top vase.*
3. Vase with applied handles, 7½", *Ozark Dawn I,* unmarked, Stoin glaze ....$400.00 – 500.00 (+/-)
   Glaze similar to Weller's Fruitone.

Second Row:

1. Vase with applied handles, 6", *Ozark Dawn I,* Hywood Art Pottery, Hywood sticker "Shape V Finish 13," Stoin glaze..$150.00 – 200.00
2. Vase with applied handles, 5½", first Hywood by Niloak, *Green and Tan Matt,* Lewis glaze ....$200.00 – 300.00
3. Vase, 6¼", first Hywood by Niloak, *Green and Tan Matte,* Lewis glaze ....$100.00 – 125.00

Third Row:

1. Vase, 5¾", Hywood Art Pottery, Stoin glaze ....$200.00 – 300.00 (+/-)
2. Vase, 5¼", first Hywood by Niloak, *Blue and Tan Matt,* Lewis glaze ....$125.00 – 175.00
3. Vase, 5", *Ozark Dawn I,* Hywood Art Pottery, Stoin glaze ....$150.00 – 200.00

Fourth Row:

1. Vase, 6¾", *Ozark Blue,* unmarked, Lewis glaze.......................$75.00 – 100.00
2. Vase, 7½", *Peacock Blue II,* Hywood incised, Lewis glaze ....$100.00 – 125.00
   "DE" in grease pencil.
3. Vase, 5", *Ozark Blue,* second Hywood by Niloak, Lewis glaze ....$25.00 – 50.00

* Letter combinations exist as both ink stamps or grease marks and refer to catalog shapes. (See pages 334 – 335.)

Plate 97

Hand-thrown Vases with Stoin or Lewis Glazes

Plate 98

(Left to right)

Top Row:

1. Vase, 6⅛", Lewis glaze, *Maroon,* first Hywood by Niloak ......$75.00 – 100.00
2. Vase with applied handles, *Ozark Blue*, Lewis glaze, 8½", Second art mark ....$150.00 – 200.00
3. Vase, 7", Lewis glaze, *Maroon*, Second art mark ....$75.00 – 100.00

Middle Row:

1. Vase, 6½", Stoin glaze, *Sea Green*, Hywood Art Pottery...$350.00 – 450.00 (+/-)
   This glaze and *Peacock Blue I* are similar to Weller's frosted matte but with less curl effects.
2. Vase, 9¼", with applied handles, *Pearled Green*, Stoin glaze, Hywood Art Pottery........................$600.00 – 700.00 (+/-)
3. Vase, 5⅛", Stoin glaze, *Sea Green*, Hywood Art Pottery...$200.00 – 300.00 (+/-)

Bottom Row:

1. Vase, 4⅛", *Green and Tan Matt*, Lewis glaze, unmarked ....$100.00 – 125.00
2. Vase with applied handles, 11¼", Stoin glaze, *Ozark Dawn I*, unmarked ....$700.00 – 800.00 (+/-)
   Shape similar to Weller's Nile shape.
3. Vase, Lewis glaze, 6", *Ozark Dawn II*, Niloak 71..........................$50.00 – 75.00

Plate 98

Hand-thrown and Castware Vases with Stoin or Lewis Glazes

Plate 99

(Left to right)

Top Row:

1. Vase with applied handles, 6½", *Green and Tan Bright,* Stoin glaze, Hywood Art Pottery ....$250.00 – 350.00 (+/-)
2. Vase, 6¼", *Peacock Blue I,* Stoin glaze, Hywood Art Pottery...$350.00 – 450.00 (+/-)
3. Vase with applied handles, 6", *Sea Green,* Stoin glaze, Hywood Art Pottery...................................$200.00 – 250.00 (+/-)

Middle Row:

1. Vase with applied handles, 6¾", Lewis glaze, unmarked ....$125.00 – 175.00
2. Vase with applied handles, 6½", *Ivory,* Lewis glaze, first Hywood by Niloak ....$75.00 – 100.00
3. Vase with handles, 6¼", *Ozark Blue,* Lewis glaze, castware, first Hywood by Niloak.......................$75.00 – 100.00

Bottom Row:

1. Vase with applied handles, 9½", *Ozark Blue,* Lewis glaze, first Hywood by Niloak ....$150.00 – 200.00
2. Vase with applied handles, 9¾", *Green and Tan Matt,* Lewis glaze, first Hywood by Niloak, "HAX" in grease pencil...................$175.00 – 225.00
3. Vase, 6¾", Lewis glaze, *Green and Tan Matt,* first Hywood by Niloak ....$75.00 – 100.00

Niloak Pottery showroom with unique Arkansas shape facade. *Courtesy of the late Hardy L. Winburn IV.*

PLATE 99

Hand-thrown Pieces with Stoin Glazes

Plate 100

Hywood Art Pottery sign, 3¾" .... N/A

Plate 101

(Left to right)

Top Row:

1. Ball Jug, 5½", *Delft Blue*, first Hywood by Niloak, Hywood incised, castware .... $125.00 – 175.00 (+/-)
2. Vase with handles, 5¼", *Wine*, Hywood mold mark, incised "B," castware .... $125.00 – 175.00 (+/-)
3. Vase, 7¼", *Delft Blue*, unmarked .... $150.00 – 200.00

Middle Row: *Delft Blue*

1. Vase, 4¾", first Hywood by Niloak .... $75.00 – 100.00 (+/-)
2. Vase, 6¼", first Hywood by Niloak .... $125.00 – 175.00 (+/-)
3. Vase, 6", Hywood Art Pottery.. $125.00 – 150.00 (+/-)

Bottom Row: *Green and Tan Bright*

1. Vase with handles, 6¼", Hywood Art Pottery .... $125.00 – 175.00 (+/-)
2. Vase with handles, 6¾", unmarked................................ $150.00 – 250.00 (+/-)
3. Vase with three applied handles, 5¾", unmarked........ $200.00 – 300.00 (+/-)

Plate 100

PLATE 101

Hand-thrown Vases with Lewis Glazes

Plate 102

(Left to right)

Top Row: *Ozark Dawn II*

1. Vase with applied handles, 9", first Hywood by Niloak........$125.00 – 175.00
2. Vase, 9¼", first Hywood by Niloak ....$125.00 – 175.00
3. Vase with applied handles, 9½", unmarked ....$125.00 – 175.00

Middle Row:

1. Vase with applied handles, 11¼", *Ozark Blue*, large Second art mark..$175.00 – 225.00
2. Vase, 9½", *Green and Tan Matt*, first Hywood by Niloak......$125.00 – 175.00
3. Vase, 11½", *Ozark Blue*, Second art mark.............................$150.00 – 200.00

Bottom Row: *Ozark Dawn II*

1. Vase with applied handles, 8¾", Potteries sticker ....$125.00 – 175.00
2. Vase, 9¾", first Hywood by Niloak ....$100.00 – 150.00
3. Vase with applied handles, 8½", unmarked ....$100.00 – 150.00

PLATE 102

HAND-THROWN PIECES WITH OZARK DAWN II GLAZE BY LEWIS

PLATE 103

(Left to right)

Top Row:

1. Vase, 5½", pink with blue overspray, unmarked * ....$50.00 – 75.00
2. Fan Vase, 7", "Potteries" sticker ....$75.00 – 100.00
3. Vase, 5", first Hywood by Niloak ....$25.00 – 50.00

Middle Row:

1. Creamer, 4¼", first Hywood by Niloak.......................................$25.00 – 50.00
2. Vase, 10", first Hywood by Niloak ....$100.00 – 150.00
3. Vase, 5½", "Potteries" sticker ....$25.00 – 50.00

Bottom Row:

1. Vase with applied handles, 9¼",
   first Hywood by Niloak..$200.00 – 300.00 (+/-)
2. Vase, 10", unmarked...$100.00 – 150.00
3. Vase with applied handles, 10",
   "Potteries" sticker ....$125.00 – 175.00

* Deb and Gini Johnson in their *Beginner's Guide to American Art Pottery* stated the pink/blue as being common. My research revealed the pink/green combination as being prevalent rather than the pink/blue.

PLATE 103

HAND-THROWN PIECES WITH LEWIS GLAZES

PLATE 104

(Left to right)

First Row:

1. Vase, 4¾", Hywood incised ....$75.00 – 100.00
2. Tumbler, 5", *Peacock Blue II*, unmarked....................................$35.00 – 55.00
3. Vase, 5", *Pearled Green*, second Hywood by Niloak.....................$50.00 – 75.00

Second Row:

1. Fan vase, 4", first Hywood by Niloak..$25.00 – 35.00
2. Bowl, 3¾", *Peacock Blue II*,
   Hywood incised (print) ....$35.00 – 55.00
3. Vase, 4", *Ozark Blue*, second Hywood by Niloak ....$25.00 – 35.00

Third Row:

1. Vase, 4½", *Ozark Blue*, first Hywood by Niloak ....$35.00 – 45.00
2. Ashtray, 3½" x 1½", *Ozark Dawn II*, unmarked ....$15.00 – 25.00
3. Vase, 2¾", *Green and Tan Matt*,
   Hywood incised (print) ....$15.00 – 25.00

Fourth Row:

1. Vase, 4", *Green and Tan Matt*, Hywood
   Art Pottery (small mark)..$15.00 – 25.00
2. Vase, 4¼", *Ozark Blue*, second Hywood by Niloak ....$15.00 – 25.00
3. Vase, 3¾", similar to *Ozark Dawn I*,
   first Hywood by Niloak..$25.00 – 50.00

PLATE 104

Hand-thrown Vases with Lewis Glazes

Plate 105

(Left to right)

First Row:

1. Vase, 5¾", unmarked .... $25.00 – 50.00
2. Vase, with applied handles, 5¾", *Ozark Dawn II*, Second art mark and Niloak 71 .... $50.00 – 75.00
3. Vase, 6", *Ozark Blue*, unmarked .... $45.00 – 55.00

Second Row:

1. Vase, 5¾", *Ozark Blue*, unmarked .... $35.00 – 45.00
2. Vase, 4⅞", *Pearled Green*, Hywood incised and "FZ" in grease pencil .... $50.00 – 75.00
3. Vase, 5¾", *Ozark Dawn II*, first Hywood by Niloak and "FZ" black ink stamp .... $35.00 – 45.00

Third Row:

1. Vase, 4¾", *Ozark Dawn II*, first Hywood by Niloak and "FZ" black ink stamp .... $35.00 – 45.00
2. Vase, 5", *Ozark Blue*, unmarked but with "FZ" black ink stamp .... $35.00 – 45.00
3. Vase, 5¼", *Ozark Dawn II*, "Potteries" sticker .... $35.00 – 45.00

Fourth Row:

1. Vase, 4½", *Peacock Blue II*, first Hywood by Niloak .... $50.00 – 75.00
2. Vase, 2¾", *Green and Tan Matt*, Hywood incised .... $15.00 – 25.00
   Also made as a molded item.
3. Vase, 4", *Ozark Dawn II*, first Hywood by Niloak .... $15.00 – 25.00

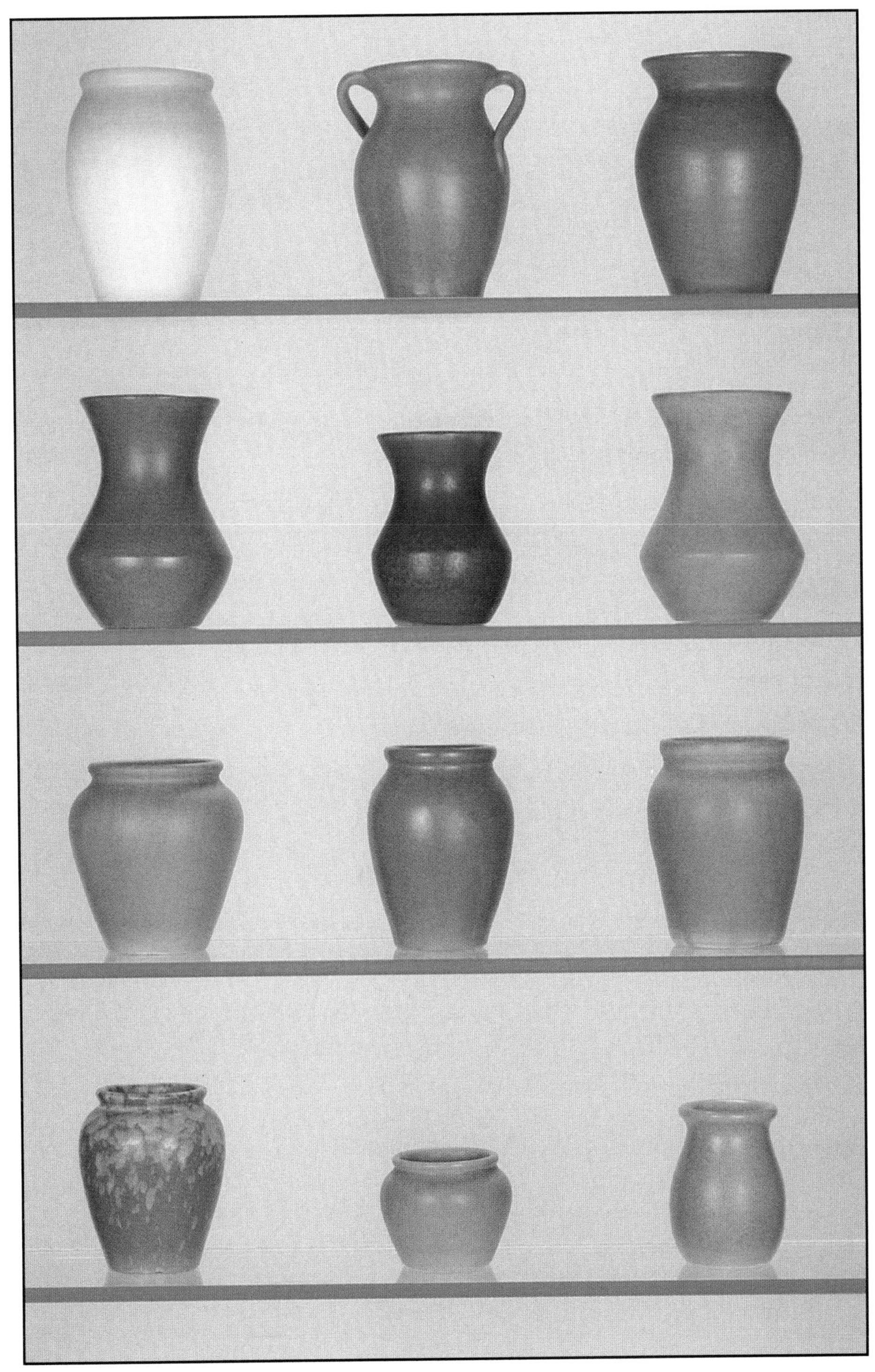

PLATE 105

Hywood Art Pottery/Hywood by Niloak

Hand-thrown and Castware Pieces with Stoin or Lewis Glazes

Plate 106

Pitcher, 6¼", casted, embossed flowers, Lewis glaze, first Hywood by Niloak..$75.00 – 100.00

Plate 107

(Left to right)

Top Row:

1. Vase, 4¾", hand thrown, Lewis glaze, *Delft Blue*, first Hywood by Niloak...$75.00 – 100.00
2. Vase with applied handles, 5", hand thrown, *Green and Tan Bright,* Stoin glaze, Hywood Art Pottery.........$200.00 – 300.00 (+/-)

Bottom Row:

1. Vase with applied handles, 8", *Green and Tan Bright,* Stoin glaze * ....$300.00 – 400.00 (+/-)
2. Cookie jar, 8½", Lewis glaze, *Delft Blue,* first Hywood by Niloak...$150.00 – 250.00 (+/-)

Plate 108

Pitcher with clay stopper, 8¾" x 7", four tumblers, 3½", *Mirror Black,* Lewis glaze, hand thrown, "Potteries" sticker on pitcher, tumblers unmarked...$175.00 – 225.00 Note: All pitchers were sold with clay stoppers and should be valued lower without it.

* Similar to shapes found in Weller's Nile line.

PLATE 106

PLATE 107

PLATE 108

Castware with Lewis and/or Stoin Glazes

Plate 109

(Left to right)

Top Row: Lewis glaze, *Peacock Blue II*

1. Handled vase, 6", first Hywood by Niloak and "EK" in grease pencil .... $50.00 – 75.00
   Note: Camark made similar shape.
2. Cabinet vase, 3¾", Second art mark .... $25.00 – 35.00
3. Handled vase, 5½", first Hywood by Niloak .... $45.00 – 55.00

Middle Row: Lewis glazes

1. Candlestick set, 6¾", *Ivory*, unmarked .... $75.00 – 125.00
2. Cabinet vase, 2¾", *Green and Tan Matt*, Hywood incised .... $15.00 – 25.00
3. Candlestick set, 6¾", *Ivory*, unmarked .... $75.00 – 125.00

Bottom Row:

1. Vase, 7½", *Peacock Blue II*, Lewis glaze, deco design, Hywood incised .... $75.00 – 100.00
2. Handled vase, 6½", *Pearled Green*, Stoin or Lewis glaze, Hywood Art Pottery * .... $75.00 – 125.00
3. Pitcher, 8¾", petal design, *Peacock Blue II*, Lewis glaze, unmarked .... $100.00 – 125.00

* *Pearled Green* was made by both S.M. Stoin and Howard Lewis. Examples with variations of this glaze can be found until the end of the 1930s.

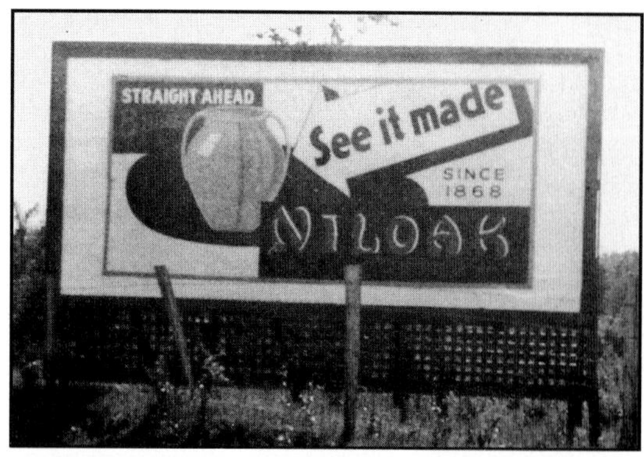

Niloak Pottery billboard, Benton, circa 1938. *Courtesy of Hardy L. Winburn IV.*

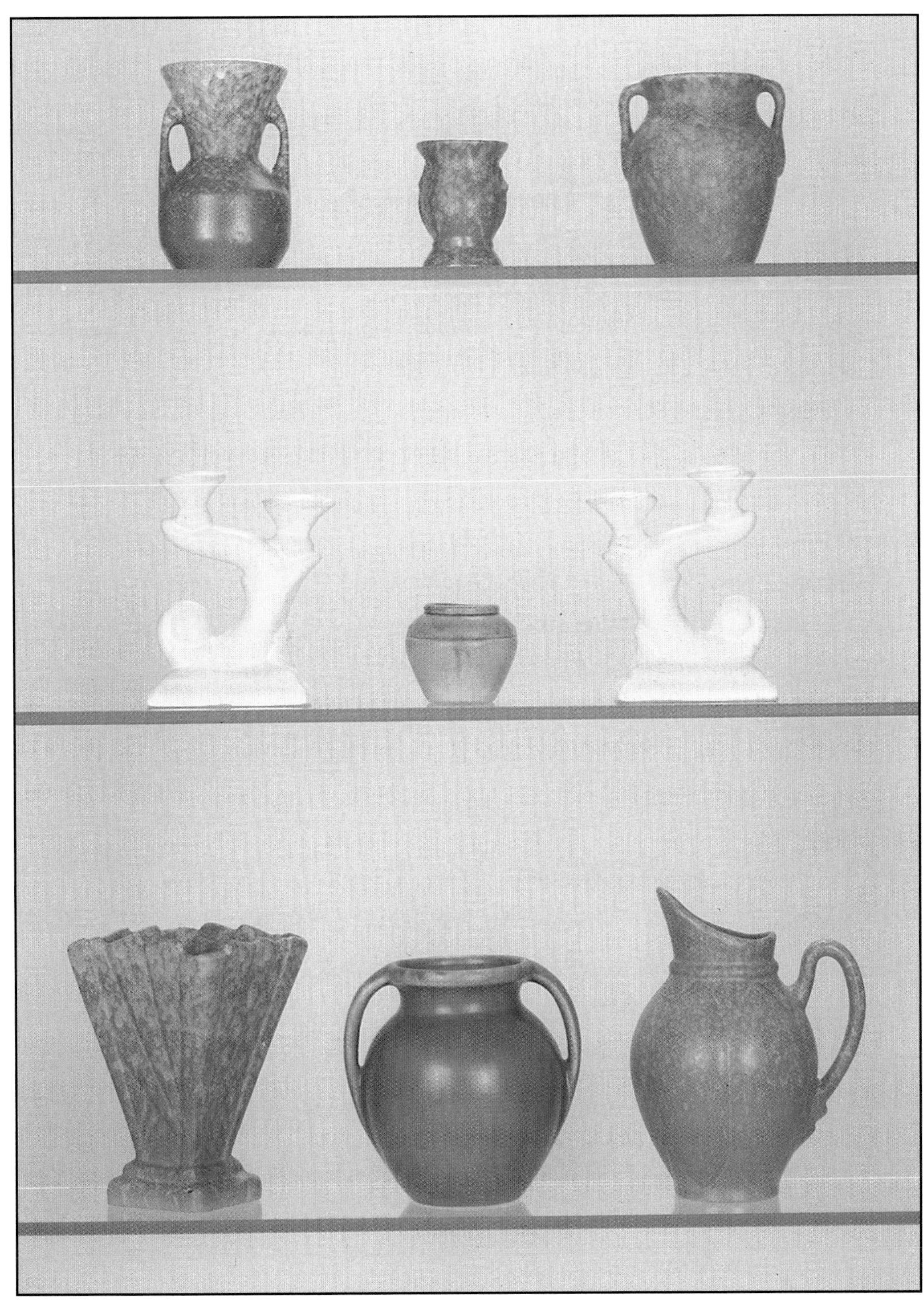

Plate 109

Hywood Art Pottery/Hywood by Niloak

Castware with Lewis and/or Stoin Glazes

Plate 110

(Left to right)

First Row:

1. Vase, 7½", embossed pine cones, *Ozark Dawn II*, Lewis glaze, Hywood mold mark..............$50.00 – 75.00
2. Horn of plenty vase, 7", *Ozark Blue*, Lewis glaze, second Hywood by Niloak..............$50.00 – 75.00
3. Handled Vase, 7¼", *Ozark Blue*, Lewis glaze, Hywood incised..............$75.00 – 100.00
   Two versions of this shape exist — one with base; one without base. See Plate 109.

Second Row:

1. Handled bowl, 4½", *Ozark Blue,* both first and second Hywood by Niloak ink stamps..............$100.00 – 125.00
2. Bud vase, 8", *Ozark Dawn II,* second Hywood by Niloak..............$25.00 – 35.00
3. Strawberry Jar, 7½", *Peacock Blue II,* plain Hywood ink stamp (fake?)..............$75.00 – 100.00

Third Row:

1. Vase with molded handles, 6¼", *Pearled Green,* Stoin or Lewis glaze, Hywood Art Pottery..............$75.00 – 100.00
2. Vase, 6", *Peacock Blue II,* first Hywood by Niloak..............$50.00 – 75.00
3. Handled Vase, 6½", *Maroon,* Lewis glaze, first Hywood by Niloak..............$35.00 – 45.00

Fourth Row:

1. Bowl with molded incisions, 8" x 3½", *Green and Tan Matt,* second Hywood by Niloak..............$50.00 – 75.00
   Also blue/silver metallic sticker "Crescent Jewelry Co., 414 Main, Little Rock, Arkansas."
2. Vase, 7", *Peacock Blue II,* unmarked..............$100.00 – 125.00
3. Planter, 10" x 3¾", *Peacock Blue II,* unmarked..............$100.00 – 125.00
   Hill and trees in relief, "W" incised.

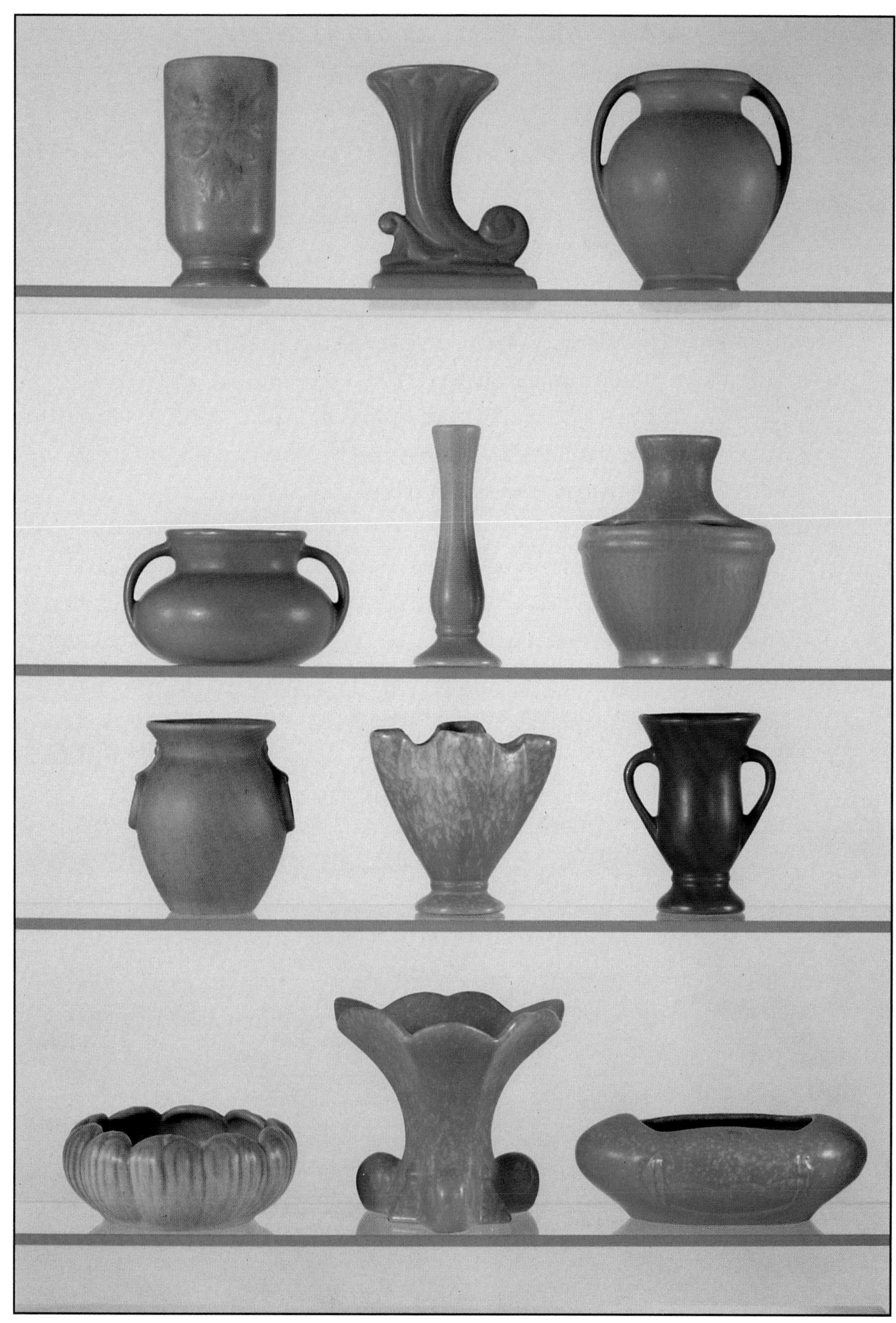

Plate 110

CASTWARE WITH LEWIS GLAZES

PLATE 111

(Left to right)

First Row:

1. Handled vase, $5\frac{1}{2}$", *Green and Tan Matt,* first Hywood by Niloak..........$35.00 – 45.00
   Note: Dickota made a similar shape.
2. Vase, $3\frac{1}{2}$", *Ozark Blue,* second Hywood by Niloak..........$25.00 – 35.00
3. Basket, $6\frac{1}{2}$", *Blue and Tan Matt,* first Hywood by Niloak..........$75.00 – 100.00
   Note: Camark Pottery made a similar piece.

Second Row:

1. Vase, $2\frac{1}{2}$", *Ozark Blue,* Hywood incised..........$15.00 – 25.00
2. Bowl, $2\frac{3}{4}$", unmarked..........$15.00 – 25.00
3. Vase, 3", *Ozark Blue,* unmarked..........$15.00 – 25.00

Third Row:

1. Vase, 3", *Green and Tan Matt,* second Hywood by Niloak..........$15.00 – 25.00
2. Scalloped bowl, $5\frac{1}{2}$" x $2\frac{3}{4}$", *Peacock Blue II,* second Hywood by Niloak..........$35.00 – 45.00
3. Vase, $4\frac{1}{2}$", *Blue and Tan Matt,* unmarked..........$25.00 – 35.00

Fourth Row:

1. Vase, $4\frac{1}{2}$", *Ozark Dawn II,* first Hywood by Niloak..........$25.00 – 35.00
2. Bud Vase, $4\frac{1}{4}$", *Peacock Blue II,* unmarked..........$15.00 – 25.00
3. Vase, $4\frac{1}{2}$", *Ozark Dawn II,* first Hywood by Niloak..........$25.00 – 35.00

Niloak Pottery billboard, Benton, circa 1938. ***Courtesy of the late Hardy L. Winburn IV.***

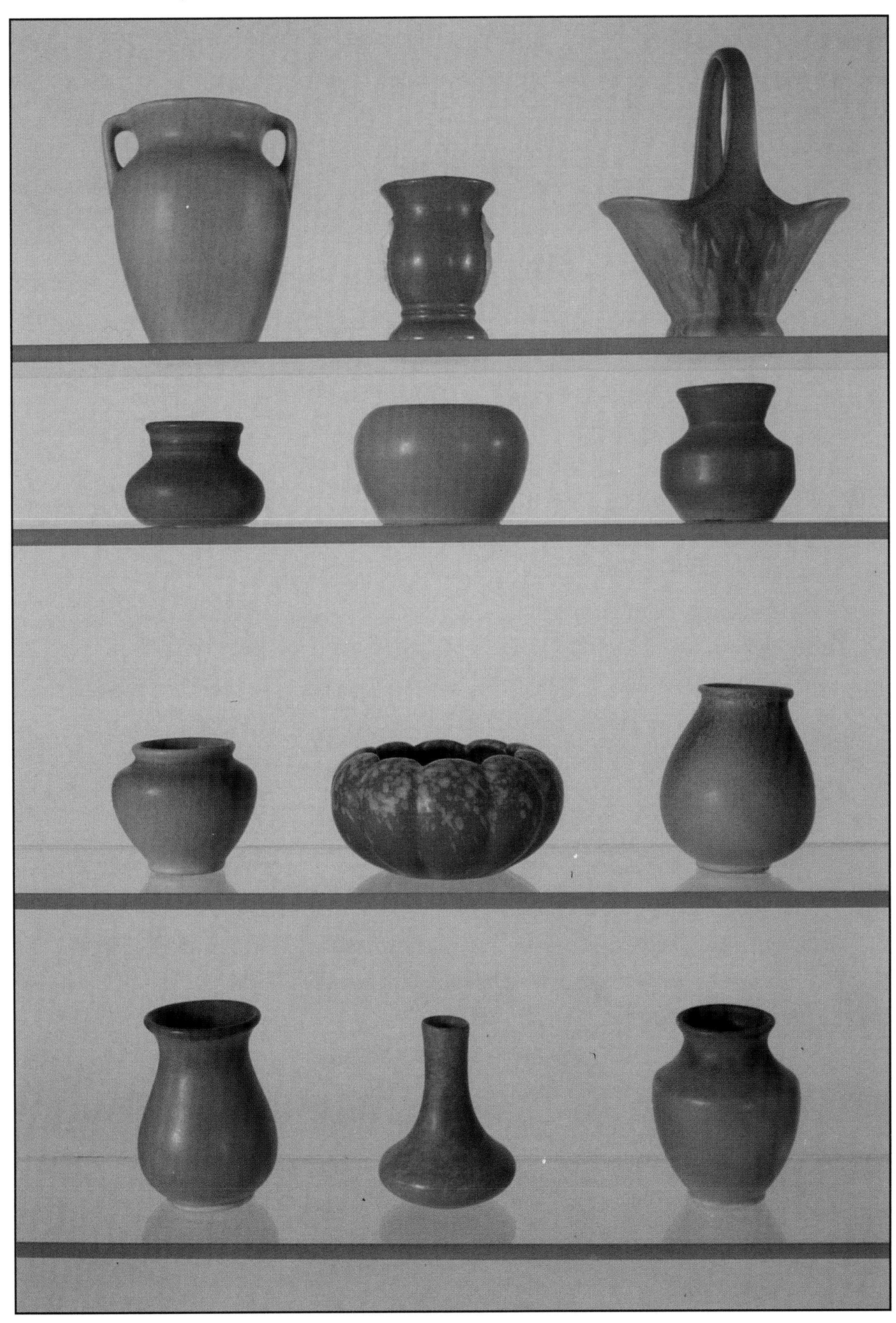

PLATE 111

NILOAK

CASTWARE, UNLESS NOTED, WITH OZARK BLUE GLAZE BY LEWIS

PLATE 112

(Left to right)

First Row:

1. Southern Belle, 7", Peterson design, unmarked .... $100.00 – 150.00 (+/-)
   Note: Other companies made similar pieces.
2. Ashtray, 4¼" x 3½", "Arkansas" with Pegasus, diamond (recessed) is a symbol of Arkansas, Niloak low relief .... $75.00 – 100.00 (+/-)
3. Vase, 7¼", freestanding, Peterson design, unmarked .... $75.00 – 125.00 (+/-)

Second Row:

1. Vase, 6", unmarked, hand thrown .... $45.00 – 65.00
2. Fan vase, 7", Niloak block letters .... $75.00 – 100.00 (+/-)
3. Pitcher with lid, 6¼", "DB" in grease pencil, unmarked, hand thrown .... $100.00 – 150.00 (+/-)

Third Row:

1. Vase with handles, 7", Niloak block letters .... $75.00 – 100.00
2. Bowl, 6¼" x 11", unmarked, hand thrown .... $100.00 – 150.00 (+/-)
3. Vase, 6¼", unmarked .... $100.00 – 150.00 (+/-)

Fourth Row:

1. Water bottle with clay stopper, 7¾", "Potteries" sticker .... $100.00 – 125.00 (+/-)
2. Ewer, 10¾", Peterson design, Niloak low relief .... $75.00 – 100.00
3. Bull's-eye pitcher, 9¼", unmarked .... $75.00 – 100.00

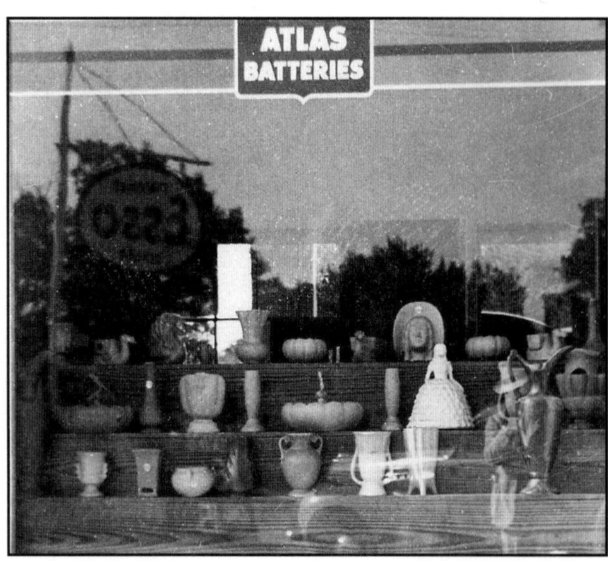

Niloak Pottery display, Esso Station, location unknown, circa late 1930s. ***Courtesy of the late Hardy L. Winburn IV.***

Plate 112

Vases with Lewis Glazes

Plate 113

(Left to right)

Top Row: Niloak Block Letters

1. Handled vase, 7½", *Ozark Blue*......$75.00 – 100.00
2. Vase, 7", *Ozark Dawn II*......$50.00 – 75.00
3. Bud Vase, 7¼", *Ozark Blue,* deco design......$50.00 – 75.00

Middle Row:

1. Fan vase, 7¼", *Ozark Dawn II,* Niloak block letters......$75.00 – 100.00
2. Vase with handles, 7¾", Niloak block letters......$75.00 – 100.00
3. Fan vase, 7", *Ozark Dawn II,* unmarked......$50.00 – 75.00

Bottom Row:

1. Handled vase, *Ozark Blue,* 6½",
   Niloak block letters......$75.00 – 100.00
2. Vase, 6¼", deco design, *Ozark Dawn II,*
   Second art mark......$50.00 – 75.00
   (Larger version in Plate 109.)
3. Vase, 6¼", *Ozark Blue,* Niloak block letters......$15.00 – 25.00

For collectors and researchers today, Alley not only identified his work, but also some of Peterson's designs as well. Throughout the following photograph plates, Peterson's and Alley's designs have been noted. Many of George Peterson's known designs coincide with the use of the Niloak block letters mark. It is also true to a lesser extent with Second art mark (found on the glazed castware pieces). It is probable then that some shapes (castware) with these marks that are not shown in the Hywood Art Pottery catalog (Ganz's designs, see pages 334 – 335) can be attributed to Peterson.

Plate 113

Ozark Blue and Maroon Glazes by Lewis

Plate 114

(Left to right)

Top Row: *Ozark Blue*

1. Vase, 6½", Niloak block letters ....$50.00 – 75.00
2. Vase, 4¼", hand thrown, unmarked ....$25.00 – 35.00
3. Vase, 6½", Niloak low relief ....$50.00 – 75.00

Middle Row: *Maroon*

1. Vase, 6½", Niloak low relief ....$50.00 – 75.00
2. Vase with handles, 6", Art Deco, Second art mark, with uncommon overspray * ....$50.00 – 75.00
3. Vase with handles, unmarked....................$75.00 – 100.00

Bottom Row: *Ozark Blue*

1. Vase, 9½", Art Deco, Niloak block letters....................$100.00 – 150.00 (+/-)
2. Vase with handles, 7", unmarked ....$75.00 – 100.00
3. Vase, 9½", Art Deco, Niloak block letters....................100.00 – 150.00 (+/-)

* Camark Pottery made a similar, if not identical vase.

PLATE 114

Hywood by Niloak/Niloak with Lewis Glazes

Hand-thrown and Hand-carved by One "Rice"

Plate 115

(Left to right)

1. Bowl, 4½", *Maroon*, incised Rice .... N/A
2. Vase, 3½", *Ozark Blue*, incised Rice .... N/A

PLATE 116

1. Vase, 6½", incised Rice .... N/A

Hywood by Niloak/Niloak

Hand-thrown and Castware with Lewis Glazes

Plate 117

(Left to right)

Top Row:

1. Pitcher, 6", *Ozark Dawn II*, first Hywood by Niloak .... $25.00 – 50.00
2. Sugar bowl w/lid, 4¼", *Green and Tan Matt*, first Hywood by Niloak, hand thrown .... $50.00 – 75.00
3. Pitcher, 5¼", *Green and Tan Matt*, hand thrown, first Hywood by Niloak .... $50.00 – 75.00

Middle Row:

1. Vase, 7", *Ozark Dawn II*, Niloak block letters .... $75.00 – 100.00
2. Vase with handles, 6¼", *Ozark Blue*, first Hywood by Niloak.... $75.00 – 100.00
3. Vase with handles, 7", *Ozark Dawn II*, unmarked .... $75.00 – 100.00

Bottom Row:

1. Vase, 8¼", *Ozark Dawn II*, Niloak block letters .... $75.00 – 100.00
2. Vase, 9½", *Ivory*, first Hywood by Niloak, hand thrown .... $75.00 – 125.00
3. Vase, 8¾", *Ozark Dawn II*, Niloak low relief .... $75.00 – 100.00

Plate 115

Plate 116

Plate 117

WATER VESSELS WITH LEWIS GLAZES

PLATE 118

(Left to right)

Top Row: Niloak Block Letters

1. Ice guard pitcher, 7¾", *Ozark Dawn II* ....$75.00 – 100.00
2. Teapot, 6½", *Ozark Dawn II,* "Potteries" sticker.....................$75.00 – 100.00
3. Ball pitcher with cork stopper, 7", *Ozark Dawn II* ....$50.00 – 75.00

Middle Row: Petal design by George Peterson in *Ozark Dawn II*

1. Open sugar bowl, 4", larger Second art mark............................$25.00 – 35.00
2. French teapot, 9", larger Second art mark ....$75.00 – 100.00 (+/-)
3. Creamer, 5", unmarked...$35.00 – 45.00

Bottom Row: George Peterson designs in *Ozark Blue*

1. Pitcher, 6", Art Deco/streamline design, Niloak block letters ....$150.00 – 200.00 (+/-)
2. Pitcher with hinged lid, 7", Art Deco design, Niloak incised and "Potteries" sticker ....$75.00 – 125.00 (+/-)

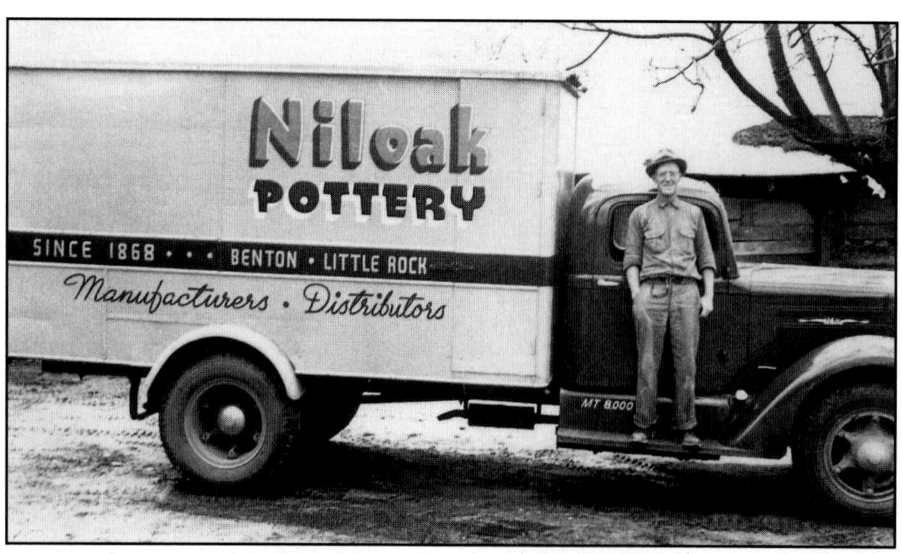

Niloak Pottery delivery truck, Jules Palmer, circa late 1930s.
Courtesy of the University of Central Arkansas Archives and Special Collections. Charles Dove Photograph Collection.

PLATE 118

CASTWARE KITCHEN/DINNERWARE ACCESSORIES WITH LEWIS GLAZES

PLATE 119

(Left to right)

Top Row: Petal design by George Peterson

1. Salad plate, 8", *Ozark Dawn II*, unmarked .... $50.00 – 75.00
2. Dinner plate, 10", *Ozark Blue*, Niloak block letters .... $75.00 – 100.00

Middle Row:

1. Bull's-eye pitcher, 10", *Blue and Tan Matt*, first Hywood by Niloak .... $50.00 – 75.00
2. Squared pitcher, 5½", Peterson design, *Green and Tan Matt*, Potteries sticker * .... $25.00 – 35.00

Bottom Row: George Peterson designs in *Ozark Blue*

1. Covered sugar bowl, 4", unmarked ** .... $50.00 – 75.00
   Very rare to locate with lid.
2. Creamer, 4", first Hywood by Niloak .... $15.00 – 25.00
3. Cup, 3", and saucer, 6", Petal design, larger Second art mark .... $50.00 – 75.00

* This squared pitcher (as well as other non-Niloak shapes) can be found on the secondary markets with a brown and white swirl pattern (similar to Weller's Marbleized line). To date, it is not known who manufactured this pitcher, but some collectors and dealers have identified this pottery as "Alaskan" made. The pitcher has also been seen with the "Hand Made Original Kentucky Pottery" ink stamp. This pitcher has been incorrectly sold as either a product of Niloak, Camark, or Weller.

** In its promotional literature, Niloak mainly sold open sugar bowls. While it is rare to find a lidded sugar bowl, bowls without a lid cannot to be considered incomplete.

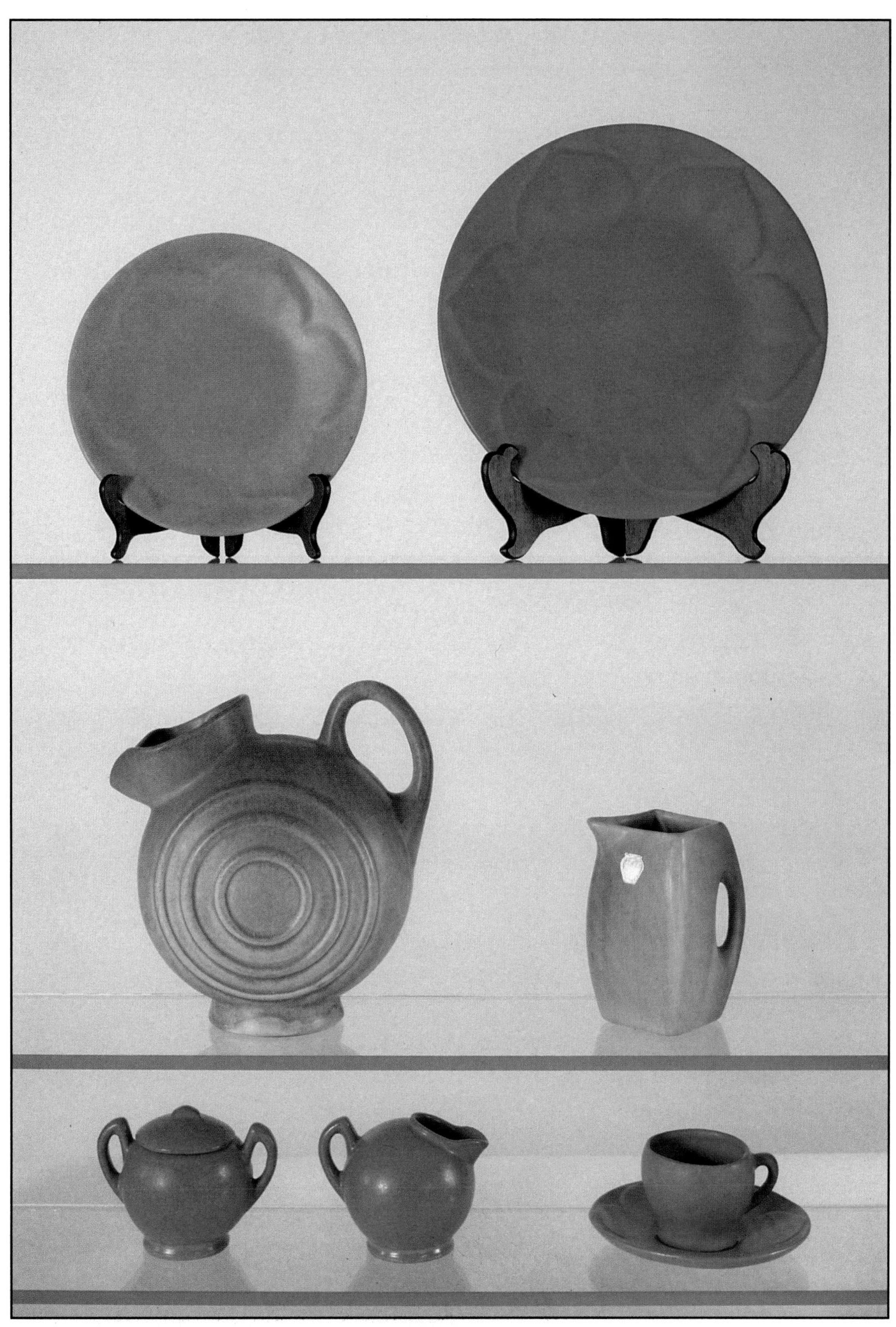

Plate 119

CASTWARE WITH LEWIS GLAZES

PLATE 120

(Left to right)

First Row:

1. Tri-fluted vase, 7¾", *Maroon*, Niloak incised............................$50.00 – 75.00
2. Scallop bowl, 4", *Ozark Blue*, Niloak block letters....................$50.00 – 75.00

Second Row:

1. Shield vase, 6", *Ozark Dawn II*, fake Hywood ink stamp and "Potteries" sticker * ....$45.00 – 55.00
2. Oblong bowl, 3" x 14", *Ozark Dawn II,* Crown design by Peterson, Niloak incised...$75.00 – 125.00 (+/-)

Third Row: Leaf Design by Joe Alley **

1. Planter, 3" x 8½", *Ozark Blue*, Niloak incised............................$50.00 – 75.00
2. Planter, 3½" x 8", half circle, *Ozark Dawn II*, Niloak incised ....$50.00 – 75.00

Fourth Row:

1. Dish, 2" x 4½" x 6¼", *Ozark Dawn II,* Niloak incised ....$45.00 – 55.00
2. Planter, 3½" x 3" x 5½", *Maroon*, Niloak incised.......................$45.00 – 55.00

* This has a fake mark. Using a modern ink stamp of simple block letters, this mimics the second Hywood by Niloak ink stamp.

** These Alley Leaf design planters were also sold in pairs, a set of four, to create an oblong table planter set or flower arranger.

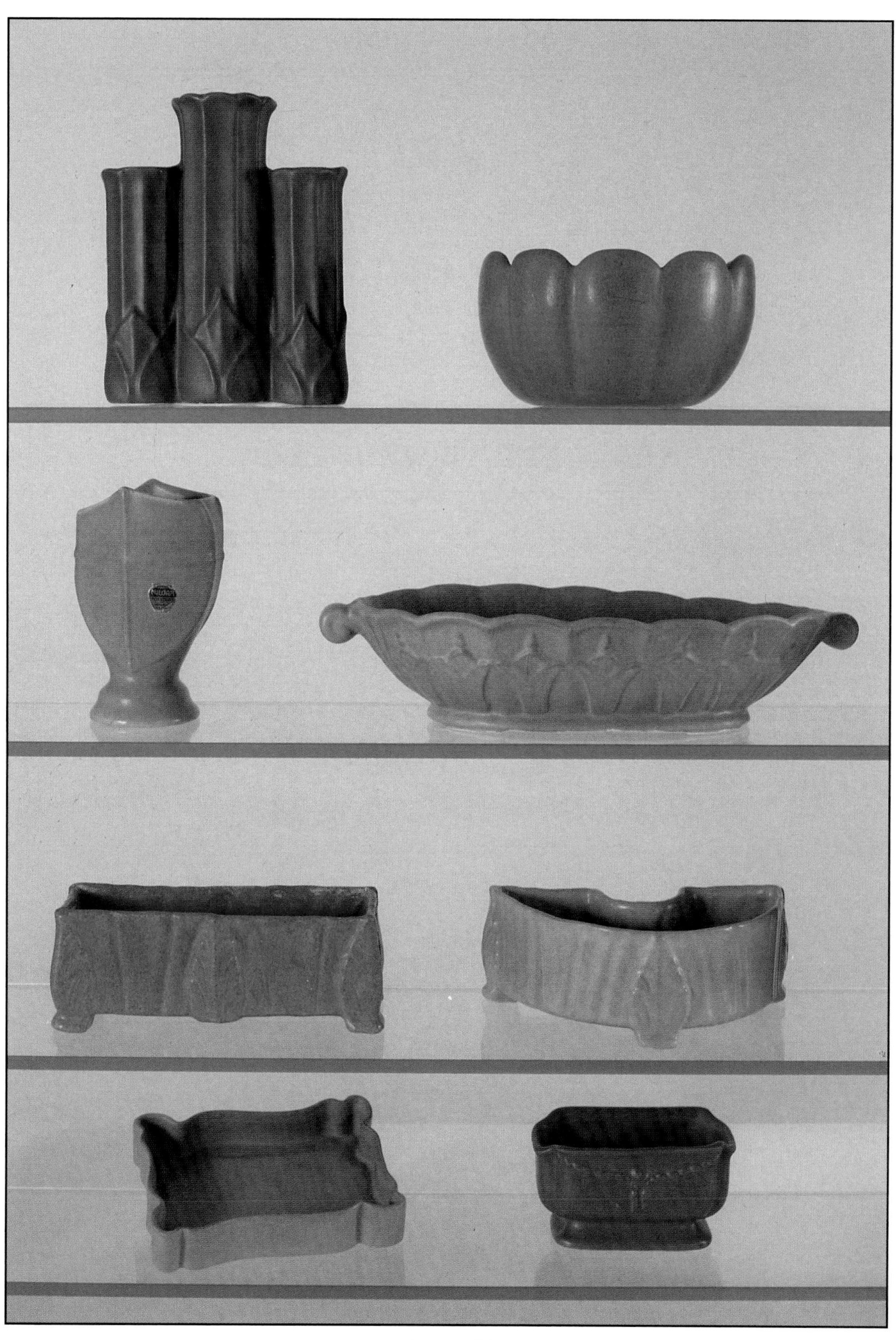

PLATE 120

Hywood by Niloak/Niloak
Castware Vases

Plate 121

(Left to right)

1. Vase, 9¾", Niloak low relief .... N/A
2. Vase, 11", *Ivory*, Lewis glaze, Hywood incised .... N/A

Hywood by Niloak
Ozark Blue Glaze by Lewis

Plate 122

Vase, 16", hand thrown, first Hywood by Niloak .... N/A

Niloak Castware
Ozark Dawn II Glaze by Lewis

Plate 123

(Left to right)

Top Row:

1. Compote, 11¼" x 7¼", Niloak low relief .... N/A

Bottom Row:

2. Goblet vase, 12", Niloak low relief .... N/A
3. Goblet vase, 12", Niloak low relief .... N/A

Plate 124

Compote's interior

PLATE 121

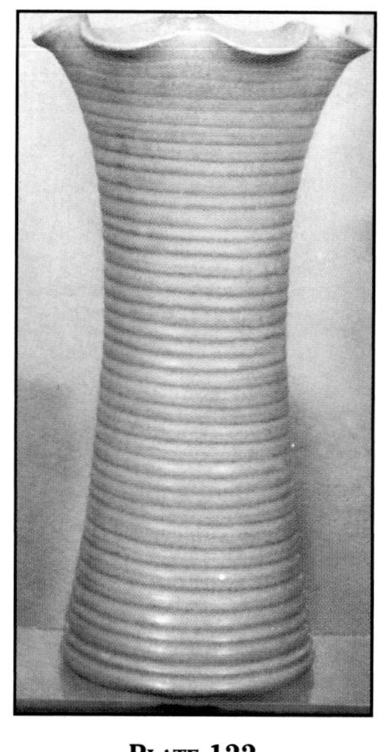

PLATE 122

PLATE 123

PLATE 124

EWERS AND VASES WITH LEWIS GLAZES

PLATE 125

(Left to right)

Top Row: *Ozark Blue*

1. Ewer, 10¾", Peterson design, Niloak incised ....$75.00 – 100.00
2. Fan vase, 14", Art Deco, Peterson design, Niloak incised ....$100.00 – 150.00
3. Ewer, 9½", Alley's Winged Victory design, Niloak ....$25.00 – 35.00

Bottom Row:

1. Vase, 11½", *Ozark Dawn II*, Niloak incised ....$75.00 – 100.00
2. Ewer, 16½", Crown design by Peterson, *Ozark Blue*, Niloak incised ....$100.00 – 125.00
3. Vase, 12", Peterson design, *Ozark Blue*, Niloak low relief ....$75.00 – 100.00

Niloak Pottery showroom, 4115 Asher Avenue, Little Rock, circa 1940. ***Courtesy of the University of Central Arkansas Archives and Special Collections. Charles Dove Photograph Collection.***

PLATE 125

Hand-thrown and Castware Pieces with Lewis Glazes

Plate 126

(Left to right)

Top Row: Hand Thrown

1. Creamer, 3½", *Ozark Dawn II*, 1868 sticker ....$35.00 – 45.00
2. Vase, 6", with applied handles, unmarked ....$50.00 – 75.00
3. Candlestick, 7⅛", *Ozark Dawn II*, unmarked, with "BX" in grease pencil ....$50.00 – 75.00

Middle Row:

1. Console set, Crown design by Peterson, *Ozark Dawn II*
2. Bud vases, pair, 8⅜", "Potteries" stickers, each ....$35.00 – 45.00
3. Bowl, 3" x 14", Niloak incised ....$75.00 – 125.00 (+/-)

Bottom Row: *Ozark Blue*

1. Bull's-eye pitcher, 9¼", unmarked ....$50.00 – 75.00
2. Bowl/flower frog set ....$75.00 – 100.00
   Bowl, 3½" x 10", Niloak incised, Duck flower frog, Alley design, 5½", unmarked.

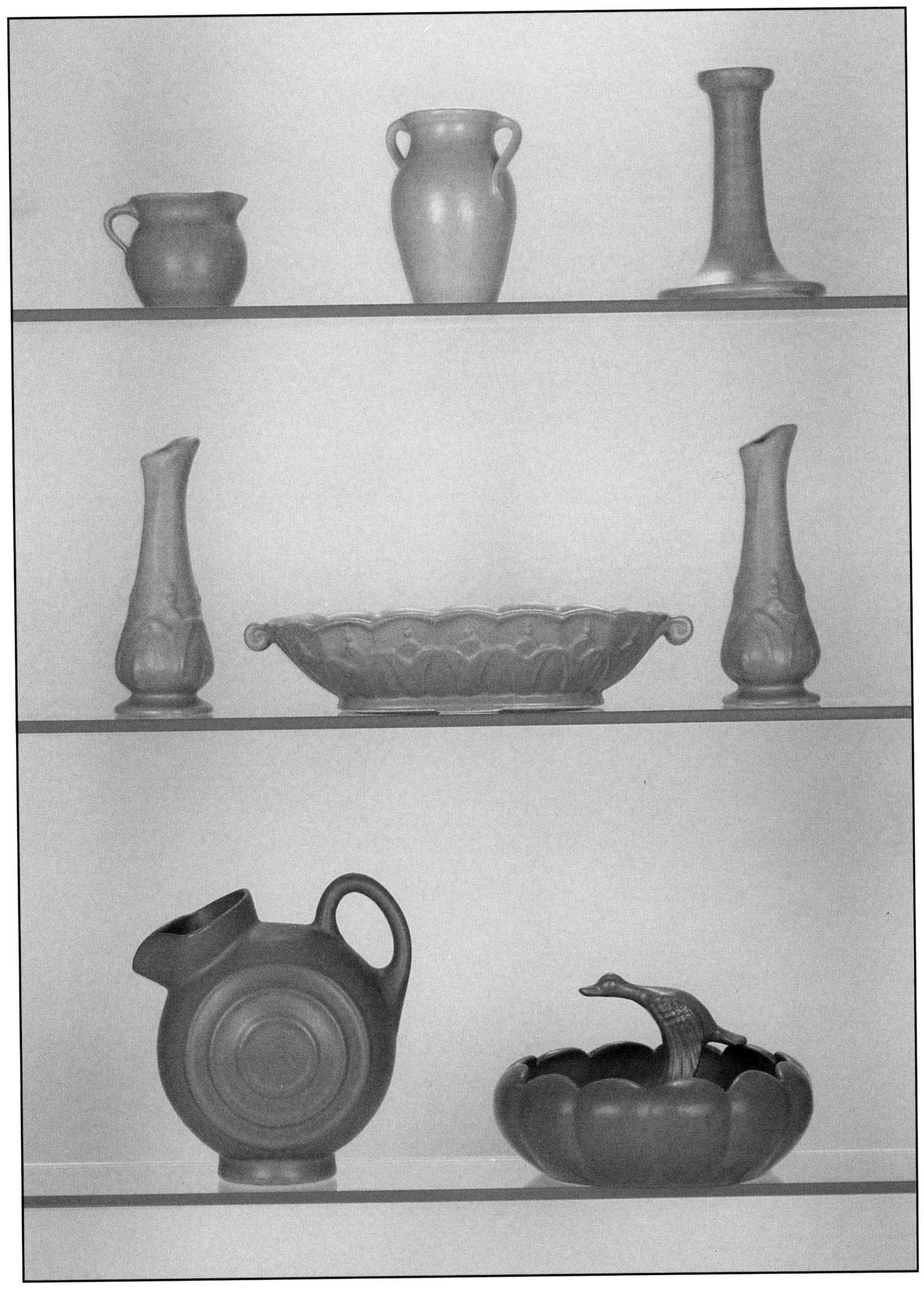

PLATE 126

Hand-thrown and Castware Pieces with Lewis Glazes

Plate 127

(Left to right)

Top Row:

1. Vase with applied handles, 5¾", Hywood incised....................$50.00 – 75.00
2. Vase, 6¾", first Hywood by Niloak ....$50.00 – 75.00
3. Vase with handles, 6", Second art mark....................................$50.00 – 75.00

Middle Row: *Ivory*

1. Compote, 6", Second Hywood by Niloak...N/A
2. Bowl, 10½" x 3¼", Imperial Niloak low relief ....N/A

Bottom Row:

1. Tray, 12¼" x 1¼", *Ozark Dawn II*, unmarked ....$25.00 – 50.00
2. Tray, 12½", *Ivory*, unmarked ....$25.00 – 50.00

PLATE 127

HAND-THROWN AND CASTWARE PIECES WITH LEWIS GLAZES

PLATE 128

(Left to right)

Top Row:

1. & 3. Candlestick set, 1¼" x 5", *Ozark Blue*, hand thrown, unmarked.......$50.00 – 75.00
2. Vase, 7".......N/A
   Carillon ware, **not** Niloak, with mutilated "Potteries" sticker. *

Middle Row:

1. Vase, 5", *Ozark Blue*, Niloak block letters and "F2" in grease pencil.......$25.00 – 35.00
2. Handled vase, 9", Alley design, *Ozark Dawn II*, unmarked.......$75.00 – 100.00
3. Vase, 5", Alley design, *Ozark Dawn II*, unmarked.......$45.00 – 55.00

Bottom Row:

1. Vase, 6½", *Pearled Green,* Niloak block letters.......$45.00 – 55.00
2. Handled vase, 11¼", Alley design, *Ozark Dawn II*, "Potteries" sticker.......$100.00 – 125.00
3. Swan, 6½", Alley design, *Ozark Blue*, "Potteries" sticker.......$15.00 – 25.00

* Identical glaze of Carillon ware to Niloak's *Ozark Dawn II.* See Notes to Collectors/Dealers.

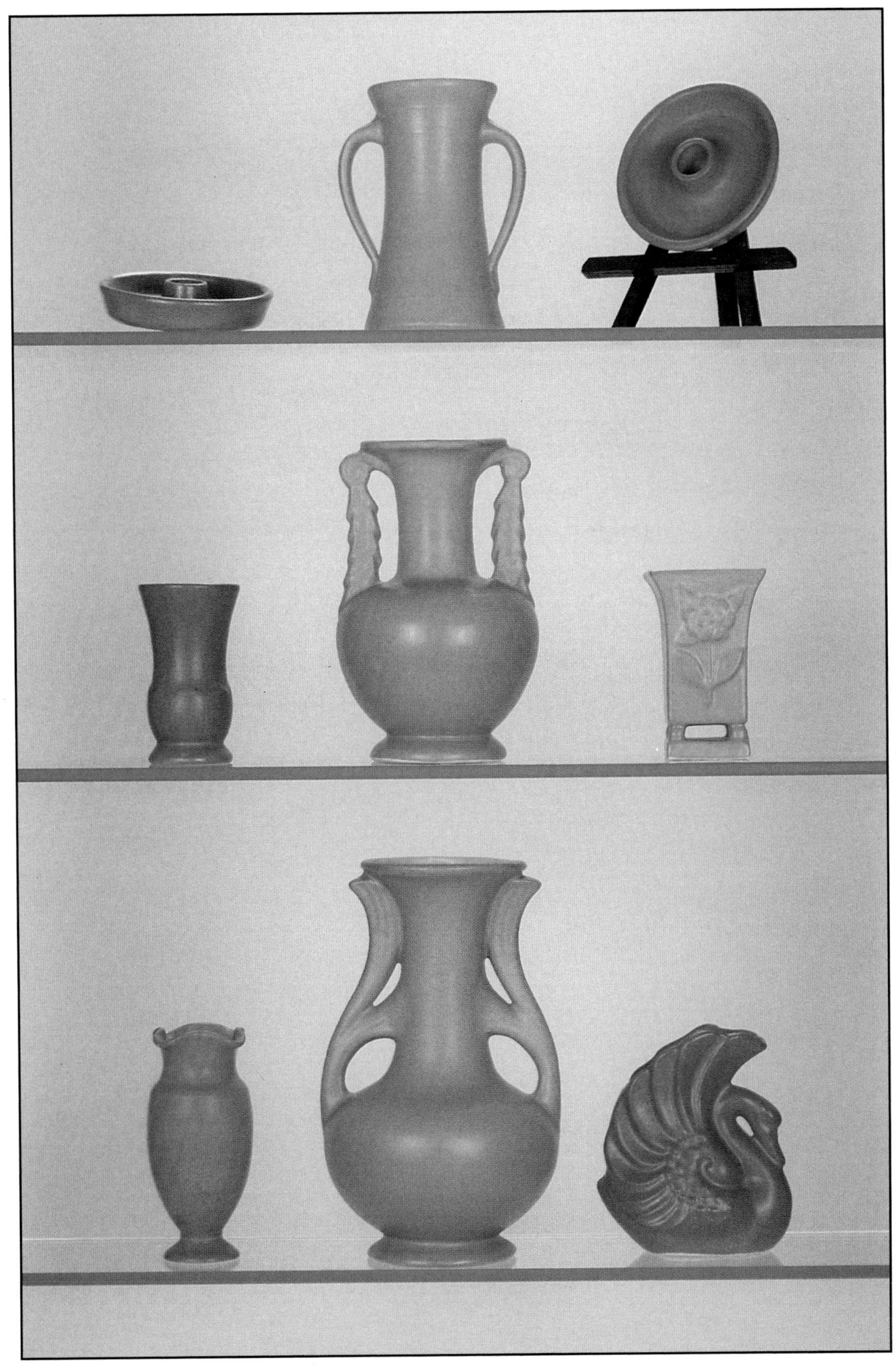

Plate 128

Hand-thrown and Castware Pieces with Lewis Glazes

Plate 129

(Left to right)

Top Row:

1. Hanging basket, $3\frac{1}{4}$", Alley design, *Maroon*, Niloak incised .... $45.00 – 55.00
2. Graceful urn, $6\frac{3}{4}$", Niloak block letters .... $35.00 – 45.00
3. Pitcher, $6\frac{1}{4}$", second Hywood by Niloak .... $25.00 – 50.00

Middle Row:

1. Vase, 8", hand thrown, *Ozark Dawn II*, unmarked .... $25.00 – 50.00
2. Vase, 5", *Maroon*, Niloak block letters .... $45.00 – 55.00
3. Vase with applied handles, $7\frac{1}{2}$", hand thrown, *Ozark Dawn II*, Second art mark .... $50.00 – 75.00

Bottom Row:

1. Speas Vinegar jar, 8", Deco design, *Ozark Dawn II*, unmarked .... $150.00 – 200.00 (+/-)
2. Cookie jar, $9\frac{1}{2}$", *Ozark Blue*, hand thrown, unmarked .... $100.00 – 150.00

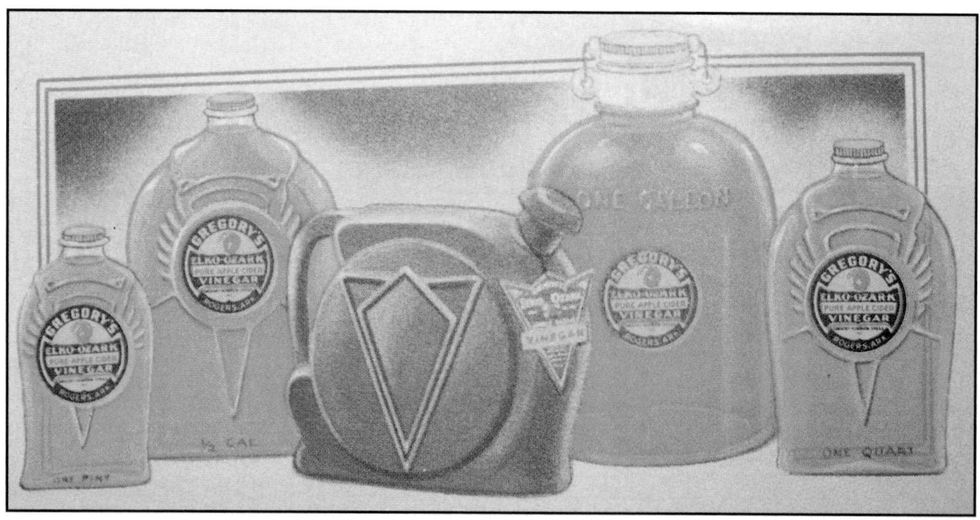

Photograph of advertisement showing Niloak's Speas Vinegar jar. This item was made by Niloak Pottery for the Gregory-Robinson Speas Company in the mid 1930s (see Niloak Production chapter). ***Courtesy of Douglas G. Hollandsworth (Speas Vinegar II).***

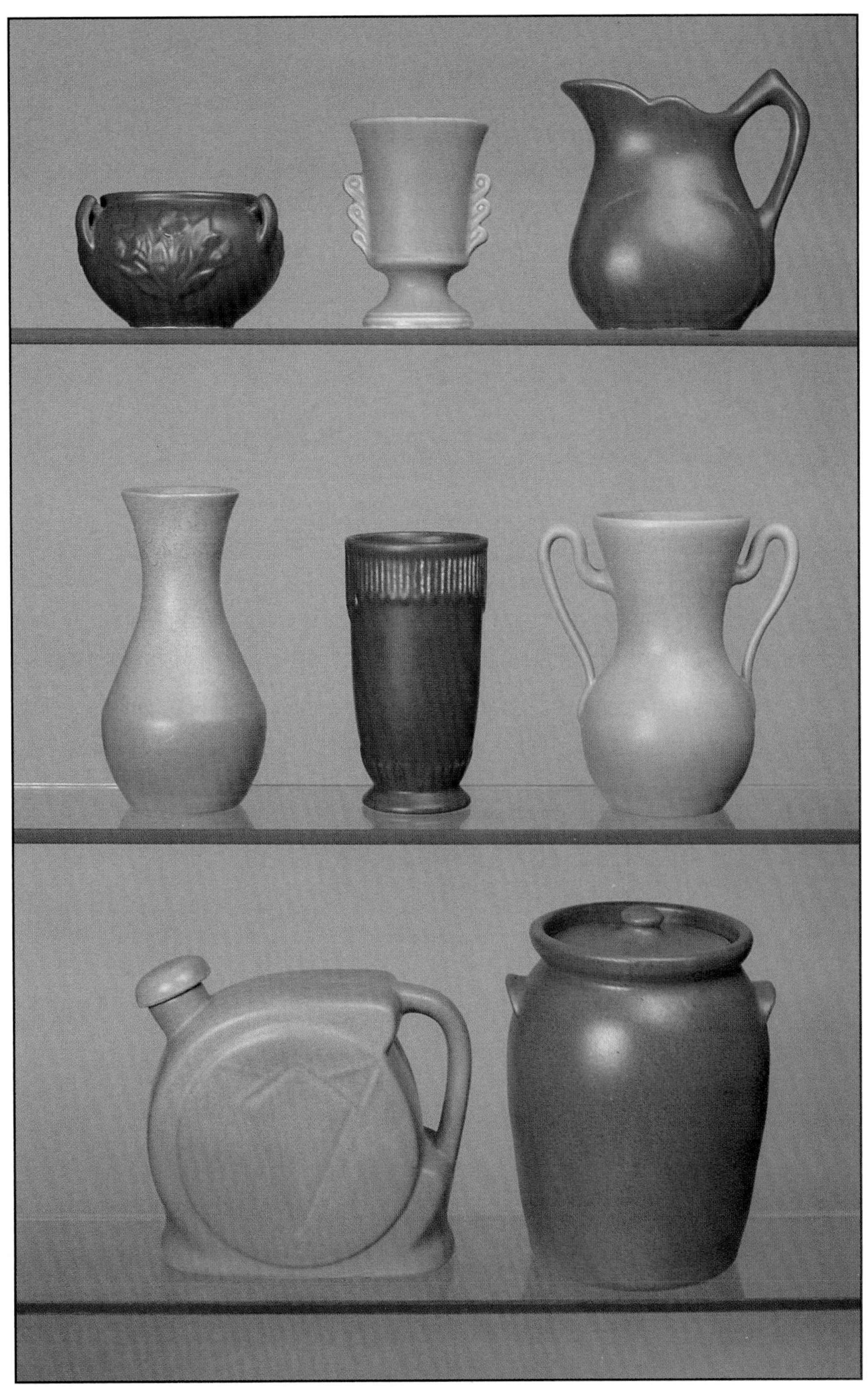

PLATE 129

Lewis's Ozark Dawn II Vases

Plate 130

(Left to right)

Top Row:

1. Handled vase, 5¾", Alley's Winged Victory design, Niloak low relief....$15.00 – 25.00
2. Handled vase, 6¼", Niloak low relief....$50.00 – 75.00
3. Handled vase, 5¼", Niloak low relief....$35.00 – 45.00

Middle Row:

1. Bud vase, 8¾", Crown design by Peterson, unmarked....$35.00 – 45.00
2. Handled vase, 7½", Alley design, Niloak incised....$50.00 – 75.00
3. Vase, 8½", Peterson design, Niloak block letters....$35.00 – 45.00

Bottom Row:

1. Handled vase, 8", Alley design, Niloak low relief....$35.00 – 45.00
2. Ewer, 8", Alley design, Niloak low relief....$35.00 – 45.00
3. Tulip vase, 7", Alley design, Niloak low relief....$25.00 – 35.00

PLATE 130

Miscellaneous Pieces with Lewis Glazes, unless noted

Plate 131

(Left to right)

Top Row:

1. Vase, 6½", *Green and Tan Matt*, Niloak for Victory ....$15.00 – 25.00
2. Scalloped bowl, 3½" x 5½", Alley design,
   Ozark Dawn II, Niloak block letters..$15.00 – 25.00
3. Vase, 6", Alley's Winged Victory design, non-Lewis glaze,
   Niloak low relief ....$15.00 – 25.00

Middle Row:

1. Strawberry jar, 5", Alley design, *Ozark Blue*,
   Niloak low relief ....$15.00 – 25.00
2. Vase, 3½", "N" low relief ....$10.00 – 15.00
3. Bull's-eye creamer, 5½", *Ozark Blue*,
   Niloak low relief ....$15.00 – 25.00

Bottom Row:

1. Vase with handles, 7", *Ozark Blue*,
   Second art mark..$35.00 – 45.00
2. Vase, 7", Peterson design, Niloak incised ....$50.00 – 75.00

PLATE 131

CABINET PIECES WITH LEWIS AND/OR STOIN GLAZES

PLATE 132

(Left to right)

First Row:

1. Cabinet vase, 3½", *Ozark Blue*, deco design, Niloak block letters .... $25.00 – 35.00
2. Cabinet vase, 4½", *Pearled Green,* Lewis or Stoin glaze, larger Second art mark .... $25.00 – 35.00
   Note: Camark made a similar shape.
3. Cabinet vase, 3½", *Ozark Blue*, Niloak block letters .... $25.00 – 35.00
4. Cabinet vase, 3¼", *Maroon*, Niloak block letters .... $25.00 – 35.00

Second Row:

1. Cabinet vase, 3¼", hand thrown, *Ozark Dawn II*, Niloak 71 .... $15.00 – 25.00
2. Basket, 3½", *Ozark Blue*, Niloak low relief .... $25.00 – 35.00
3. Cabinet vase, 3", Alley design, *Ozark Blue*, Niloak incised .... $25.00 – 35.00
4. Cabinet vase, 3½", solid pink, Niloak block letters .... $15.00 – 25.00

Third Row:

1. Cabinet vase, 3½", Niloak block letters .... $15.00 – 25.00
2. Cabinet vase, 5", *Ozark Blue*, Niloak block letters .... $25.00 – 35.00
3. Cabinet vase, 4", *Ozark Blue*, Niloak low relief .... $25.00 – 35.00
4. Cabinet vase, 4", Alley design, Niloak block letters .... $15.00 – 25.00

Fourth Row:

1. Cabinet vase, 4", *Ozark Blue*, Niloak block letters and "Potteries" sticker .... $10.00 – 15.00
2. Basket, 4", Alley design, *Ozark Blue*, "N" low relief .... $25.00 – 35.00
3. Cabinet vase, 3½", Niloak block letters .... $15.00 – 25.00
4. Cabinet vase, *Ozark Blue*, 4¾", "N" low relief .... $25.00 – 35.00

PLATE 132

Hand-thrown and Cast Pieces with Lewis Glazes

Plate 133

(Left to right)

First Row:

1. Vase, 4¼", *Ozark Dawn II*, second Hywood by Niloak ....$15.00 – 25.00
2. Candlestick, 2½", *Ozark Blue*, "Potteries" sticker ....$25.00 – 35.00
3. Cannon, *Ozark Dawn II*, 2¾", Niloak low relief ....$50.00 – 75.00
4. Cannon, large unusual size, *Ozark Dawn II*, 3½", Niloak low relief ....$75.00 – 100.00

Second Row: *Ozark Blue*

1. Vase, 4¼", Hywood Art Pottery (smallest)...............................$25.00 – 35.00
2. Vase, 3½", first Hywood by Niloak, *Peacock Blue II* ....$25.00 – 35.00
3. Cone vase, 3½", second Hywood by Niloak.............................$25.00 – 35.00
4. Fan vase, 4¾", first Hywood by Niloak ....$25.00 – 35.00

Third Row:

1. Bowl, 1¾", *Ozark Blue*, Niloak block letters, Blue....................$15.00 – 25.00
2. Candlestick, 3½" x 6" dia., *Ozark Dawn II*, second Hywood by Niloak..$25.00 – 50.00
3. Jug, 3½", *Ozark Blue*, Second art mark.....................................$35.00 – 45.00

Fourth Row: *Ozark Dawn II*

1. Pin tray, 1" x 4" dia., unmarked ....$15.00 – 25.00
2. Bowl/flower frog (bowl) 8¾" x 2½", Niloak low relief (frog) 5" x 1¼", Niloak low relief ....$50.00 – 75.00
3. Vase, 4", "Potteries" sticker ....$15.00 – 25.00

Plate 133

VARIOUS CASTWARE PIECES, UNLESS NOTED

PLATE 134

(Left to right)

First Row:

1. Vase, 2", "N" low relief ....$5.00 – 10.00
2. Vase, 5", *Ivory*, Lewis glaze, large Second art mark ....$25.00 – 35.00
3. Jug, 3¾", hand thrown, unmarked ....$35.00 – 45.00
4. Pitcher, 2", *Maroon*, Lewis glaze, "Potteries" sticker ....$10.00 – 15.00

Second Row: Lewis Glazes

1. Sugar bowl, 3" x 4½", *Ozark Blue*, Niloak block letters ....$15.00 – 20.00
2. Ashtray, 1½", *Ozark Dawn II*, Niloak block letters ....$15.00 – 20.00
3. Pitcher, 1¾", *Ozark Blue*, hand thrown, "Potteries" sticker ...$15.00 – 20.00
4. Pitcher, 3", *Ozark Dawn II*, hand thrown, "Potteries" sticker..$15.00 – 20.00

Third Row:

1. Flower/Frog, 4¼" x 1½", *Ozark Dawn II*, Lewis glaze, unmarked ....$15.00 – 25.00
2. Cup, 2¾", Niloak block letters, unusual glaze ....$15.00 – 25.00
3. Pitcher, 2½", *Ivory*, Lewis glaze, hand thrown, "Potteries" sticker, "Souvenir of Lake of Ozarks, Mo." ....$15.00 – 20.00
4. Pitcher, 2½", *Ivory*, Lewis glaze, hand thrown, Second art mark ....$15.00 – 20.00

Fourth Row * : Lewis Glazes

1. Planter, 4" x 2½", *Ozark Dawn II*, Niloak low relief ....$10.00 – 15.00
2. Planter, 4" x 2¼", *Ozark Blue*, Niloak low relief ....$10.00 – 15.00
3. Planter, 4" x 2¼", *Ozark Dawn II*, Niloak low relief ....$10.00 – 15.00

* These items are the planters from the Pacific Planters group.

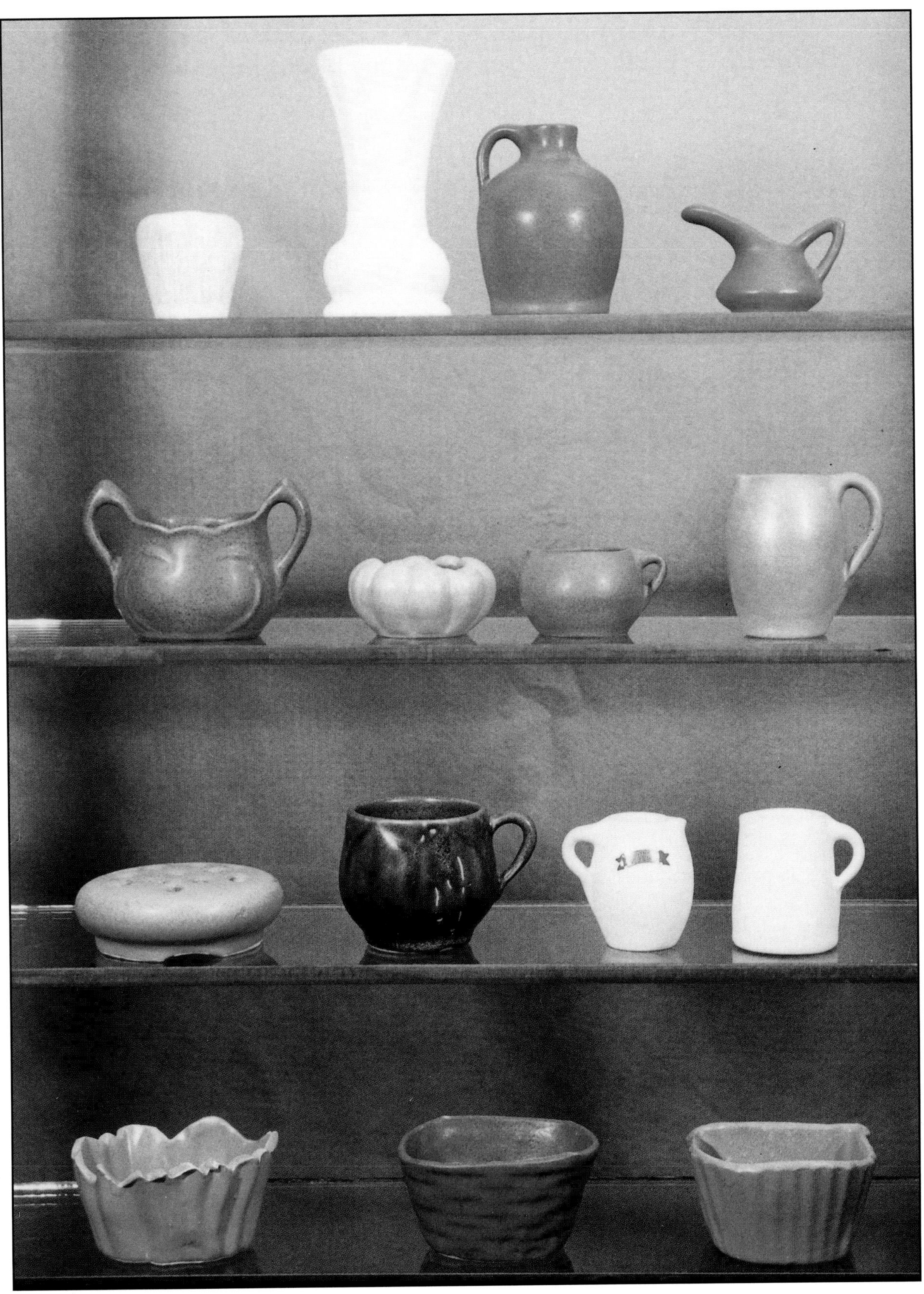

PLATE 134

Novelty and Figural Items with Lewis Glazes

Plate 135

(Left to right)

First Row:

1. Southern Belle, standing with hat, 7¼", Peterson design, *Ozark Dawn II*, Niloak low relief................................$100.00 – 125.00
2. Cart, 4¼", Alley design, *Ozark Blue*, Niloak low relief..$35.00 – 45.00
3. Southern Belle, sitting, 4¾", Peterson design, *Ozark Dawn II*, Niloak low relief...$75.00 – 100.00

Second Row:

1. Wishing Well, covered, 8", Alley design, *Ozark Dawn II*, Niloak low relief...$35.00 – 45.00
2. Southern Belle, standing, 10", Peterson design, *Ozark Blue*, Niloak low relief....................................$125.00 – 175.00
3. Wishing Well, opened, 8½", Alley design, *Ozark Blue*, Niloak low relief...$75.00 – 100.00

Third Row: *Ozark Dawn II*

1. Vase with "Wagon Wheel" handles, 5", Niloak block letters..$15.00 – 25.00
2. Scalloped bowl, 3½" x 10½", Niloak block letters....................$35.00 – 45.00
3. Ivory bowl, 5", Peterson design, Niloak block letters...$15.00 – 25.00

Fourth Row: *Ozark Dawn II*

1. Wooden Shoe, 2½" x 5", unmarked ....$5.00 – 10.00
2. Indian Canoe, 3½" x 11", Niloak block letters ....$45.00 – 55.00
3. Indian Canoe, 2" x 5½", Niloak low relief..................................$50.00 – 75.00

Plate 135

NOVELTY ITEMS AND PLANTERS WITH LEWIS GLAZES

PLATE 136 *

(Left to right)

1. Elephant, 2¼", *Ozark Blue*, hollow inside, unmarked ....$50.00 – 75.00
2. Elephant, 2", swirl, unmarked ....$400.00 – 600.00 (+/-)

* Another connection between Niloak and Denver's White Pottery is their production of seemingly identical elephants. See Not Necessarily Niloak.

PLATE 137

Rocking Horse, 6¼", Joe Alley design, *Ozark Blue,* Niloak low relief ..$75.00 – 100.00

PLATE 138

(Left to right)

First Row: *Ozark Blue*

1. Elephant, 3½" x 6½", Alley design, Niloak incised ....$75.00 – 100.00 (+/-)
2. Frog, 3¼", Peterson design, unmarked ....$35.00 – 45.00
3. Camel, 3¾", Alley design, unmarked ....$50.00 – 75.00

Second Row:

1. Elephant, 4¼", *Ozark Dawn II,* Niloak block letters ....$45.00 – 65.00
2. Elephant, 3¾", Second art mark ....$75.00 – 100.00
3. Elephant, 6", Alley design, *Ozark Dawn II,* "N" for Niloak on base, Niloak low relief ....$45.00 – 65.00
   First circus planter of this kind.

Third Row: *Maroon*

1. Razorback Hog, 3¾", unmarked ....$100.00 – 200.00 (+/-)
2. Duck, 1¾", unmarked, "Turner Falls, Okla." on bill in black ink ....$50.00 – 100.00 (+/-)
3. Razorback Hog, 5", Niloak block letters ....$100.00 – 200.00 (+/-)
   Note: Either of the razorbacks can be found with or without Arkansas on the side.

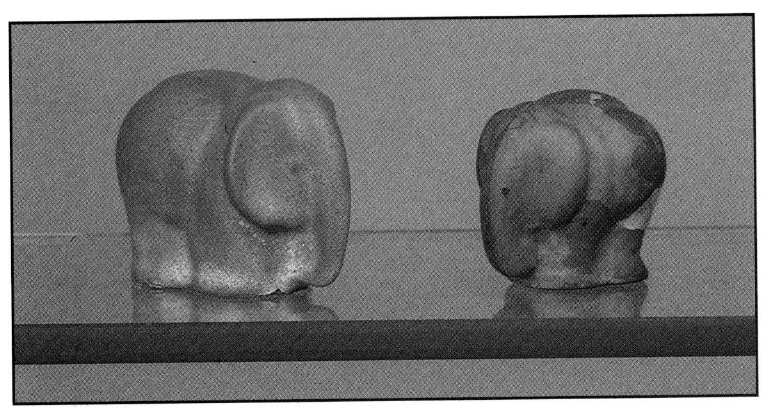

Plate 136

Plate 137

Plate 138

NOVELTY ITEMS AND PLANTERS WITH LEWIS GLAZES

PLATE 139

(Left to right)

1. Swan, 2¾", hollow, *Ozark Blue*, "Potteries" sticker ....$50.00 – 100.00 (+/-)
2. Frog, 3¼", first Hywood by Niloak ....$50.00 – 100.00 (+/-)
3. Duck, 3½", first Hywood by Niloak, "FD" ink stamp ....$50.00 – 100.00 (+/-)
   Similar to a Weller item.

PLATE 140

(Left to right)

First Row: Joe Alley designs

1. Squirrel planter, 5", earliest, with opening between its arms, *Ozark Blue*, Niloak low relief.......................$50.00 – 75.00
2. Bulldog, 2" x 5¾", *Blue and Tan Matt*, Niloak low relief ....$50.00 – 75.00
3. Squirrel planter, 6", *Blue and Tan Matt*, Niloak low relief.........$35.00 – 45.00

Second Row:

1. Pigeon, 4¾", *Ozark Dawn II*, not a planter, Hywood incised.$100.00 – 150.00 (+/-)
2. Scottie, 3½", Alley design, *Ozark Blue*, Niloak incised ....$35.00 – 45.00
3. Double rabbits, 5", Alley design, *Ozark Dawn II*, Niloak low relief ....$50.00 – 75.00

Third Row: George Peterson Designs in *Ozark Dawn II*

1. Bird, 3" x 3", turned head, Niloak low relief...............................$15.00 – 25.00
2. Bird, 2½" x 3½", Niloak low relief...$15.00 – 25.00
3. Bird, 2½" x 4", Niloak low relief ....$15.00 – 25.00

Fourth Row: *Ozark Dawn II*

1. Retriever, 4½", Alley design, Niloak low relief ....$45.00 – 65.00
2. Duck, 4", turned head, Peterson design Niloak low relief........$25.00 – 35.00
3. Poodle, 3½", Alley design, Niloak low relief ....$100.00 – 150.00 (+/-)

PLATE 139

Plate 140

ALLEY DESIGNED DEER PLANTERS

PLATE 141

(Left to right)

Top Row: Lewis Glazes

1. 5", facing left, *Ozark Blue*, Niloak low relief..............................$15.00 – 25.00
2. 5¼", *Ozark Dawn II*, unmarked...$75.00 – 100.00 (+/-)
3. 5", facing right, *Ivory*, Niloak low relief ....$15.00 – 25.00

Middle Row: Lewis's *Ozark Blue*

1. 10", free standing, Niloak low relief...............................$100.00 – 200.00 (+/-)
2. 8", in grass, Niloak low relief ....$25.00 – 35.00

Bottom Row:

1. 7", in grass, Niloak low relief ....$25.00 – 35.00
2. 6½", *Ozark Blue*, Lewis glaze, unmarked..................................$25.00 – 35.00

Note: Many other companies made similar deer items.

PLATE 141

PETERSON DESIGNED NOVELTY ITEMS *

PLATE 142

(Left to right)

Top Row:

1. Donkey, 2¾", on base..$75.00 – 125.00 (+/-)
2. Donkey, 3½"..$100.00 – 150.00 (+/-)
3. Donkey, 2¾", on base..$75.00 – 125.00 (+/-)

Middle Row:

1. Dog, 2½"...$75.00 – 100.00 (+/-)
2. Cow, 3", decal "Souvenir of Little Rock Arkansas".........$75.00 – 125.00 (+/-)
3. Dog, 2½"...$75.00 – 100.00 (+/-)

Bottom Row:

1. Dog, 2¾", with black circle ink stamp
   "Stateline Pottery, Texarkana, U.S.A." ....$75.00 – 100.00 (+/-)
2. Dog, 2"..$75.00 – 100.00 (+/-)
3. Dog, 2¼"...$75.00 – 100.00 (+/-)

Note: All have smallest Niloak block letters mark.

* The novelty animals in this plate and others are unique in that the bodies are molded with their features tooled individually. While Peterson is responsible for the creation of these items, his replacement, Joe Alley, is known to have made some as well.

Plate 142

Novelty Items

Plate 143

Donkey with baskets, on base, 2¾", *Fox Red*, smallest Niloak block letters ....N/A

Plate 144

(Left to right)

First Row:

1. Lion, 14½" x 5½", *Green & Tan Matt*, Lewis Glaze, "Potteries" sticker ...N/A

Second Row: Handmade by George Peterson and Joe Alley

1. Dog, 2¼", smallest Niloak block letters............................$75.00 – 100.00 (+/-)
2. Panther, 4½" x 1¾", unmarked, "11-9-42" * ....N/A
3. Dog, 2¼", smallest Niloak block letters..$75.00 (+/-)

Third Row:

1. Pig, 2", *Ozark Blue*, Lewis glaze, Hywood incised......................................N/A
2. Frog, 3½", first Hywood by Niloak..................................$50.00 – 100.00 (+/-)

Fourth Row:

1. Owl, 4¼", *Wine*, Stoin glaze, Hywood incised ....N/A
2. Swan, 4½", *Ozark Dawn II*, Lewis glaze, unmarked..................$25.00 – 35.00

* The panther is the mascot of the Benton High School.

Plate 143

PLATE 144

Niloak/Joe Alley Designs
One-of-a-Kind Castware, unless noted

Plate 145

(Left to right)

Top Row:

1. Dog, 5" x 4", handmade, unmarked, grease pencil "Niloak" .... N/A
2. Hat, 5", *Ivory,* Lewis glaze, hand thrown, unmarked, grease pencil "1940" .... N/A
3. Policeman, 6½", unmarked .... N/A

Bottom Row:

1. Keystone Cop, 6¼", Niloak incised , grease pencil "1939," one of six known to exist .... N/A
2. Goblet, 6¼", *Fox Red,* unmarked, grease pencil "1939" .... N/A
3. Trojan Horse, 10¼", unmarked, grease pencil "1941" .... N/A

Niloak Castware
Peterson's Angel and Christmas Bells

Plate 146

(Left to right)

1. Angel, 4¼", unmarked .... N/A
2. Christmas Bells, 3¼" x 3", 2" x 2", 1¼" x 1¼", unmarked .... N/A
3. Angel, 4", unmarked .... N/A

PLATE 145

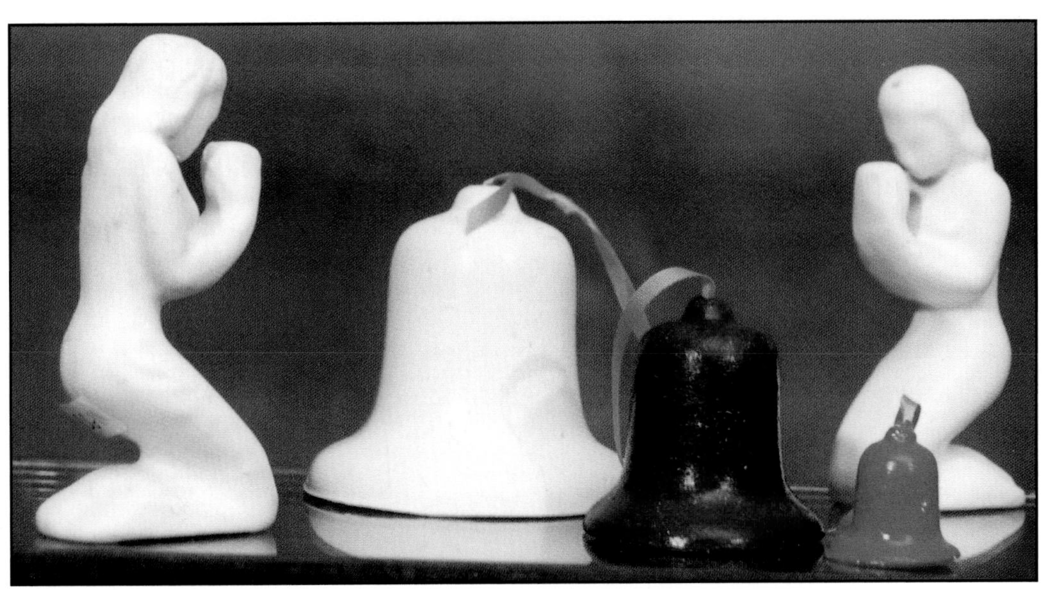

PLATE 146

NOVELTY ITEMS WITH LEWIS GLAZES, UNLESS NOTED

PLATE 147

(Left to right)

First Row: *Ozark Dawn II*

1. Geese salt & pepper shakers, 2", Alley design, "Potteries" sticker .... $35.00 – 45.00
2. Tumbler, 4", hand thrown, Niloak block letters .... $15.00 – 25.00
3. Ball salt & pepper shakers, 2½", unmarked .... $15.00 – 25.00

Second Row: Joe Alley Designs

1. Tank, 2¼", *Ozark Blue*, Niloak low relief and "Potteries" sticker .... $50.00 – 75.00
2. Airplane, 2", *Ozark Dawn II*, Niloak low relief .... $100.00 – 150.00 (+/-)
3. Bullets salt & pepper shakers, 2¾", *Ozark Dawn II*, "Potteries" sticker .... $100.00 – 150.00 (+/-)
4. Cannon, 3¼", *Ozark Blue*, Niloak low relief .... $50.00 – 75.00

Third Row:

1. Birds salt & pepper shakers, 2¼", Alley design, *Maroon*, unmarked .... $35.00 – 45.00
2. Candlestick, 7", hand thrown, "Potteries" sticker .... $45.00 – 65.00
3. Penguins salt & pepper shakers, 2¾", Alley design, *Ozark Blue*, "Potteries" sticker .... $35.00 – 45.00

Fourth Row:

1. Tumbler with gazelle, 5½", deco, Peterson design, *Ozark Blue*, Niloak block letters .... $35.00 – 45.00
2. Pitcher, 7½", Arkansas flag and USA on sides in relief, Alley design, *Ozark Blue*, Niloak low relief * .... $75.00 – 125.00 (+/-)
3. Cradle, 4" x 6" x 3", Alley design, *Ozark Dawn II*, Niloak low relief .... $50.00 – 75.00

* Other states known to exist include Louisiana, Mississippi, Missouri, Kansas, Texas, as well as the city of Memphis. Also found with USA on the sides only. (See page 43.)

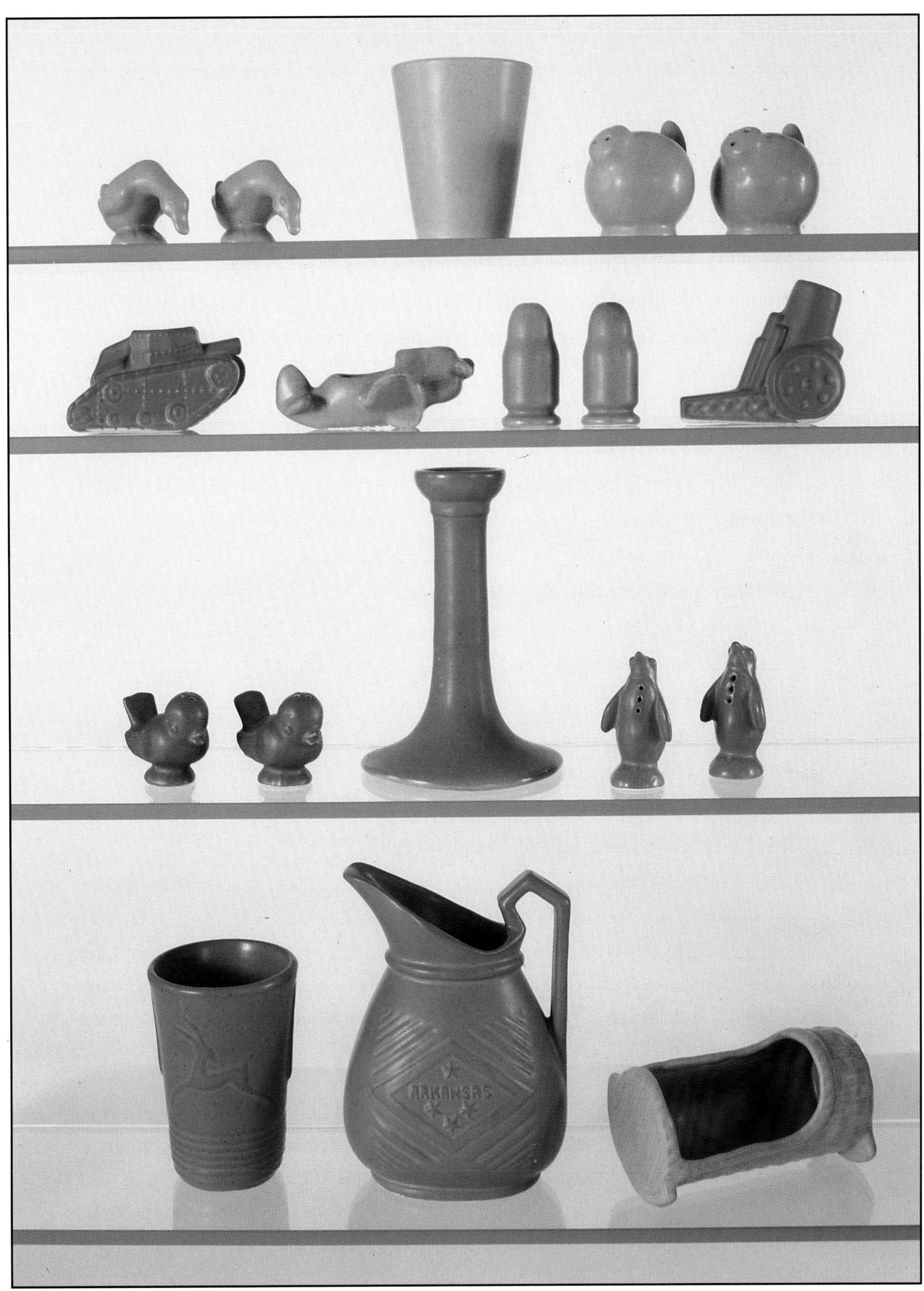

Plate 147

Novelty Items

Plate 148

(Left to right)

Top Row:

1. Elephant, 2¼", hollow inside with round Niloak sticker (commonly found on swirl) in the inside .... $50.00 – 75.00
   Also the remnants of rectangular red and white sticker with "Benton" written in ink on it.
2. Standard Niloak Elephant (?), 3¾", *Maroon*, Lewis glaze, unmarked, with "Hand Made Original Kentucky Pottery" black ink stamp * .. $45.00 – 65.00
3. Deer, 4¾", *Ivory*, Lewis glaze, Niloak low relief .... $50.00 – 75.00

Middle Row:

1. Shoe, 2¾", unmarked ** .... N/A
2. Kitchenware flower pot, 3¼", Alley design, Niloak block letters .... $25.00 – 35.00
3. Horn of Plenty, 3¼", unmarked ** .... N/A

Bottom Row:

1. Cabinet vase, 3¾", Niloak block letters .... $10.00 – 15.00
2. Pin dish, ¾" x 4", Alley design, *Ozark Dawn II*, Lewis glaze, unmarked .... $15.00 – 25.00
3. Bowl, 2¼", *Ivory*, Lewis glaze, Niloak incised and "Potteries" sticker .... $15.00 – 25.00

* Question: Did the designer of this particular shape make an elephant mold for Niloak and a Kentucky firm? Or did Niloak make this item and sell it wholesale for other retailers' tourist trade? It is not, however, a handmade item. (See pages 53 and 54.)

** With the publication of the first edition, collectors debated whether or not this Shoe and the Horn of Plenty were indeed Niloak. In interviews and correspondence with Niloak designer Joe Alley, he neither offered nor took responsibility as the designer of these items (their production came too late to be Peterson's designs). Therefore, upon reflection, it is possible, maybe probable, that these two items are not Niloak.

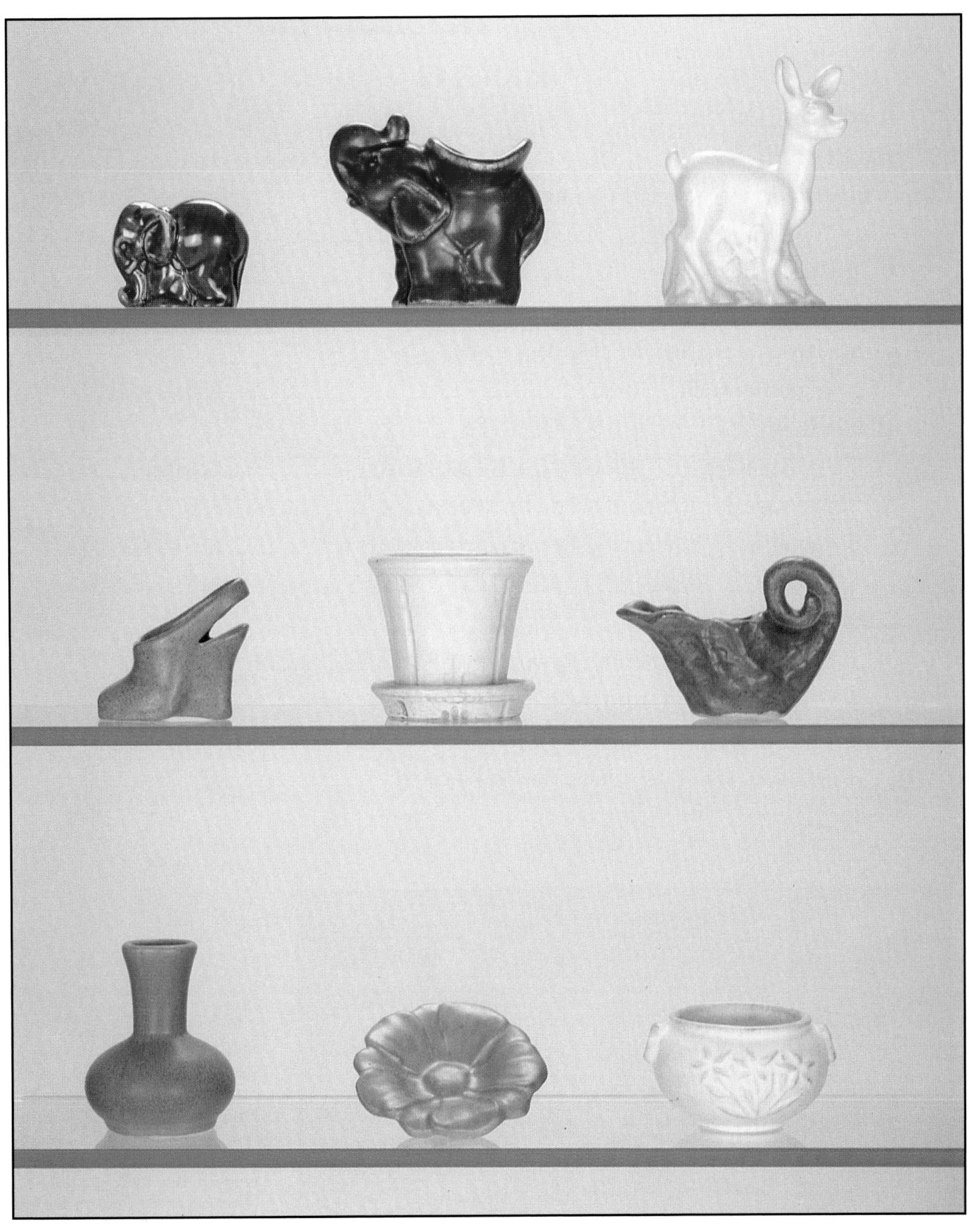

PLATE 148

CASTWARE, UNLESS NOTED, WITH LEWIS IVORY GLAZE

PLATE 149

(Left to right)

Top Row:

1. Planter, 3½" x 3" x 5½", Niloak incised and "Potteries" sticker .... $45.00 – 55.00
2. Trojan Horse figurine, 8¾", larger Second art mark .... $125.00 – 175.00 (+/-)
3. Basket, 3½", Alley design, Niloak low relief .... $25.00 – 35.00
4. Planter of girl leaning over basket, 4¾", Niloak low relief .... $50.00 – 75.00

Middle Row:

1. Swan planter, 7½", Alley design, Niloak incised .... $15.00 – 25.00
2. Bud vase, 9", second Hywood by Niloak .... $25.00 – 35.00
3. Rabbit, 3½", Peterson design, Niloak block letters .... $15.00 – 25.00
4. Winged Victory vase, 7¼", Alley design, Niloak .... $15.00 – 25.00

Bottom Row:

1. Handled vase, 7", second Hywood by Niloak .... $75.00 – 100.00
2. Vase, 9½", hand thrown with applied handles, first Hywood by Niloak .... $100.00 – 150.00
3. Fan vase, 7¼", Pine Cones, Hywood incised .... $50.00 – 75.00

Niloak Pottery plant, interior, Pearl Street, Benton, circa early 1940s. Photo caption reads: "China mugs for the Navy and a brand new product for Arkansas, as Miss Bardwell makes coffee mugs of Niloak's 'Porsaline.'" ***Courtesy of the late Hardy L. Winburn IV.***

PLATE 149

CASTWARE WITH IVORY GLAZE BY LEWIS

PLATE 150

(Left to right)

Top Row: Joe Alley Designs

1. Winged Victory vase, 7¼", Niloak low relief .... $25.00 – 35.00
2. Dove or Pigeon planter, 9", Niloak incised .... $150.00 – 200.00 (+/-)
3. Strawberry jar, 7½", Niloak low relief .... $25.00 – 35.00

Middle Row:

1. Fan vase, 7", Niloak block letters .... $50.00 – 75.00
2. Strawberry jar, 5", Niloak block letters .... $15.00 – 25.00
3. Swan ashtray, 5", Niloak block letters and "Potteries" sticker .... $50.00 – 75.00
4. Pelican flower frog, 6¾", Alley design, "Potteries" sticker .... $25.00 – 35.00

Bottom Row: Joe Alley Designs

1. Ewer, 9", Niloak low relief .... $25.00 – 35.00
2. Bowl, 4½" x 12¼", with bird flower frog, 7¼", set .... $100.00 – 150.00 (+/-)
   Niloak low relief on bowl and "Potteries" sticker on both the bowl and flower frog.
3. Ewer, 10", profiles of colonial man and woman on either side, unmarked .... $35.00 – 45.00

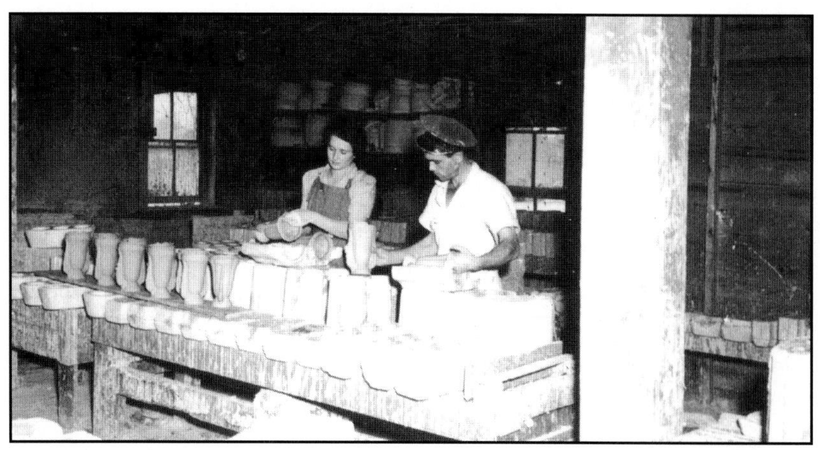

Niloak Pottery plant, interior, Pearl Street, Benton, circa early 1940s. *Courtesy of the late Hardy L. Winburn IV.*

PLATE 150

Niloak Castware, unless noted

Joe Alley Designs, unless noted, Canary Yellow Bright by Lewis

Plate 151

(Left to right)

First Row:

1. Winged Victory bud vase, 7", Niloak .... $10.00 – 15.00
2. Swan planter, 3¾", Niloak low relief .... $10.00 – 15.00
3. Bud vase, 7¼", Niloak low relief .... $20.00 – 25.00

Second Row:

1. Pitcher, 4¼", Niloak .... $10.00 – 15.00
2. Wallpocket, 5¼", Bouquet pattern, Niloak low relief .... $25.00 – 35.00

Third Row: George Peterson Designs

1. Turtle flower frog, 1½" x 4¾",
   smallest Niloak block letters .... $50.00 – 100.00 (+/-)
2. Rabbit planter, 3", Niloak incised .... $50.00 – 75.00

Fourth Row:

1. Basket, 6", Niloak low relief .... $45.00 – 65.00
2. Miniature jug, 4½", hand thrown, Niloak 71 .... $35.00 – 45.00
3. Cannon, 3", Niloak low relief .... $50.00 – 75.00

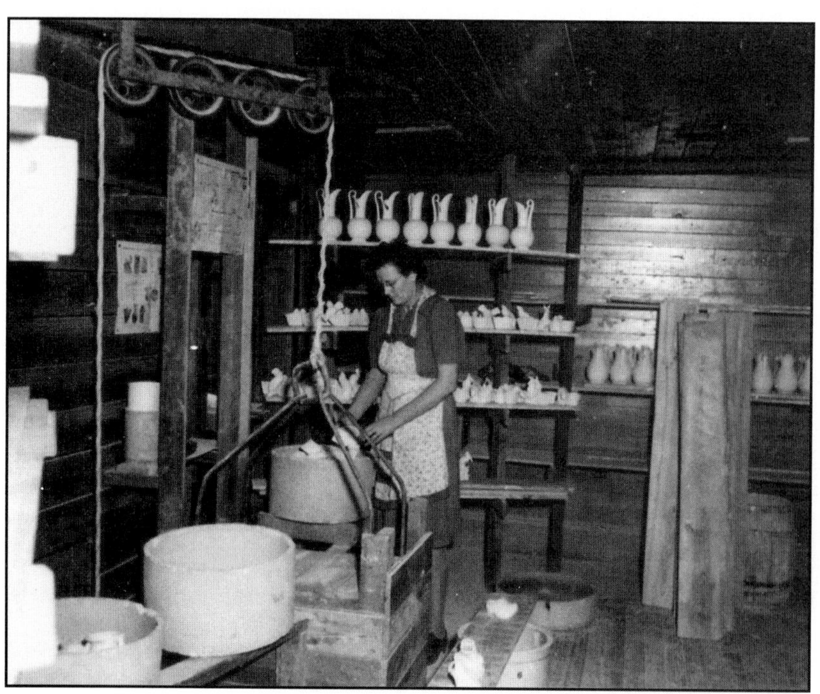

Niloak Pottery plant, interior, Pearl Street, Benton, circa early 1940s. Note castware catalog page on left wall. *Courtesy of the late Hardy L. Winburn IV.*

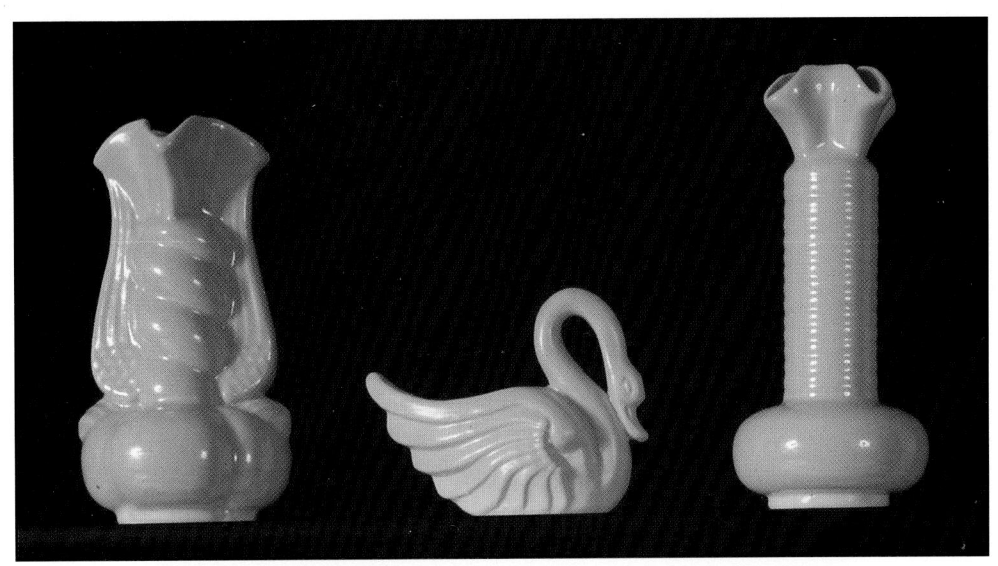

Plate 151

ALLEY DESIGNED VASES AND PLANTERS

PLATE 152

(Left to right)

First Row: *Ozark Dawn II*

1. Duck flower frog, 6", unmarked..$45.00 – 65.00
2. Swan planter, 6¼", Niloak incised ....$15.00 – 25.00
   Rosemeade made a similar item.

Second Row:

1. Handled vase, 7", Niloak low relief ....$35.00 – 45.00
2. Winged Victory vase, 7½", Niloak incised.................................$25.00 – 35.00

Third Row * : Pacific Planters

1. Siberia Polar Bear, 3½", Niloak low relief.................................$35.00 – 45.00
2. China Bird, 5½", Niloak low relief...$35.00 – 45.00
3. Aleutian Islands Seal, 4¾", Niloak low relief ....$35.00 – 45.00

Fourth Row * : Pacific Planters

1. Burma Camel, 3¼", Niloak low relief...$35.00 – 45.00
2. Malay Parrot, 4½", Niloak low relief...$35.00 – 45.00
3. Australia Kangaroo, 5", Niloak low relief....................................$35.00 – 45.00

* These popular animal planters were first made during World War II. Designed by Joe Alley, these were called the Pacific Planters and some were made using Niloak's Porsaline clay. The brown/tan color, not a typical color for Niloak Pottery, resulted from the war shortage of other oxides. These hand decorations are "cold water" decorations added after firing. The decorations are not permanent, therefore, and can be washed off.

PLATE 152

Miniature Pitchers with Lewis Glazes

Plate 153

(Left to right)

Top Row:

1. Pitcher, 3", *Ozark Dawn II*, "Potteries" sticker, hand thrown .... $15.00 – 20.00
2. Pitcher, 3¾", Alley design, *Yellow Canary Bright*, Niloak low relief, castware .... $10.00 – 15.00
3. Pitcher, 3½", Alley design, *Green and Tan Matt*, Niloak low relief, castware .... $15.00 – 20.00
4. Pitcher, 3¼", *Ozark Dawn II*, Second art mark, hand thrown .... $15.00 – 20.00

Middle Row: Hand Thrown

1. Pitcher, 2¾", *Ozark Dawn II*, "Potteries" sticker .... $15.00 – 20.00
2. Pitcher, 2", *Ozark Dawn II*, unmarked .... $15.00 – 20.00
3. Pitcher, 2¾", *Ozark Blue*, Second art mark .... $15.00 – 20.00
4. Pitcher, 2½", *Ozark Blue*, unmarked .... $15.00 – 20.00

Bottom Row: Castware of Joe Alley Designs

1. Pitcher, 3½", *Ozark Blue*, Niloak low relief .... $10.00 – 15.00
2. Pitcher, 3¼", *Maroon*, Niloak low relief .... $10.00 – 15.00
3. Pitcher, 3¼", *Ozark Blue*, Niloak low relief .... $15.00 – 20.00

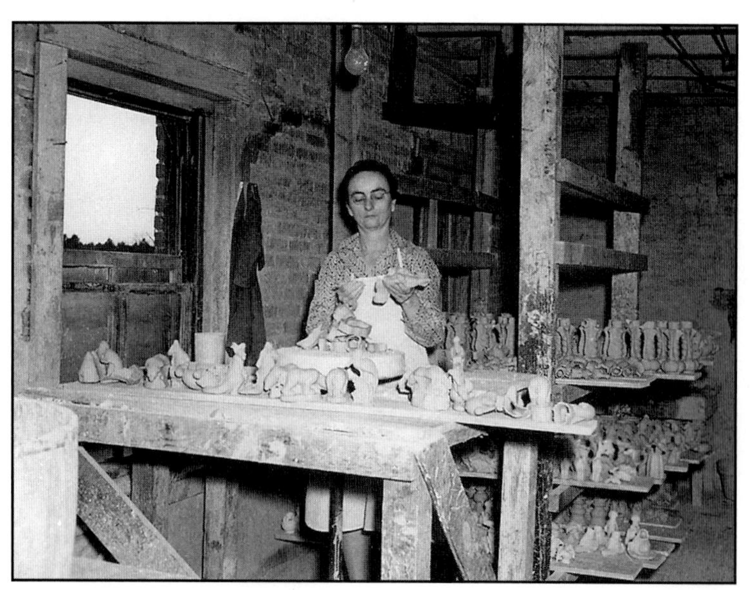

Niloak Pottery plant, interior, Pearl Street, Benton, circa early 1940s. *Courtesy of the late Hardy L. Winburn IV.*

PLATE 153

Miniature Pitchers with Lewis Glazes

Plate 154

(Left to right)

Top Row: Hand Thrown

1. Pitcher, 2¼", *Ozark Blue*, "Potteries" sticker ....$15.00 – 20.00
2. Pitcher, 3", *Maroon,* Second art mark ....$25.00 – 30.00
3. Jug, 3", *Ozark Dawn II*, unmarked ....$35.00 – 45.00

Middle Row: Castware with *Ozark Dawn II*

1. Pitcher, 2¼", Niloak block letters ....$10.00 – 15.00
2. Pitcher, 3", Alley design, Niloak block letters ....$10.00 – 15.00
3. Pitcher, 3", Alley design, unmarked ....$10.00 – 15.00

Bottom Row: Castware

1. Pitcher, 2¾", *Ozark Dawn II,* "Potteries" stickers ....$10.00 – 15.00
2. Pitcher, 2¾", Alley design, *Ozark Blue,* unmarked ....$10.00 – 15.00
3. Pitcher, 2¾", *Ozark Dawn II*, "Potteries" stickers ....$10.00 – 15.00

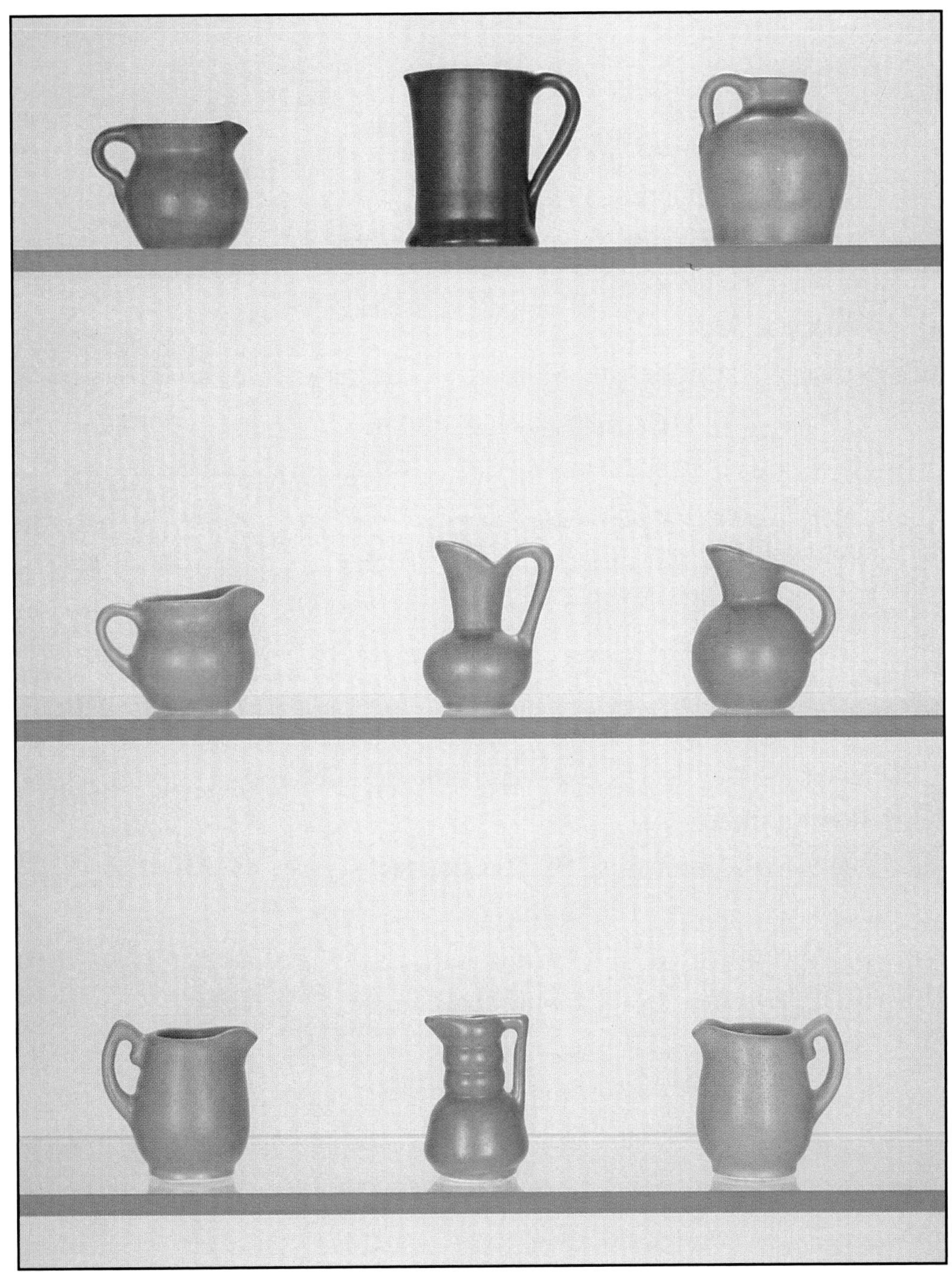

PLATE 154

Miniature Pitchers with Lewis Glazes, unless noted

Plate 155

(Left to right)

First Row: Hand Thrown

1. Pitcher, 3¼", *Fox Red,* Second art mark....$15.00 – 20.00
2. Pitcher, 3¼", "Potteries" sticker....$15.00 – 20.00
3. Pitcher, 2½", *Delft Blue,* Stoin glaze, Second art mark and "Potteries" sticker....$15.00 – 20.00

Second Row: *Fox Red*

1. Pitcher, 3½", Alley design, "N" low relief, castware....$10.00 – 15.00
2. Pitcher, 2", "Potteries" sticker, hand thrown....$10.00 – 15.00
3. Pitcher, 3½", Alley design, Niloak low relief, castware....$10.00 – 15.00

Third Row: Castware

1. Pitcher, 2¾", Alley design, *Cobalt Blue,* "Potteries" sticker....$10.00 – 15.00
2. Pitcher, 3", *Canary Yellow Bright,* Niloak low relief and "Potteries" sticker....$10.00 – 15.00
3. Pitcher, 3", Alley design, *Fox Red,* "Potteries" sticker....$10.00 – 15.00

Fourth Row: Castware

1. Pitcher, 3½", Alley design, *Fox Red,* flowers and "Ozarks" painted decoration on to the glaze, 1868 sticker....$10.00 – 15.00
2. Jug, 2½", *Fox Red,* salt or pepper shaker, 1868 sticker....$10.00 – 15.00
3. Pitcher, 2½", Alley design, non-Lewis glaze, "N" low relief....$10.00 – 15.00

PLATE 155

VARIOUS HAND-THROWN MINIATURES, UNLESS NOTED

PLATE 156

(Left to right)

First Row: Castware

1. Bowl, 2¼" x 1½", unmarked .... $10.00 – 15.00
2. Creamer, 2½", Alley design, Niloak incised .... $15.00 – 25.00
3. Bowl, 2¾" x 1¾", Niloak incised .... $10.00 – 15.00

Second Row: Lewis glazes

1. Pitcher, 2½", *Yellow Canary Bright,* "Potteries" sticker .... $15.00 – 20.00
2. Pitcher, 2½", *Delft Blue,* unmarked .... $15.00 – 20.00
3. Pitcher, 2¼", *Yellow Canary Bright,* unmarked .... $15.00 – 20.00

Third Row: *Fox Red*

1. Pitcher, 2½", "Potteries" sticker .... $25.00 – 30.00
2. Pitcher, 2¾", Second art mark .... $15.00 – 20.00
3. Shot glass, 2½", unmarked .... $15.00 – 20.00

Charles Dove at kiln opening, Niloak Pottery Plant, Pearl Street, Benton, circa late 1930s. ***Courtesy of the University of Central Arkansas Archives and Special Collections, Charles Dove Photograph Collection.***

PLATE 156

HAND-THROWN AND CASTWARE PIECES WITH LEWIS GLAZES, UNLESS NOTED

PLATE 157

(Left to right)

Top Row:

1. Vase, 4½", *Delft Blue*, Stoin glaze, first Hywood by Niloak and "EZ" ink stamp, hand thrown ....$75.00 – 100.00 (+/-)
2. Ashtray or relish dish, 9¾" x 9¾" x 9¾", *Fox Red*, unmarked, castware ....$50.00 – 75.00
3. Vase, 4½", first Hywood by Niloak and "FZ" ink stamp, hand thrown ....$50.00 – 75.00

Middle Row: Hand Thrown

1. Vase, 5", *Delft Blue*, Stoin glaze, first Hywood by Niloak and "DL" in grease pencil (?)..............................$125.00 – 175.00 (+/-)
2. Vase with handles, 9", *Mirror Black*, first Hywood by Niloak..$125.00 – 175.00 (+/-)
3. Jug, 8", *Fox Red*, Second art mark..$50.00 – 75.00

Bottom Row: Castware

1. Salt and pepper shakers with letters "S" and "P" as handles, 3", *Fox Red*, unmarked ....$15.00 – 25.00
2. Classic Vase, 5", *Canary Yellow Bright*, Niloak block letters..$15.00 – 25.00
3. Rooster, 6¼", *Fox Red*, Niloak incised..$15.00 – 25.00
   Camark Pottery made similar item.
4. Dish, 3¼", non-Lewis glaze, Niloak incised ....$10.00 – 15.00

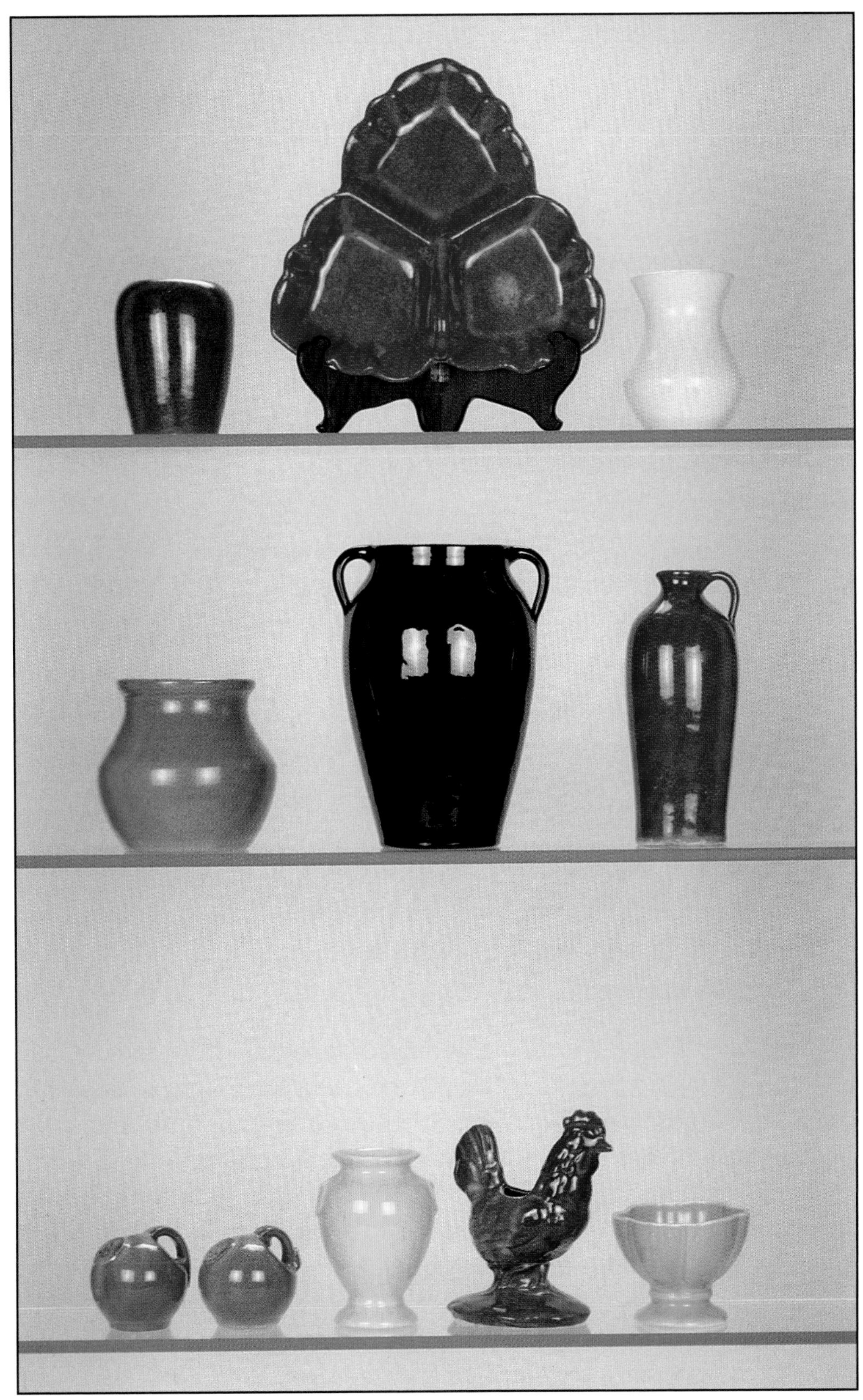

Plate 157

Niloak Castware
Miscellaneous Pieces with Fox Red by Lewis *

Plate 158

(Left to right)

First Row:

1. Ashtray, promotional, 5¾" x 3½", "Parts and Equipment, Crow Burlingame Co.," Niloak low relief ....$50.00 – 75.00
2. Winged Victory vase, 7½", Alley design, Niloak ....$15.00 – 25.00
3. Ashtray, 4¼" x 3½", "Arkansas" with Pegasus and recessed diamond (the symbol on the Arkansas flag), Niloak low relief ....$75.00 – 100.00 (+/-)

Second Row: Joe Alley Designs

1. Squirrel planter, 6", turned left, Niloak incised ....$15.00 – 25.00
2. Wallpocket, 5", Bouquet pattern, Niloak low relief ....$25.00 – 35.00
3. Squirrel planter, 6", turned right, Niloak incised ....$15.00 – 25.00

Third Row: Aladdin Tea Set **

1. Creamer, 2½", unmarked ....$15.00 – 25.00
2. Teapot, 6½", unmarked..$75.00 – 100.00
3. Sugar bowl, 3¾", "Potteries" sticker ....$25.00 – 35.00

Fourth Row: Joe Alley Designs

1. Cornucopia cabinet vase, 3¼", Niloak low relief........................$5.00 – 10.00
2. Fox planter, 4½", turned right, Niloak low relief.......................$35.00 – 45.00
3. Creamer, 5", Niloak low relief, 1868 sticker...............................$10.00 – 15.00
4. Dog, 3¾", unmarked..$50.00 – 75.00

* Howard Lewis's *Fox Red* glaze was introduced in the mid 1930s and used until the 1950s, the longest use of any Niloak glaze. There are varying shades to *Fox Red* and it can be found with or without a green overspray. Austelle Lloyd, an employee who came to Niloak with Hardy Winburn, commented about her personal feelings regarding *Fox Red* with the green overspray. As Niloak's operation supervisor in the late 1940s and early 1950s, she said "it came through (the firing process) looking a little (like) tobacco spit."

** Since the Niloak Pottery Company jobbed for the Hall China Company in the 1940s, this is obviously a copy of Hall's Aladdin teapot. Moreover, Niloak Pottery even marketed its teapot under the name Aladdin.

PLATE 158

PLANTERS AND VASES WITH FOX RED BY LEWIS

PLATE 159

(Left to right)

Top Row:

1. Deer planter, 7", Alley design, Niloak low relief ....$25.00 – 35.00
2. Bud vase, $6\frac{3}{4}$", Second art mark ....$25.00 – 35.00
3. Deer and Fawn planter, $7\frac{1}{2}$", Niloak low relief * ....$25.00 – 35.00

Middle Row:

1. Turtle planter, $2\frac{1}{2}$" x 6" x $8\frac{1}{2}$", unmarked ....$45.00 – 65.00
2. Cabinet vase, 4", Niloak low relief...$15.00 – 25.00
3. Fish plant bowl, $4\frac{3}{4}$" x 5" x 9", Niloak incised * ....$35.00 – 45.00

Bottom Row:

1. Horn vase, $8\frac{1}{4}$", Niloak incised ....$15.00 – 25.00
2. Moccasin, $1\frac{3}{4}$" x 5" x $2\frac{1}{4}$", Peterson design,
   Niloak low relief ....$50.00 – 75.00 (+/-)
3. Shell-like vase, $2\frac{1}{2}$", "N" low relief...$10.00 – 15.00
4. Tulip vase, decorated, $7\frac{1}{4}$", Alley design,
   Niloak low relief..$15.00 – 25.00

* Two of Joe Alley's Bright Whimsies designs.

PLATE 159

VARIOUS CASTWARE PIECES, UNLESS NOTED

PLATE 160

(Left to right)

First Row:

1. Creamer, 4¾", Niloak low relief....................$10.00 – 15.00
2. Sugar bowl, 4½", Niloak low relief....................$10.00 – 15.00
3. Indian Canoe, 9¼", "1868" sticker....................$25.00 – 35.00

Second Row:

1. Rooster, 6½", Niloak incised....................$15.00 – 25.00
2. China planter, 5½", unmarked....................$15.00 – 25.00
3. Ewer, 7", Niloak incised....................$10.00 – 15.00

Third Row:

1. Vase, 5", Second Hywood by Niloak, large Second art mark...$15.00 – 25.00
2. Cup, 2¾", and saucer, 5¾", Petal design, cup, unmarked; saucer, Niloak block letters....................$25.00 – 35.00
3. Tumbler, 5¼", hand thrown, second Hywood by Niloak.........$35.00 – 55.00

Fourth Row:

1. Dish, 8¾", Niloak incised....................$15.00 – 25.00
2. Dish, 10½" x 11", Second art mark....................$25.00 – 35.00

PLATE 160

Hand-thrown and Castware with Mirror Black Glaze by Lewis

Plate 161

(Left to right)

Top Row: Castware

Scottie dog figurine, 3¾", Alley design, unmarked ....$50.00 – 75.00 (+/-)

Not a planter.

Middle Row:

1. Ewer, 6¾", castware, Alley design, "Potteries" sticker ....$10.00 – 15.00
2. Strawberry jar, 9", both first and second Hywood by Niloak ....$150.00 – 200.00 (+/-)
3. Ewer, 7½", Alley design, *Gun Metal,* Niloak low relief ....$15.00 – 25.00

Bottom Row:

1. Bowl, 2¾", first Hywood by Niloak, hand thrown ....$15.00 – 25.00
2. Vase, 3½", first Hywood by Niloak, hand thrown ....$25.00 – 50.00
3. Duck, 3¾", unusual with two colors, Peterson design, "1868" sticker, castware..$25.00 – 35.00

PLATE 161

PLATE 162

(Left to right)

Top Row:

1. Pitcher with lid, 6½", Second art mark, hand thrown ....$75.00 – 100.00
2. Petal pitcher, 8¼", petal design, Niloak block letters ....$100.00 – 125.00

Middle Row:

1. Tank, 2½", Alley design, Niloak low relief.................................$50.00 – 75.00
2. Ball pitcher, 7½", Niloak low relief ....$35.00 – 45.00
   Similar item made by many other pottery companies.
3. Fox planter, 4½", Alley design, Niloak low relief.......................$35.00 – 45.00

Bottom Row:

1. Salt & pepper shakers, 2¼", "Potteries" sticker * ....$25.00 – 35.00
2. Bathtub, 1½", "Hot Springs, Arkansas,"
   Niloak low relief * ....$25.00 – 35.00
3. Creamer, 2", Alley design, Niloak low relief ....$15.00 – 25.00

* Camark Pottery produced an identical salt & pepper set as well as the miniature bathtub. The sticker on the salt and pepper is in mint condition. Although both the glaze and clay body is similar to Niloak's, we cannot exclude the possibility that these items, otherwise unmarked, are Camark and the result of an unscrupulous person. The bathtub shown has a permanent mark. It has also been manufactured by numerous other companies (including Camark) up to the present day.

Plate 162

Various Castware Pieces, unless noted

Plate 163

(Left to right)

Top Row:

1. Lamp, 10½", unmarked .... $50.00 – 100.00
2. Razorback ashtray, 1" x 5½" dia., *Maroon*, Lewis glaze, Niloak block letters .... N/A
3. Tulip vase, 7 holes, 7¼", *Ozark Blue*, Lewis glaze, Niloak low relief * .... 25.00 – 50.00

Middle Row:

1. Bowl, 9¼" x 1½", unmarked .... $15.00 – 25.00
2. Dish, 14" x 2¼", unmarked ** .... $25.00 – 35.00

Bottom Row:

1. Bowl, 7" x 3¾", Niloak low relief .... $15.00 – 25.00
2. Tray, 11" x 1½", *Ivory*, Lewis glaze, unmarked .... $25.00 – 50.00

* Uncommon tulip vase with seven holes.

** Camark Pottery made a similar item. This piece is probably a Joe Alley design as Alley performed free-lance work for the Camden-based plant. Alley did design Camark's three comical dogs (the most popular being the pointer and setter) as well as the three figurines, the old man, the old woman, and the hillbilly.

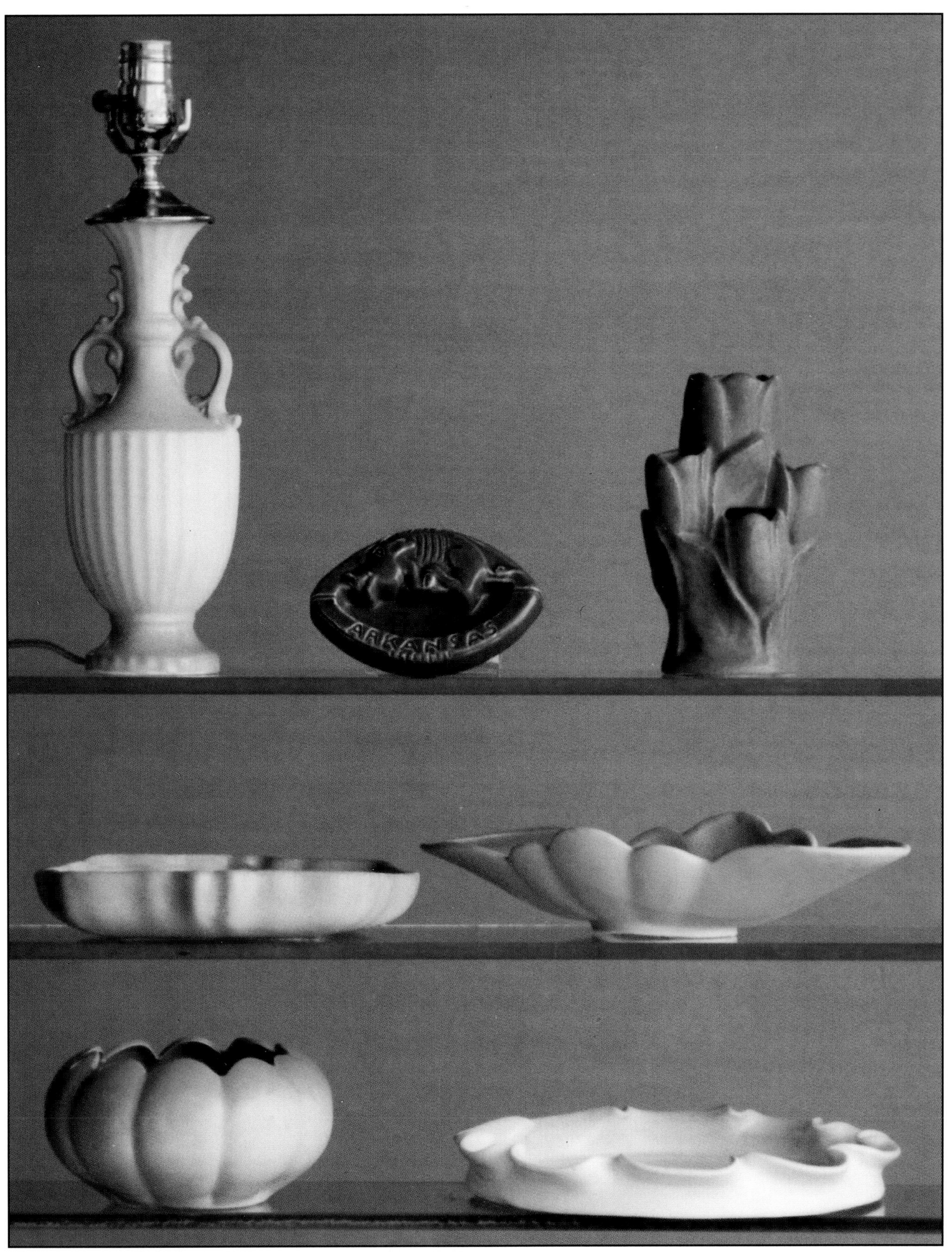

Plate 163

PLATE 164

(Left to right)

First Row: Joe Alley Designs

1. Cornucopia, 6", Niloak incised .... $15.00 – 25.00
2. Rose jar, 9", bouquet dinnerware, Niloak incised .... $50.00 – 75.00
3. Creamer, 4", Niloak low relief .... $10.00 – 15.00

Second Row:

1. Bird planter, 2¼", Peterson design, Niloak incised .... $10.00 – 15.00
2. Cup, 3", with saucer, 5", Bouquet dinnerware, Alley design, unmarked .... $15.00 – 25.00
3. Cannon, 2", Joe Alley design, unmarked * .... $15.00 – 25.00

Third Row:

1. Vase, 6¼", Niloak incised .... $10.00 – 15.00
2. Frog planter with hole in back, 5", Alley design, Niloak low relief and "1868" sticker .... $15.00 – 25.00
3. Squirrel planter, 6", Alley design, Niloak incised .... $10.00 – 15.00

Fourth Row:

1. Duck planter, 4½", Peterson design, Niloak low relief .... $10.00 – 15.00
2. Cabinet vase, 4", "N" low relief .... $10.00 – 15.00
3. Goat planter, 4¼", Peterson design, Niloak incised .... $100.00 – 150.00 (+/-)

* Since the publication of the first edition of this book, debate has ensued on whether or not this cannon was a product of Niloak Pottery. Joe Alley, Niloak's designer in the late 1930s and early 1940s, both offered and took responsibility for this cannon's design in correspondence and interviews with the author.

PLATE 164

Plate 165

(Left to right)

First Row: Joe Alley's Winged Victory Designs

1. Fan vase, 5¼", Niloak incised....................$15.00 – 25.00
2. Vase, 5½", Niloak low relief....................$15.00 – 25.00

Second Row:

1. Creamer, 4", Niloak low relief....................$15.00 – 25.00
2. Pitcher, 7", Bouquet dinnerware, Alley design, Niloak incised....................$25.00 – 35.00
3. Cow creamer, 4½", "Potteries" sticker *....................N/A

Third Row: Joe Alley Designs

1. Frog planter, 4¼", Niloak incised....................$15.00 – 25.00
2. Clown Drummer planter, 7½", Niloak incised **....................$25.00 – 35.00
3. Elephant planter, 6", "N" on drum, Niloak incised....................$10.00 – 15.00

Fourth Row:

1. Rabbit planter, 4¼", "1868" sticker....................$10.00 – 15.00
2. Shell-like vase, 3", "N" low relief....................$10.00 – 15.00
3. Bird planter, 2¼", Peterson design, Niloak incised....................$10.00 – 15.00
4. Cat planter, 4¼", "Potteries" sticker....................$10.00 – 15.00

* A similar cow creamer has been made by many companies, especially Japanese firms. This cow, located in the Gann Museum of Benton, has the Niloak characteristics of color glaze and clay. Although the "Potteries" sticker is not mutilated, no other piece has surfaced with or without a permanent mark.

** One of Joe Alley's "Stars of the Big Top" designs.

PLATE 165

Niloak
Castware

Plate 166

(Left to right)

Top Row:

1. Rooster planter, 8½", Niloak low relief ....$35.00 – 45.00
   Camark Pottery made similar item.
2. Peter Pan bowl, 7½", Alley design, Niloak low relief * ....$15.00 – 25.00
3. Mug, 6¾", "1868" sticker ....$15.00 – 25.00

Middle Row:

1. Cornucopia vase, 6½", Alley design, Niloak incised ....$15.00 – 25.00
2. Duck planter, 4½", wings extended (unusual),
   Niloak low relief ....$25.00 – 35.00
3. Cornucopia vase, 7", Alley design, Niloak incised ....$15.00 – 25.00

Bottom Row:

1. Scottie dog planter, 3½", Alley design, Niloak incised............$35.00 – 45.00
2. Frog on Lily Pad planter, 4", "Dicky Clay"
   in relief on pad, unmarked ** ....$50.00 – 75.00 (+/-)
3. Rabbit planter, 3¾", Peterson design, Niloak incised.............$10.00 – 15.00

* One of Joe Alley's "Bright Whimsies" designs.

** Dicky Clay, with manufacturing plant in Texarkana, Arkansas, produced clay piping and sewer connections. This is a promotional item for this company.

PLATE 166

PLATE 167

(Left to right)

First Row:

1. Monkey planter, 4", "Potteries" sticker .... $10.00 – 15.00
2. Creamer, 4", Niloak incised .... $10.00 – 15.00
3. Pitcher, 5", Alley design, painted flowers (underglaze decoration), Niloak incised, "1868" sticker .... $15.00 – 25.00

Second Row: Joe Alley Designs

1. Cornucopia vase, 7", Niloak incised .... $15.00 – 25.00
2. Handled vase, 6¾", Niloak incised .... $25.00 – 35.00
3. Shell vase, 5½", Niloak incised .... $15.00 – 25.00

Third Row: Joe Alley Designs

1. Siberia Polar Bear, 3¼", Niloak low relief * .... $35.00 – 45.00
2. Elephant planter, 6¼", on plain drum with trimmed ears, "1868" sticker .... $10.00 – 15.00
3. Double Rabbit planter, 4¾", Niloak low relief .... $15.00 – 25.00

Fourth Row: Joe Alley Designs

1. Clown and Donkey planter, 7", Niloak incised ** .... $35.00 – 45.00
   Surviving pieces with painted faces are the most desirable but the hardest to find.
2. Rabbit planter, 3½", Peterson design, Niloak incised .... $10.00 – 15.00
3. Circus Elephant planter, 7", from Circus Planter Group, Niloak incised** .... $35.00 – 45.00

* One of Joe Alley's Pacific Planters.

** Two of Joe Alley's "Stars of the Big Top" designs.

PLATE 167

Various Pieces

Plate 168

(Left to right)

Top Row:

1. Vase, 7¾", "Potteries" sticker .... $25.00 – 50.00
2. Pen holder, 3½" x 1½", unmarked .... $15.00 – 25.00
3. Pen holder, 3½" x 1¼", unmarked .... $15.00 – 25.00
4. Vase, 7", Joe Alley's Winged Victory design, Niloak .... $10.00 – 15.00

Middle Row: OOPS! *

1. Vase, 5¾", Niloak low relief ** .... $10.00 – 15.00
2. Vase, 5½", unmarked ** .... $10.00 – 15.00
3. Teddy Bear planter, 3¾", Niloak low relief .... $50.00 – 75.00
4. Vase, 5¾", Niloak low relief ** .... $10.00 – 15.00
5. Vase, 5¾", Niloak low relief ** .... $10.00 – 15.00

Bottom Row:

1. Mustard jar w/lid, 3½", unmarked .... $25.00 – 50.00
2. Sugar bowl, 3½" x 2½", "Potteries" sticker .... $15.00 – 25.00
3. Creamer, 4¼" x 3¼", "Potteries" sticker .... $15.00 – 25.00
4. Sugar bowl, 3", Niloak incised .... $10.00 – 15.00

* I simply failed to photograph these very common vases for the first Niloak book. The Teddy Bear planter, on the other hand, is rare!

** These vases are Joe Alley's Winged Victory designs.

Plate 168

Various Pieces

Plate 169

(Left to right)

Top Row:

1. Lamp, 9¾", Joe Alley's Winged Victory design, unmarked...$50.00 – 100.00
2. Double Deer, 7¼", Niloak incised ....$25.00 – 35.00
3. Vase, 6", "N" incised............$10.00 – 15.00

Middle Row: Colonial Teapot set

1. Sugar bowl w/lid, 3½", "Potteries" sticker ....$25.00 – 50.00
2. Teapot w/lid, 6½", "Potteries" sticker............$50.00 – 75.00
3. Creamer, 3", "Potteries" sticker............$25.00 – 50.00

Bottom Row:

1. Bowl, 2" x 5¾" dia., Niloak incised ....$10.00 – 15.00
2. Tray, 11½" x 6½" x 2¼", Niloak low relief............$25.00 – 35.00
3. Ashtray with fish, 3½" x 4", Niloak block letters ....N/A

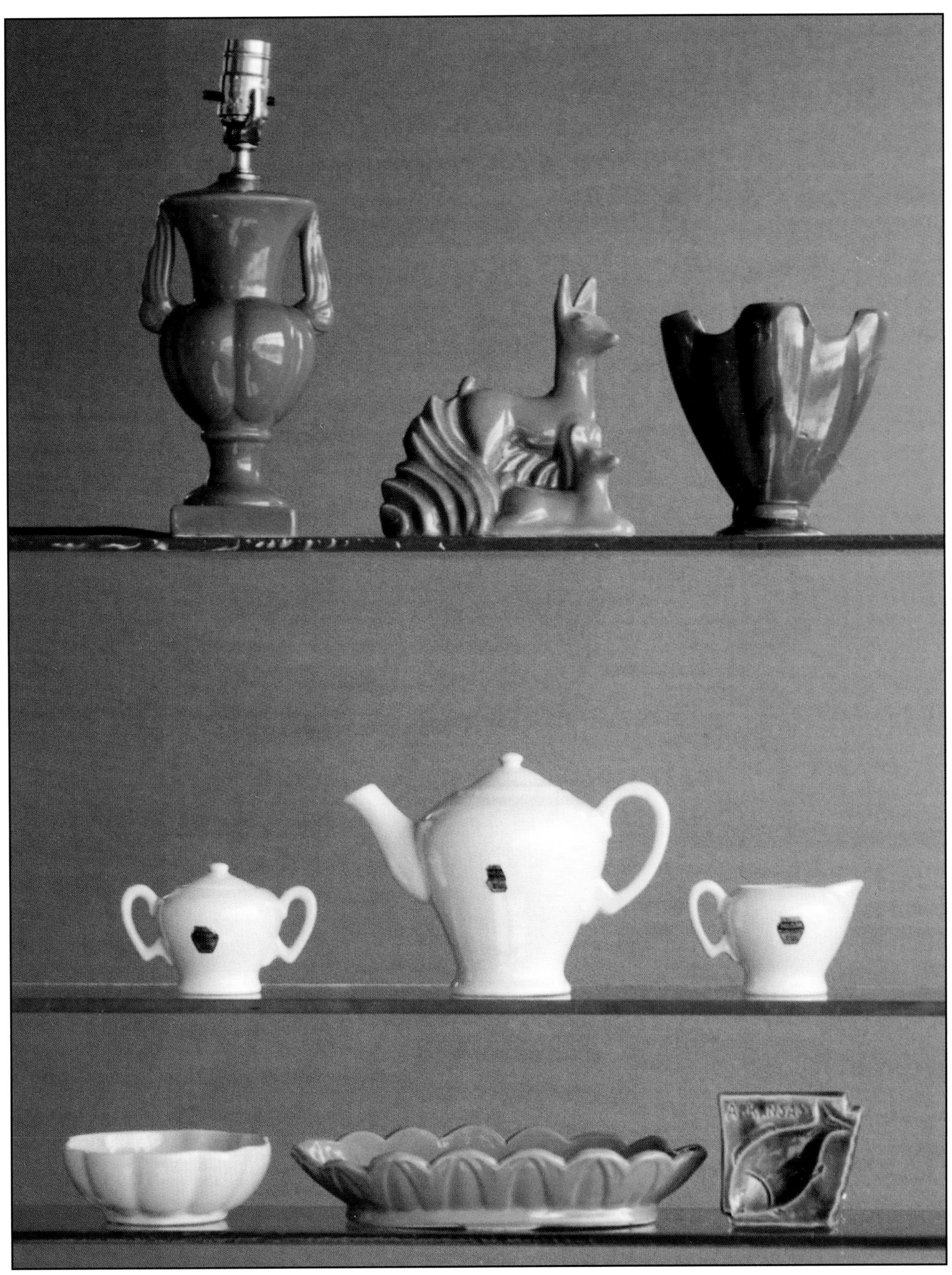

Plate 169

Alley's Bouquet Dinnerware

Plate 170

(Left to right)

Top Row:

1. Plate, 7¾", unmarked ....N/A
2. Pitcher, 7", Niloak incised ....$25.00 – 35.00

Middle Row:

1. Pitcher, 7¼", Niloak incised..N/A
2. Rose jar, 9¼", unmarked..$50.00 – 75.00

Bottom Row:

1. Serving bowl, 2½" x 10¼", unmarked ....N/A
2. Platter, 13" x 10¼", unmarked ....N/A

PLATE 170

Alley's Bouquet Dinnerware

Plate 171

(Left to right)

Top Row:

1. Plate, 6½" square, unmarked .... N/A
2. Bowl, 5½" square, "Bouquet" ink stamp .... N/A

Middle Row:

1. Mug, 3½", Niloak incised .... $5.00 – 10.00
2. Mug, 3½", Niloak incised .... $5.00 – 10.00
3. Mug, 3½", Niloak incised .... $5.00 – 10.00

Bottom Row:

1. Creamer, 6¾" x 2¾", "Bouquet" ink stamp .... N/A
2. Cup, 3" & saucer, 5", Niloak incised .... $15.00 – 25.00
3. Sugar bowl, 2¾" x 6¾" dia., unmarked .... N/A

PLATE 171

Eagle Stoneware

Plate 172

(Left to right)

1. Jug, 3 gallons, Eagle circle ink stamp ....$200.00 – 250.00
2. Crock, 2 gallons, Eagle circle ink stamp................................$150.00 – 200.00

Plate 173

(Left to right)

1. Jug, 5 gallons, Eagle circle ink stamp ....$250.00 – 300.00
2. Crock, 3 gallons, Eagle circle ink stamp................................$200.00 – 250.00

Eagle and Niloak Stoneware

Plate 174

(Left to right)

1. Water cooler, 6 gallons, Eagle circle ink stamp...N/A
2. Water cooler, 6 gallons, Niloak block ink stamp ....N/A

PLATE 172

PLATE 173

PLATE 174

PLATE 175

Cookie jar, 8½", mold mark "Niloak"...N/A

PLATE 176*

(Left to right)

Top Row:

1. Bowl, 11¾" x 5½", mold mark "Niloak 3" ....$75.00 – 100.00
2. Candlestick, 8¼", unmarked ....$25.00 – 50.00

Middle Row:

1. Bowl/lid, 4¾" x 10", mold mark "Niloak 2, Benton, Ark.".....$100.00 – 150.00
2. Canister/lid, 5¼", Niloak block letters ....$50.00 – 100.00
3. Bowl/lid, 4" x 8¼", mold mark "Niloak 100, Benton, Ark.".....$75.00 – 125.00

Bottom Row:

1. Water cooler, 10½", unmarked...$100.00 – 150.00
2. Chicken waterer, 7½", mold mark, "Niloak 147, Benton, Ark." ..$50.00 – 100.00
3. Churn, 11", mold mark "Niloak" ....$100.00 – 150.00

PLATE 175

* With the exception of the Navy coffee mug (see page 297), the mold marks for these items are not included in this publication. The marks are located either on the lids, bottoms, or on the outer part of a particular piece. They are similar in style to the Niloak circular mold mark (see page 51). It is common to find the canister with the standard Niloak block letters mark.

Plate 176

NILOAK
ALLEY'S NAVY MUG

PLATE 177

Navy coffee mug, 3¾", mold mark "Niloak, Benton, Ark." ....N/A

NILOAK FAKE
VASE

PLATES 178 & 179

Vase, 8½", die stamp mark ....Worthless!

Within the last year or so, this Grueby-like, mustard glaze vase appeared on the secondary market. Norman Haas, past president of the American Art Pottery Association bought it (knowing it was a fake) and sent it to me. Yes, it is a fake big time! Not only is the shape out of character for Niloak Pottery, but the mark is totally different from any marks Niloak created. As for the glaze, it could vaguely resemble a 1940s Niloak glaze.

In addition, the small bunny rabbit planter (see plate 166) has been reproduced with a glossy black glaze. It is super lightweight, made with bright white clay, and the black glossy glaze in no way compares to Niloak's *Mirror Black*. Finally, as with most tangible things, there is a certain feel or a certain way something looks or appears. The best defense is to learn these intangible aspects. Be careful!

PLATE 177

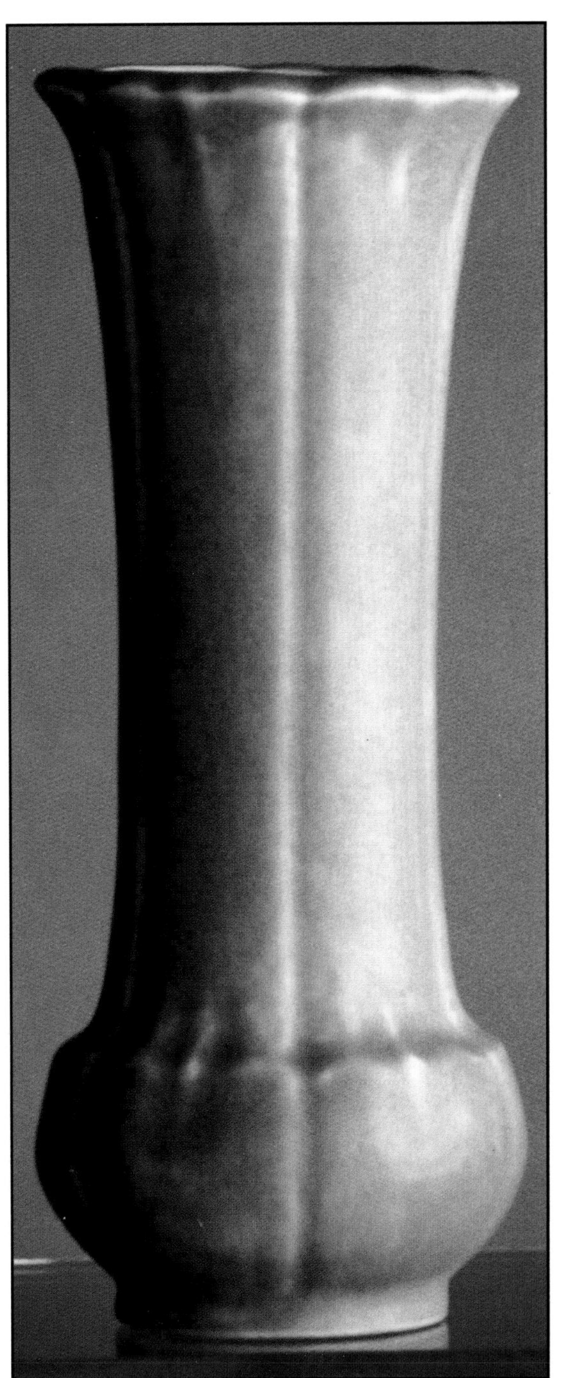

PLATE 179

PLATE 178

NILOAK/HYWOOD POTTERY CATALOGS

NILOAK
Pottery
MADE IN ARKANSAS
F. W. Sanders & Co.
LITTLE ROCK, ARK.

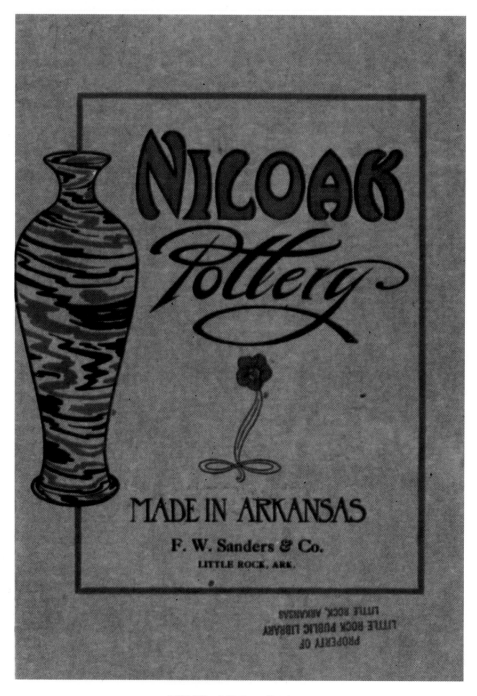

1910 Niloak Pottery Catalog.
Courtesy of the Butler Center for Arkansas Studies, Central Arkansas Library System.

THE soft and soothing blends of a bit of NILOAK POTTERY are readily appreciated by people of refinement and taste, and is in direct contrast to the gaudy and high-colored imported wares with which the market has recently been flooded. Furthermore, it is unique, inexpensive, and cannot be duplicated. As a souvenir from Arkansas, a wedding or anniversary gift, can you think of anything that would be more acceptable?

1910 Niloak Pottery Catalog.
Courtesy of the Butler Center for Arkansas Studies, Central Arkansas Library System.

Niloak Pottery

ITS ORIGIN AND MANUFACTURE

COMMON pottery wares have been manufactured in Arkansas for many years, but it may be of interest to the reader to know that the manufacture of Art Pottery in Arkansas, as well as in the entire South, is entirely new; the first successful line of Art Pottery being turned out by this pottery early in January, 1910. The pottery, located near Benton, Arkansas, twenty-two miles from Little Rock, is in the heart of large fields of potter's clay, and thus commands the world's attention for what may be expected from Arkansas in Art Pottery.

NILOAK POTTERY is made from kaolin (clay without sand), from which it derives its name, the word being spelled backward. It closely resembles the pottery made by the Indians, and, we judge by specimens of their pottery that the same clay must have been used, and, like their pottery, each piece is moulded by hand. Their crudeness being overcome by modern methods gives to our pottery perfect symmetry and individuality.

The process of coloring and mixing the clay which brings out the unique effects obtained is the secret of the manufacturer. No two pieces take the distribution of the coloring matter alike, thereby rendering each piece distinct. The prevailing colors are blue, brown, slate intermingled with white, forming a grain effect, and resembles petrified wood. The illustrations herein contained, while being the best obtainable, fail to do justice to the beauty of the ware itself. Fully realizing the possibilities and merits of this ware, we have secured the sole selling agency for NILOAK POTTERY.

In making your selections from the catalogue, please bear in mind that we cannot duplicate the cuts exactly, but will endeavor to do so as nearly as possible.

F. W. SANDERS & CO.
Little Rock, Ark.

1910 Niloak Pottery Catalog.
Courtesy of the Butler Center for Arkansas Studies, Central Arkansas Library System.

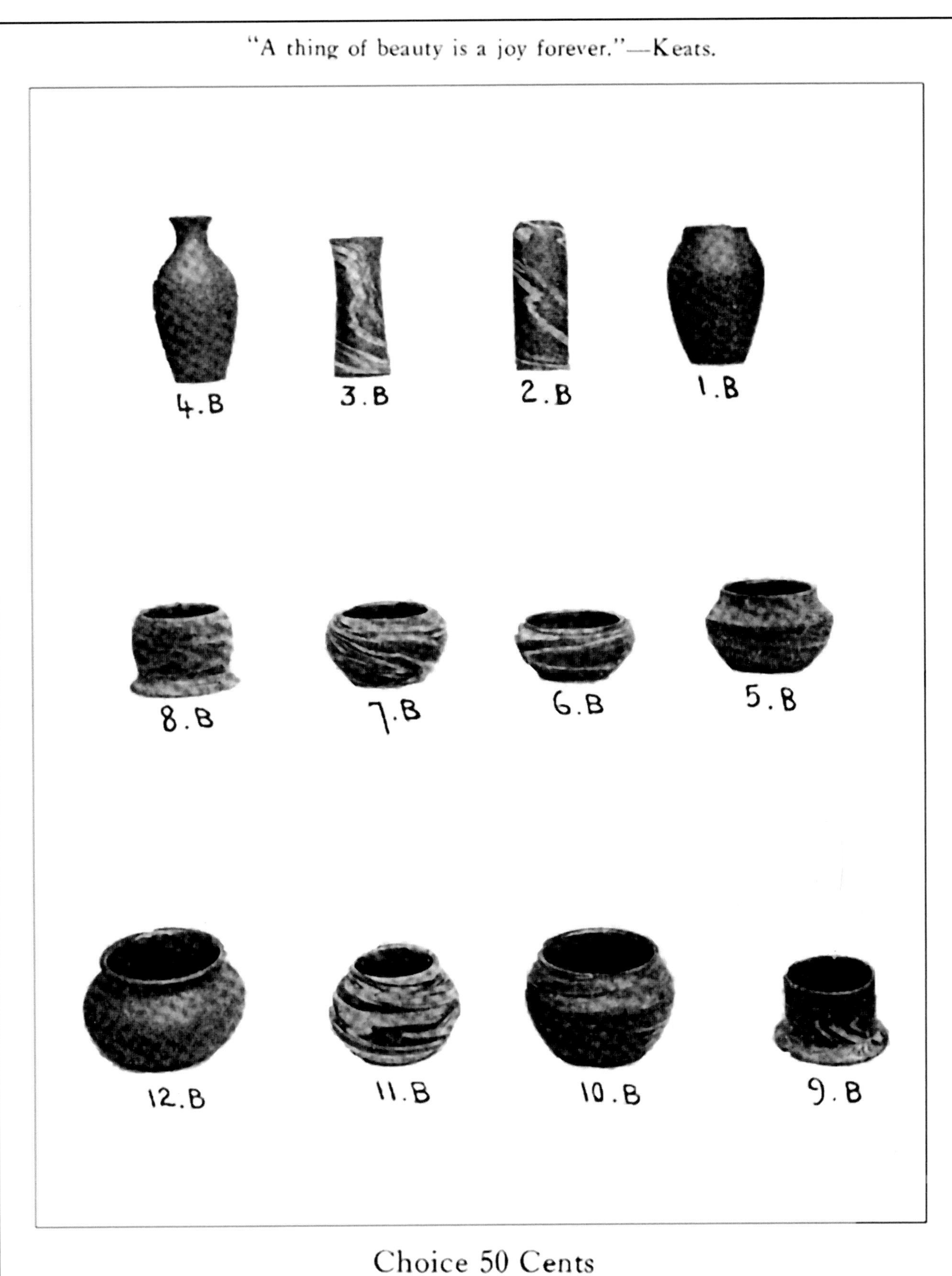

"A thing of beauty is a joy forever."—Keats.

Choice 50 Cents

Illustrations one-fifth actual size

1910 Niloak Pottery Catalog.
Courtesy of the Butler Center for Arkansas Studies, Central Arkansas Library System.

"Beauty is truth, truth beauty."—Keats.

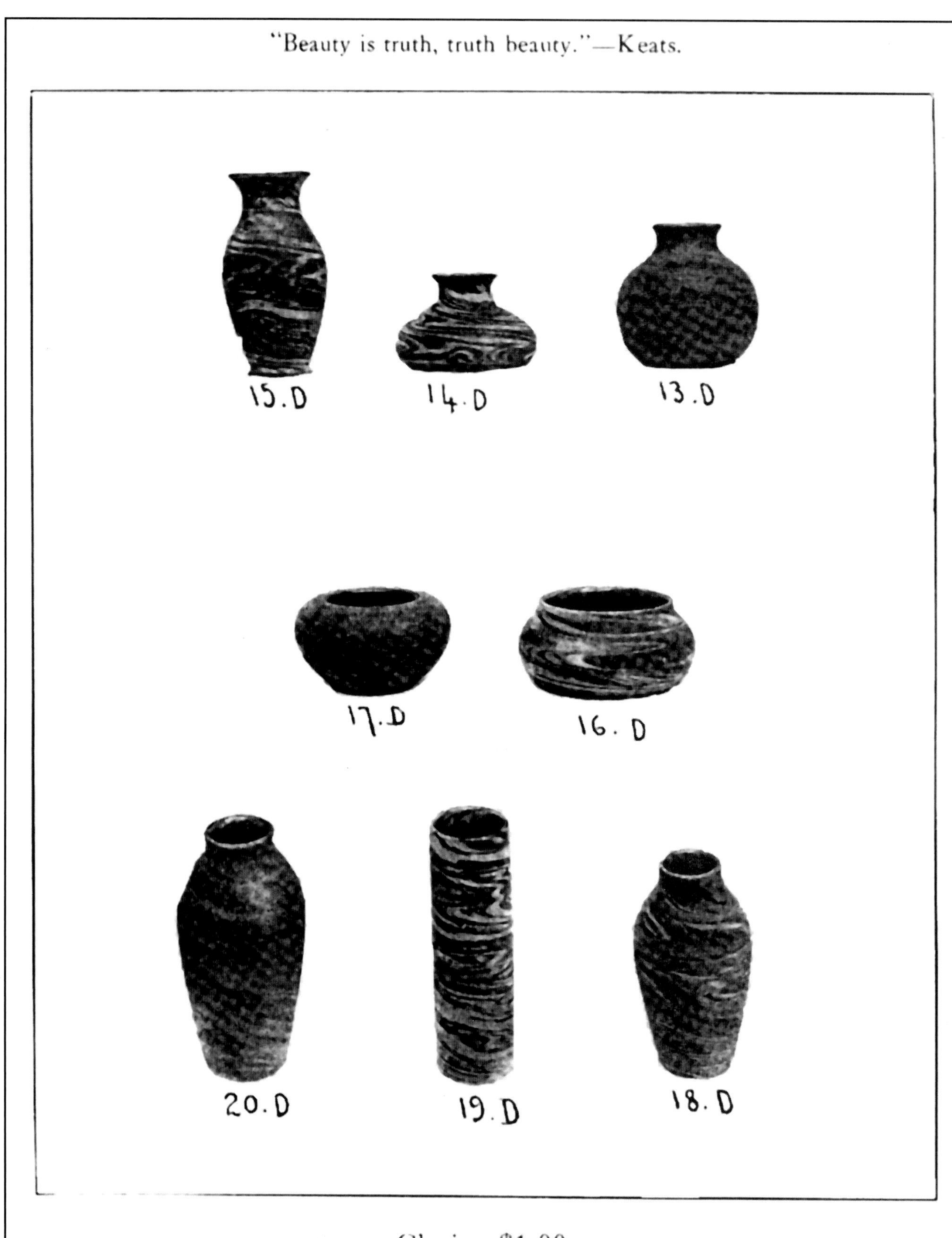

Choice $1.00

Illustrations one-fifth actual size.

1910 Niloak Pottery Catalog.
Courtesy of the Butler Center for Arkansas Studies, Central Arkansas Library System.

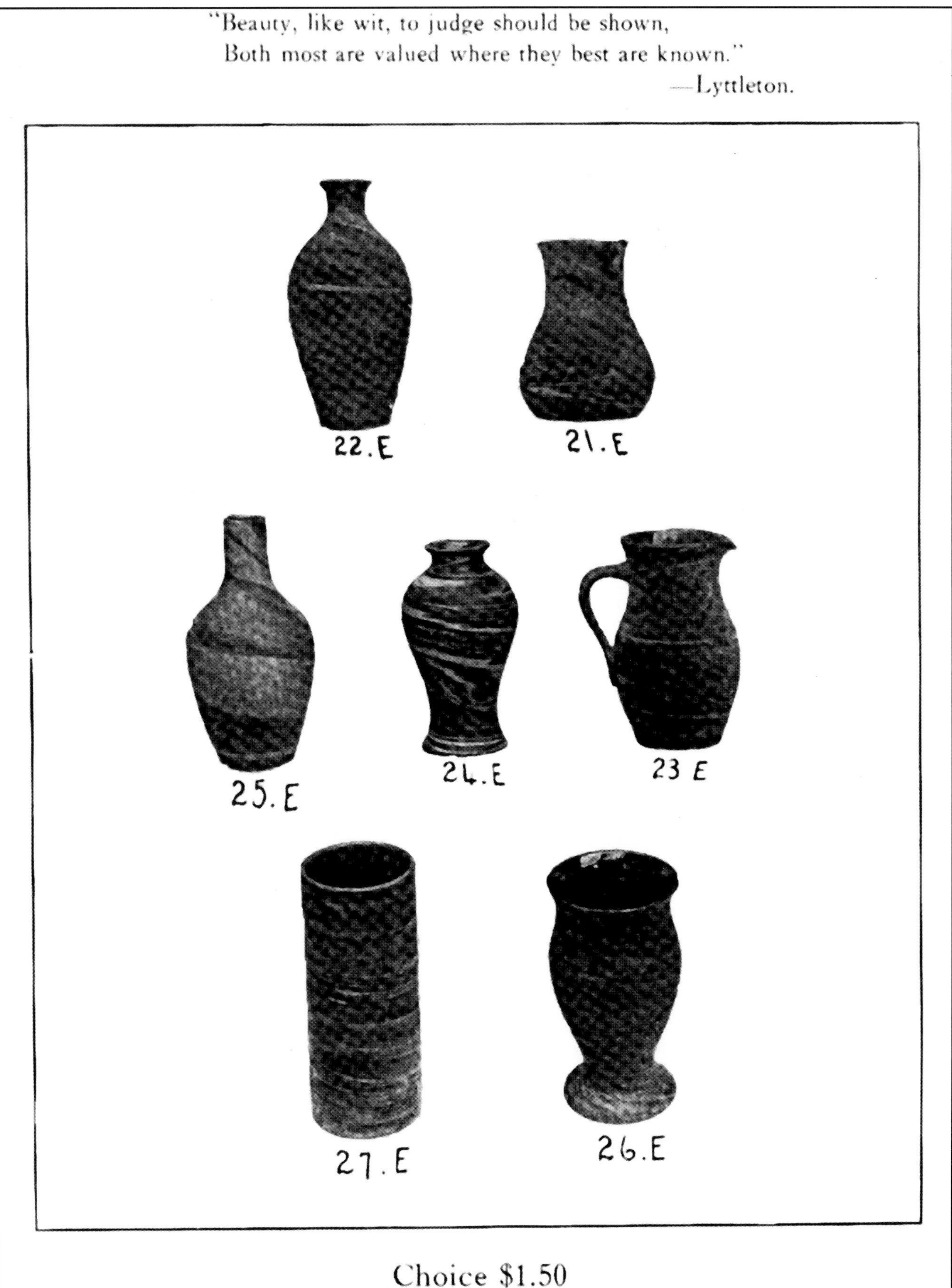

"Beauty, like wit, to judge should be shown,
Both most are valued where they best are known."

—Lyttleton.

Choice $1.50

1910 Niloak Pottery Catalog.
Courtesy of the Butler Center for Arkansas Studies, Central Arkansas Library System.

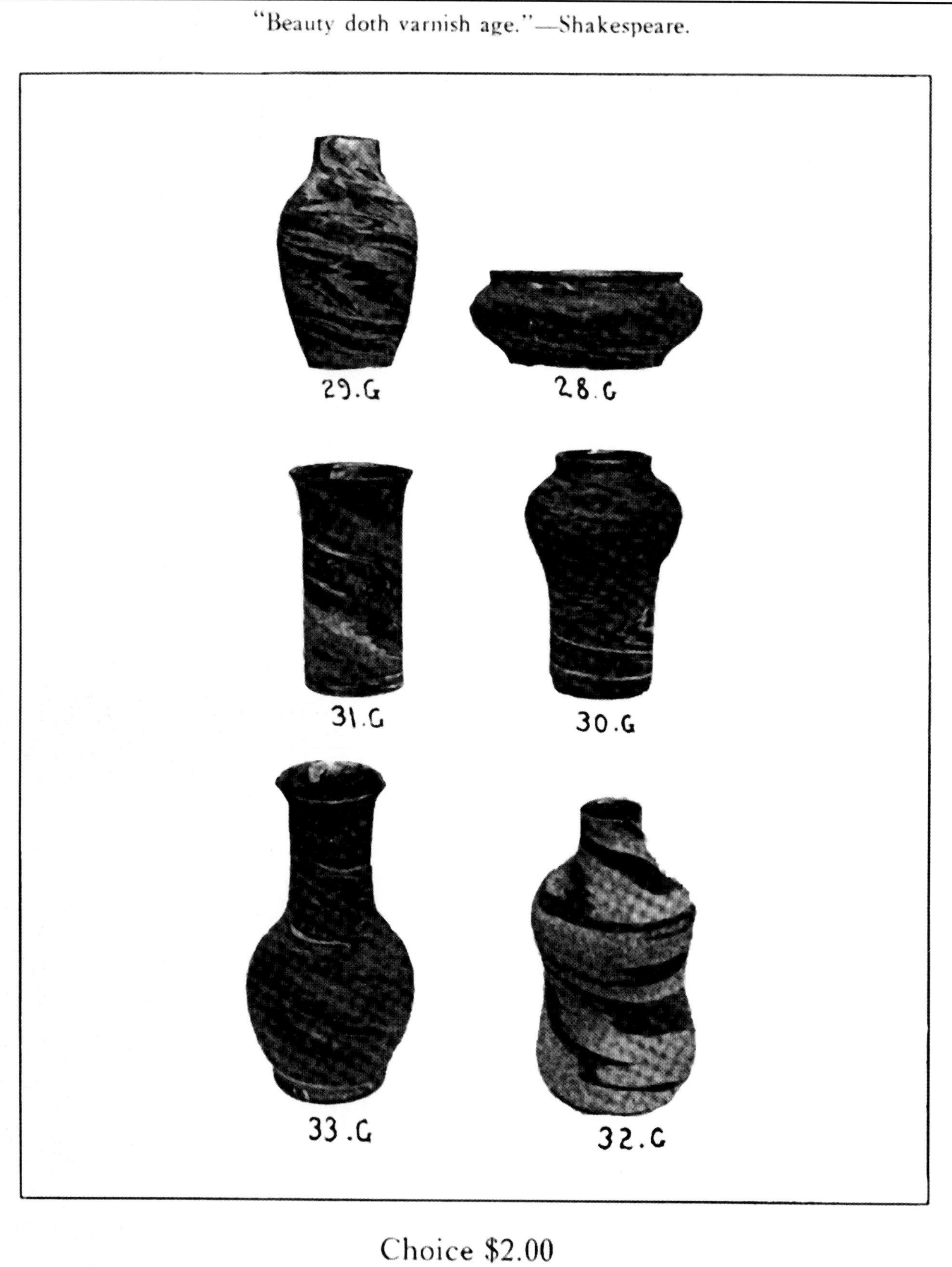

"Beauty doth varnish age."—Shakespeare.

29.G 28.G

31.G 30.G

33.G 32.G

Choice $2.00

Illustrations one-fifth actual size.

1910 Niloak Pottery Catalog.
Courtesy of the Butler Center for Arkansas Studies, Central Arkansas Library System.

"Beauty was lent to nature as the type of heaven's unspeakable and holy joy."—S. J. Hale.

36.H 35.H 34.H

39.H 38.H 37.H

42.H 41.H 40.H

Choice $2.50

Illustrations one-fifth actual size.

1910 Niloak Pottery Catalog.
Courtesy of the Butler Center for Arkansas Studies, Central Arkansas Library System.

Niloak Pottery—Useful, Ornamental, Unique—Made in Arkansas.

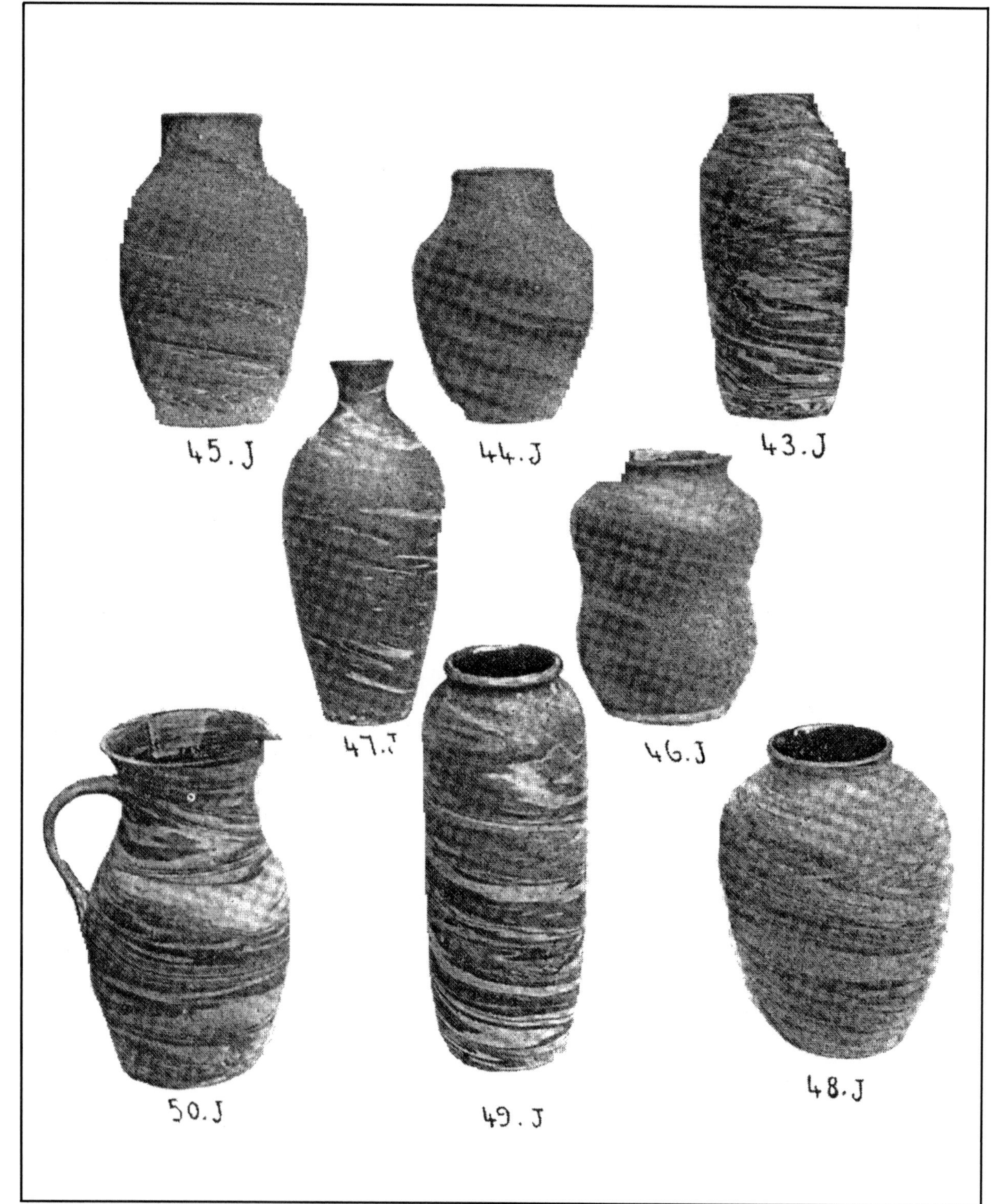

Choice $3.50

Illustrations one-fifth actual size.

1910 Niloak Pottery Catalog.
Courtesy of the Butler Center for Arkansas Studies, Central Arkansas Library System.

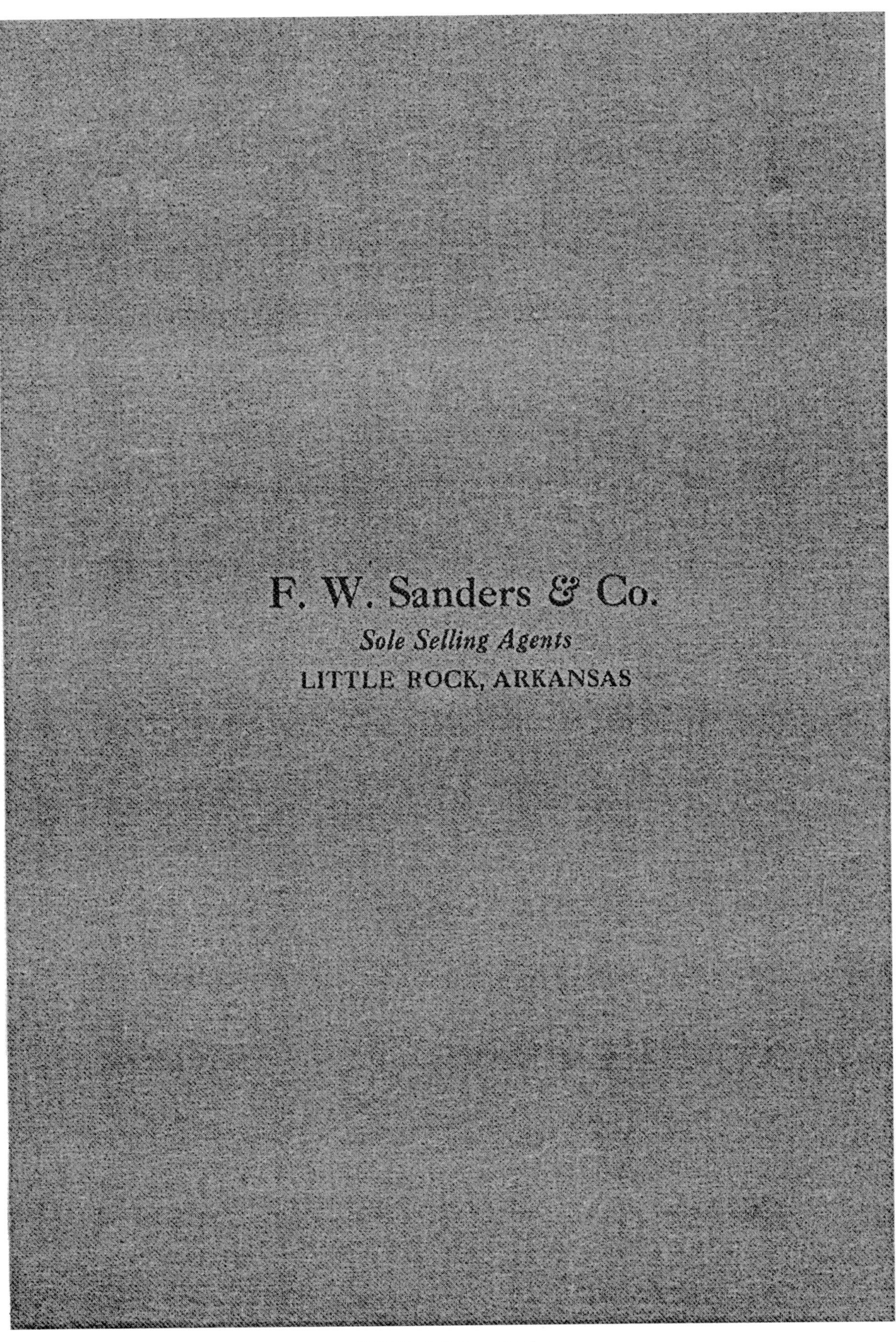

1910 Niloak Pottery Catalog.
Courtesy of the Butler Center for Arkansas Studies, Central Arkansas Library System.

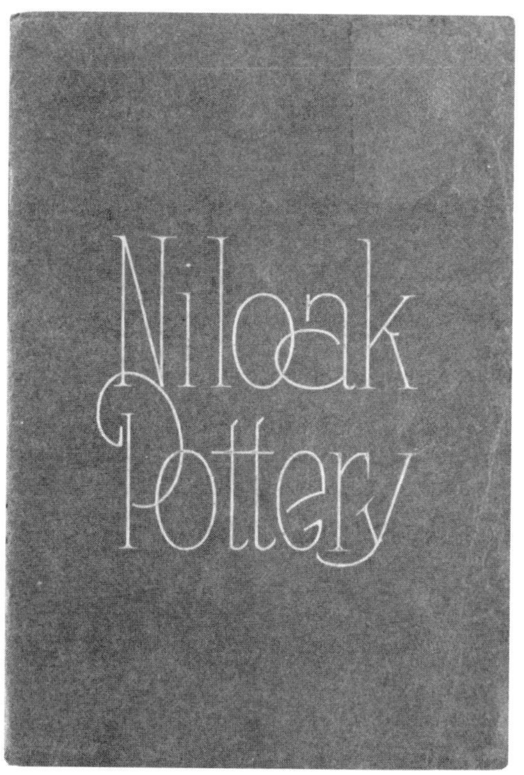

NILOAK Pottery is made by hand from natural color clays found in restricted beds in the foot hills of the Ozark Mountains. It is probable that no other part of the world contains so desirable a class of clay for the making of art pottery. No color seen in other pottery, either natural or artificial, is as beautiful in tone or decorative in value as are the beautiful colors seen in Niloak.

For several years the designers and potters creating this unique ware have been studying and experimenting, with the result that Niloak has been raised to the highest point of art excellence. Quite recently the pottery has been standardized as to shapes, sizes and colors and is now being offered to collectors and fine art shops at as moderate prices as are consistent with uniform excellence and artistic worth.

Niloak Pottery is based upon classic designs, avoiding the commonplace, yet introducing forms of practical usefulness, such as vases, bowls, ash trays, candlesticks, etc. The surface of the ware shows a charming and irregular variety of tones, no two pieces of the pottery ever occurring the same in this particular. The general tone, however, is uniform employing a wonderfully soft subtle blue with one or two shades of brown, containing also occasional grays produced by the combining of these colors.

1913 Niloak Pottery Catalog.
Courtesy of Kenneth Mauney.

Niloak Pottery is thoroughly artistic, is different from any other class of art ware and is reasonable as to price. These three facts are sufficient explanation of the remarkable vogue attending the pottery at this time. Each individual piece is shaped and finished by an artist and the process is a slow and careful one. Therefore the output is limited and in offering this catalogue we urge everyone who has not seen examples of the ware to send immediately 80 cents in stamps for a small exquisite vase especially prepared at this time to acquaint the public with the colors and texture and general character of Niloak Pottery.

Address all communications to

~~BROWN-ROBERTSON-COMPANY~~
~~707 Fifth Avenue, New York City, N. Y.~~

THE NILOAK POTTERY.
BENTON, ARK

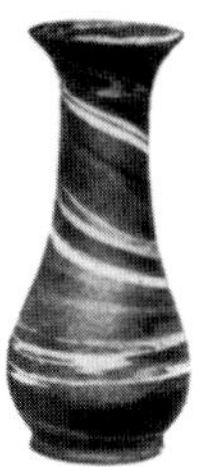

A B VASE
Sizes from 8 to 18 inches
Prices from \$2.00 to \$11.00

E B VASE
Sizes from 6 to 18 inches
Prices from \$1.50 to \$11.00

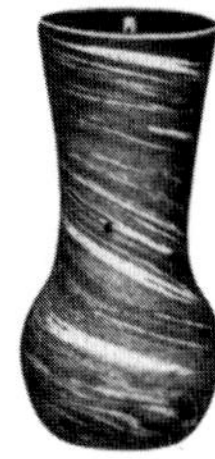

B B VASE
Sizes from 8 to 18 inches
Prices from \$2.00 to \$11.00

F B VASE
Sizes from 6 to 14 inches
Prices from \$1.50 to \$7.00

1913 Niloak Pottery Catalog.
Courtesy of Kenneth Mauney.

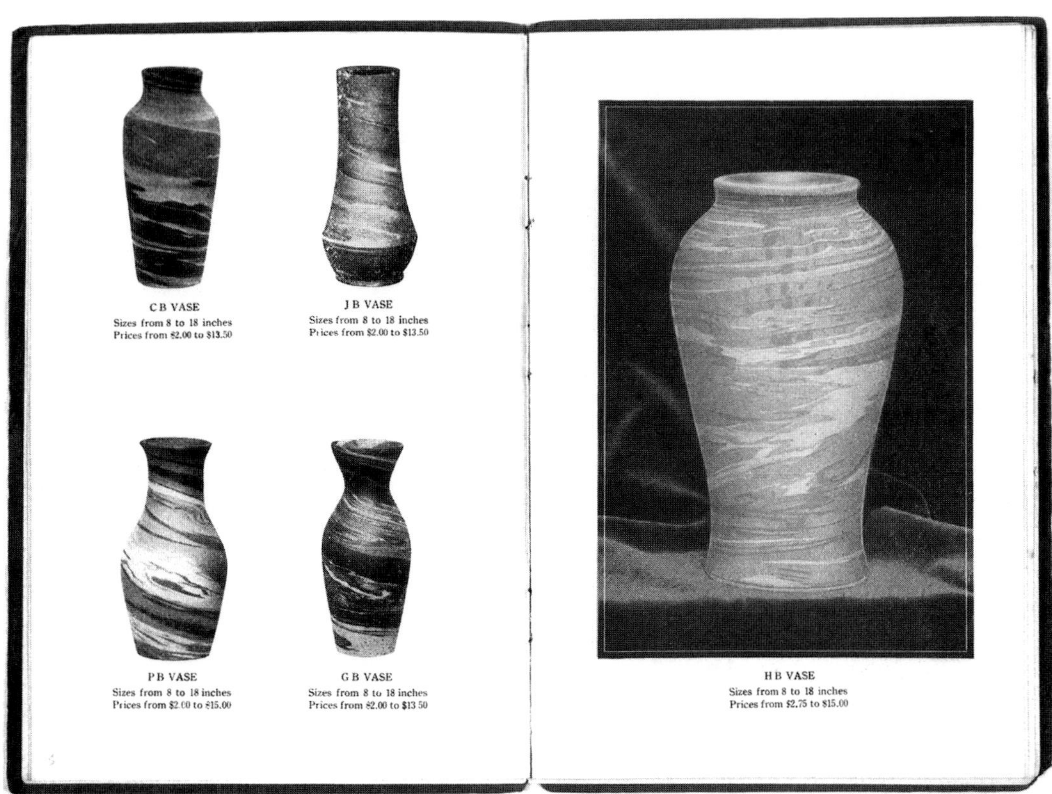

1913 Niloak Pottery Catalog.
Courtesy of Kenneth Mauney.

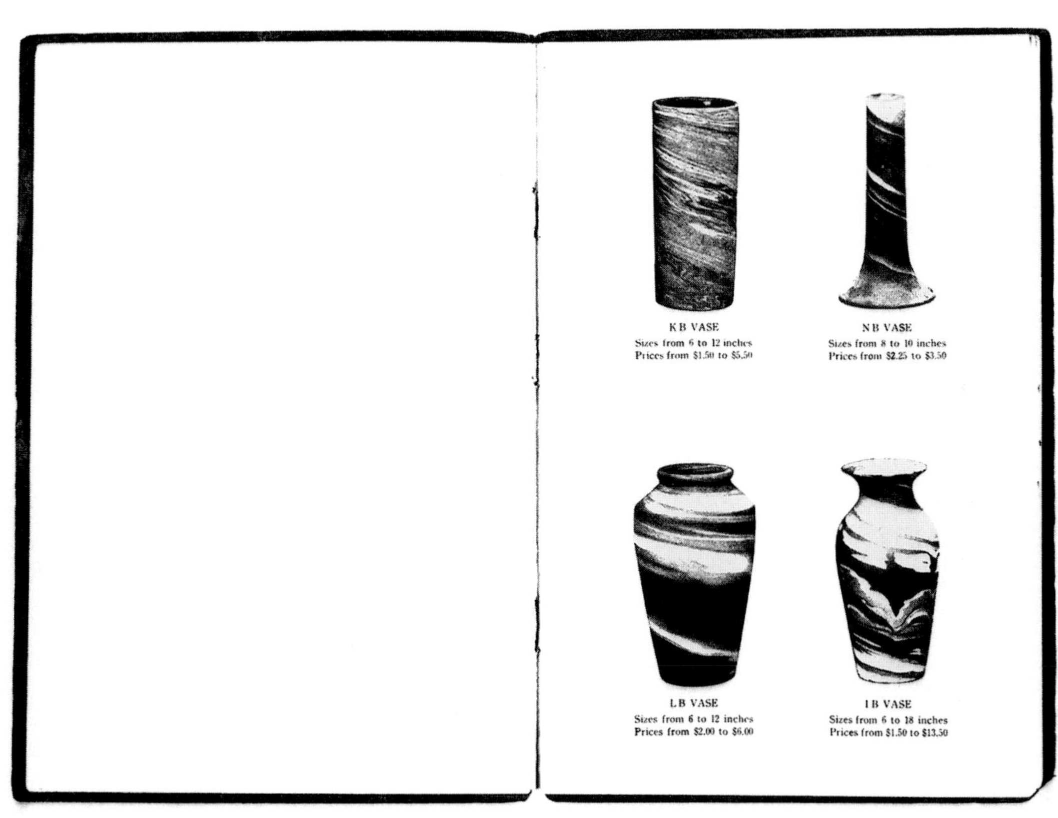

1913 Niloak Pottery Catalog.
Courtesy of Kenneth Mauney.

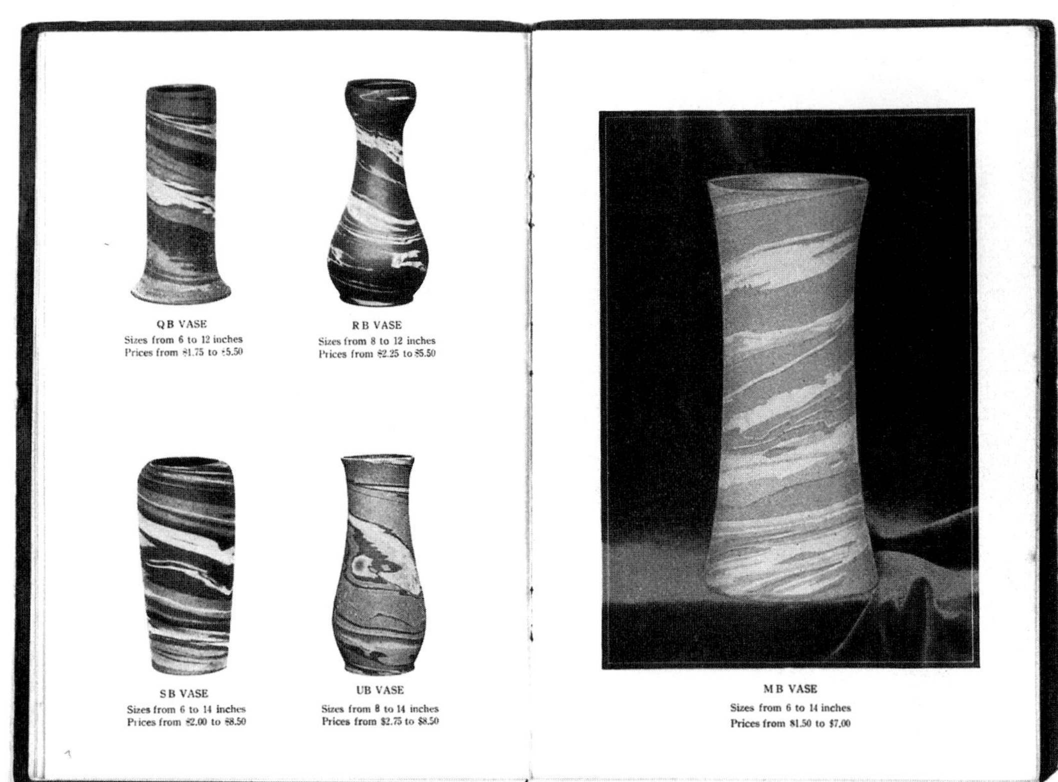

Q B VASE
Sizes from 6 to 12 inches
Prices from $1.75 to $5.50

R B VASE
Sizes from 8 to 12 inches
Prices from $2.25 to $5.50

S B VASE
Sizes from 6 to 14 inches
Prices from $2.00 to $8.50

UB VASE
Sizes from 8 to 14 inches
Prices from $2.75 to $8.50

M B VASE
Sizes from 6 to 14 inches
Prices from $1.50 to $7.00

1913 Niloak Pottery Catalog.
Courtesy of Kenneth Mauney.

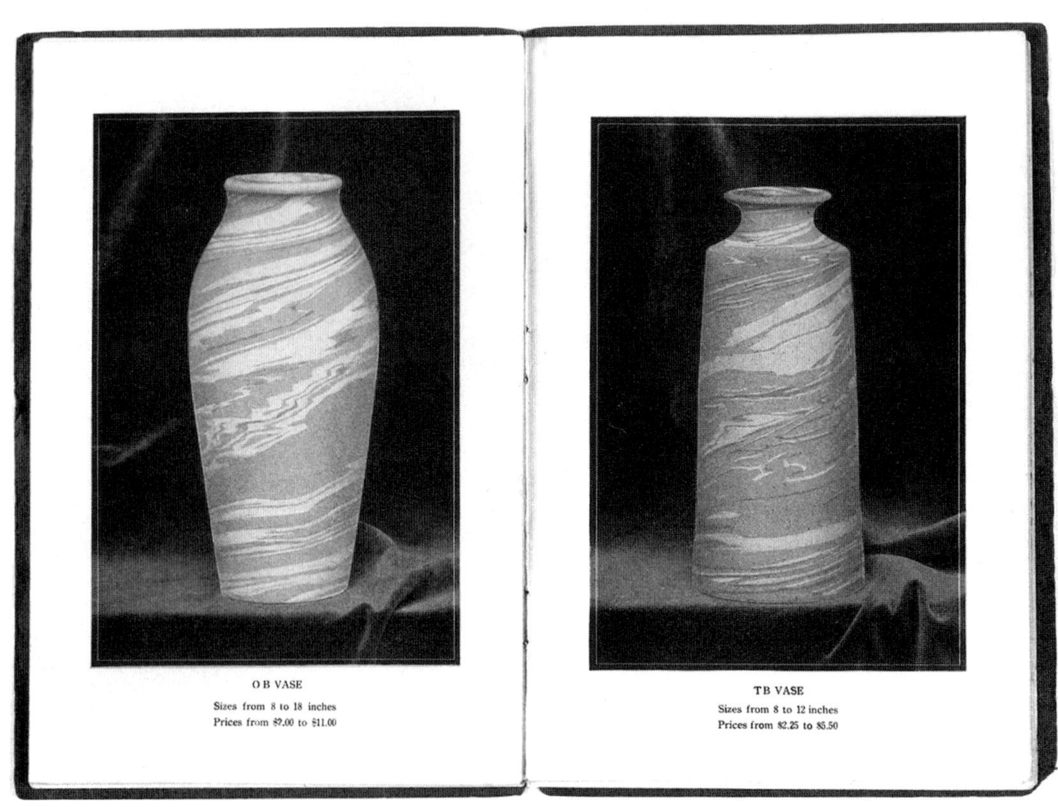

O B VASE
Sizes from 8 to 18 inches
Prices from $7.00 to $11.00

TB VASE
Sizes from 8 to 12 inches
Prices from $2.25 to $5.50

1913 Niloak Pottery Catalog.
Courtesy of Kenneth Mauney.

No.1110 CANDLESTICK 10 inches high
Price $3.25

V B VASE
Sizes from 6 to 16 inches
Prices from $2.00 to $14.00

W B VASE
Sizes from 2 to 6 inches
Prices from $1.00 to $3.25

X B VASE
Sizes from 3 to 6 inches
Prices from $1.00 to $2.75

Z B BOWL
Sizes from 2 to 6 inches
Prices from $1.00 to $5.50

1913 Niloak Pottery Catalog.
Courtesy of Kenneth Mauney.

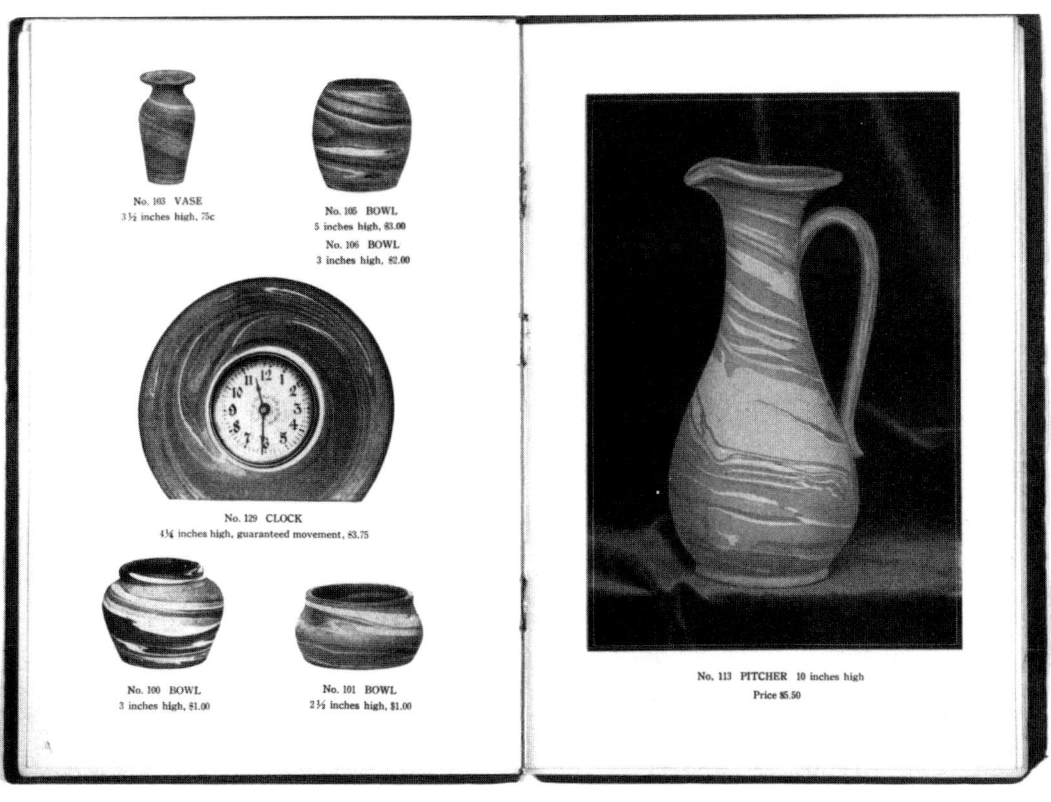
No. 103 VASE
3½ inches high, 75c

No. 105 BOWL
5 inches high, $3.00
No. 106 BOWL
3 inches high, $2.00

No. 129 CLOCK
4¾ inches high, guaranteed movement, $3.75

No. 100 BOWL
3 inches high, $1.00

No. 101 BOWL
2½ inches high, $1.00

No. 113 PITCHER 10 inches high
Price $5.50

1913 Niloak Pottery Catalog.
Courtesy of Kenneth Mauney.

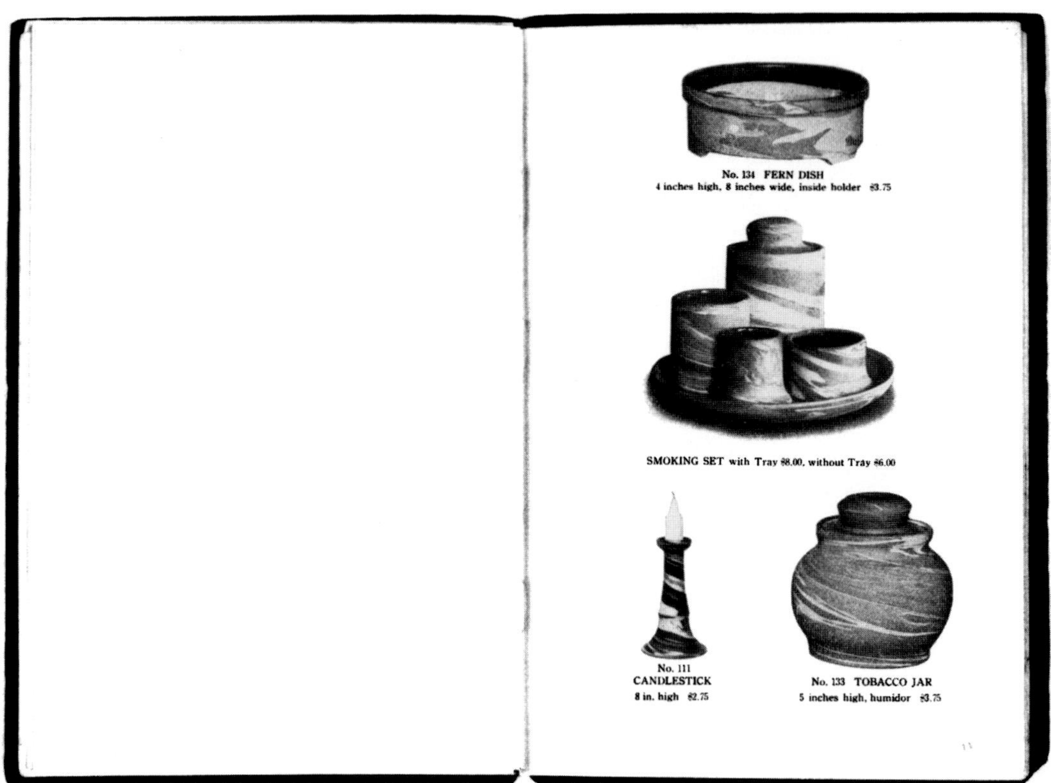

No. 134 FERN DISH
4 inches high, 8 inches wide, inside holder $3.75

SMOKING SET with Tray $8.00, without Tray $6.00

No. 111
CANDLESTICK
8 in. high $2.75

No. 133 TOBACCO JAR
5 inches high, humidor $3.75

1913 Niloak Pottery Catalog.
Courtesy of Kenneth Mauney.

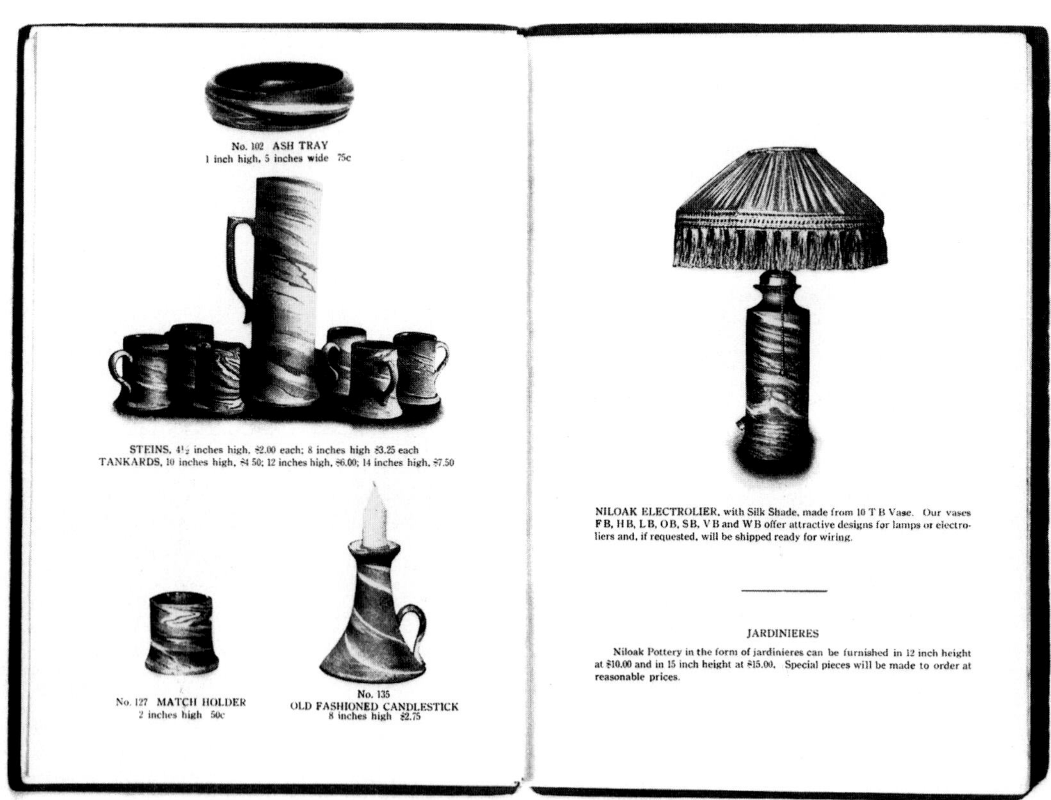

No. 102 ASH TRAY
1 inch high, 5 inches wide 75c

STEINS, 4½ inches high, $2.00 each; 8 inches high $3.25 each
TANKARDS, 10 inches high, $4.50; 12 inches high, $6.00; 14 inches high, $7.50

No. 127 MATCH HOLDER
2 inches high 50c

No. 135
OLD FASHIONED CANDLESTICK
8 inches high $2.75

NILOAK ELECTROLIER, with Silk Shade, made from 10 T B Vase. Our vases F B, H B, L B, O B, S B, V B and W B offer attractive designs for lamps or electroliers and, if requested, will be shipped ready for wiring.

JARDINIERES

Niloak Pottery in the form of jardinieres can be furnished in 12 inch height at $10.00 and in 15 inch height at $15.00. Special pieces will be made to order at reasonable prices.

1913 Niloak Pottery Catalog.
Courtesy of Kenneth Mauney.

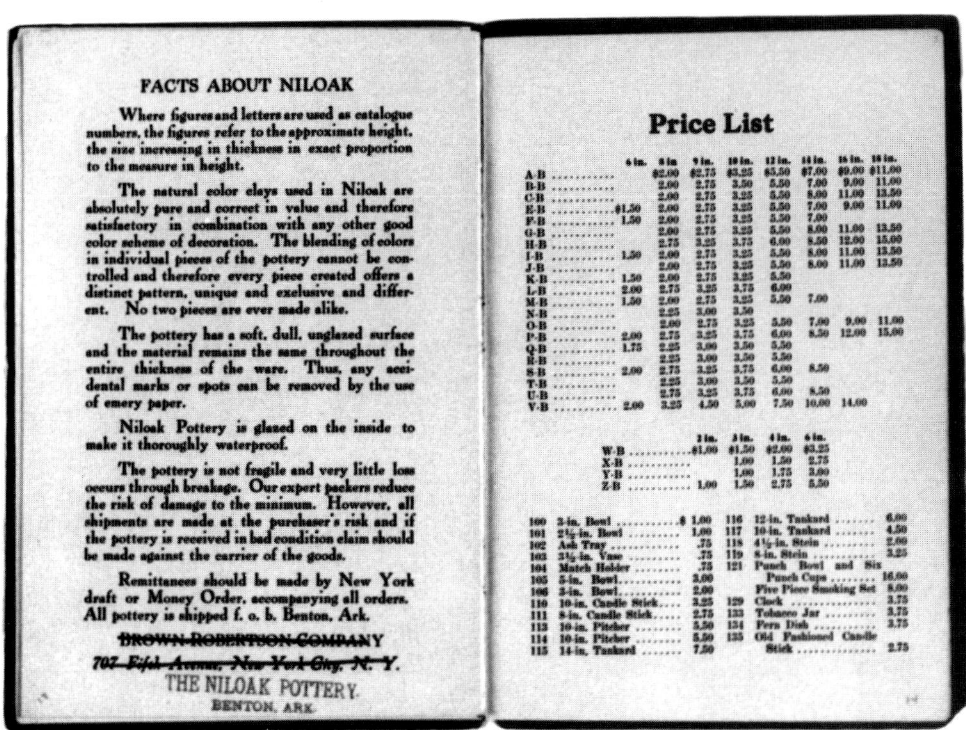

FACTS ABOUT NILOAK

Where figures and letters are used as catalogue numbers, the figures refer to the approximate height, the size increasing in thickness in exact proportion to the measure in height.

The natural color clays used in Niloak are absolutely pure and correct in value and therefore satisfactory in combination with any other good color scheme of decoration. The blending of colors in individual pieces of the pottery cannot be controlled and therefore every piece created offers a distinct pattern, unique and exclusive and different. No two pieces are ever made alike.

The pottery has a soft, dull, unglazed surface and the material remains the same throughout the entire thickness of the ware. Thus, any accidental marks or spots can be removed by the use of emery paper.

Niloak Pottery is glazed on the inside to make it thoroughly waterproof.

The pottery is not fragile and very little loss occurs through breakage. Our expert packers reduce the risk of damage to the minimum. However, all shipments are made at the purchaser's risk and if the pottery is received in bad condition claim should be made against the carrier of the goods.

Remittances should be made by New York draft or Money Order, accompanying all orders. All pottery is shipped f. o. b. Benton, Ark.

~~BROWN-ROBERTSON-COMPANY~~

~~707 Fifth Avenue, New York City, N. Y.~~

THE NILOAK POTTERY.
BENTON, ARK.

Price List

	6 in.	8 in	9 in.	10 in.	12 in.	14 in.	16 in.	18 in.
A-B		$2.00	$2.75	$3.25	$5.50	$7.00	$9.00	$11.00
B-B		2.00	2.75	3.50	5.50	7.00	9.00	11.00
C-B		2.00	2.75	3.25	5.50	8.00	11.00	13.50
E-B	$1.50	2.00	2.75	3.25	5.50	7.00	9.00	11.00
F-B	1.50	2.00	2.75	3.25	5.50	7.00		
G-B		2.00	2.75	3.25	5.50	8.00	11.00	13.50
H-B		2.75	3.25	3.75	6.00	8.50	12.00	15.00
I-B	1.50	2.00	2.75	3.25	5.50	8.00	11.00	13.50
J-B		2.00	2.75	3.25	5.50	8.00	11.00	13.50
K-B	1.50	2.00	2.75	3.25	5.50			
L-B	2.00	2.75	3.25	3.75	6.00			
M-B	1.50	2.00	2.75	3.25	5.50	7.00		
N-B		2.25	3.00	3.50				
O-B		2.00	2.75	3.25	5.50	7.00	9.00	11.00
P-B	2.00	2.75	3.25	3.75	6.00	8.50	12.00	15.00
Q-B	1.75	2.25	3.00	3.50	5.50			
R-B		2.25	3.00	3.50	5.50			
S-B	2.00	2.75	3.25	3.75	6.00	8.50		
T-B		2.25	3.00	3.50	5.50			
U-B		2.75	3.25	3.75	6.00	8.50		
V-B	2.00	3.25	4.50	5.00	7.50	10.00	14.00	

	2 in.	3 in.	4 in.	6 in.
W-B	$1.00	$1.50	$2.00	$3.25
X-B		1.00	1.50	2.75
Y-B		1.00	1.75	3.00
Z-B	1.00	1.50	2.75	5.50

No.	Item	Price	No.	Item	Price
100	2-in. Bowl	$ 1.00	116	12-in. Tankard	6.00
101	2½-in. Bowl	1.00	117	10-in. Tankard	4.50
102	Ash Tray	.75	118	4½-in. Stein	2.00
103	3½-in. Vase	.75	119	8-in. Stein	3.25
104	Match Holder	.75	121	Punch Bowl and Six Punch Cups	16.00
105	5-in. Bowl	3.00		Five Piece Smoking Set	8.00
106	3-in. Bowl	2.00	129	Clock	3.75
110	10-in. Candle Stick	3.25	133	Tobacco Jar	3.75
111	8-in. Candle Stick	2.75	134	Fern Dish	3.75
113	10-in. Pitcher	5.50	135	Old Fashioned Candle Stick	2.75
114	10-in. Pitcher	5.50			
115	14-in. Tankard	7.50			

1913 Niloak Pottery Catalog.
Courtesy of Kenneth Mauney.

1920 Niloak Pottery Catalog.
Courtesy of the University of Central Arkansas Archives and Special Collections.

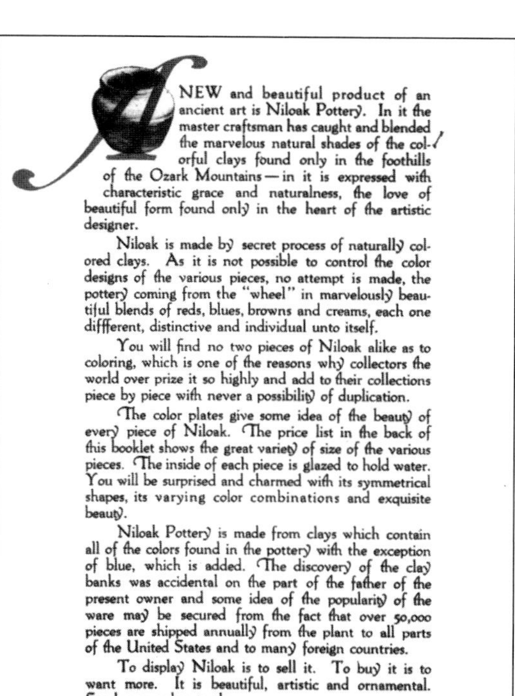

A NEW and beautiful product of an ancient art is Niloak Pottery. In it the master craftsman has caught and blended the marvelous natural shades of the colorful clays found only in the foothills of the Ozark Mountains — in it is expressed with characteristic grace and naturalness, the love of beautiful form found only in the heart of the artistic designer.

Niloak is made by secret process of naturally colored clays. As it is not possible to control the color designs of the various pieces, no attempt is made, the pottery coming from the "wheel" in marvelously beautiful blends of reds, blues, browns and creams, each one diffferent, distinctive and individual unto itself.

You will find no two pieces of Niloak alike as to coloring, which is one of the reasons why collectors the world over prize it so highly and add to their collections piece by piece with never a possibility of duplication.

The color plates give some idea of the beauty of every piece of Niloak. The price list in the back of this booklet shows the great variety of size of the various pieces. The inside of each piece is glazed to hold water. You will be surprised and charmed with its symmetrical shapes, its varying color combinations and exquisite beauty.

Niloak Pottery is made from clays which contain all of the colors found in the pottery with the exception of blue, which is added. The discovery of the clay banks was accidental on the part of the father of the present owner and some idea of the popularity of the ware may be secured from the fact that over 50,000 pieces are shipped annually from the plant to all parts of the United States and to many foreign countries.

To display Niloak is to sell it. To buy it is to want more. It is beautiful, artistic and ornamental. Send your orders to the

NILOAK POTTERY
BENTON, ARK.

1920 Niloak Pottery Catalog.
Courtesy of the University of Central Arkansas Archives and Special Collections.

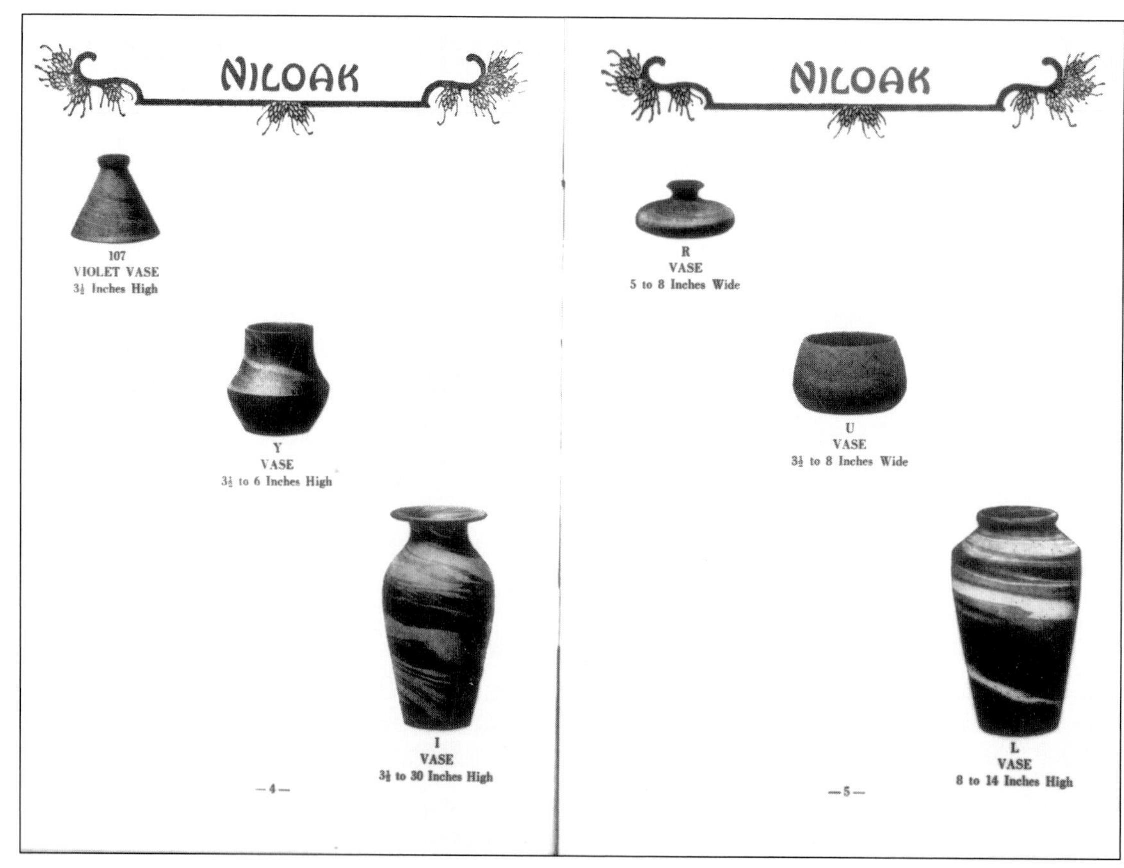

NILOAK

107
VIOLET VASE
3½ Inches High

Y
VASE
3½ to 6 Inches High

I
VASE
3½ to 30 Inches High

—4—

NILOAK

R
VASE
5 to 8 Inches Wide

U
VASE
3½ to 8 Inches Wide

L
VASE
8 to 14 Inches High

—5—

1920 Niloak Pottery Catalog.
Courtesy of the University of Central Arkansas Archives and Special Collections.

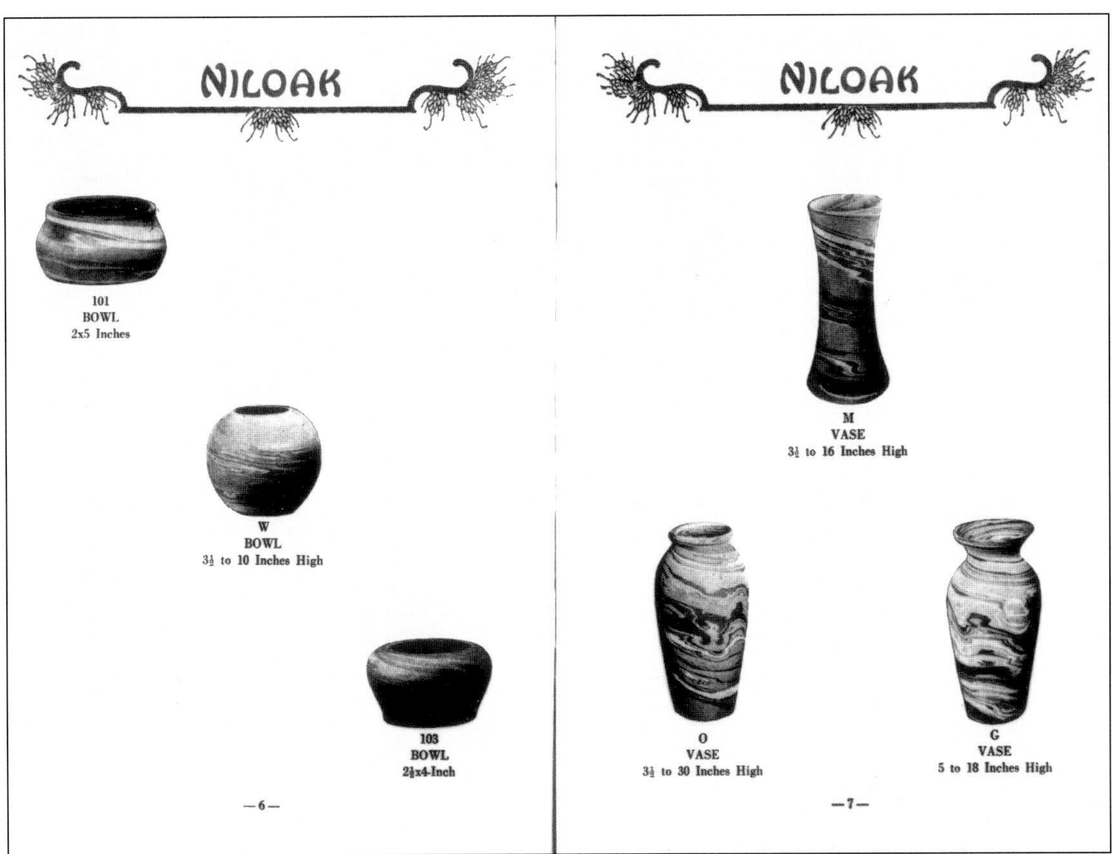
NILOAK

101
BOWL
2x5 Inches

W
BOWL
3½ to 10 Inches High

103
BOWL
2½x4-Inch

—6—

NILOAK

M
VASE
3½ to 16 Inches High

O
VASE
3½ to 30 Inches High

G
VASE
5 to 18 Inches High

—7—

1920 Niloak Pottery Catalog. ***Courtesy of the University of Central Arkansas Archives and Special Collections.***

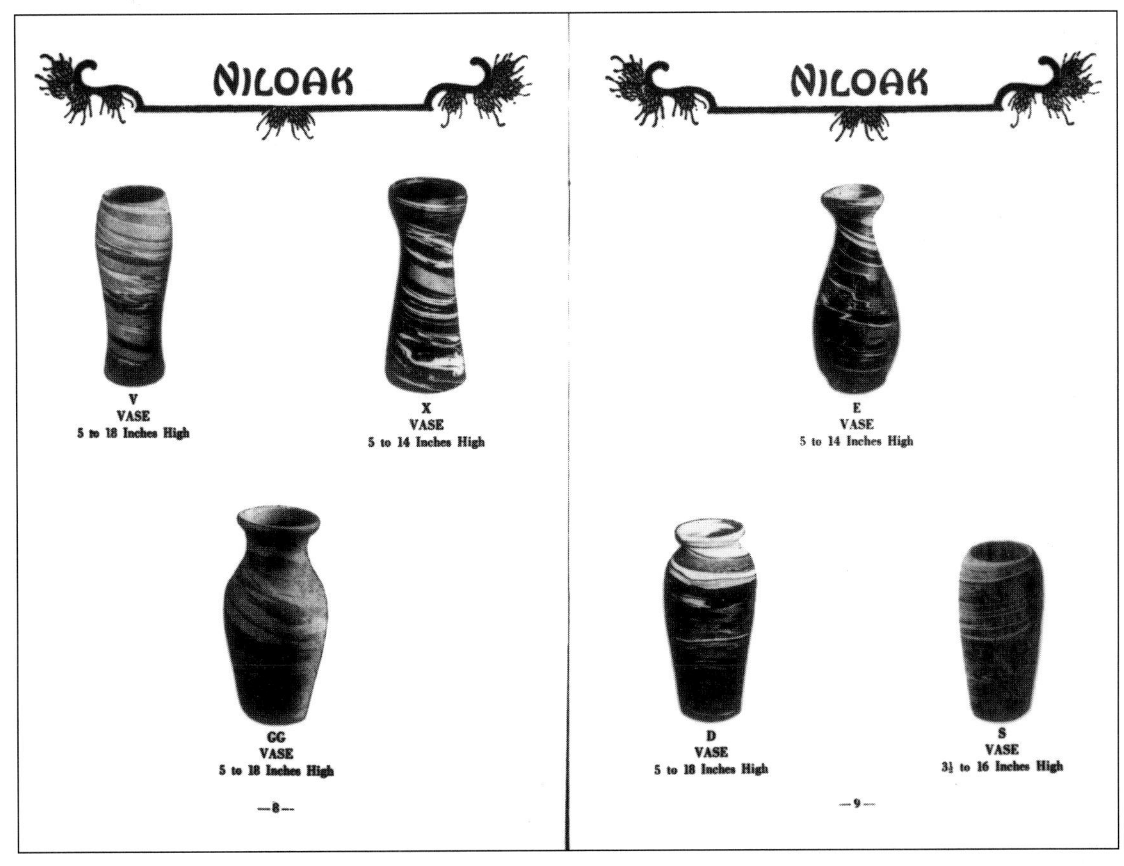
NILOAK

V
VASE
5 to 18 Inches High

X
VASE
5 to 14 Inches High

GG
VASE
5 to 18 Inches High

—8—

NILOAK

E
VASE
5 to 14 Inches High

D
VASE
5 to 18 Inches High

S
VASE
3½ to 16 Inches High

—9—

1920 Niloak Pottery Catalog. ***Courtesy of the University of Central Arkansas Archives and Special Collections.***

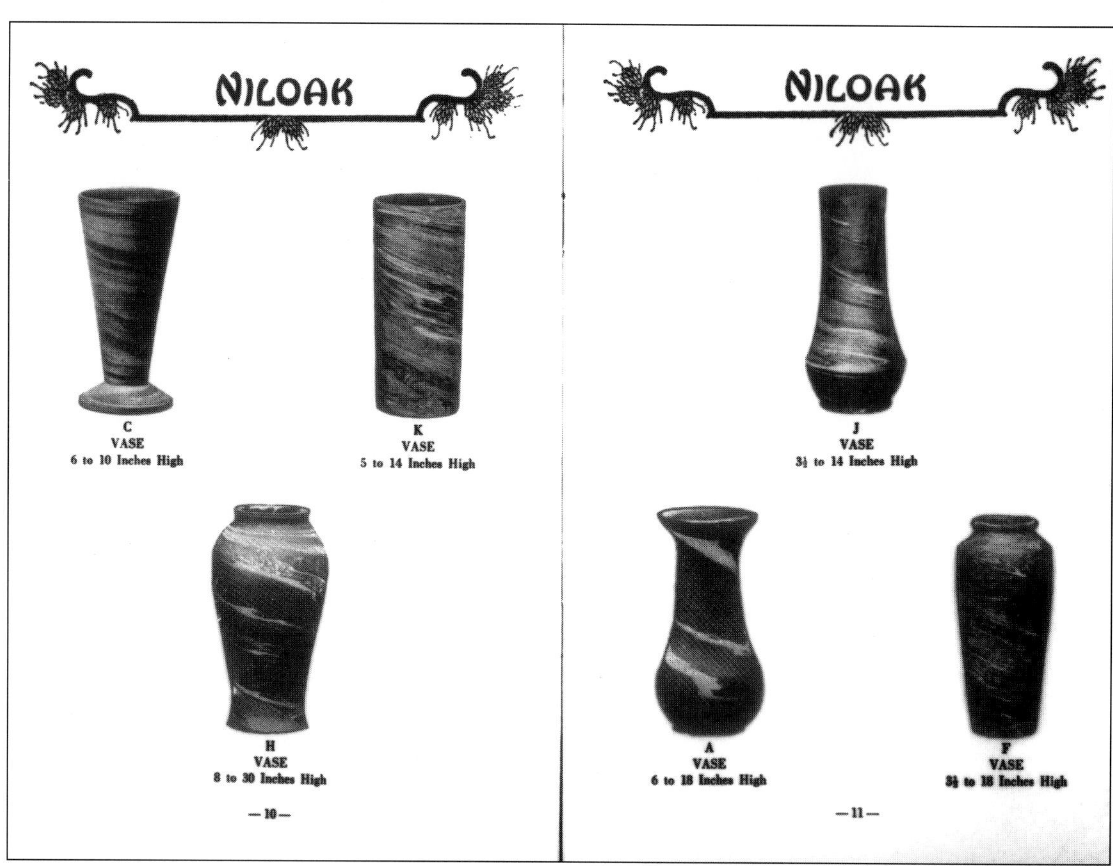

NILOAK

C
VASE
6 to 10 Inches High

K
VASE
5 to 14 Inches High

H
VASE
8 to 30 Inches High

—10—

NILOAK

J
VASE
3½ to 14 Inches High

A
VASE
6 to 18 Inches High

F
VASE
3½ to 18 Inches High

—11—

1920 Niloak Pottery Catalog. ***Courtesy of the University of Central Arkansas Archives and Special Collections.***

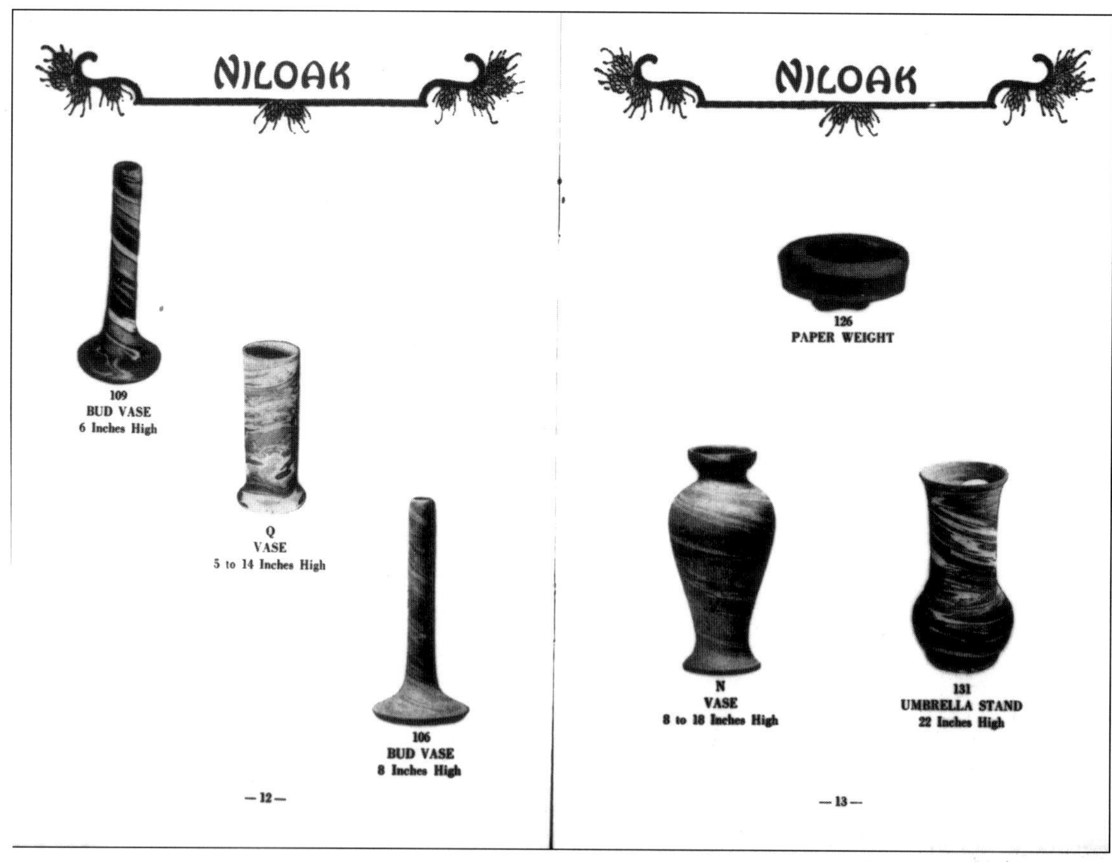

NILOAK

109
BUD VASE
6 Inches High

Q
VASE
5 to 14 Inches High

106
BUD VASE
8 Inches High

—12—

NILOAK

126
PAPER WEIGHT

N
VASE
8 to 18 Inches High

131
UMBRELLA STAND
22 Inches High

—13—

1920 Niloak Pottery Catalog. ***Courtesy of the University of Central Arkansas Archives and Special Collections.***

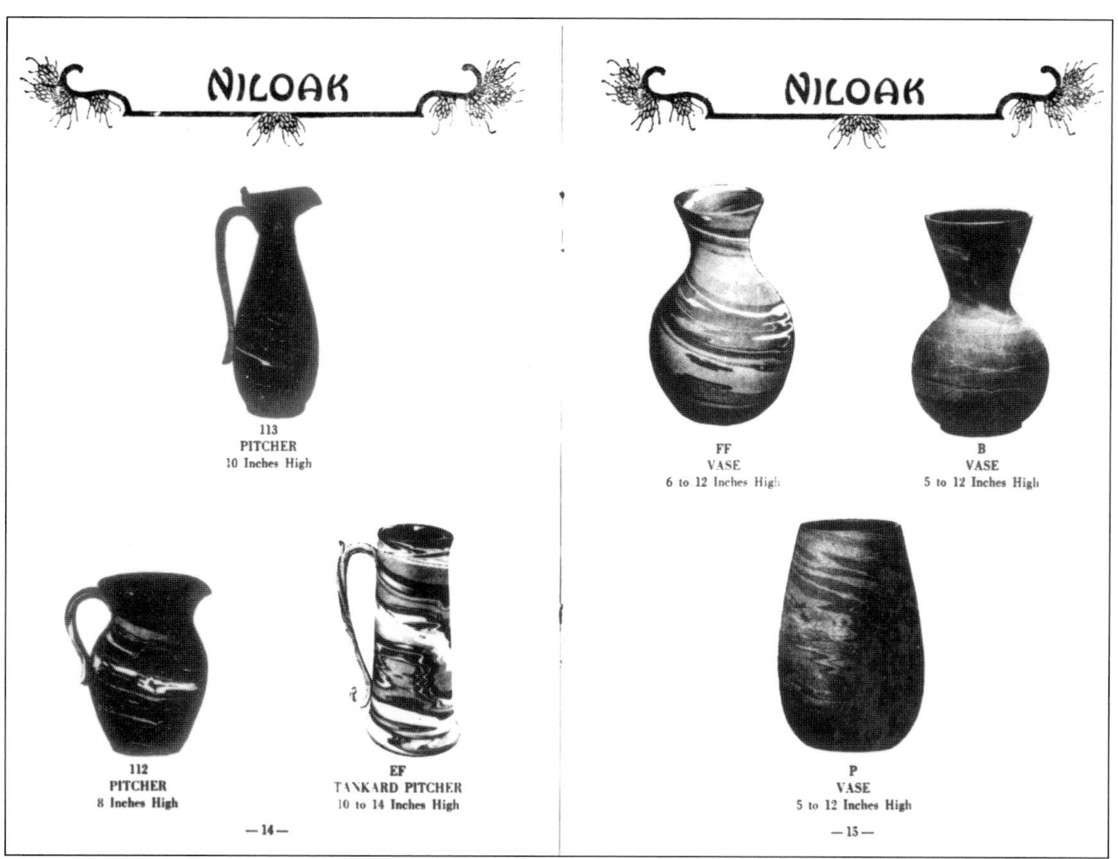

NILOAK

113
PITCHER
10 Inches High

112
PITCHER
8 Inches High

EF
TANKARD PITCHER
10 to 14 Inches High

—14—

NILOAK

FF
VASE
6 to 12 Inches High

B
VASE
5 to 12 Inches High

P
VASE
5 to 12 Inches High

—15—

1920 Niloak Pottery Catalog. ***Courtesy of the University of Central Arkansas Archives and Special Collections.***

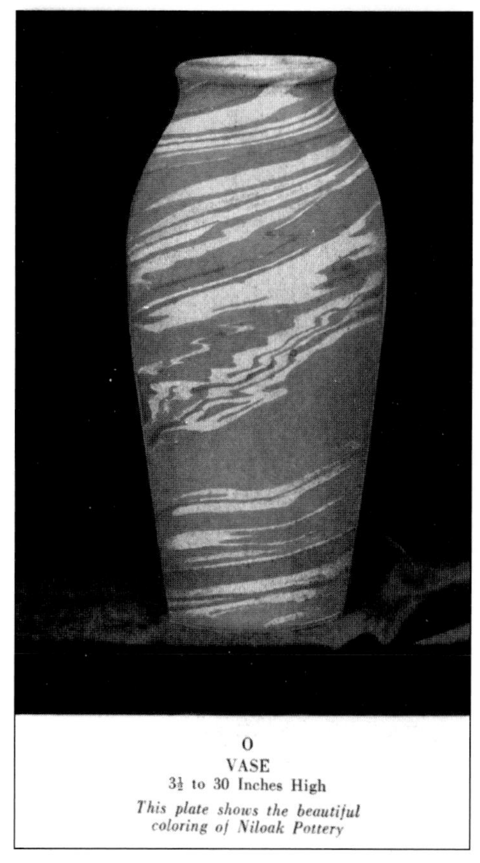

O
VASE
3½ to 30 Inches High

This plate shows the beautiful coloring of Niloak Pottery

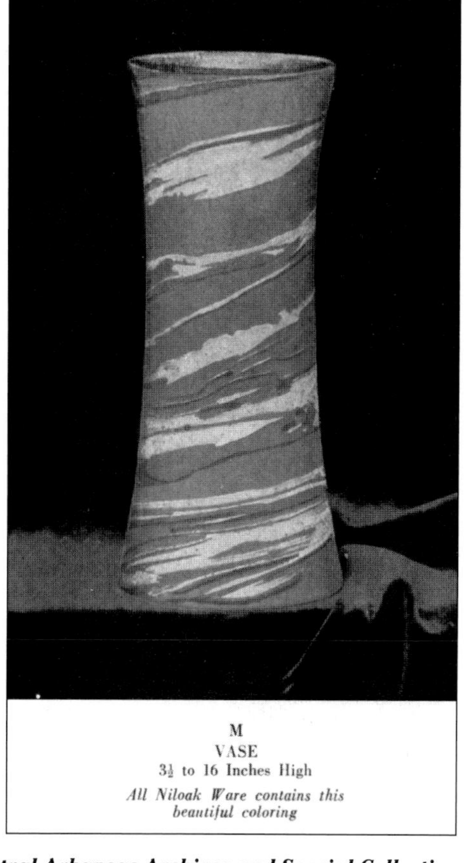

M
VASE
3½ to 16 Inches High

All Niloak Ware contains this beautiful coloring

1920 Niloak Pottery Catalog. ***Courtesy of the University of Central Arkansas Archives and Special Collections.***

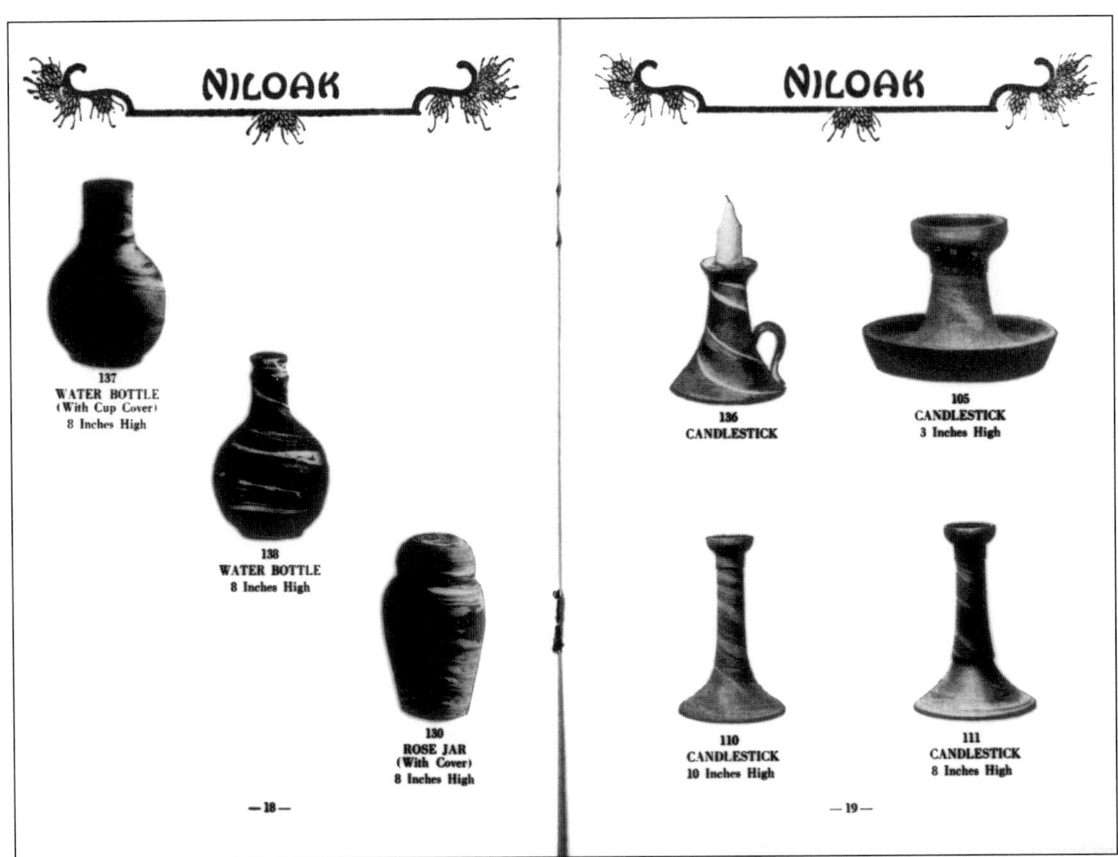

NILOAK

137
WATER BOTTLE
(With Cup Cover)
8 Inches High

138
WATER BOTTLE
8 Inches High

130
ROSE JAR
(With Cover)
8 Inches High

—18—

NILOAK

136
CANDLESTICK

105
CANDLESTICK
3 Inches High

110
CANDLESTICK
10 Inches High

111
CANDLESTICK
8 Inches High

—19—

1920 Niloak Pottery Catalog. *Courtesy of the University of Central Arkansas Archives and Special Collections.*

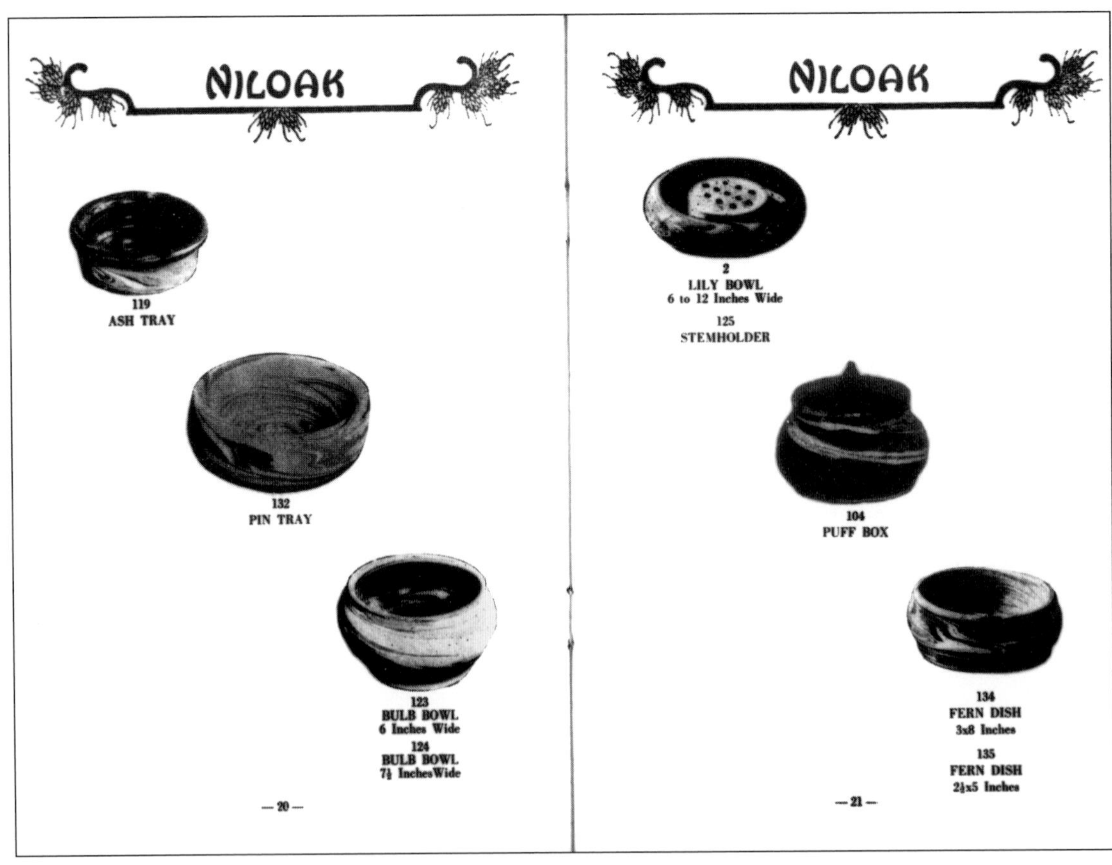

NILOAK

119
ASH TRAY

132
PIN TRAY

123
BULB BOWL
6 Inches Wide

124
BULB BOWL
7½ Inches Wide

—20—

NILOAK

2
LILY BOWL
6 to 12 Inches Wide

125
STEMHOLDER

104
PUFF BOX

134
FERN DISH
3x8 Inches

135
FERN DISH
2½x5 Inches

—21—

1920 Niloak Pottery Catalog. *Courtesy of the University of Central Arkansas Archives and Special Collections.*

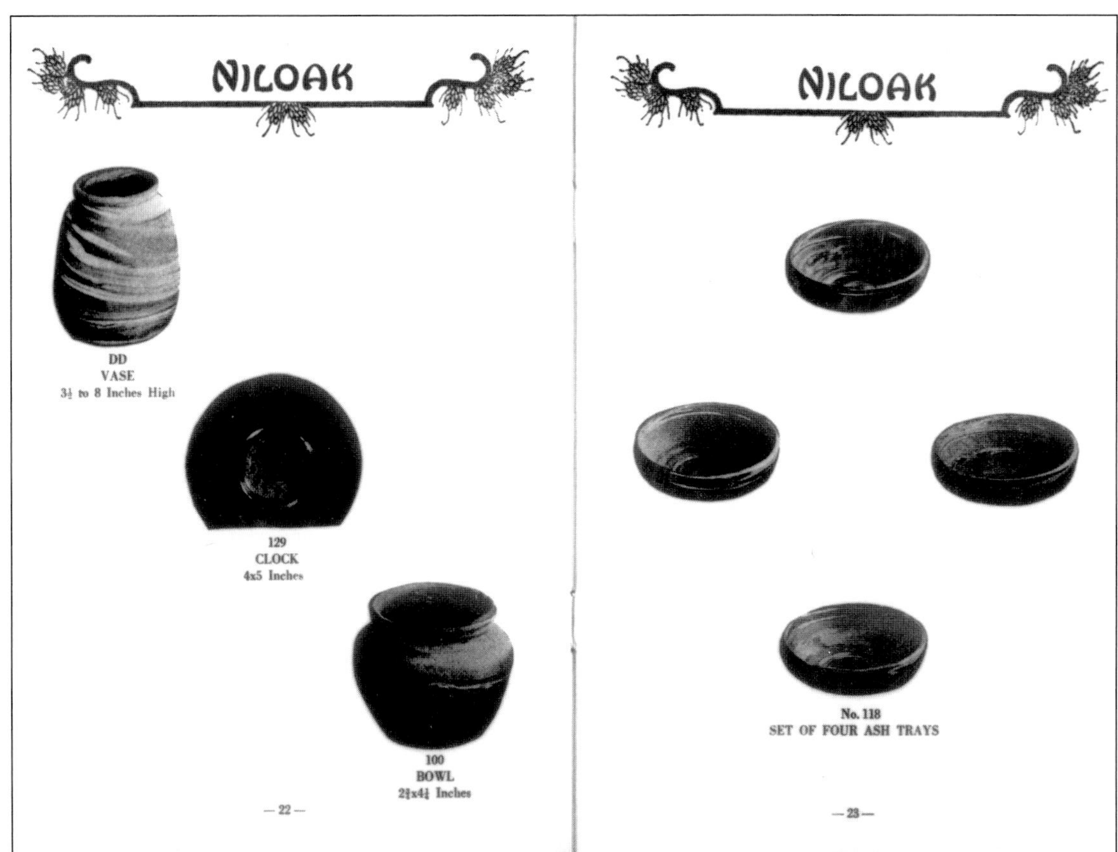

1920 Niloak Pottery Catalog. *Courtesy of the University of Central Arkansas Archives and Special Collections.*

1920 Niloak Pottery Catalog. *Courtesy of the University of Central Arkansas Archives and Special Collections.*

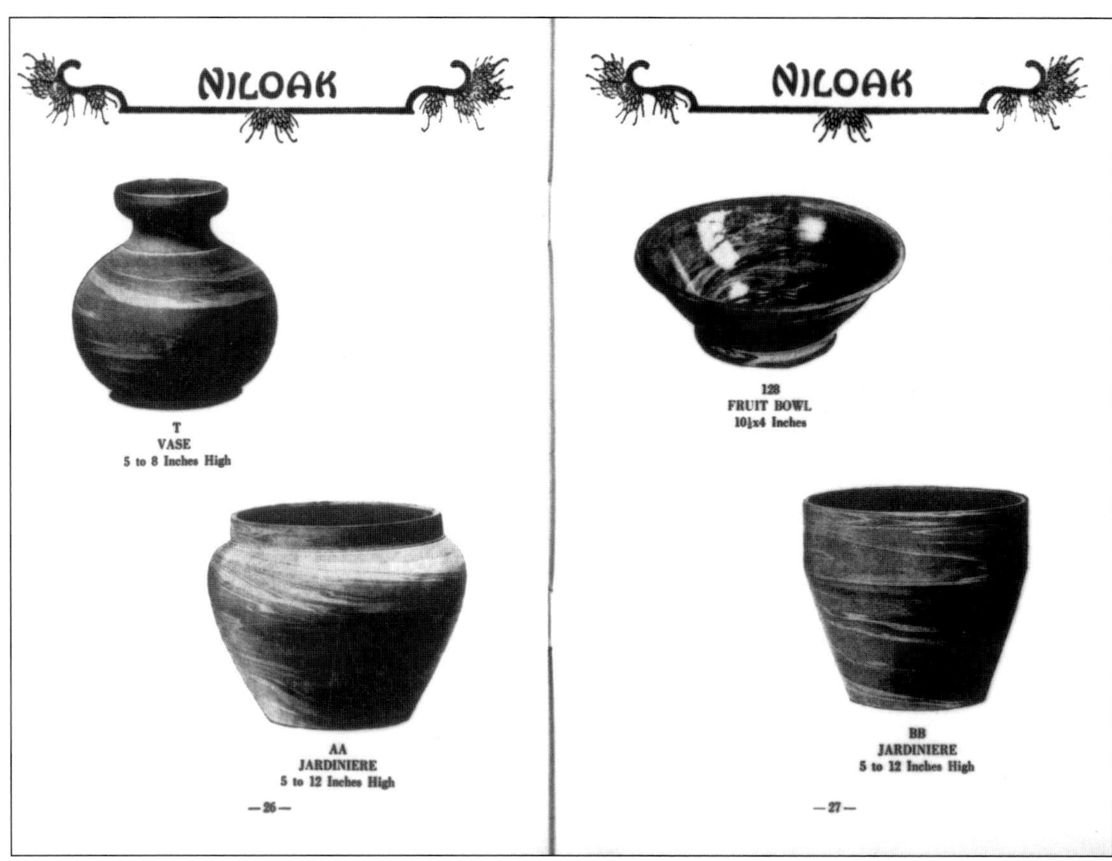

1920 Niloak Pottery Catalog. *Courtesy of the University of Central Arkansas Archives and Special Collections.*

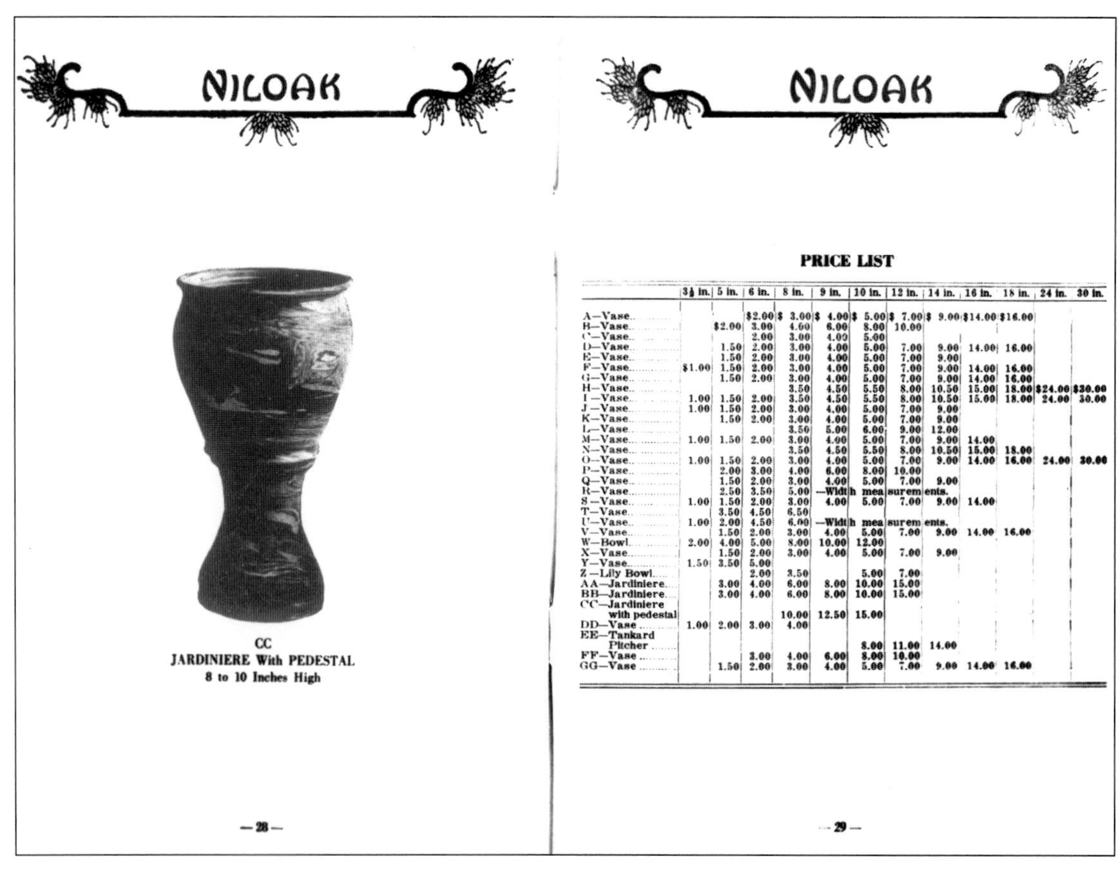

PRICE LIST

	3½ in.	5 in.	6 in.	8 in.	9 in.	10 in.	12 in.	14 in.	16 in.	18 in.	24 in.	30 in.
A—Vase			$2.00	$ 3.00	$ 4.00	$ 5.00	$ 7.00	$ 9.00	$14.00	$16.00		
B—Vase		$2.00	3.00	4.00	6.00	8.00	10.00					
C—Vase			2.00	3.00	4.00	5.00						
D—Vase		1.50	2.00	3.00	4.00	5.00	7.00	9.00	14.00	16.00		
E—Vase		1.50	2.00	3.00	4.00	5.00	7.00	9.00				
F—Vase	$1.00	1.50	2.00	3.00	4.00	5.00	7.00	9.00	14.00	16.00		
G—Vase		1.50	2.00	3.00	4.00	5.00	7.00	9.00	14.00	16.00		
H—Vase				3.50	4.50	5.50	8.00	10.50	15.00	18.00	$24.00	$30.00
I—Vase	1.00	1.50	2.00	3.50	4.50	5.50	8.00	10.50	15.00	18.00	24.00	30.00
J—Vase	1.00	1.50	2.00	3.00	4.00	5.00	7.00	9.00				
K—Vase		1.50	2.00	3.00	4.00	5.00	7.00	9.00				
L—Vase				3.50	5.00	6.00	9.00	12.00				
M—Vase	1.00	1.50	2.00	3.00	4.00	5.00	7.00	9.00	14.00			
N—Vase				3.50	4.50	5.50	8.00	10.50	15.00	18.00		
O—Vase	1.00	1.50	2.00	3.00	4.00	5.00	7.00	9.00	14.00	16.00	24.00	30.00
P—Vase		2.00	3.00	4.00	6.00	8.00	10.00					
Q—Vase		1.50	2.00	3.00	4.00	5.00	7.00	9.00				
R—Vase		2.50	3.50	5.00	—Widt	h mea	surem	ents.				
S—Vase	1.00	1.50	2.00	3.00	4.00	5.00	7.00	9.00	14.00			
T—Vase		3.50	4.50	6.50								
U—Vase	1.00	2.00	4.50	6.00	—Widt	h mea	surem	ents.				
V—Vase		1.50	2.00	3.00	4.00	5.00	7.00	9.00	14.00	16.00		
W—Bowl	2.00	4.00	5.00	8.00	10.00	12.00						
X—Vase		1.50	2.00	3.00	4.00	5.00	7.00	9.00				
Y—Vase	1.50	3.50	5.00									
Z—Lily Bowl			2.00	3.50		5.00	7.00					
AA—Jardiniere		3.00	4.00	6.00	8.00	10.00	15.00					
BB—Jardiniere		3.00	4.00	6.00	8.00	10.00	15.00					
CC—Jardiniere with pedestal				10.00	12.50	15.00						
DD—Vase	1.00	2.00	3.00	4.00								
EE—Tankard Pitcher						8.00	11.00	14.00				
FF—Vase			3.00	4.00	6.00	8.00	10.00					
GG—Vase		1.50	2.00	3.00	4.00	5.00	7.00	9.00	14.00	16.00		

—29—

1920 Niloak Pottery Catalog. *Courtesy of the University of Central Arkansas Archives and Special Collections.*

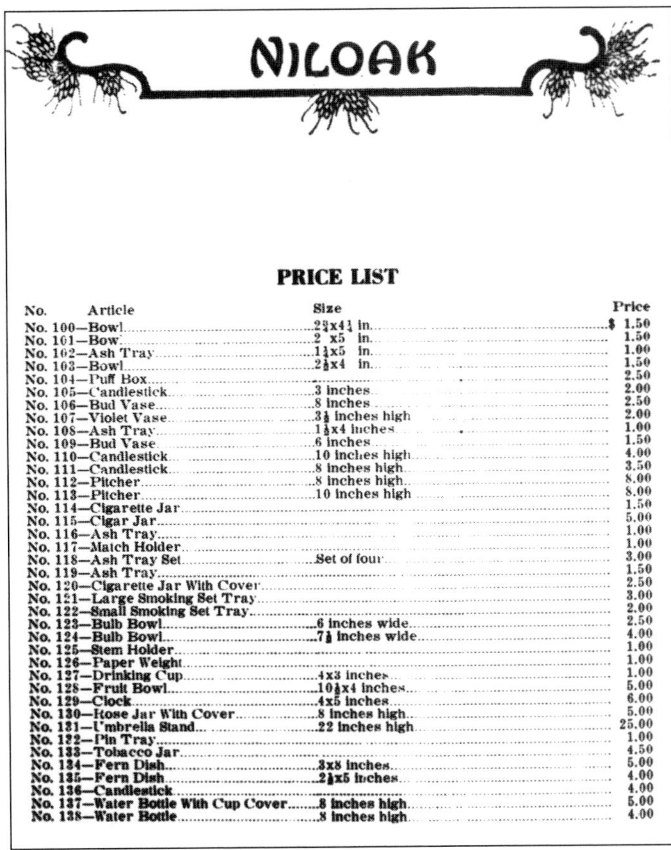

NILOAK

PRICE LIST

No. Article	Size	Price
No. 100—Bowl	2¾x4¼ in.	$ 1.50
No. 101—Bow	2 x5 in.	1.50
No. 102—Ash Tray	1¼x5 in.	1.00
No. 103—Bowl	2½x4 in.	1.50
No. 104—Puff Box		2.50
No. 105—Candlestick	3 inches	2.00
No. 106—Bud Vase	8 inches	2.50
No. 107—Violet Vase	3½ inches high	2.00
No. 108—Ash Tray	1½x4 inches	1.00
No. 109—Bud Vase	6 inches	1.50
No. 110—Candlestick	10 inches high	4.00
No. 111—Candlestick	8 inches high	3.50
No. 112—Pitcher	8 inches high	8.00
No. 113—Pitcher	10 inches high	8.00
No. 114—Cigarette Jar		1.50
No. 115—Cigar Jar		5.00
No. 116—Ash Tray		1.00
No. 117—Match Holder		1.00
No. 118—Ash Tray Set	Set of four	3.00
No. 119—Ash Tray		1.50
No. 120—Cigarette Jar With Cover		2.50
No. 121—Large Smoking Set Tray		3.00
No. 122—Small Smoking Set Tray		2.00
No. 123—Bulb Bowl	6 inches wide	2.50
No. 124—Bulb Bowl	7½ inches wide	4.00
No. 125—Stem Holder		1.00
No. 126—Paper Weight		1.00
No. 127—Drinking Cup	4x3 inches	1.00
No. 128—Fruit Bowl	10½x4 inches	5.00
No. 129—Clock	4x5 inches	6.00
No. 130—Rose Jar With Cover	8 inches high	5.00
No. 131—Umbrella Stand	22 inches high	25.00
No. 132—Pin Tray		1.00
No. 133—Tobacco Jar		4.50
No. 134—Fern Dish	3x8 inches	5.00
No. 135—Fern Dish	2½x5 inches	4.00
No. 136—Candlestick		4.00
No. 137—Water Bottle With Cup Cover	8 inches high	5.00
No. 138—Water Bottle	8 inches high	4.00

1920 Niloak Pottery Catalog. *Courtesy of the University of Central Arkansas Archives and Special Collections.*

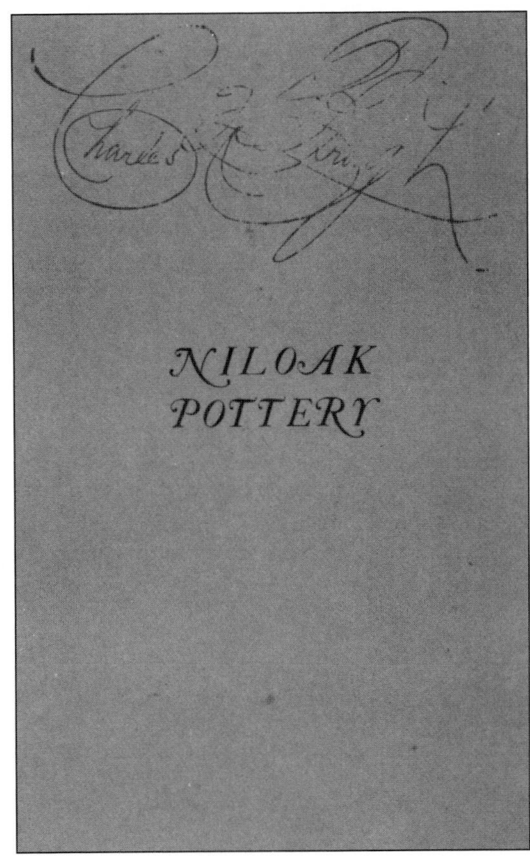

1929 Niloak Pottery Catalog. *Courtesy of the Butler Center for Arkansas Studies, Central Arkansas Library System.*

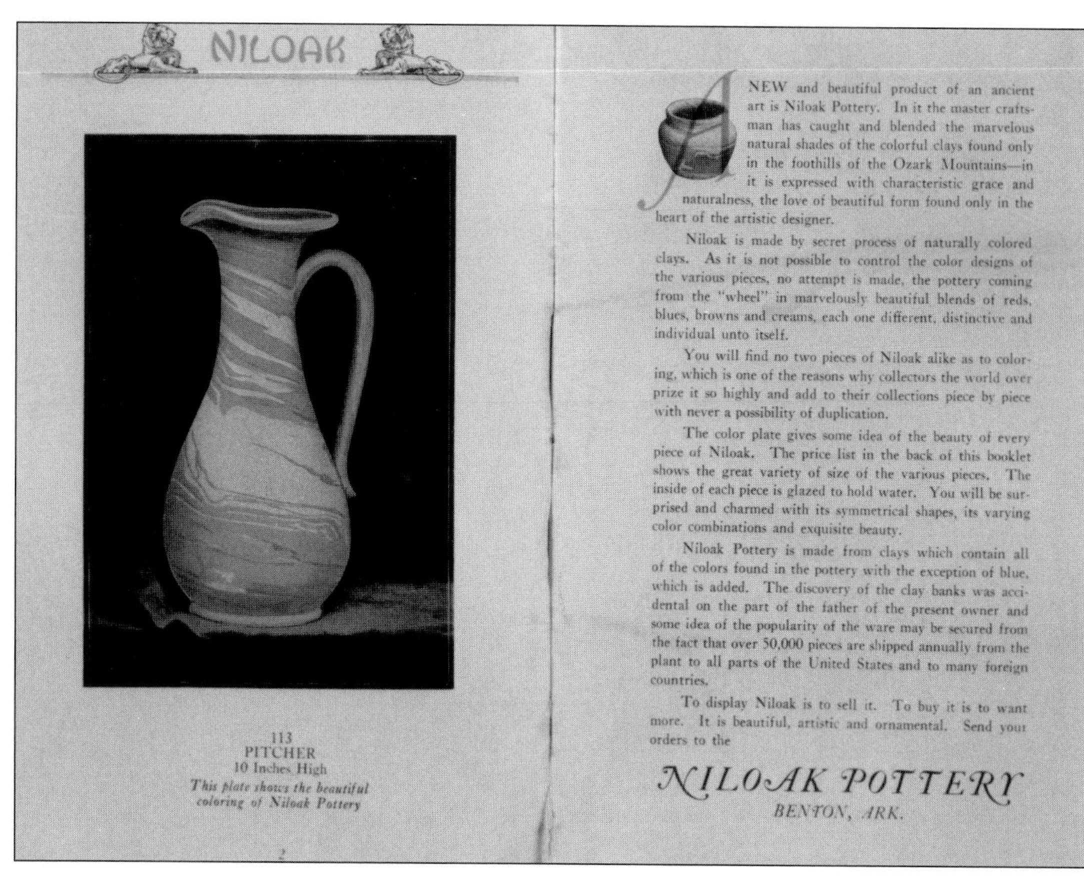
NILOAK

113
PITCHER
10 Inches High
This plate shows the beautiful coloring of Niloak Pottery

2

NILOAK

A NEW and beautiful product of an ancient art is Niloak Pottery. In it the master craftsman has caught and blended the marvelous natural shades of the colorful clays found only in the foothills of the Ozark Mountains—in it is expressed with characteristic grace and naturalness, the love of beautiful form found only in the heart of the artistic designer.

Niloak is made by secret process of naturally colored clays. As it is not possible to control the color designs of the various pieces, no attempt is made, the pottery coming from the "wheel" in marvelously beautiful blends of reds, blues, browns and creams, each one different, distinctive and individual unto itself.

You will find no two pieces of Niloak alike as to coloring, which is one of the reasons why collectors the world over prize it so highly and add to their collections piece by piece with never a possibility of duplication.

The color plate gives some idea of the beauty of every piece of Niloak. The price list in the back of this booklet shows the great variety of size of the various pieces. The inside of each piece is glazed to hold water. You will be surprised and charmed with its symmetrical shapes, its varying color combinations and exquisite beauty.

Niloak Pottery is made from clays which contain all of the colors found in the pottery with the exception of blue, which is added. The discovery of the clay banks was accidental on the part of the father of the present owner and some idea of the popularity of the ware may be secured from the fact that over 50,000 pieces are shipped annually from the plant to all parts of the United States and to many foreign countries.

To display Niloak is to sell it. To buy it is to want more. It is beautiful, artistic and ornamental. Send your orders to the

NILOAK POTTERY
BENTON, ARK.

1929 Niloak Pottery Catalog. ***Courtesy of the Butler Center for Arkansas Studies, Central Arkansas Library System.***

NILOAK

R
VASE
5 to 8 Inches Wide

U
VASE
3½ to 8 Inches Wide

105
CANDLESTICK
3 Inches High

4

NILOAK

107
VIOLET VASE
3½ Inches High

Y
VASE
3½ to 6 Inches High

103
BOWL
2¼ x 4 Inches

5

1929 Niloak Pottery Catalog. ***Courtesy of the Butler Center for Arkansas Studies, Central Arkansas Library System.***

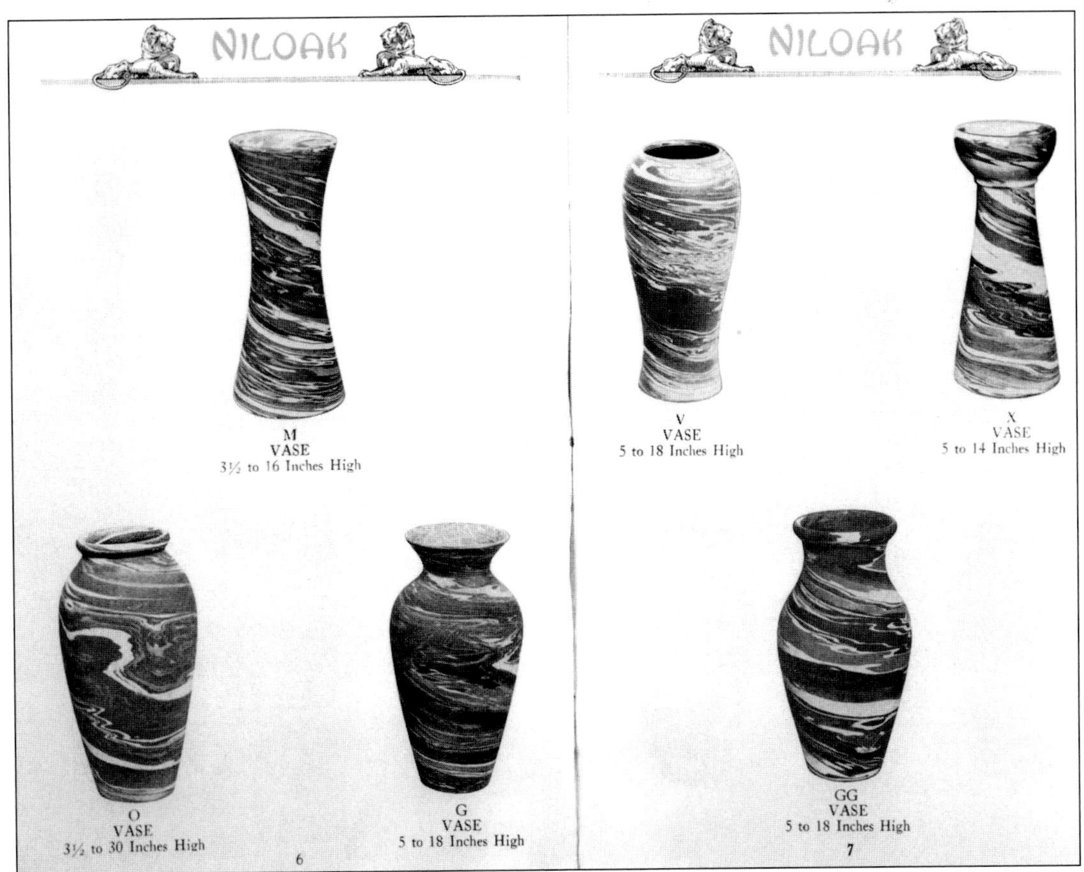
NILOAK

M
VASE
3½ to 16 Inches High

O
VASE
3½ to 30 Inches High

G
VASE
5 to 18 Inches High

6

NILOAK

V
VASE
5 to 18 Inches High

X
VASE
5 to 14 Inches High

GG
VASE
5 to 18 Inches High

7

1929 Niloak Pottery Catalog. ***Courtesy of the Butler Center for Arkansas Studies, Central Arkansas Library System.***

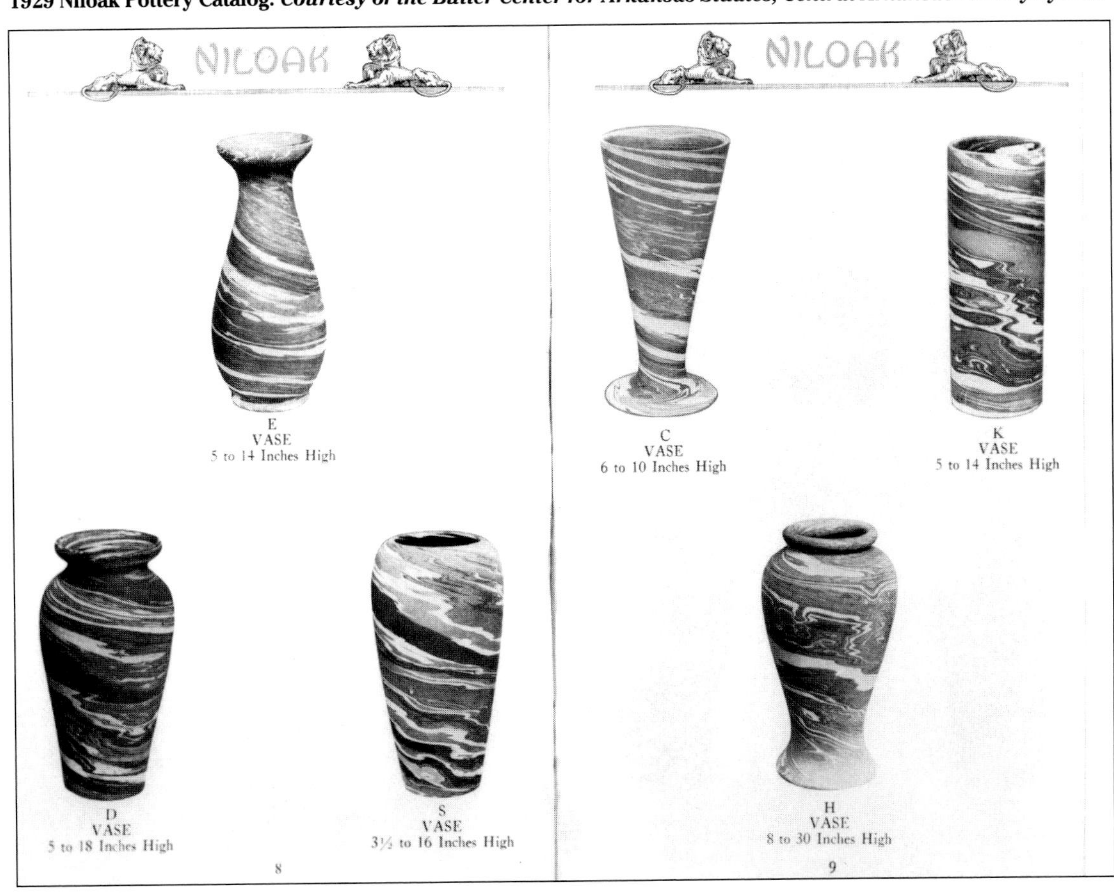
NILOAK

E
VASE
5 to 14 Inches High

D
VASE
5 to 18 Inches High

S
VASE
3½ to 16 Inches High

8

NILOAK

C
VASE
6 to 10 Inches High

K
VASE
5 to 14 Inches High

H
VASE
8 to 30 Inches High

9

1929 Niloak Pottery Catalog. ***Courtesy of the Butler Center for Arkansas Studies, Central Arkansas Library System.***

1929 Niloak Pottery Catalog. ***Courtesy of the Butler Center for Arkansas Studies, Central Arkansas Library System.***

1929 Niloak Pottery Catalog. ***Courtesy of the Butler Center for Arkansas Studies, Central Arkansas Library System.***

1929 Niloak Pottery Catalog. ***Courtesy of the Butler Center for Arkansas Studies, Central Arkansas Library System.***

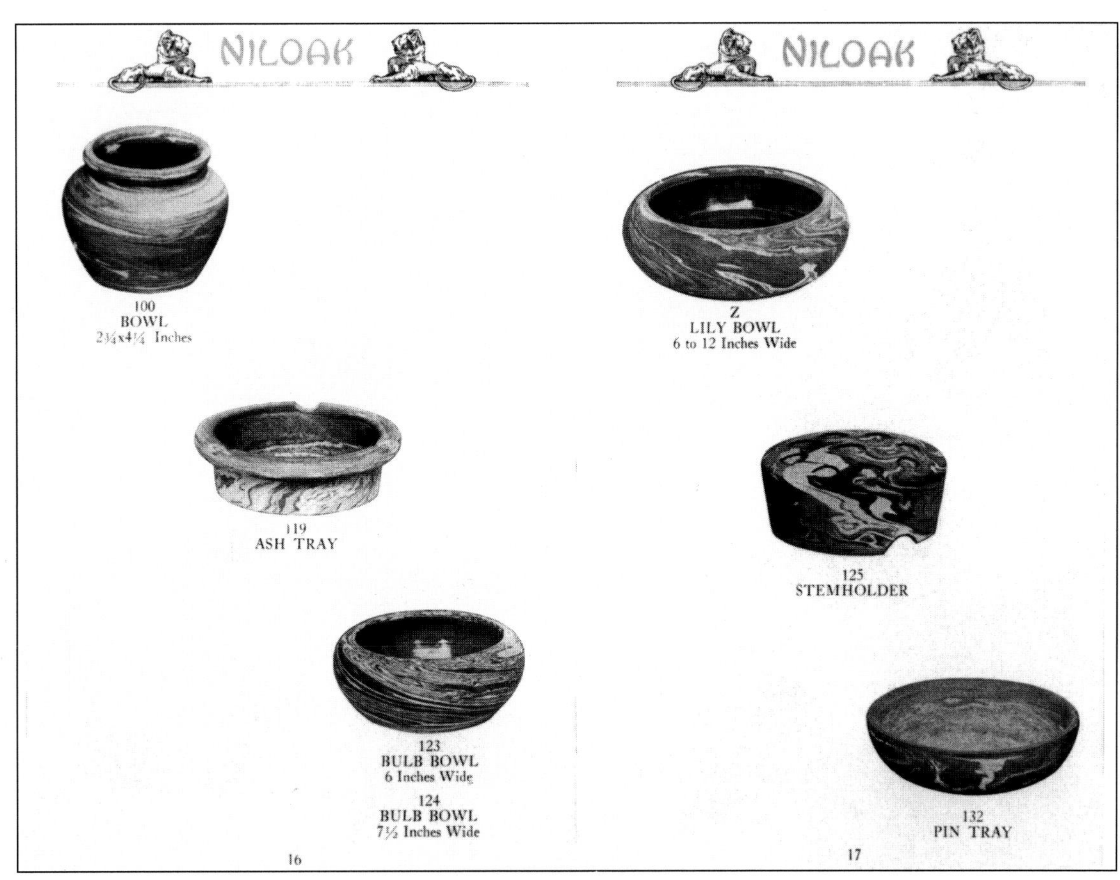

1929 Niloak Pottery Catalog. ***Courtesy of the Butler Center for Arkansas Studies, Central Arkansas Library System.***

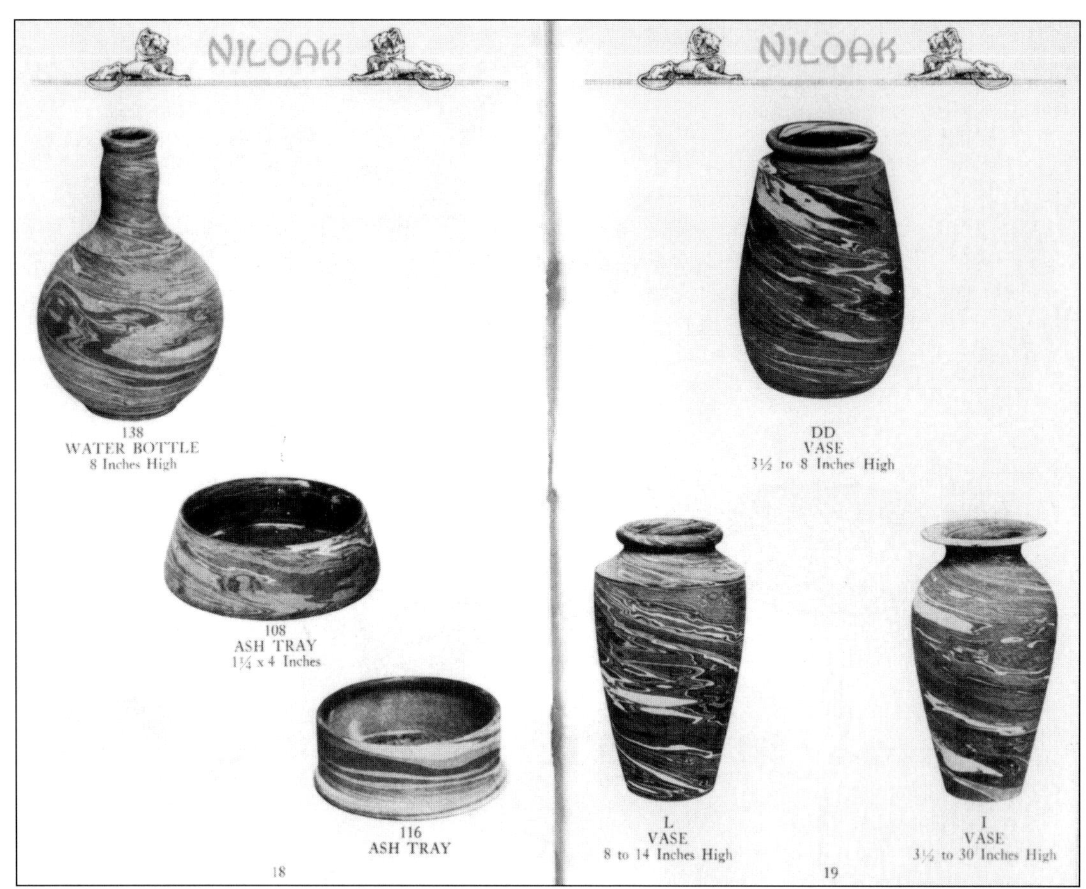

NILOAK

138
WATER BOTTLE
8 Inches High

108
ASH TRAY
1¾ x 4 Inches

116
ASH TRAY

18

NILOAK

DD
VASE
3½ to 8 Inches High

L
VASE
8 to 14 Inches High

I
VASE
3½ to 30 Inches High

19

1929 Niloak Pottery Catalog. ***Courtesy of the Butler Center for Arkansas Studies, Central Arkansas Library System.***

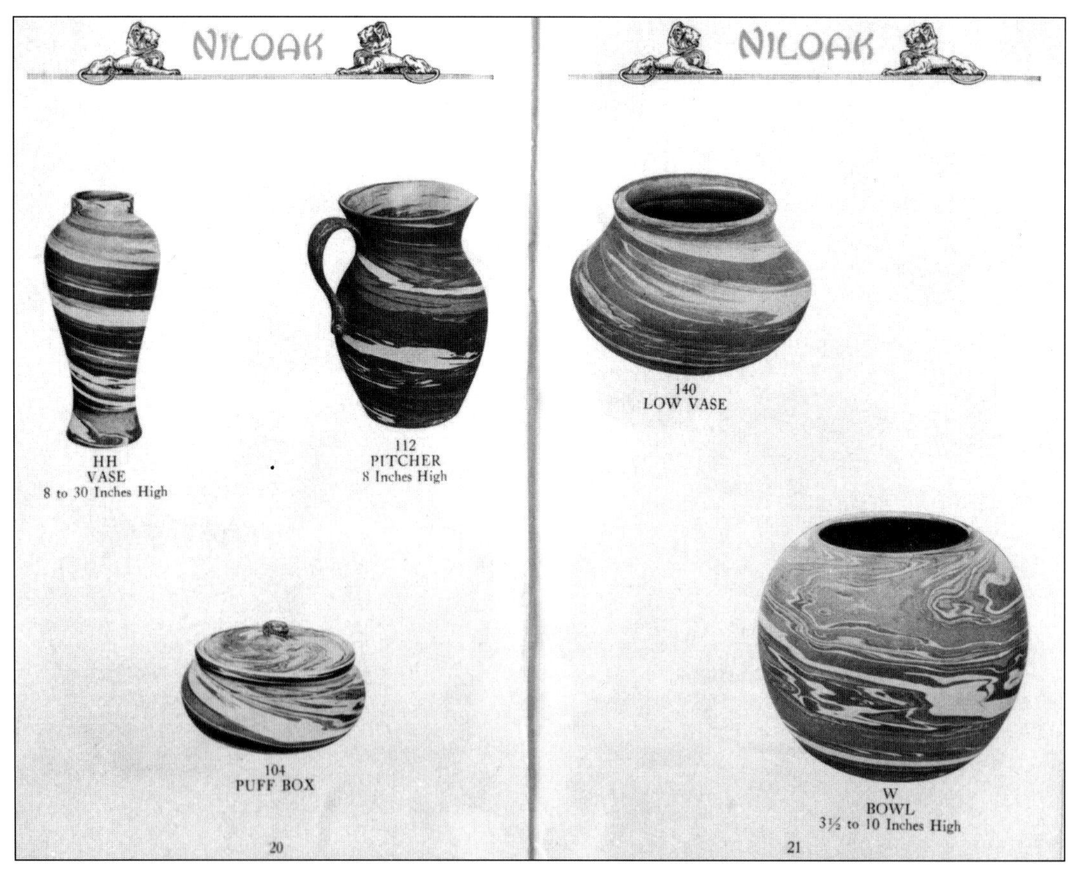

NILOAK

HH
VASE
8 to 30 Inches High

112
PITCHER
8 Inches High

104
PUFF BOX

20

NILOAK

140
LOW VASE

W
BOWL
3½ to 10 Inches High

21

1929 Niloak Pottery Catalog. ***Courtesy of the Butler Center for Arkansas Studies, Central Arkansas Library System.***

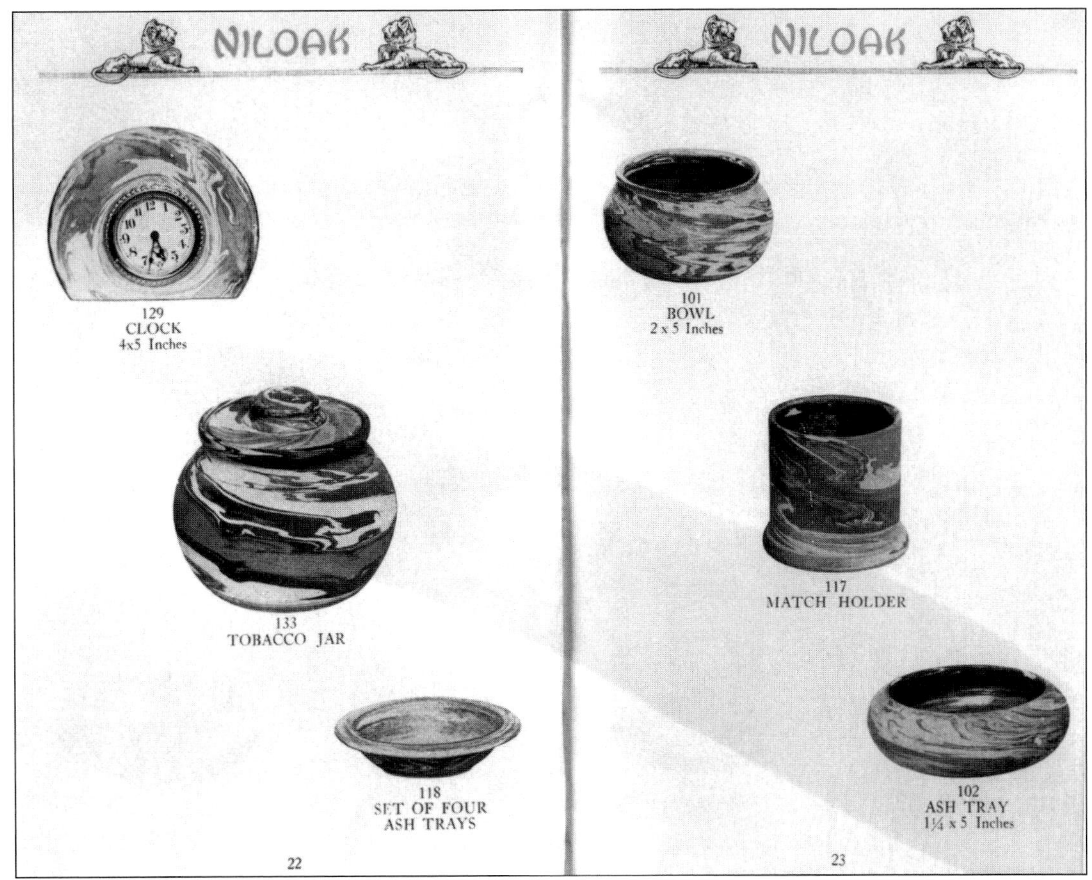

1929 Niloak Pottery Catalog. ***Courtesy of the Butler Center for Arkansas Studies, Central Arkansas Library System.***

1929 Niloak Pottery Catalog. ***Courtesy of the Butler Center for Arkansas Studies, Central Arkansas Library System.***

NILOAK

127
DRINKING CUP
4 x 3 Inches

134
FERN DISH
3 x 8 Inches
135
FERN DISH
2½ x 5 Inches

139
INFANT'S CHAMBER

26

NILOAK

126
PAPER WEIGHT

119—ASH TRAYS
120—Cigarette Jar with Cover
122—Small Smoking Set Tray

27

1929 Niloak Pottery Catalog. ***Courtesy of the Butler Center for Arkansas Studies, Central Arkansas Library System.***

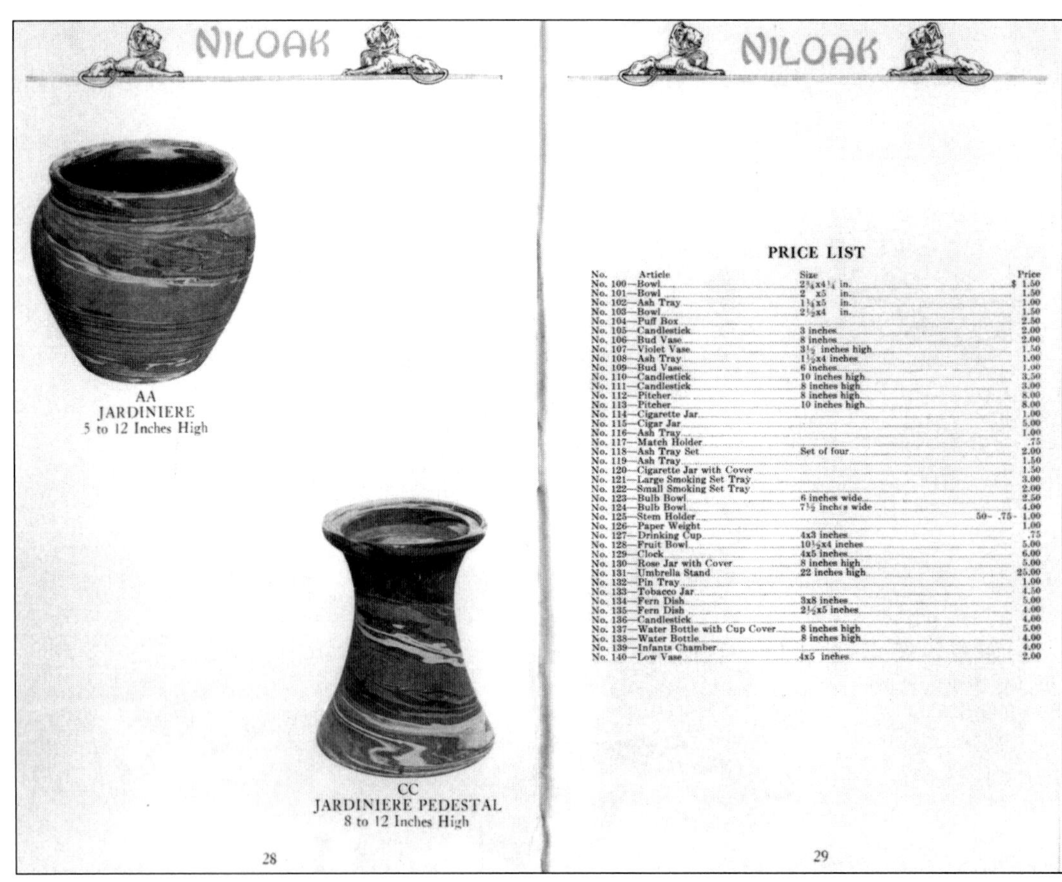

NILOAK

AA
JARDINIERE
5 to 12 Inches High

CC
JARDINIERE PEDESTAL
8 to 12 Inches High

28

NILOAK

PRICE LIST

No.	Article	Size	Price
No. 100	Bowl	2¾x4¼ in.	$ 1.50
No. 101	Bowl	2 x5 in.	1.50
No. 102	Ash Tray	1¼x5 in.	1.00
No. 103	Bowl	2½x4 in.	1.50
No. 104	Puff Box		2.50
No. 105	Candlestick	3 inches	2.00
No. 106	Bud Vase	8 inches	2.00
No. 107	Violet Vase	3½ inches high	1.50
No. 108	Ash Tray	1½x4 inches	1.00
No. 109	Bud Vase	6 inches	1.00
No. 110	Candlestick	10 inches high	3.50
No. 111	Candlestick	8 inches high	3.00
No. 112	Pitcher	8 inches high	8.00
No. 113	Pitcher	10 inches high	8.00
No. 114	Cigarette Jar		1.00
No. 115	Cigar Jar		5.00
No. 116	Ash Tray		1.00
No. 117	Match Holder		.75
No. 118	Ash Tray Set	Set of four	2.00
No. 119	Ash Tray		1.50
No. 120	Cigarette Jar with Cover		1.50
No. 121	Large Smoking Set Tray		3.00
No. 122	Small Smoking Set Tray		2.00
No. 123	Bulb Bowl	6 inches wide	2.50
No. 124	Bulb Bowl	7½ inches wide	4.00
No. 125	Stem Holder		.50- .75- 1.00
No. 126	Paper Weight		1.00
No. 127	Drinking Cup	4x3 inches	.75
No. 128	Fruit Bowl	10½x4 inches	5.00
No. 129	Clock	4x5 inches	6.00
No. 130	Rose Jar with Cover	8 inches high	5.00
No. 131	Umbrella Stand	22 inches high	25.00
No. 132	Pin Tray		1.00
No. 133	Tobacco Jar		4.50
No. 134	Fern Dish	3x8 inches	5.00
No. 135	Fern Dish	2½x5 inches	4.00
No. 136	Candlestick		4.00
No. 137	Water Bottle with Cup Cover	8 inches high	5.00
No. 138	Water Bottle	8 inches high	4.00
No. 139	Infants Chamber		4.00
No. 140	Low Vase	4x5 inches	2.00

29

1929 Niloak Pottery Catalog. ***Courtesy of the Butler Center for Arkansas Studies, Central Arkansas Library System.***

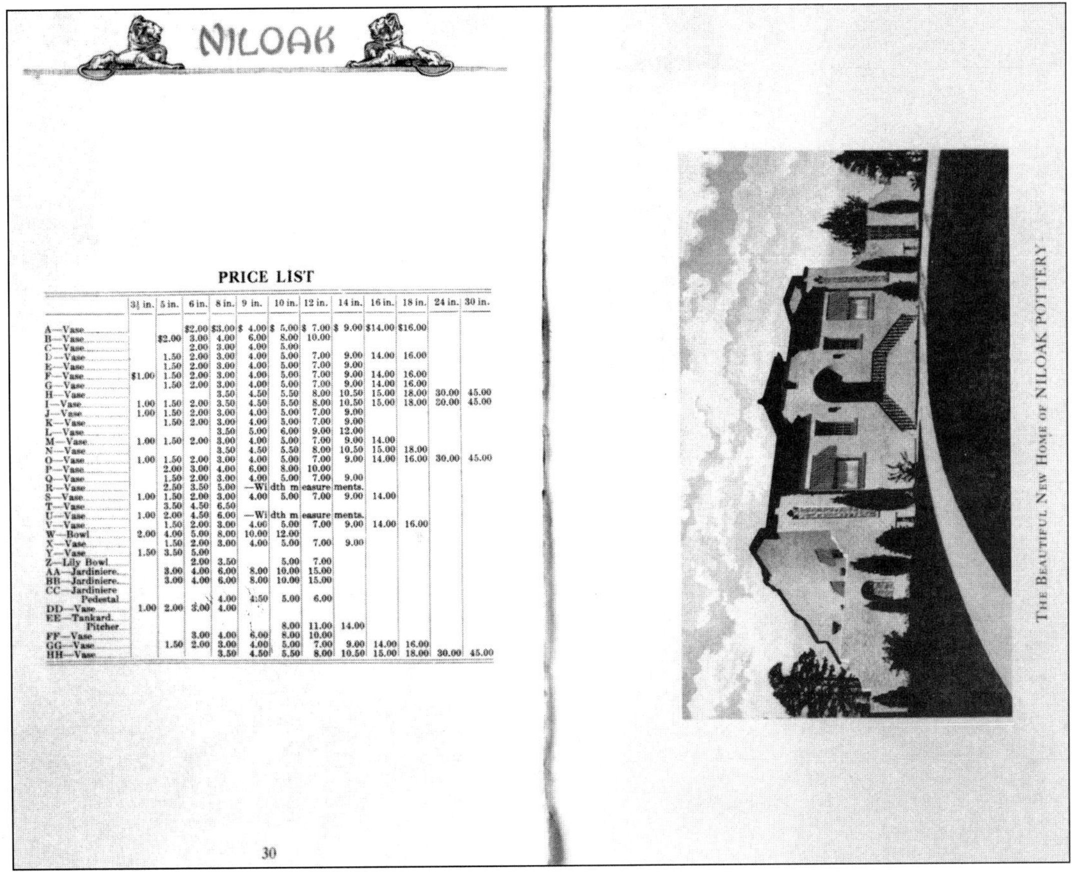

NILOAK

PRICE LIST

	3½ in.	5 in.	6 in.	8 in.	9 in.	10 in.	12 in.	14 in.	16 in.	18 in.	24 in.	30 in.
A—Vase			$2.00	$3.00	$ 4.00	$ 5.00	$ 7.00	$ 9.00	$14.00	$16.00		
B—Vase		$2.00	3.00	4.00	6.00	8.00	10.00					
C—Vase			2.00	3.00	4.00	5.00						
D—Vase		1.50	2.00	3.00	4.00	5.00	7.00	9.00	14.00	16.00		
E—Vase		1.50	2.00	3.00	4.00	5.00	7.00	9.00				
F—Vase	$1.00	1.50	2.00	3.00	4.00	5.00	7.00	9.00	14.00	16.00		
G—Vase		1.50	2.00	3.00	4.00	5.00	7.00	9.00	14.00	16.00		
H—Vase				3.50	4.50	5.50	8.00	10.50	15.00	18.00	30.00	45.00
I—Vase	1.00	1.50	2.00	3.50	4.50	5.50	8.00	10.50	15.00	18.00	20.00	45.00
J—Vase	1.00	1.50	2.00	3.00	4.00	5.00	7.00	9.00				
K—Vase		1.50	2.00	3.00	4.00	5.00	7.00	9.00				
L—Vase				3.50	5.00	6.00	9.00	12.00				
M—Vase	1.00	1.50	2.00	3.00	4.00	5.00	7.00	9.00	14.00			
N—Vase				3.50	4.50	5.50	8.00	10.50	15.00	18.00		
O—Vase	1.00	1.50	2.00	3.00	4.00	5.00	7.00	9.00	14.00	16.00	30.00	45.00
P—Vase		2.00	3.00	4.00	6.00	8.00	10.00					
Q—Vase		1.50	2.00	3.00	4.00	5.00	7.00	9.00				
R—Vase		2.50	3.50	5.00	—Wi	dth m	easure	ments.				
S—Vase	1.00	1.50	2.00	3.00	4.00	5.00	7.00	9.00	14.00			
T—Vase		3.50	4.50	6.50								
U—Vase	1.00	2.00	4.50	6.00	—Wi	dth m	easure	ments.				
V—Vase		1.50	2.00	3.00	4.00	5.00	7.00	9.00	14.00	16.00		
W—Bowl	2.00	4.00	5.00	8.00	10.00	12.00						
X—Vase		1.50	2.00	3.00	4.00	5.00	7.00	9.00				
Y—Vase	1.50	3.50	5.00									
Z—Lily Bowl			2.00	3.50		5.00	7.00					
AA—Jardiniere		3.00	4.00	6.00	8.00	10.00	15.00					
BB—Jardiniere		3.00	4.00	6.00	8.00	10.00	15.00					
CC—Jardiniere Pedestal				4.00	4.50	5.00	6.00					
DD—Vase	1.00	2.00	3.00	4.00								
EE—Tankard Pitcher						8.00	11.00	14.00				
FF—Vase			3.00	4.00	6.00	8.00	10.00					
GG—Vase		1.50	2.00	3.00	4.00	5.00	7.00	9.00	14.00	16.00		
HH—Vase				3.50	4.50	5.50	8.00	10.50	15.00	18.00	30.00	45.00

30

THE BEAUTIFUL NEW HOME OF NILOAK POTTERY

1929 Niloak Pottery Catalog. *Courtesy of the Butler Center for Arkansas Studies, Central Arkansas Library System.*

1930s Niloak Pottery Catalog.
Courtesy of Walter Wright, Sr.

VASE
Showing the Beautiful Coloring of
Niloak Pottery

1930s Niloak Pottery Catalog.
Courtesy of Walter Wright, Sr.

Niloak of the Ozarks

IT HAS been said that no man has ever looked on the face of beauty without being changed for the better. If this be true, then C. D. Hyten, producer of the now world-famous Niloak pottery from the natural clays of the Ozark section of Arkansas has placed all mankind in his debt.

For certainly, since his father first discovered the colorful clay banks from which comes the raw material, through all the years in which the family has been making the pottery and sending it out to all parts of the world, the sum total of genuine and distinctive beauty has been steadily increasing. So that there are now but few corners of this civilized planet in which some of these exquisitely colored shapes, each with its priceless individuality, have not found an honored place in the eyes of men.

Indeed, so rapidly has the demand increased that at present more than 50,000 pieces are shipped each year to all points of the compass, and

1930s Niloak Pottery Catalog. *Courtesy of Walter Wright, Sr.*

NILOAK POTTERY

PRICE LIST

Nó.	Article	Size	Price
No. 100	Bowl	2¾x4¼ inches	$ 1.50
No. 101	Bowl	2 x5 inches	1.50
No. 102	Ash Tray	1¼x5 inches	1.00
No. 103	Bowl	2½x4 inches	1.50
No. 104	Puff Box		2.50
No. 105	Candlestick	3 inches	2.00
No. 106	Bud Vase	8 inches	2.00
No. 107	Violet Vase	3½ inches high	1.50
No. 108	Ash Tray	1½x4 inches	1.00
No. 109	Bud Vase	6 inches	1.00
No. 110	Candlestick	10 inches high	3.50
No. 111	Candlestick	8 inches high	3.00
No. 112	Pitcher	8 inches high	3.00
No. 113	Pitcher	10 inches high	3.00
No. 114	Cigarette Jar		1.00
No. 115	Cigar Jar		5.00
No. 116	Ash Tray		1.00
No. 117	Match Holder		.75
No. 118	Ash Tray Set	Set of four	2.00
No. 119	Ash Tray		1.50
No. 120	Cigarette Jar with Cover		1.50
No. 121	Large Smoking Set Tray		3.00
No. 122	Small Smoking Set Tray		2.00
No. 123	Bulb Bowl	6 inches wide	2.50
No. 124	Bulb Bowl	7½ inches wide	4.00
No. 125	Stem Holder	.50- .75-	1.00
No. 126	Paper Weight		1.00
No. 127	Drinking Cup	4x3 inches	.75
No. 128	Fruit Bowl	10½x4 inches	5.00
No. 129	Clock	4x5 inches	6.00
No. 130	Rose Jar with Cover	8 inches high	5.00
No. 131	Umbrella Stand	22 inches high	25.00
No. 132	Pin Tray		1.00
No. 133	Tobacco Jar		4.50
No. 134	Fern Dish	3x8 inches	5.00
No. 135	Fern Dish	2½x5 inches	4.00
No. 136	Candlestick		4.00
No. 137	Water Bottle with Cup Cover	8 inches high	5.00
No. 138	Water Bottle	8 inches high	4.00
No. 139	Infants Chamber		4.00
No. 140	Low Vase	4x5 inches	2.00
No. 141	Decanter Set		10.00
No. 142	Wall Pocket	6 inches high	1.00
	Wall Pocket	8 inches high	2.50
No. 143	Flower Bowl	4 inches high	2.50
	Flower Bowl	5 inches high	4.50
	Flower Bowl	6 inches high	5.50
No. 144	Low Candlestick	3 inches high	1.00

18

1930s Niloak Pottery Catalog. *Courtesy of Walter Wright, Sr.*

NILOAK POTTERY

thousands of tourists, attracted to Arkansas by the lure of health in the radium-charged waters of Hot Springs, pause in their journey along U. S. Highway No. 70 at Benton long enough to explore the mysteries of the pottery and marvel at the unusual processes by which beauty is here conjured out of shapeless clay.

It is significant of the appeal of these unique examples of ceramic art that few of those who stop to witness the operation of the pottery go their way without taking with them some individual specimen which meets their fancy.

It is also significant that a very high percentage of such "accidental" or "incidental" sales result in subsequent re-orders, when the "sample" piece has had an opportunity to add its refreshing touch to some corner of the home in which it is placed.

In fact, the tremendous volume of production attained in recent years has been largely due to this one factor, rather than to the use of the high-pressure methods of modern salesmanship.

Among the earliest of all the arts developed by man, the art of pottery has never before achieved so distinctive a natural beauty as that to be

4

NILOAK POTTERY

found in Niloak. Even such notable civilizations as the Egyptian, Grecian, Roman, Chinese and Japanese, with their creations of varied craftmanship, failed to get away from the artificial and the "traditional" as does Niloak, of which the word "natural" can be used in its truest and most complete sense.

Everything about Niloak is just as Nature, collaborating with the Potter, around the potter's wheel, has made possible. The clay itself, found here in quantity, quality, color and workability as nowhere else in the world, provides the natural elements ready for the potter's hand.

As his wheel is turned by the chained-lightning generated by the impounded Ouachita near at hand, there rises from its revolving table a distinctive and inimitable blend of rainbow colors, taking shape under the fortuitous permutations and combinations of the streaked and variegated clay.

No color plate and no catalog can picture these results as they reveal themselves in ever-changing lines and hues. No well-laid plans can guarantee in advance the exact elements of beauty and form that will be found in any particular piece since Chance,

5

1930s Niloak Pottery Catalog. *Courtesy of Walter Wright, Sr.*

NILOAK POTTERY

that God whose finger is to be found in most human activities, stands untiringly at the potter's wheel.

It is this feature, perhaps, more than any other, which is responsible for the interest taken in Niloak by collectors, who delight in the unlimited variety to be met with, even in pieces planned along the same general design.

To those fortunate enough to visit this magic fairyland of multi-colored clay, the sight is unforgetable, one always to be remembered with wonderment and pleasure.

Under the heavy demand of the increasing interest in this notable Arkansas product, the little pottery of years ago, motivated by an Arkansas mule, has given place to a modern plant in which gas and electricity heat all the ovens, and turn all the wheels necessary for the finishing and polishing of the perfected ware.

One does not have to come to Arkansas, however, or stop at the pottery at Benton, to see Niloak. In the delightful little art shops of the East or in the art corners of colossal modern emporia of merchandise, one is sure to find an interesting collection of these vari-colored products, the handicraft of our expert workmen.

6

NILOAK POTTERY

Even in England, on the Continent and in Asia they may easily be found by the art-seeker, but undoubtedly the joy of meeting these objects of art must always be greatest to those travelers who in their journeyings have chanced once to visit their place of origin and recall the magic of their birth.

To such favored ones this little booklet is inscribed, in the hope that when next they meet a piece of Niloak pottery, wherever it may be, the natural joy which its beauty brings may be warmed and accentuated by the always pleasurable feeling of meeting old friends and renewing old acquaintances.

There are to be found herewith a number of designs from which the approximate shape desired may be selected. However, as we have pointed out, no catalog can adequately describe or guarantee the exact lines or color of the piece which may be secured, since Niloak, like Shakespeare's "woman", must ever remain "infinite in its variety".

PAUL GRABIEL

7

1930s Niloak Pottery Catalog. *Courtesy of Walter Wright, Sr.*

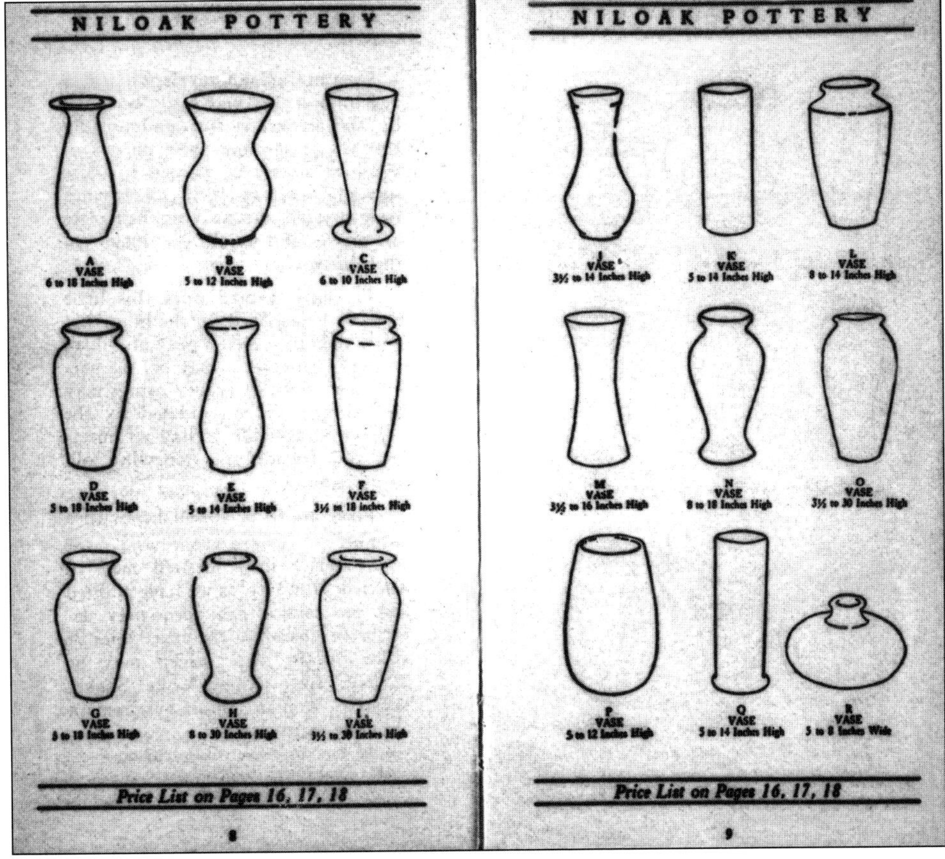
NILOAK POTTERY

A VASE 6 to 18 Inches High

B VASE 5 to 12 Inches High

C VASE 6 to 10 Inches High

D VASE 5 to 18 Inches High

E VASE 5 to 14 Inches High

F VASE 3½ to 18 inches High

G VASE 5 to 18 Inches High

H VASE 8 to 30 Inches High

I VASE 3½ to 30 Inches High

Price List on Pages 16, 17, 18

8

NILOAK POTTERY

J VASE 3½ to 14 Inches High

K VASE 5 to 14 Inches High

L VASE 8 to 14 Inches High

M VASE 3½ to 16 Inches High

N VASE 8 to 18 Inches High

O VASE 3½ to 30 Inches High

P VASE 5 to 12 Inches High

Q VASE 5 to 14 Inches High

R VASE 5 to 8 Inches Wide

Price List on Pages 16, 17, 18

9

1930s Niloak Pottery Catalog. *Courtesy of Walter Wright, Sr.*

NILOAK POTTERY

S VASE 3½ to 16 Inches High
T VASE 5 to 8 Inches High
U VASE 3½ to 8 Inches Wide
V VASE 5 to 18 Inches High
W BOWL 3½ to 10 Inches High
X VASE 5 to 14 Inches High
Z LILY BOWL 6 to 12 Inches Wide
Y VASE 3½ to 6 Inches High
AA JARDINIERE 5 to 12 Inches High

Price List on Pages 16, 17, 18

10

NILOAK POTTERY

BB JARDINIERE 5 to 12 Inches High
CC JARDINIERE PEDESTAL 8 to 12 Inches High
DD VASE 3½ to 8 Inches High
EE TANKARD PITCHER 10 to 14 Inches High
FF VASE 6 to 12 Inches High
GG VASE 5 to 18 Inches High
HH VASE 8 to 30 Inches High
100 BOWL 2½x4½ Inches
101 BOWL 2x5 Inches

Price List on Pages 16, 17, 18

11

1930s Niloak Pottery Catalog. *Courtesy of Walter Wright, Sr.*

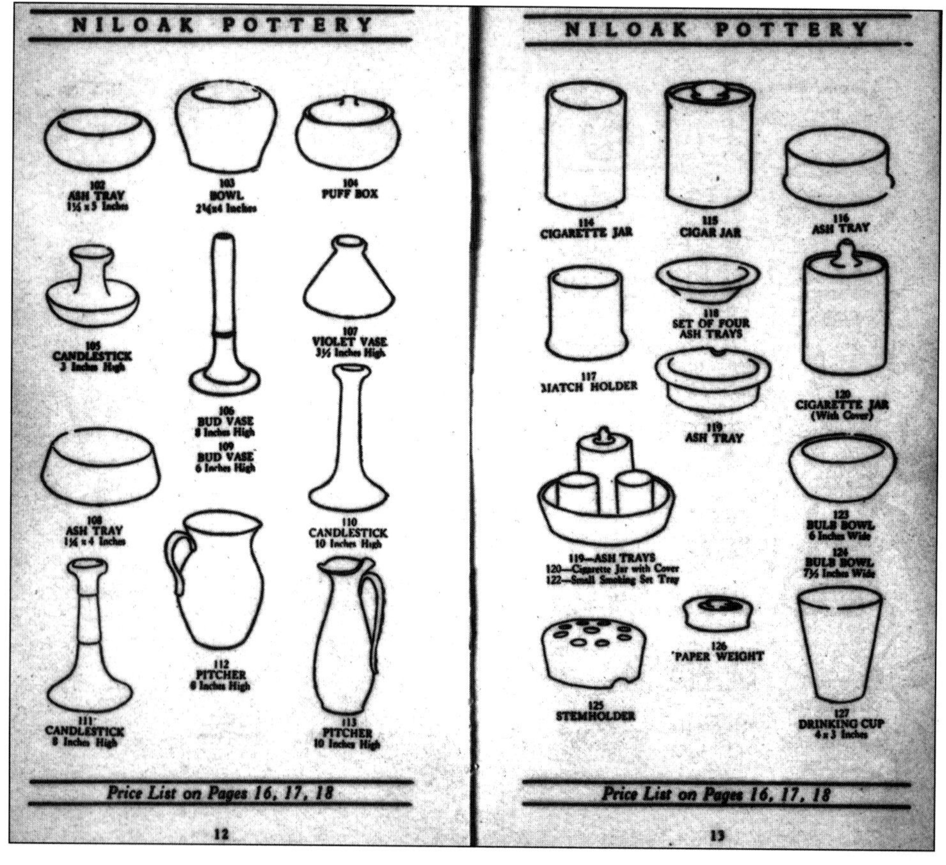
NILOAK POTTERY

102 ASH TRAY 1½x5 Inches
103 BOWL 2¾x4 Inches
104 PUFF BOX
105 CANDLESTICK 3 Inches High
106 BUD VASE 8 Inches High
109 BUD VASE 6 Inches High
107 VIOLET VASE 3½ Inches High
108 ASH TRAY 1½x4 Inches
110 CANDLESTICK 10 Inches High
111 CANDLESTICK 8 Inches High
112 PITCHER 8 Inches High
113 PITCHER 10 Inches High

Price List on Pages 16, 17, 18

12

NILOAK POTTERY

114 CIGARETTE JAR
115 CIGAR JAR
116 ASH TRAY
117 MATCH HOLDER
118 SET OF FOUR ASH TRAYS
119 ASH TRAY
120 CIGARETTE JAR (With Cover)
119—ASH TRAYS
120—Cigarette Jar with Cover
122—Small Smoking Set Tray
123 BULB BOWL 6 Inches Wide
124 BULB BOWL 7½ Inches Wide
125 STEMHOLDER
126 PAPER WEIGHT
127 DRINKING CUP 4x3 Inches

Price List on Pages 16, 17, 18

13

1930s Niloak Pottery Catalog. *Courtesy of Walter Wright, Sr.*

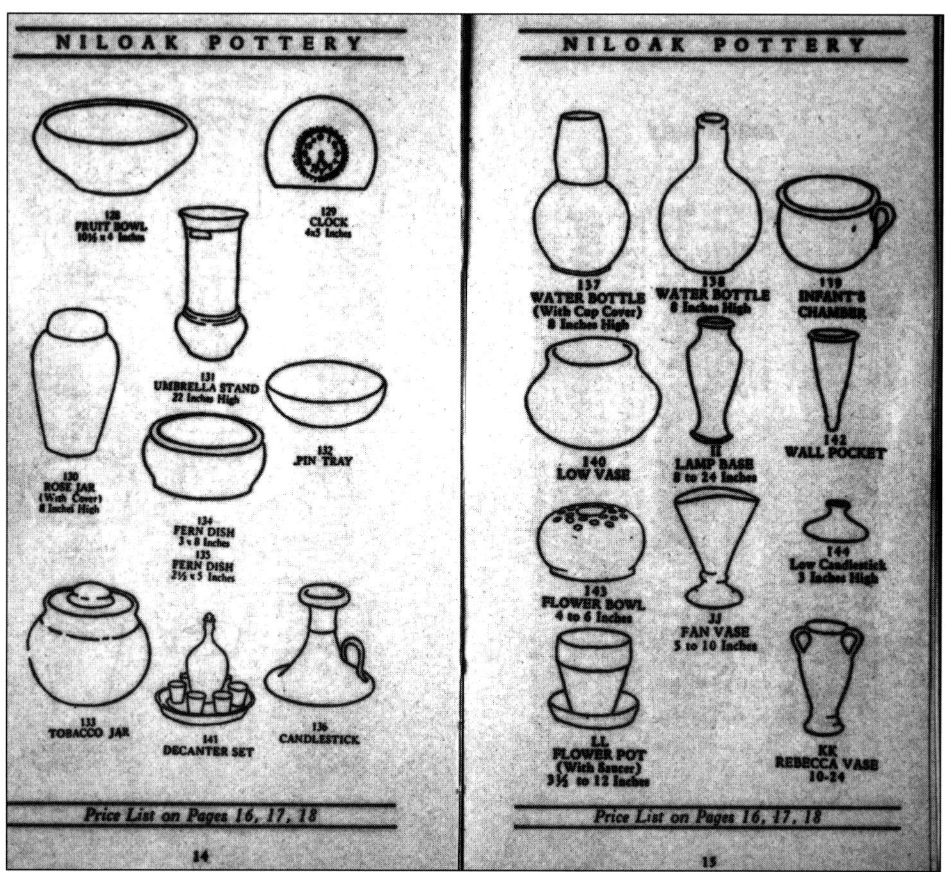

1930s Niloak Pottery Catalog. *Courtesy of Walter Wright, Sr.*

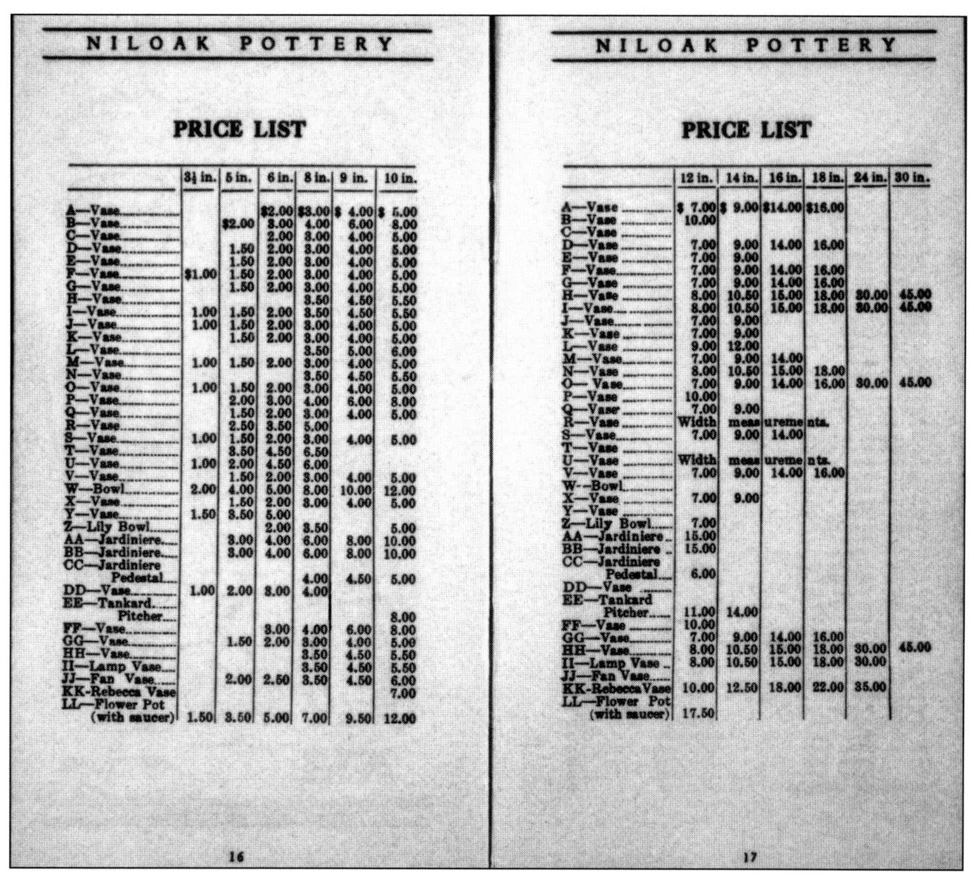

NILOAK POTTERY

PRICE LIST

	3½ in.	5 in.	6 in.	8 in.	9 in.	10 in.
A—Vase			$2.00	$3.00	$ 4.00	$ 5.00
B—Vase		$2.00	3.00	4.00	6.00	8.00
C—Vase			2.00	3.00	4.00	5.00
D—Vase		1.50	2.00	3.00	4.00	5.00
E—Vase		1.50	2.00	3.00	4.00	5.00
F—Vase	$1.00	1.50	2.00	3.00	4.00	5.00
G—Vase		1.50	2.00	3.00	4.00	5.00
H—Vase				3.50	4.50	5.50
I—Vase	1.00	1.50	2.00	3.50	4.50	5.50
J—Vase	1.00	1.50	2.00	3.00	4.00	5.00
K—Vase		1.50	2.00	3.00	4.00	5.00
L—Vase				3.50	5.00	6.00
M—Vase	1.00	1.50	2.00	3.00	4.00	5.00
N—Vase				3.50	4.50	5.50
O—Vase	1.00	1.50	2.00	3.00	4.00	5.00
P—Vase		2.00	3.00	4.00	6.00	8.00
Q—Vase		1.50	2.00	3.00	4.00	5.00
R—Vase		2.50	3.50	5.00		
S—Vase	1.00	1.50	2.00	3.00	4.00	5.00
T—Vase		3.50	4.50	6.50		
U—Vase	1.00	2.00	4.50	6.00		
V—Vase		1.50	2.00	3.00	4.00	5.00
W—Bowl	2.00	4.00	5.00	8.00	10.00	12.00
X—Vase		1.50	2.00	3.00	4.00	5.00
Y—Vase	1.50	3.50	5.00			
Z—Lily Bowl			2.00	3.50		5.00
AA—Jardiniere		3.00	4.00	6.00	8.00	10.00
BB—Jardiniere		3.00	4.00	6.00	8.00	10.00
CC—Jardiniere Pedestal				4.00	4.50	5.00
DD—Vase	1.00	2.00	3.00	4.00		
EE—Tankard Pitcher						8.00
FF—Vase			3.00	4.00	6.00	8.00
GG—Vase		1.50	2.00	3.00	4.00	5.00
HH—Vase				3.50	4.50	5.50
II—Lamp Vase				3.50	4.50	5.50
JJ—Fan Vase		2.00	2.50	3.50	4.50	6.00
KK-Rebecca Vase						7.00
LL—Flower Pot (with saucer)	1.50	3.50	5.00	7.00	9.50	12.00

16

NILOAK POTTERY

PRICE LIST

	12 in.	14 in.	16 in.	18 in.	24 in.	30 in.
A—Vase	$ 7.00	$ 9.00	$14.00	$16.00		
B—Vase	10.00					
C—Vase						
D—Vase	7.00	9.00	14.00	16.00		
E—Vase	7.00	9.00				
F—Vase	7.00	9.00	14.00	16.00		
G—Vase	7.00	9.00	14.00	16.00		
H—Vase	8.00	10.50	15.00	18.00	30.00	45.00
I—Vase	8.00	10.50	15.00	18.00	30.00	45.00
J—Vase	7.00	9.00				
K—Vase	7.00	9.00				
L—Vase	9.00	12.00				
M—Vase	7.00	9.00	14.00			
N—Vase	8.00	10.50	15.00	18.00		
O—Vase	7.00	9.00	14.00	16.00	30.00	45.00
P—Vase	10.00					
Q—Vase	7.00	9.00				
R—Vase	Width	meas	ureme	nts.		
S—Vase	7.00	9.00	14.00			
T—Vase						
U—Vase	Width	meas	ureme	nts.		
V—Vase	7.00	9.00	14.00	16.00		
W—Bowl						
X—Vase	7.00	9.00				
Y—Vase						
Z—Lily Bowl	7.00					
AA—Jardiniere	15.00					
BB—Jardiniere	15.00					
CC—Jardiniere Pedestal	6.00					
DD—Vase						
EE—Tankard Pitcher	11.00	14.00				
FF—Vase	10.00					
GG—Vase	7.00	9.00	14.00	16.00		
HH—Vase	8.00	10.50	15.00	18.00	30.00	45.00
II—Lamp Vase	8.00	10.50	15.00	18.00	30.00	
JJ—Fan Vase						
KK-Rebecca Vase	10.00	12.50	18.00	22.00	35.00	
LL—Flower Pot (with saucer)	17.50					

17

1930s Niloak Pottery Catalog. *Courtesy of Wa!ter Wright, Sr.*

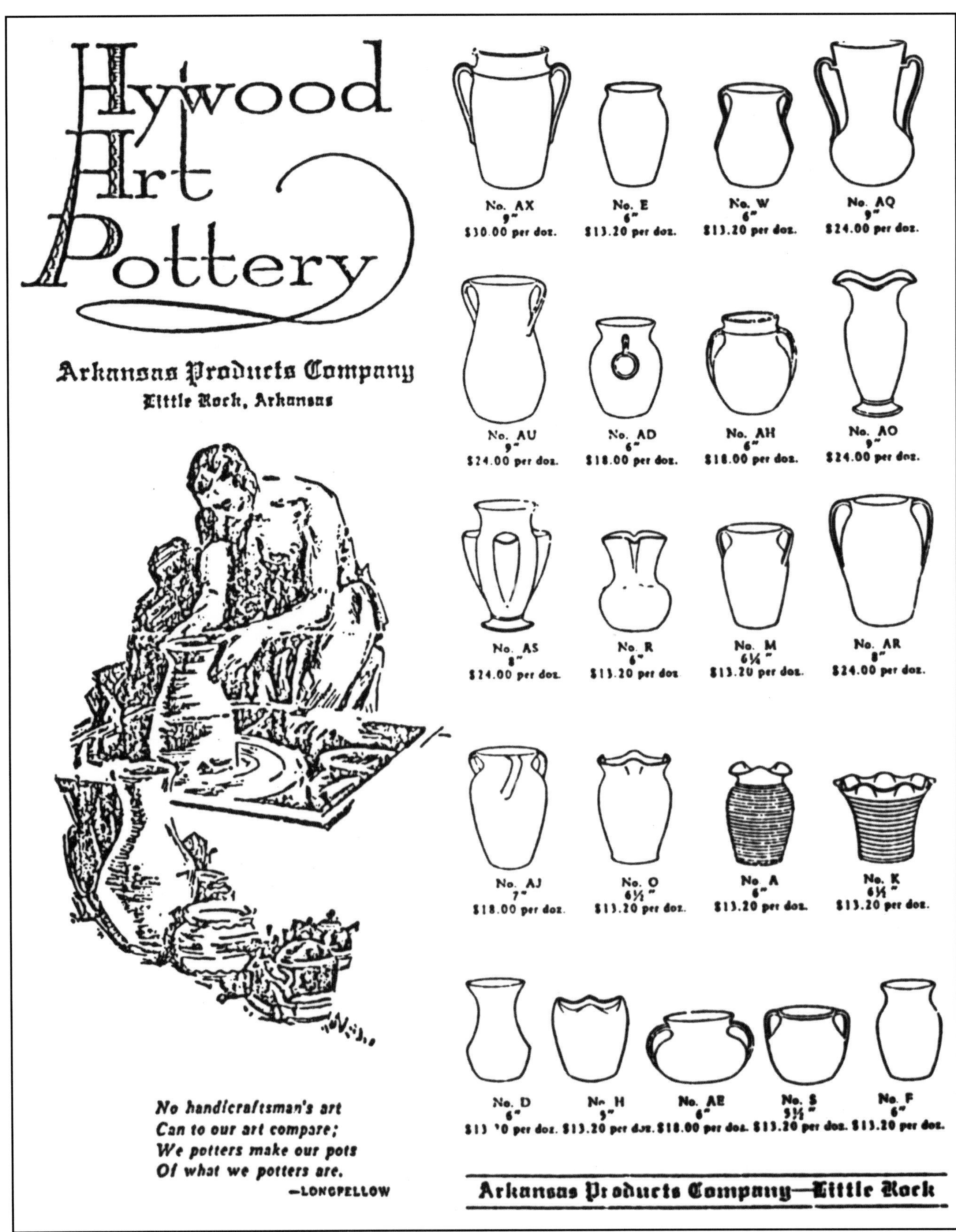

Hywood Art Pottery Catalog, Arkansas Products Company, 1931.
Courtesy of Margaret Kinney.

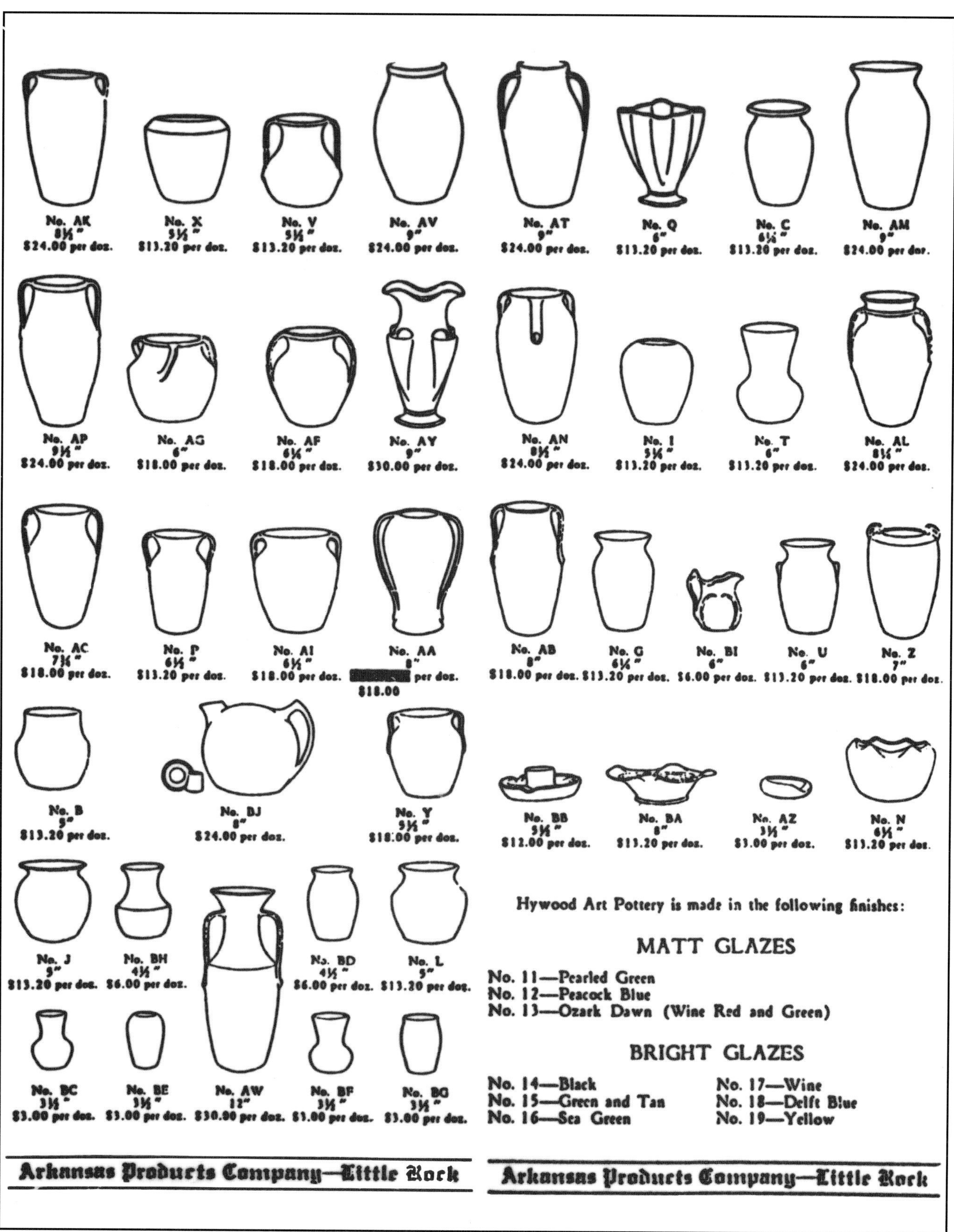

No. AK 8½" $24.00 per doz.
No. X 5½" $13.20 per doz.
No. V 5½" $13.20 per doz.
No. AV 9" $24.00 per doz.
No. AT 9" $24.00 per doz.
No. Q 6" $13.20 per doz.
No. C 6½" $13.20 per doz.
No. AM 9" $24.00 per doz.

No. AP 9½" $24.00 per doz.
No. AG 6" $18.00 per doz.
No. AF 6½" $18.00 per doz.
No. AY 9" $30.00 per doz.
No. AN 8½" $24.00 per doz.
No. I 5½" $13.20 per doz.
No. T 6" $13.20 per doz.
No. AL 8½" $24.00 per doz.

No. AC 7¾" $18.00 per doz.
No. P 6½" $13.20 per doz.
No. AI 6½" $18.00 per doz.
No. AA 8" [illegible] per doz. $18.00
No. AB 8" $18.00 per doz.
No. G 6½" $13.20 per doz.
No. BI 6" $6.00 per doz.
No. U 6" $13.20 per doz.
No. Z 7" $18.00 per doz.

No. B 5" $13.20 per doz.
No. BJ 8" $24.00 per doz.
No. Y 9½" $18.00 per doz.
No. BB 5½" $12.00 per doz.
No. BA 8" $13.20 per doz.
No. AZ 3½" $3.00 per doz.
No. N 6½" $13.20 per doz.

No. J 5" $13.20 per doz.
No. BH 4½" $6.00 per doz.
No. BD 4½" $6.00 per doz.
No. L 5" $13.20 per doz.

No. BC 3½" $3.00 per doz.
No. BE 3½" $3.00 per doz.
No. AW 12" $30.00 per doz.
No. BF 3½" $3.00 per doz.
No. BG 3½" $3.00 per doz.

Hywood Art Pottery is made in the following finishes:

MATT GLAZES

No. 11—Pearled Green
No. 12—Peacock Blue
No. 13—Ozark Dawn (Wine Red and Green)

BRIGHT GLAZES

No. 14—Black
No. 15—Green and Tan
No. 16—Sea Green
No. 17—Wine
No. 18—Delft Blue
No. 19—Yellow

Arkansas Products Company—Little Rock

Arkansas Products Company—Little Rock

Hywood Art Pottery Catalog, Arkansas Products Company, 1931.

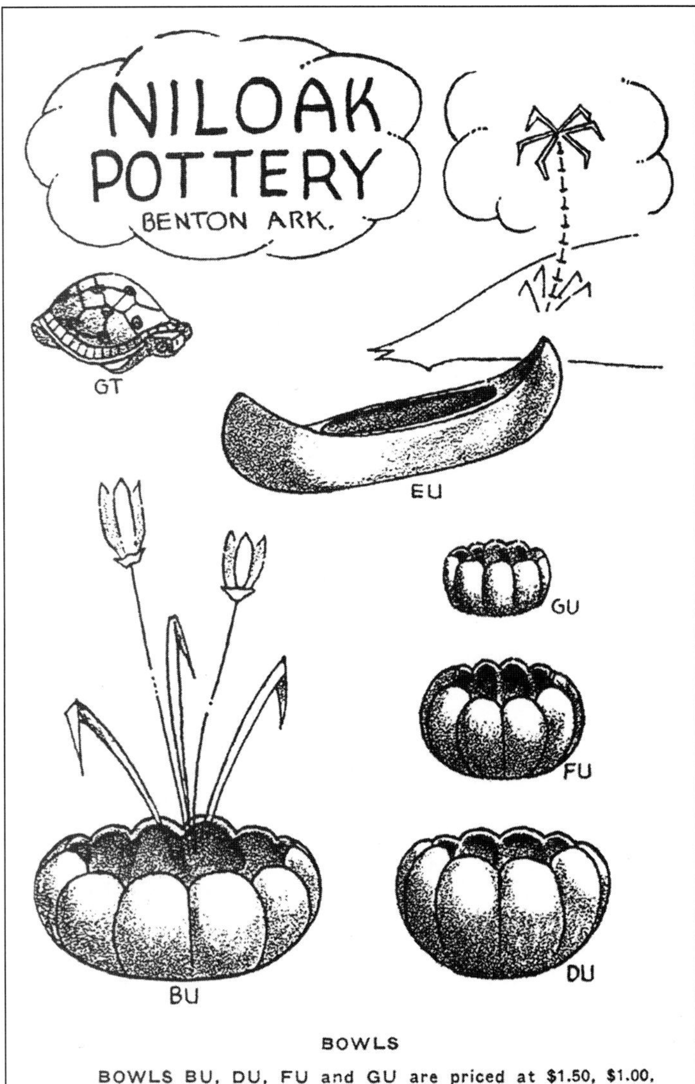

Advertising Card, c. 1935. *Author's Collection.*

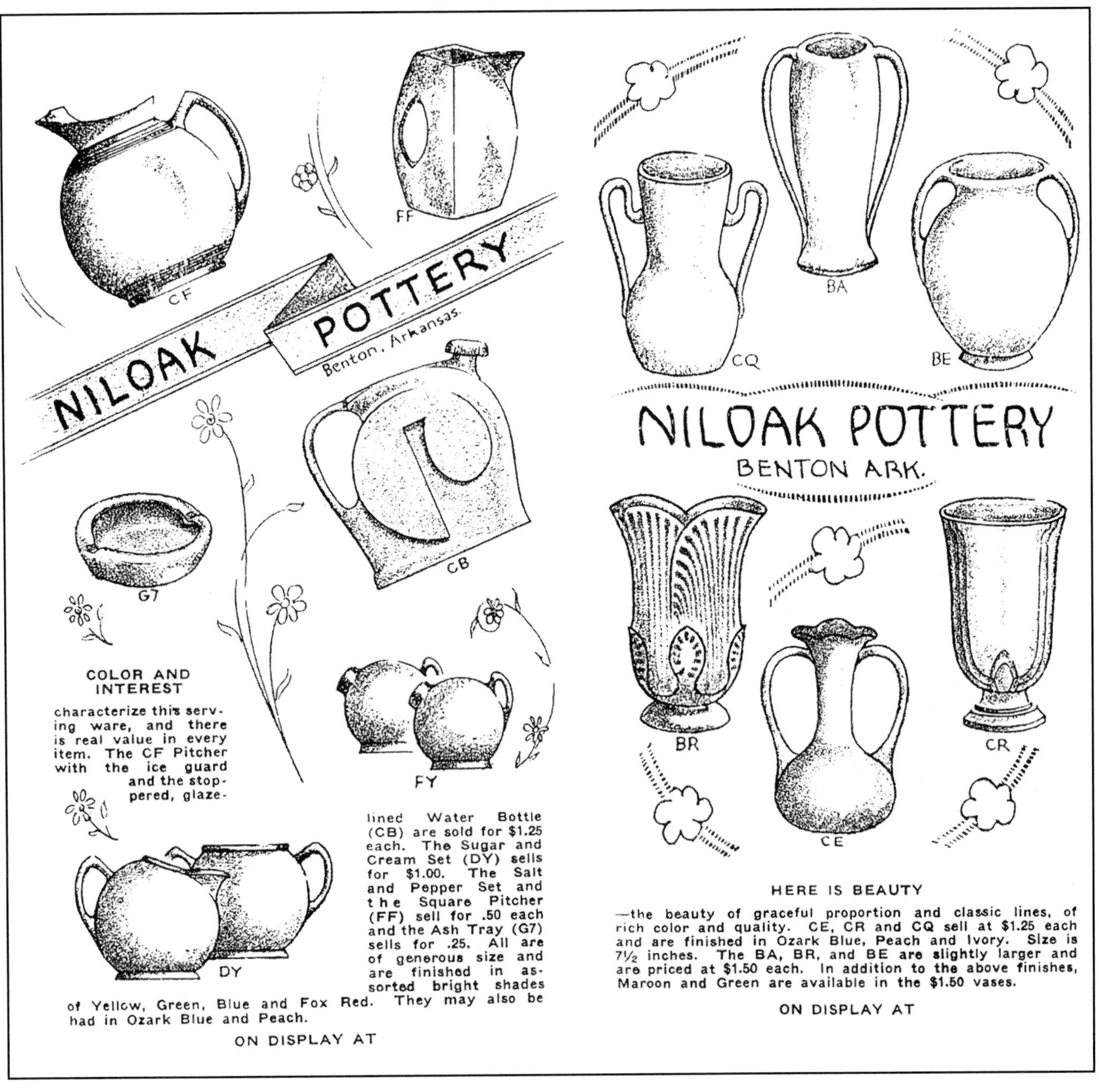

NILOAK POTTERY
Benton, Arkansas
CF
FF
CB
G7
FY
DY
COLOR AND INTEREST
characterize this serving ware, and there is real value in every item. The CF Pitcher with the ice guard and the stoppered, glaze-lined Water Bottle (CB) are sold for $1.25 each. The Sugar and Cream Set (DY) sells for $1.00. The Salt and Pepper Set and the Square Pitcher (FF) sell for .50 each and the Ash Tray (G7) sells for .25. All are of generous size and are finished in assorted bright shades of Yellow, Green, Blue and Fox Red. They may also be had in Ozark Blue and Peach.
ON DISPLAY AT
BA
CQ
BE
NILOAK POTTERY
BENTON ARK.
BR
CR
CE
HERE IS BEAUTY
—the beauty of graceful proportion and classic lines, of rich color and quality. CE, CR and CQ sell at $1.25 each and are finished in Ozark Blue, Peach and Ivory. Size is 7½ inches. The BA, BR, and BE are slightly larger and are priced at $1.50 each. In addition to the above finishes, Maroon and Green are available in the $1.50 vases.
ON DISPLAY AT

Advertising Cards, c. 1935. ***Author's Collection.***

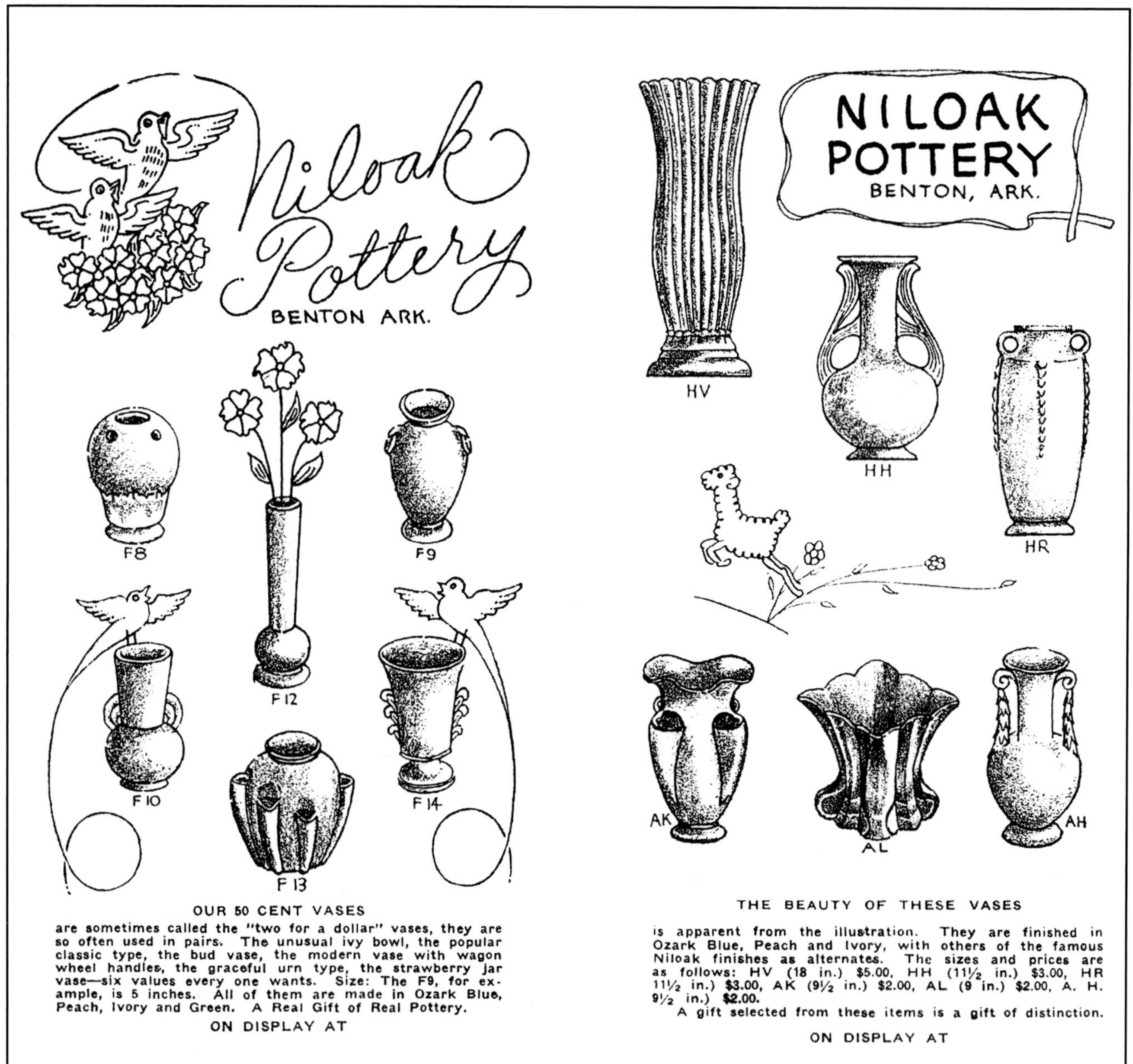

Niloak Pottery
BENTON ARK.
F8
F12
F9
F10
F13
F14
OUR 50 CENT VASES
are sometimes called the "two for a dollar" vases, they are so often used in pairs. The unusual ivy bowl, the popular classic type, the bud vase, the modern vase with wagon wheel handles, the graceful urn type, the strawberry jar vase—six values every one wants. Size: The F9, for example, is 5 inches. All of them are made in Ozark Blue, Peach, Ivory and Green. A Real Gift of Real Pottery.
ON DISPLAY AT
NILOAK
POTTERY
BENTON, ARK.
HV
HH
HR
AK
AL
AH
THE BEAUTY OF THESE VASES
is apparent from the illustration. They are finished in Ozark Blue, Peach and Ivory, with others of the famous Niloak finishes as alternates. The sizes and prices are as follows: HV (18 in.) $5.00, HH (11½ in.) $3.00, HR 11½ in.) $3.00, AK (9½ in.) $2.00, AL (9 in.) $2.00, A. H. 9½ in.) $2.00.
A gift selected from these items is a gift of distinction.
ON DISPLAY AT

Advertising Cards, c. 1935. ***Author's Collection.***

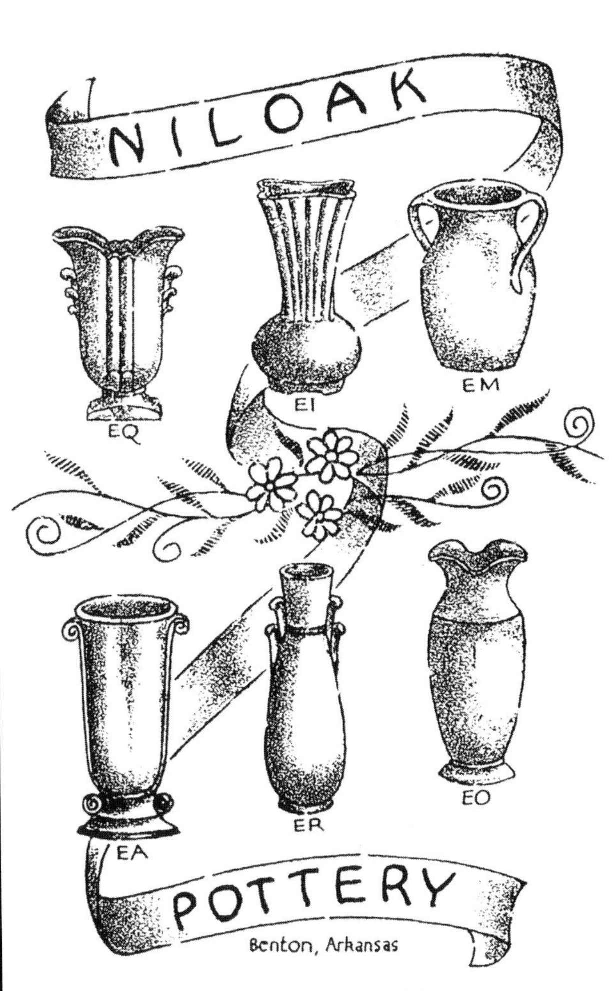

AT SEVENTY-FIVE CENTS

we offer the six entirely different vase types everyone should have. Sizes vary from 6 inches to 8 inches, as you may notice from the illustration, and floral accomodations vary from a spray to a single bud.

Colors may be selected from unusual shades of Blue, Peach, Maroon, Ivory and Green, to harmonize or contrast with any interior.

Gifts that will continue to give Beauty and Interest wherever they are used.

ON DISPLAY AT

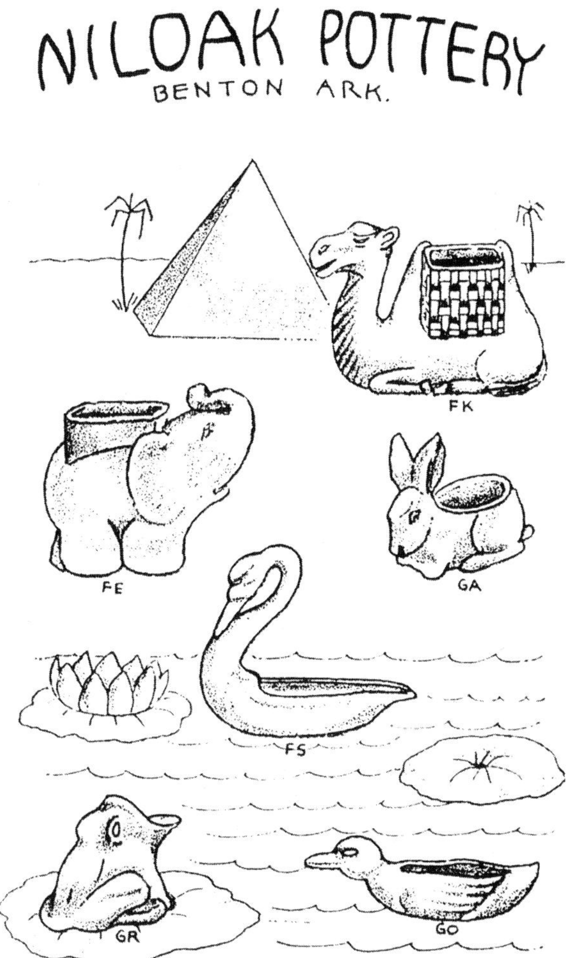

POTTERY ANIMALS

for plant and flower holders, trays and ornaments. The Frog, Duck and Rabbit are .25 each, and the Swan, Elephant and Camel are .50 each. They are made in Blue, Ivory and Peach., together with other assorted selected finishes. The Swan is 5½ inches in length, and the other shapes are shown in scale. Here is color, novelty and value in just the shapes you have always wanted.

ON DISPLAY AT

Advertising Cards, c. 1935. ***Author's Collection.***

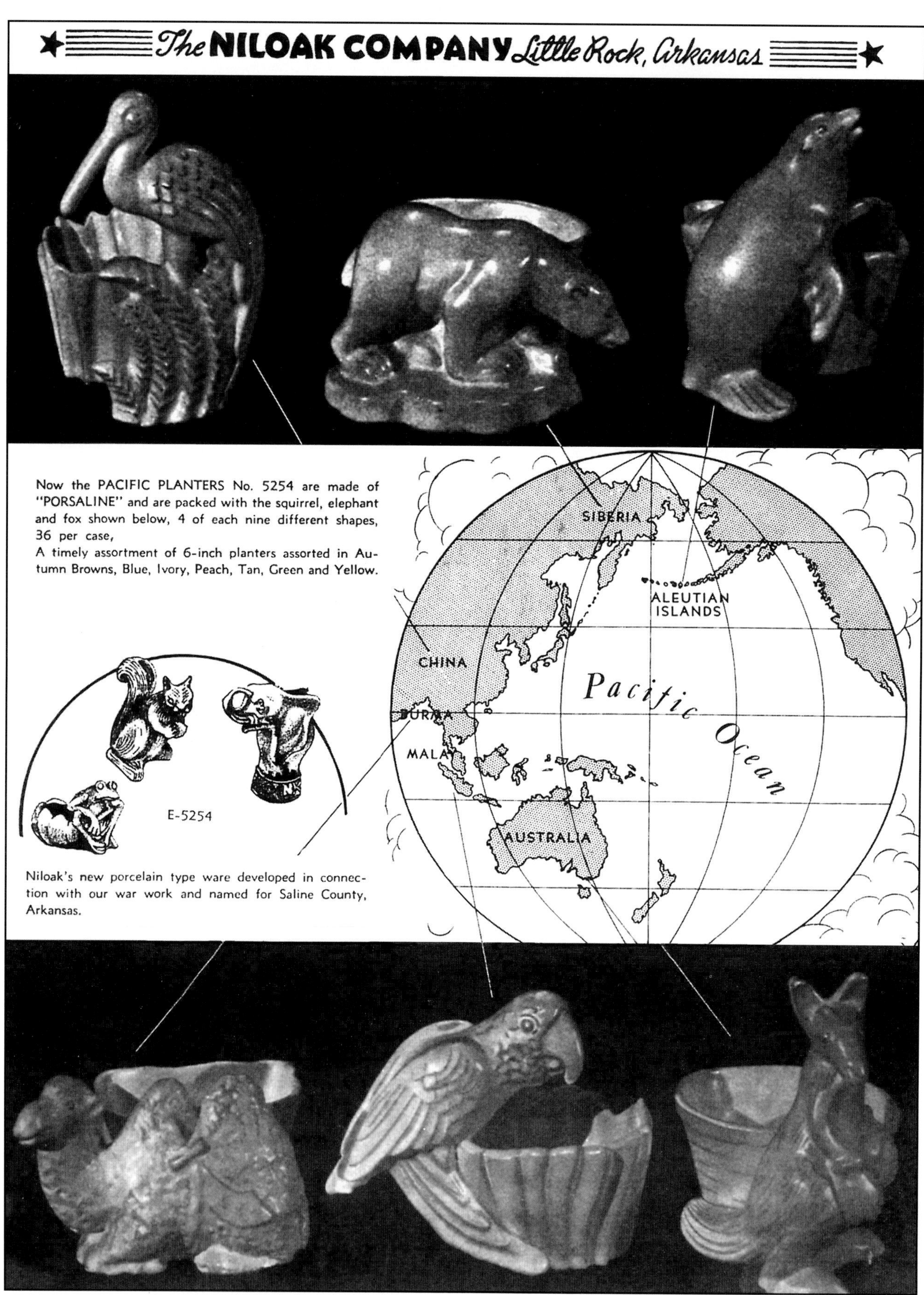

The NILOAK COMPANY Little Rock, Arkansas
Now the PACIFIC PLANTERS No. 5254 are made of "PORSALINE" and are packed with the squirrel, elephant and fox shown below, 4 of each nine different shapes, 36 per case,
A timely assortment of 6-inch planters assorted in Autumn Browns, Blue, Ivory, Peach, Tan, Green and Yellow.
E-5254
Niloak's new porcelain type ware developed in connection with our war work and named for Saline County, Arkansas.
SIBERIA
ALEUTIAN ISLANDS
CHINA
Pacific Ocean
MALA
AUSTRALIA

Advertising Sheet, Pacific Planters, c. 1942. *Courtesy of Melvin and Pat Minton.*

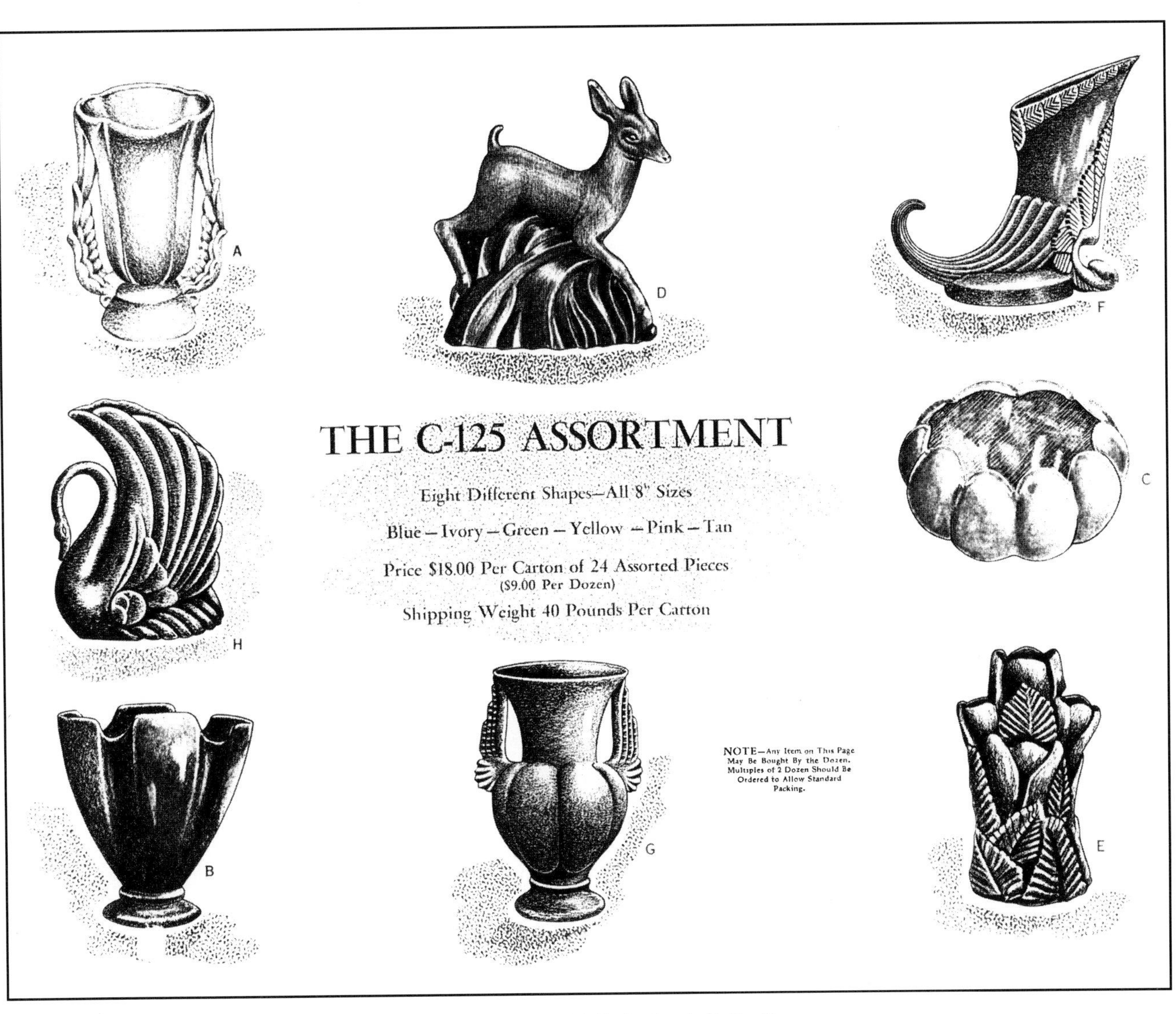

A
D
F
THE C-125 ASSORTMENT
Eight Different Shapes—All 8" Sizes
Blue – Ivory – Green – Yellow – Pink – Tan
Price $18.00 Per Carton of 24 Assorted Pieces
($9.00 Per Dozen)
Shipping Weight 40 Pounds Per Carton
C
H
NOTE—Any Item on This Page May Be Bought By the Dozen. Multiples of 2 Dozen Should Be Ordered to Allow Standard Packing.
B
G
E

Advertising Sheet, c. 1945. *Author's Collection.*

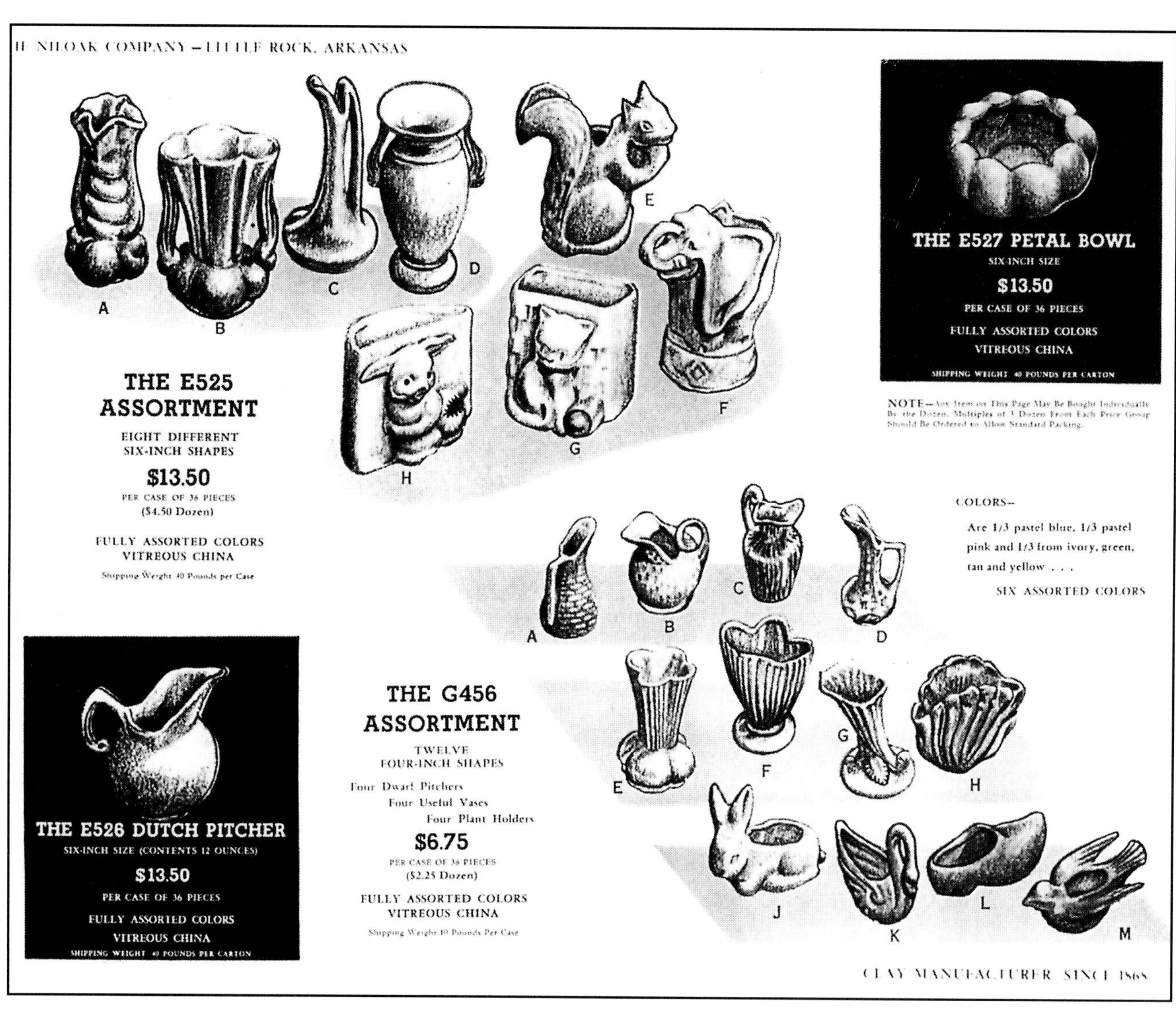

THE NILOAK COMPANY – LITTLE ROCK, ARKANSAS
A
B
C
D
E
F
G
H
THE E525 ASSORTMENT
EIGHT DIFFERENT SIX-INCH SHAPES
$13.50
PER CASE OF 36 PIECES
($4.50 Dozen)
FULLY ASSORTED COLORS
VITREOUS CHINA
Shipping Weight 40 Pounds per Case
THE E527 PETAL BOWL
SIX-INCH SIZE
$13.50
PER CASE OF 36 PIECES
FULLY ASSORTED COLORS
VITREOUS CHINA
SHIPPING WEIGHT 40 POUNDS PER CARTON
NOTE—Any Item on This Page May Be Bought Individually By the Dozen. Multiples of 3 Dozen From Each Price Group Should Be Ordered to Allow Standard Packing.
COLORS—
Are 1/3 pastel blue, 1/3 pastel pink and 1/3 from ivory, green, tan and yellow . . .
SIX ASSORTED COLORS
THE E526 DUTCH PITCHER
SIX-INCH SIZE (CONTENTS 12 OUNCES)
$13.50
PER CASE OF 36 PIECES
FULLY ASSORTED COLORS
VITREOUS CHINA
SHIPPING WEIGHT 40 POUNDS PER CARTON
THE G456 ASSORTMENT
TWELVE FOUR-INCH SHAPES
Four Dwarf Pitchers
Four Useful Vases
Four Plant Holders
$6.75
PER CASE OF 36 PIECES
($2.25 Dozen)
FULLY ASSORTED COLORS
VITREOUS CHINA
Shipping Weight 10 Pounds Per Case
A
B
C
D
E
F
G
H
J
K
L
M
CLAY MANUFACTURER SINCE 1868

Advertising Sheet, c. 1945. *Author's Collection.*

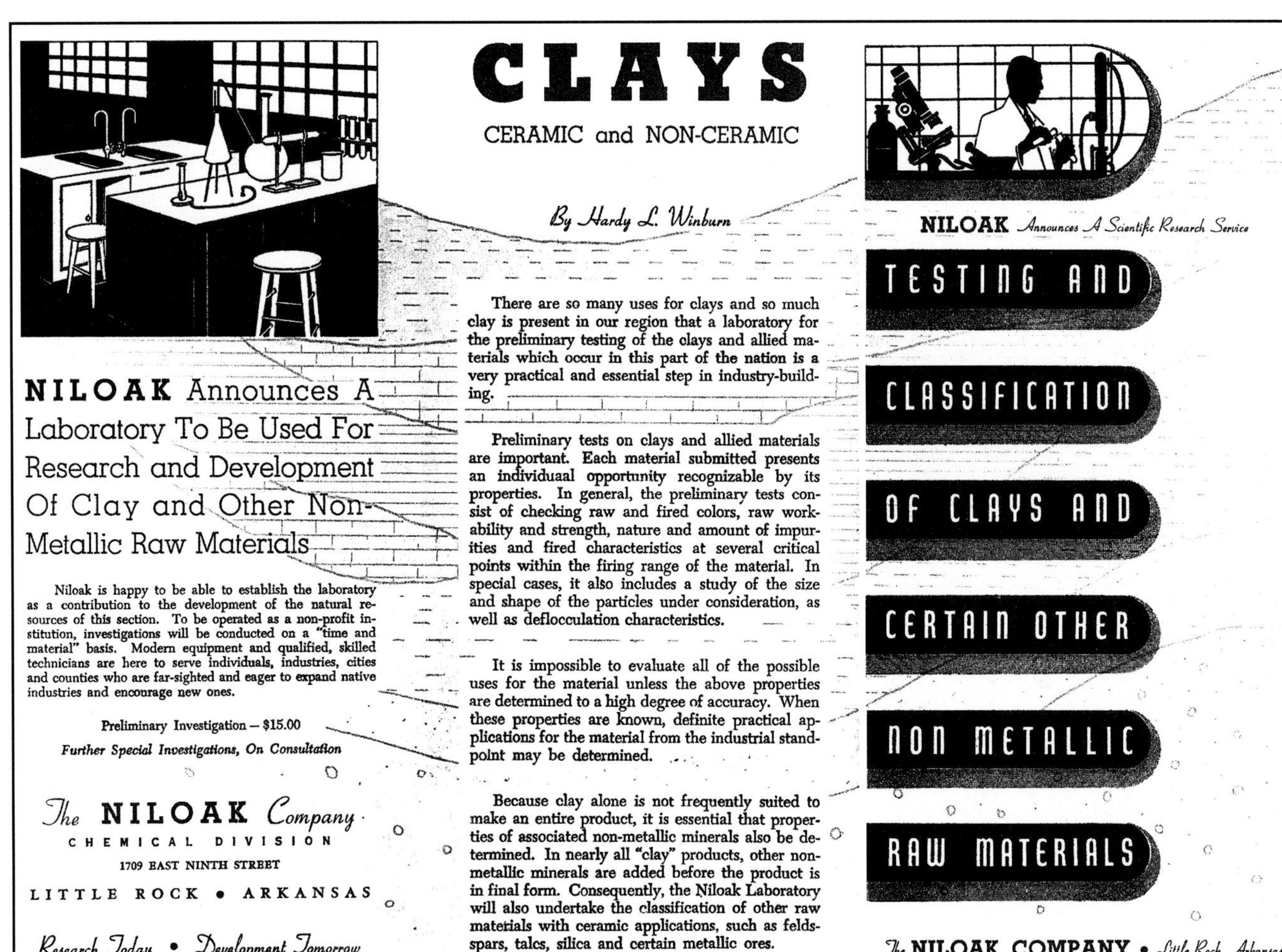

Advertising Sheet, Niloak Chemical Division, front view, c. 1945. ***Author's Collection.***

Research Today - - -

Development Tomorrow

Native industry is expanding . . . study now of raw materials will insure their successful use in the future . . . use in native industries as they reconvert from war work . . . use as foundations for the new industries of a secure peace.

Laboratory Under Direction of

Wm. E. Crockett, C. E.

CERAMIC ENGINEER

University of Missouri — Clay Technologist

Assisted by E. S. AMOS,

Ceramic Engineer, Ohio State University

Is the term "Clay Technologist" new to you? Briefly, a clay technologist is a scientist trained with respect to the testing of non-metallic minerals, especially clay minerals. He knows not only *how* to test the materials but also knows the type of plant and the application wherein the materials being tested will be best used. He not only finds materials for known markets but also finds markets for known materials.

A Commercial Necessity

•

a. Ceramic Uses of Clays

ABRASIVES—Clays are used in vitreous grinding wheel bonds.

ARTWARE—Clays are used in the manufacture of vases, lamps, costume jewelry, figurines, novelties, sculpture, etc.

CHEMICAL WARE—Battery jars, acid jars, porcelain crucibles, etc.

DINNERWARE—Semi-vitreous and vitreous, for domestic use.

ELECTRICAL PORCELAIN—High and low tension, as used on highlines and in domestic applications respectively.

FLOOR AND WALL TILE—Artistic, durable, sanitary floor and wall coverings for baths, public buildings, etc.

GLASS—Clays enter into the refractories in which glass is melted and in special cases enter into the glass batch proper.

HOTEL CHINA—Durable vitreous china for hotel and allied institutional use.

PORCELAIN ENAMEL—Clays are used to suspend enamel frits and to produce certain bubble structures in the enameling of hollowware, bathtubs, etc.

REFRACTORIES—High temperature cements, fire brick, insulating fire brick, radiants, stove and flue liners, etc.

SANITARYWARE—Lavatories, toilet assemblies, etc.

STEATITE—High frequency Radar insulation, as a plasticizer and bonding agent.

STRUCTURAL CLAY PRODUCTS—Common brick, building tile, roofing tile, sewer tile, etc.

b. Non-Ceramic Uses of Clays

ADHESIVES—Filler and plasticizer in many cements, glues, etc.

ABSORBENTS—Clays with high absorptive properties are used to remove oils, etc., from factory floors.

DETERGENTS—Many types of washing powders, etc., employ certain types of clay.

EMULSIONS—Certain clay types act as emulsifying agents with asphalt and other substances of an allied nature.

FILTRATION PLANTS—Clays are used to clarify and purify water, oils, etc.

INSECTICIDES—Clays are used as carriers and diluents in many insecticidal dusts.

INSULATION—Certain clay types are used as a reacting agent and bonding agent in the manufacture of special lightweight insulation.

LINOLEUM—The linoleum industry uses clay as a filling agent; also to produce certain desirable working characteristics.

MEDICINAL—Special types of clay are used as extenders and diluents for active ingredients.

PAINTS—Clays are used as fillers for interior paints and in certain instances as fillers for camouflage paints, etc., for exterior use.

PAPER—Clays are used to fill and coat many types of paper.

PETROLEUM INDUSTRY—Clays are used for filtering and bleaching oils and in certain applications as catalytic agents.

RUBBER—Clays are used in many rubber compounds as a filler.

TEXTILES—Many textiles employ clay as a filler.

The above lists are by no means complete, but are intended to illustrate the diversity of products into which clay is incorporated.

CLAY

Is Yours Worthless - - - or Do You Have Valuable Raw Material Waiting To Be Developed?

Write, Wire or Phone

The NILOAK Company

CHEMICAL DIVISION

1709 EAST NINTH STREET

LITTLE ROCK • ARKANSAS

•

(Excerpts From Letter of November 13, 1944.)

STATE OF ARKANSAS

GEOLOGICAL SURVEY

"The matter of a ceramic laboratory . . . impresses me more and more as the need for such a laboratory becomes increasingly apparent.

"The Survey is equipped to do a limited amount of field investigation . . . but is not provided with specialized personnel and equipment necessary to continue the investigation of a clay to that stage where it is possible to absolutely demonstrate its utility.

"The State Geological Survey will welcome an opportunity to co-operate with the public in all phases of field sampling and evaluation and such other aid as we may give incidental to laboratory testing.

Respectfully,

(Signed) JOE W. KIMZEY,

State Geologist."

Advertising Sheet, Niloak Chemical Division, back view, c. 1945. ***Author's Collection.***

Glossary

This glossary has been adapted from Sharon and Bob Huxford's book, *Collector's Encyclopedia of Roseville Pottery* and Jack Chipman's *Collector's Encyclopedia of California Pottery.*

Airbrush Decoration (Overspray): Decorative process whereby an atomizer employing compressed air is used to spray paint in a fine mist.

Art Pottery: True form of art, unique in shape or decoration, motivated by free expression of one's artistic abilities.

Body: Term referring to the particular type and characteristics of the material forming a vessel. Structure of a ceramic object.

Cast: Objects which are duplicated by pouring liquid clay into plaster production molds.

Ceramics: Term used to cover a variety of fired, clay products. All-inclusive term for the art of making objects of fired clay.

Crazing: The crackled appearance of certain glazes caused by uneven expansion and contraction between body and glaze.

Designer: One who develops proposed shapes for molds.

Embossed: Raised design formed on the surface of an item within the mold.

Finishing: Process of smoothing out rough spots and removing incidental defects in swirl/Missionware prior to firing.

Glaze: The finish applied to the surface of pottery as a liquid and fired in the kiln until it becomes a hard and protective covering for the pottery.

Hand Thrown: Objects formed by hand on a potter's wheel.

Jigger: Type of molding machine whereby the clay is pressed into the sides of the mold while it is spinning on the wheel, and the object is formed. Semi-automated pottery.

Jobber: Individual or organization which obtains ware directly from producers (sometimes under exclusive contract) and sells it to retailers and individuals.

Kaolin: A white to yellowish, non-plastic clay which burns white.

Kiln: Oven designed specifically for the high temperatures required for baking and glazing clay objects.

Models: An original object from which molds are made for production purposes.

Molds: Sectional forms which are used to shape pottery, either by casting, in which case liquid clay or slip is poured into the mold, allowed to stand until desired thickness adheres to the wall of the mold, the excess then poured out; or by jiggering. A hollow plaster of Paris form into which plastic clay is pressed or liquid clay is poured.

Periodic Kiln: Kiln in which ware is heated in a gradual cycle and allowed to cool before removal.

Pottery: Objects, especially vessels, which are made from fired clay. General term that includes earthenware, stoneware, and porcelain.

Second: Any item not meeting standard quality control as first grade, but not having serious imperfections.

Utilitarian: General term for stoneware. Includes crocks, urns, jugs for use in and around the home.

Bibliography

A historical study of this nature requires extensive research. Visiting nearly all the archives and many libraries in Arkansas and throughout the nation, over 10,000 issues of Arkansas and clay-related publications were surveyed, and more than 50 years worth of newspapers were read. Moreover, an extensive search was undertaken to locate people to interview who were associated one way or another with Niloak. Among the secondary works, I found *Art Pottery of the United States* by Paul Evans to be helpful. While Evans's accounts represent the nearest to overall correctness in context, other writers' histories were helpful in showing me the diversity of contradicting information which existed.

The following bibliography is broken down into books, articles, advertisements, miscellaneous historical records, and interviews. Among the primary sources were city and state directories, state histories, geological surveys, and industry directories for Arkansas. The largest commitment of time was reading local and state newspapers. The *Arkansas Gazette* was read from 1908 to 1914 completely, and December Sundays up to 1923 resulting in the location of several articles as well as the many Niloak Pottery advertisements.

As for Benton's local paper, it is unfortunate that the continuous back issues of the *Benton Courier* do not exist until 1914. For this book, I read from 1914 to the early 1950s, yielding vast amounts of Niloak Pottery history and personal accounts of Hyten, the Winburns, Frank Long, and others. Most importantly, the history of the 1920s is based on these accounts from the *Benton Courier*. In addition, articles in both the *Gazette* and *Courier* led to finding additional information in other Arkansas newspapers and publications.

Journals of many kinds were surveyed. The most fruitful one was the *Dixie Magazine*. Also, The *Clay-Worker* from 1908 to 1932 held various Niloak Pottery articles and Arkansas clay-related information. Last, Niloak information was secured through various bibliographies.

I was fortunate to locate Niloak Pottery information in the Charles Dove Photograph Collection at the University of Central Arkansas Archives and Special Collections; the Governor Futrell papers and the Sanborn Insurance Maps at the Arkansas History Commission; and the Mary Hudgins Collection at the Univeristy of Arkansas Special Collections. As for private materials, I accessed the Niloak Pottery and Tile Corporation records from the Winburn Tile Company (courtesy of its past president, the late Hardy L. Winburn IV). These private records provided, along with information gained from the *Benton Courier,* much of the information used in recounting Niloak Pottery's history from 1934 to the late 1950s.

Lastly, I relied on several important interviews conducted with Lee Joe Alley, Howard S. Lewis, Mrs. Beatrice Sanders, Lydia Stoin, and the late William F. Long for information on various aspects concerning Niloak pottery.

Books

Anderson, Richard J. *Mineral Resources of Montgomery, Garland, Saline, and Pulaski Counties.* Little Rock: Arkansas Geological Survey, 1942.

Annual Directory of Women's Organizations, Greater Little Rock, 1934–35. Little Rock: Women's City Club, 1934.

Arkansas State Gazetteer and Business Directory for 1884–5. Saint Louis: R.L. Polk and Company, 1884.

Arkansas State Gazetteer and Business Directory for 1888–9. Atlanta: R.L. Polk and Company, 1888.

Arkansas State Gazetteer and Business Directory for 1892–3. Detroit: R.L. Polk and Company, 1892.

Arkansas State Gazetteer and Business Directory for 1898–9. Detroit: R.L. Polk and Company, 1898.

Baker, T. Harri, and Jane Browning. *An Arkansas History for Young People.* Fayetteville: The University of Arkansas Press, 1991.

Bennett, Swannee and William B. Worthen. Ark*ansas Made: A Survey of the Decorative, Mechanical, Fine Arts Produced in Arkansas 1819–1870.* 2 Vols. Fayetteville: University of Arkansas Press, 1990.

Blasberg, Robert W. *George E. Ohr and His Biloxi Art Pottery.* Port Jervis, NY: J. W. Carpenter, 1973.

Blasberg, Robert W., Robert Ellison, Jr., and Eugene Hecht. *The Mad Potter of Biloxi: The Art and Life of George E. Ohr.* New York: Abbeville Press, 1989.

Branner, John C. *Clays of Arkansas.* Washington, D.C.: Government Printing Office – United States Geological Survey, 1908.

____. *Outlines of Arkansas' Mineral Resources.* Little Rock: Bureau of Mines, Manufacturers and Agriculture and State Geological Survey, 1927.

Burnett, Fred Mark. *The Evans Family Pottery of Southeast Missouri, 1858–1969.* Cape Girardeau, MO: Southeast Missouri State University, 1978.

Business Directory of the State of Arkansas, 1900. Little Rock: Southern Directory Company, 1900.

Community Progress. Publisher unknown, 1942.Curran, Pamela Duvall. *Shawnee Pottery: The Full Encyclopedia.* Atglen, PA: Schiffer Publishing LTD, 1955.

Duke, Harvey. *Official Guide to Pottery and Porcelain.* Eighth edition. New York: House, of Collectibles, 1995.

Ellis, Anita J. *Rookwood Pottery: The Glaze Lines.* Atglen, PA: Schiffer Publishing LTD, 1995.

____. *Rookwood Pottery, the Glorious Gamble.* New York: Rizzoli International Publications, Inc., 1992.

Evans, Paul. *Art Pottery of the United States: An Encyclopedia of Producers and Their Marks.* 2nd edition. New York: Feingold and Lewis, 1987.

Ferguson, Jim G. *Arkansas Marketing and Industrial Guide and Directory of Manufacture.* Little Rock: Department of Mines, Manufacturers and Agriculture, 1921.

____. *Directory of Arkansas Industries.* Little Rock: Department of Mines, Manufacturing and Agriculture, 1924.

Gifford, David Edwin. *Arkansas Art Pottery Bibliography.* Bibliography Series 3. Conway, Arkansas: University of Central Arkansas Archives and Special Collections, 1989.

____. *The Collector's Encyclopedia of Niloak Pottery: A Reference and Value Guide.* First edition. Paducah, KY: Collector Books, 1993.

____. *The Collector's Guide to Camark Pottery: Identification and Values.* Paducah, KY: Collector Books, 1997.

____. *The Collector's Guide to Camark Pottery: Identification and Values, Book II.* Paducah, KY: Collector Books, 1997.

Goodspeed. *Biographical and Historical Memoirs of Pulaski, Jefferson, Lonoke, Faulkner, Grant, Saline, Perry, Garland, and Hot Springs Counties, Arkansas Comprising a Condensed History of the State, a number of Biographies of Distinguished Citizens of the Same, a Brief Descriptive History of Each of the Counties above Named, and Numerous Biographical Sketches of their Prominent Citizens.* Chicago: Goodspeed Publishing Company, 1889.

Herndon, Dallas T. *Centennial History of Arkansas.* 3 Volume. Chicago-Little Rock: S.J. Clarke Publishing Company, 1922.

Houdeshell, James. *Houghton and Dalton Pottery.* Finley, Ohio: By the author, 1983.

Huxford, Sharon and Bob. *Collector's Encyclopedia of Weller Pottery.* Paducah, KY: Collector Books 1979.

Hyten, Robert S., Jr. *Hyten: An American Family.* Second edition. N. P., 1988.

Johnson, Deb and Gini. *Beginner's Book of American Pottery.* Des Moines: Wallace-Homestead Book Company, 1974.

Kovel, Ralph and Terry. *The Kovels' Collector's Guide to American Art Pottery.* New York: Crown Publishing Incorporated, 1974.

Lehner, Lois. *Lehner's Encyclopedia of U.S. Marks on Pottery, Porcelain, and Clay.* Paducah, KY: Collector Books, 1988.

Levin, Elaine. *The History of American Ceramic, 1607 to the Present.* New York: Harry N. Abrams, Inc., 1988.

Nelson, Marion John. *Art Pottery of the Midwest.* University of Minnesota, Minneapolis: University Art Museum, 1988.

Newman, Marvin J. *Recollections of Saline County compiled by the Benton Courier.* Marceline, MO: D-Books Publishing Co., 1997.

Official Gazette of the Patent and Trademark Office, trademark #195,889 (March 3, 1925) and patent #1,657,997 (January 31, 1928). Washington: United States Government Printing Office.

Poesch, Jessie. *Newcomb Pottery: An Enterprise for Southern Women, 1895–1940.* Exton, Pennsylvania: Schiffer Publishing Ltd, 1984.

Polk's Arkansas State Gazetteer and Business Directory, 1906–1907. Volume V. Memphis: R.L. Polk and Company, 1906.

Polk's Arkansas State Gazetteer and Business Directory, 1912–1913. Volume VI. Memphis: R.L. Polk and Company, 1912.

Sayers, Robert. "Potters in a Changing South." *In The Not So Solid South: Anthropological Studies in a Regional Subculture.* J. Kenneth Moreland, ed. Athens, GA: Southern Anthropological Society, 1971.

Tuchman, Mitch. *Bauer: Classic American Pottery.* San Francisco: Chronicle Books, 1995.

Turnquist, Thomas G. *Denver's White Pottery.* Tulsa: The Homestead Press, 1980.

United Commercial Travelers of America. Little Rock Council *No.167 Building Fund Souvenir.* Publisher Unknown, 1909.

Williams, Norman F., and Norman Plummer. *Clay Resources of the Wilcox Group in Arkansas.* Little Rock: Arkansas Resources and Development Commission, 1951.

Winburn, Hardy L. III. *Seventy Years of Saline County Pottery.* Benton: Niloak Pottery Company, 1938.

ARTICLES/PRESS RELEASES

"Advertising Niloak." Benton Courier, 17 April 1924, 1.

"Arkansas Boosters Are Received by Coolidge." Arkansas Gazette, 25 November 1923, 1.

"Arkansas Brick Men Experiencing a Busy Season." *The Clay-Worker* 84 (July 1925): 30.

"Arkansas Clay Situation." *Dixie Magazine* 3 (September 1927): 35–37.

"Arkansas Is Noted as Mineral State." *Arkansas Gazette,* 16 June 1929, 15B.

"Arkansas Pottery is Feature of Show." Arkansas Gazette, 30 November 1910, 6.

"The Arkansas Products Company." *The Gift and Art Shop* [Volume number unknown] (March 1932): 113.

"Arkansas' Wonderful Mineral Resources." *Arkansas Gazette,* 14 July 1912, 12.

"At Benton." *Arkansas Gazette,* 17 January 1909, 3 (Section II).

"At Benton." *Arkansas Gazette,* 17 January 1909, 5.

Atkinson, J.W. "J.W. Atkinson Tells of Benton at the Present." *Benton Courier,* 30 April 1931, 1, 8.

"Beautiful Niloak Pottery An Exclusive Product of Arkansas Clay Deposit." *Arkansas Democrat,* 6 November 1921, 10.

"Benton." *Benton Courier,* 27 March 1913, 1, 5.

"Benton, Capital of Saline, Prosperous and Progressive." *Arkansas Democrat,* 5 June 1904, 10–11(Section II).

"Benton to Manufacture Art Pottery." *Arkansas Gazette,* 1 February 1909, 6.

Bott, Leo Paul, Jr. "The Niloak Pottery, Benton Ark." *Ceramic Age* 11 (June 1928): 219–220.

Branner, George C. "Expansion in Arkansas Clay, 1926 and 1927." *Ceramic Age* 10 (July 1927): 22.

"Brick Makers Convene Today." *Arkansas Gazette,* 28 March 1910, 14.

"Busy Benton and its Development." *Arkansas Gazette,* 9 January 1909, 10.

"C.D. Hyten Loses Life by Drowning in Saline River." *Benton Courier,* 7 September 1944, 1.

Carney, Margaret. "Henan Marbled Ware." *Oriental Art* 34 (Winter 1988–89): 245–254.

"Ceramic at the Century of Progress Exposition." *The Clay-Worker* 95 (February 1931): 117.

Chenault, Fletcher. "Artistic Pottery Made at Benton." *Arkansas Gazette,* 7 January 1926, 3, 11.

"Clays of Benton." *Arkansas Gazette,* 23 March 1910, 10.

Cox, Paul E. "Clay Working by Amateurs in Arkansas With Arkansas Clays." *Dixie Magazine* 2 (October 1926): 40.

Crowley, Lillian H. "It's Now the Potter's Turn." *International Studio* 75 (September 1922): 539–540.

"Damage at Eagle Pottery Is Repaired." *Benton Courier,* 24 March 1932, 1.

Davidson, Clair. "The Ridge Pottery of Evans Crowley." *Antique Journal* [Volume number unknown] (August 1972): 17–18.

"Department of Ceramic Engineering of Iowa State College Entertains its Friends." *The Clay-Worker* 91 (June 1929): 582.

Doherty, Bob. "Niloak Swirl Production." *American Clay Exchange* 4 (March 1984): 2.

"Editorial Notes and Clippings." *The Clay-Worker* 51 (February 1909): 358.

Dunnahoo, Pat. "Made From Arkansas Clays: Pottery Making Dates Back to Early Indians Days." *Arkansas Democrat Magazine,* 7 January 1962, 3.

"Editorial Notes and Clippings." *The Clay-Worker* 60 (December 1913): 686.

"Fair Brought to Successful Close." *Arkansas Gazette,* 16 October 1910, 1.

"Famed Potter, C.D. Hyten, of Benton, Drowns." *Arkansas Democrat,* 7 September 1944, 3.

"The Famous Niloak Pottery, Benton, Using Arkansas Kaolin." *Arkansas Democrat UCV Reunion Edition,* 16–18 May 1911, 35.

Forester, Bobbie. "Workers in Clay." *Arkansas Gazette,* 11 September 1932, 5.

Forster, Ken. "Some Notes on Southern Pottery." *Journal of the American Art Pottery Association* 2(September/October 1987): 4, 16.

[Funk, Erwin].
"Arkansas Editors Learn Facts About State." *The Rodgers Democrat,* 3 June 1926, 2.

____. "F.W. Sanders and Co." *Arkansas Gazette,* 16 May 1911, 4.

Gifford, David Edwin, "Arkansas Art Pottery: A Historical Perspective." *Journal of the American Art Pottery Association.* 6 (January/February 1991): 1, 3–9, 12.

____. "Howard S. Lewis." *Journal of the American Art Pottery Association* 8 (September/October 1993): 4.

____. "Not Necessarily Niloak." *Journal of American Art Pottery Association* 8 (January/February 1991): 8–11.

____. "The Ouachita Pottery Company of Hot Springs: The Beginning of the Arkansas Art Pottery Industry." *The Record* (Garland County Historical Society, 1990), 42–49.

"Ground Is Broken For Niloak Plant." *Benton Courier,* 6 September 1928, 1.

Hamm, Jo. "Desert Sands Pottery." *Antique Journal* [Volume number unknown] (February 1971), 24–25.

"Handmade 'Ozark Pottery,' Made from Native Clays, New Northwest Arkansas Industry." *Fayetteville Daily Democrat,* 19 February 1926, 1.

"Hardy Lathan Winburn IV: Ceo at 37, Took Firm to Top of Tile Making." *Arkansas Democrat-Gazette,* 10 August 1997, 4B.

"Has Paper Printed Twenty Years Ago." *Benton Courier,* 4 October 1917, 7.

"Here, There, Everywhere." *The Clay-Worker,* 87 (May 1927): 484, 486.

"Here, There, Everywhere." *The Clay-Worker,* 88 (September

1927): 218.

"Here, There, Everywhere." *The Clay-Worker,* 90 (October 1928): 316.

"Here, There, Everywhere." *The Clay-Worker,* 90 (December 1928): 488.

Herrington, Gene. "Little Rock Pottery Firm Sets Reconversion Record after Wartime Contract Is Canceled." *Arkansas Democrat,* 17 March 1946, 7B.

"The Hytens Are Home." *Benton Courier,* 4 September 1924, 1.

"In Arkansas." *Benton Courier,* 15 October 1925, 1.

"Iowa State Clay Worker's Conference." *The Clay-Worker,* 97 (February 1932): 108.

"Iowa State College Celebrates Annual Spring Festival." *The Clay-Worker* 97 (May 1932): 326.

"J. W. Atkinson Tells of Benton at the Present." *Benton Courier,* 30 April 1931, 1, 8.

"Kau-Ling – High Ridge." *Dixie Magazine* 2 (January 1926): 15.

"Latest News from Benton." *Arkansas Democrat,* 1 May 1904, 8.

"Latest Pottery on Display Here." *Arkansas Gazette,* 15 December 1931, 10.

"Local News." *Benton Courier,* 31 May 1917, 5.

"Local News." *Benton Courier,* 19 July 1917, 5.

"Local News." *Benton Courier,* 2 August 1917, 4.

"Local News." *Benton Courier,* 20 September 1917, 5.

"Local News." *Benton Courier,* 19 June 1919, 5.

"Local News." *Benton Courier,* 14 August 1919, 5.

"Local News." *Benton Courier,* 2 October 1919, 5.

"Locals." *Benton Courier,* 12 January 1922, 5.

"Locals." *Benton Courier,* 2 August 1923, 5.

"Locals." *Benton Courier,* 23 August 1923, 5.

"Locals." *Benton Courier,* 4 October 1923, 5.

"Locals." *Benton Courier,* 15 November 1923, 5.

"Locals." *Benton Courier,* 20 December 1923, 5.

"Locals." *Benton Courier,* 1 January 1925, 5.

"Locals." *Benton Courier,* 2 July 1925, 5.

"Locals." *Benton Courier,* 22 October 1925, 5.

"Locals." *Benton Courier,* 29 October 1925, 5.

"Locals." *Benton Courier,* 1 April 1926, 5.

"Locals." *Benton Courier,* 23 September 1926, 5.

"Locals." *Benton Courier,* 31 March 1927, 5.

"Locals." *Benton Courier,* 21 April 1927, 5.

"Locals." *Benton Courier,* 29 September 1927, 5.

"Locals." *Benton Courier,* 13 October 1927, 5.

"Locals." *Benton Courier,* 20 October 1927, 5.

"Locals." *Benton Courier,* 19 January 1928, 5.

"Locals." *Benton Courier,* 23 February 1928, 5.

"Locals." *Benton Courier,* 13 December 1928, 5.

"Locals." *Benton Courier,* 18 April 1929, 5.

"Locals." *Benton Courier,* 17 October 1929, 5.

"Locals." *Benton Courier,* 8 May 1930, 5.

"Locals." *Benton Courier,* 28 September 1933, 5.

"Locals." *Benton Courier,* 21 June 1934, 5.

"Locals." *Benton Courier,* 21 February 1935, 5.

"Locals." *Benton Courier,* 26 September 1935, 5.

"Locals." *Benton Courier,* 30 May 1940, 5.

"Locals." *Benton Courier,* 26 September 1940, 5.

"LR Woman Is Christmas Card Decorator." *Arkansas Gazette,* 21 December 1919, 7, (section II).

"Machinery for a Pottery: Equipment Purchased in Little Rock Yesterday by Benton Men." *Arkansas Gazette,* 2 February 1909, 10.

"Members Benton Lions Club Visit Plastic Plant at Pottery." *Benton Courier,* 22 July 1948, 1.

Moore, Caruth S. "Making of Pottery One of Arkansas' Oldest Industries." *Arkansas Gazette,* 26 December 1937, 15.

"A New American Pottery." *The Clay-Worker* 59 (May 1913): 739–741.

"New Niloak Plant Formerly Opened." *Benton Courier,* 21 February 1929, 1.

"News and Views." *Dixie Magazine* 4 (March 1928): 14.

"News and Views." *Dixie Magazine* 4 (April 1929): 10.

"News From All Over Arkansas." *Arkansas Gazette,* 1 February 1909, 6.

"News From Dixie Land." *The Clay-Worker* 87 (March 1927): 326.

"News Notes on One of Benton's Main Industries – Niloak Pottery." *Benton Courier,* 24 November 1940, 1.

"Niloak, An Exclusive Arkansas Product." *Y.W.C.A. News* 9 (April 19, 1922): 3.

"Niloak Contracts to Supply Government with Clay 'Pigeons.'" *Benton Courier,* 9 September 1943, 1.

"Niloak in CA." *Benton Courier,* 18 October 1923, 1.

"Niloak on Arkansas." *Benton Courier,* 7 June 1923, 1.

"Niloak Manufacturing Necessary Equipment for Rubber Research." *Benton Courier,* 11 October 1942, 1.

"Niloak Opens Plant on Little Rock Highway." *Benton Courier,* 26 June 1947, 1.

"Niloak Pottery Appoints Bakster Representative." *Giftwares & Decorative Furnishings* Volume unknown (November 1931): 55.

"Niloak Pottery Because of Its Color Patterns Is Unique in Art." *Arkansas Democrat,* 17 April 1921, 3 (section II).

"Niloak Pottery Is Unique Product." *Arkansas Gazette,* 19 July 1926, 9.

"Niloak Pottery On Display at Convention." *Benton Courier,* 27 December 1928, 4 .

"Niloak Pottery Sold to School of Plastics." *Benton Courier,* 8 July 1948, 1.

"Niloak Pottery to Erect New Warehouse in Benton: 4,000 Square Feet." *Benton Courier,* 4 September 1947, 1.

"Our Traveling Boosters." *Benton Courier,* 22 November 1923, 1.

Parker, E. L. "Benton is One of the Towns Which Do Things. " *Arkansas Gazette,* 19 August 1906, 11(Section II).

"Pottery Clays Near This City." *Arkansas Gazette,* 3 September 1908, 1.

"Pottery Is Made in Home State Mr. Houck Learns in Colorado." *Benton Courier,* 12 April 1923, 1.

"Pottery Miscellaneous." *Crockery and Glass Journal* Volume Unknown (July 30, 1925): 23.

"Pottery Originator Drowns Near Benton." *Arkansas Gazette,* 8 September 1944, 5.

"President and Secretary to Represent Benton on Arkansas Traveling Exposition." *Benton Courier,* 15 November 1923, 1.

Rainey, Arlene. "The History of Niloak Pottery." In four weekly parts. *Saline County Pacesetter,* March 21 & 28/April 4 & 11, 1973; 2A, 2A, 2A, & 1B.

____. "The Hytens of Saline County, 111 years." *The Saline* 2 (June 1987): 64–69.

Ries, Heinrich. "Kaolin – Its Composition and Use – Peculiar Methods of Gathering and Preparing It for Market." *The Clay-Worker* 33 (March 1900): 243

"Rudy Ganz Sculptural Work Attracts Attention in Ft. Smith." *Benton Courier,* 25 January 1934, 8.

Russo, Susan. "A Collaboration in Clay: Iowa State's Prairie Pottery." *The Palimpsest* 68 (Fall 1987): 112–129.

"Saline's Winnings at the Arkansas State Fair." *Benton Courier,* 3 December 1914, 1.

"Selling Pottery Out of State." *Benton Courier,* 15 February 1923, 1.

Sherwood, Diana. "Arkansas Clay Goes to War." *Arkansas Gazette,* Magazine Section, 28 March 1943, 1–2.

"Tells of Arkansas, The Resourceful." *Arkansas Gazette,* 5 February 1911, 1.

"Tells of his Visit with Mr. Coolidge." *Arkansas Gazette,* 16 December 1923, 15 (section I).

"Theodore Roosevelt, Foremost Citizen of the World, visits the foremost health Resort of the World." *Sentinel Record,* 10 October 1910, 1.

"Third Annual Directory of the China, Earthenware, and Glassware Industries." *Crockery and Glass Journal* 119 (December 1936): Special issue.

"To Be Ready for Centennial Celebration." *Benton Courier,* 28 August 1919, 1.

"To Demostrate Pottery." *Benton Courier,* 7 June 1923, 5.

ADVERTISEMENTS

"Bush Brothers Advertisement." *Benton Courier,* 10 December 1925, 5.

"Eagle Pottery Advertisement." *Benton Courier,* 18 July 1918, 5.

"Eagle Pottery Advertisement." *Benton Courier,* 11 July 1918, 5.

"Hyten's Pottery and Gift Shop Advertisement." *The Panther,* Benton High School, 1945–46 edition.

"Hywood Art Pottery Advertisement." *Benton Courier,* 3 December 1931, 8.

"Hywood Art Pottery Advertisement." *Arkansas Democrat,* 14 December 1931, 7.

"Hywood Art Pottery Advertisement." *Benton Courier,* 17 December 1931, 12.

"Niloak Pottery Advertisement." *Arkansas Gazette,* 13 March 1910, 17.

"Niloak Pottery Advertisement." R.O. Schaefer and Frank N. Henderson. eds. *National Editors' Magazine.* Little Rock: National Editorial Association, 1918.

"Niloak Pottery Advertisement." *Arkansas Gazette: 100 Years; Supplement Commemorating the Founding of Arkansas First Newspaper.* Little Rock: Gazette Publishing Company, 20 November 1919, 220.

"Niloak Pottery Advertisement." *Benton Courier,* 2 January 1919, 5.

"Niloak Pottery Advertisement." *Benton Courier,* 23 September 1926, 4.

"Niloak Pottery Advertisement." *Benton Courier,* 9 December 1926, 5.

"Niloak Pottery Advertisement." *Benton Courier,* 3 November 1932, 8.

"Niloak Pottery Advertisements." *The Pottery, Glass, and Brass Salesman* volume unknown (February and March 1923): pages unknown.

Papers

George C. Merkel, Secretary-Manager, Pine Bluff Chamber of Commerce, Pine Bluff Arkansas to A.W. Parks, Secretary, Arkansas Commission, Century of Progress, Little Rock, Arkansas, September 11, 1933. "Century of Progress Exposition," file 443 of the J.M. Futrell Papers, Governor's Papers, *Guides to the Arkansas History Commission Manuscript Collection,* Book 1, page 103.

Mary D. Hudgins, Hot Springs, Arkansas to Paul Evans, Mill Valley, CA, November 24, 1970. Mary D. Hudgins Collection. Special Collections, University of Arkansas, Fayetteville, Arkansas.

Miscellaneous Records

"A Historical Sketch of Saline County, Arkansas." The Business and Professional Woman's Club, Benton, Arkansas, April 1935.

"Albert Pike Memorial Temple, Inventory of June 2, 1928."

"Article of Agreement and Incorporation." 31 July 1911, Office of Corporate Records, Commercial Filing Division, Secretary of State Office, State Capitol, Little Rock.

"Benton–Insurance Map." The Sanborn Map Company. New York, New York, March 1915.

"Benton–Insurance Map." The Sanborn Map Company. New York, New York, May 1921.

"Benton–Insurance Map." The Sanborn Map Company. New York, New York, July 1930.

"Little Rock Telephone Directory." Southwestern Bell Telephone Company,

Little Rock, January 1933.

"Niloak Business Records, 1940–1950." Private Collection, Benton, Arkansas.

"Record of the Organization and Incorporation of the Niloak Pottery and Tile Company, 1928–1948." Winburn Tile Company Records, Little Rock.

"Saline County." Arkansas Census, 1880.

"Saline County." Arkansas Census, 1910.

"Surrendered of Charter Record." 21 January 1918, Office of Corporate Records, Commercial Filing Division, Secretary of State Office, State Capitol, Little Rock.

Interviews

Alley, Joe. Letter to author, October 1993.

Alley, Joe. Interview by author, 28 December 1992.

Heiss, Virginia. Letter to author, 16 January 1991.

Hutcheson, Albert Vernon. Interview by author, December 1992.

Lewis, Kathy. Letter to author, 30 June 1993.

Long, William F. Interview by author, 17 January 1992.

Leveritt, Joe. Interviewed by author, 1996.

Lewis, Howard S. Six interviews by author: 15 July 1990, 16 September 1990, 12 October 1990, 22 October 1990, 29 October 1990, and 25 April 1991.

Mooney, Lois Evans. Interview by author, 27 February 1991.

Rainey, Arlene Hyten. Interview by author, 13 March 1986.

Sanders, the late Mrs. Frederick (Beatrice). Interview by the author, Little Rock, 4 October 1990.

Stoin, Dale. Letter to author, 24 April 1996.

Stoin, Lydia E. Interview by author, 10 August 1990.

Whiten, Mary F. Interview by author, 27 November 1992.

Winburn, Hardy L., IV. Three interviews by author: 6 March 1989, 10 October 1989, and 5 February 1992.

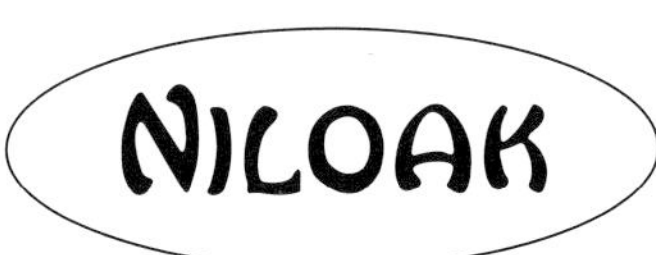

INDEX

This limited index does not include entries such as Charles Hyten, Missionware, Niloak Pottery, locations etc. as they appear throughout the text. Pottery pieces such as vases, bowls, candlesticks, etc. are not indexed as they appear throughout the photographs. Items with (P) at the end designate that the entry is a photograph or image. The entries in this index are arranged alphabetically letter by letter regardless of punctuation.

About the Author

David Edwin Gifford is a historian of Arkansas's early twentieth century pottery companies: Ouachita Pottery of Hot Springs; Niloak Pottery of Benton; and the Camark Pottery of Camden. Gifford has a bachelor of arts in history (1988) from the University of Central Arkansas (Conway) and a master's of arts in public history (1998) from the University of Arkansas at Little Rock. After nearly fifteen years of exhaustive, pioneering research, Gifford is also the author of the *Collector's Guide to Camark Pottery,* Book II (1999), the *Collector's Guide to Camark Pottery* (1997), and the first edition of the *Collector's Encyclopedia of Niloak Pottery* (1993). Mr. Gifford has lectured across the nation and has written articles for publications (national, state, and local) detailing the history of pottery making in Arkansas, including the *Journal of the American Art Pottery Association.* He won the national award, Certificate of Commendation, from the National Association for State and Local History for his *Collector's Encyclopedia of Niloak Pottery* and the "Best Business History" award for his article "The Art of Camark" from the Arkansas Historical Association. He has curated four Arkansas pottery exhibits for the nationally recognized Old State House Museum as well as an Arts and Crafts exhibit for the Arkansas Art Center's Decorative Arts Museum, both in Little Rock. Gifford's current exhibit, "Arkansas Art Pottery: Art, Tradition, and Industry" is at the Old State House Museum until June 2001. David Edwin Gifford is currently working on publishing his 1998 master's thesis entitled: "The Development of and Influences on the Commercial Manufacture of Art Pottery in Arkansas During the Early Twentieth Century." He lives in the historic Hillcrest neighborhood in Little Rock, Arkansas.

COLLECTOR BOOKS

Informing Today's Collector

5035 Standard Encyclopedia of **Carnival Glass**, 6th Ed., Edwards/Carwile $24.95
5036 Standard **Carnival Glass** Price Guide, 11th Ed., Edwards/Carwile $9.95
5272 Standard Encyclopedia of **Opalescent Glass**, 3rd ed., Edwards $24.95
4731 **Stemware Identification**, Featuring Cordials with Values, Florence $24.95
3326 **Very Rare Glassware** of the Depression Years, 3rd Series, Florence $24.95
4732 **Very Rare Glassware** of the Depression Years, 5th Series, Florence $24.95
4656 **Westmoreland Glass**, Wilson $24.95

POTTERY

4927 **ABC Plates & Mugs**, Lindsay $24.95
4929 **American Art Pottery**, Sigafoose $24.95
4630 **American Limoges**, Limoges $24.95
1312 **Blue & White Stoneware**, McNerney $9.95
1958 So. Potteries **Blue Ridge Dinnerware**, 3rd Ed., Newbound $14.95
1959 **Blue Willow**, 2nd Ed., Gaston $14.95
4848 Ceramic **Coin Banks**, Stoddard $19.95
4851 Collectible **Cups & Saucers**, Harran $18.95
4709 Collectible **Kay Finch**, Biography, Identification & Values, Martinez/Frick $18.95
1373 Collector's Encyclopedia of **American Dinnerware**, Cunningham $24.95
4931 Collector's Encyclopedia of **Bauer Pottery**, Chipman $24.95
4932 Collector's Encyclopedia of **Blue Ridge Dinnerware**, Vol. II, Newbound $24.95
4658 Collector's Encyclopedia of **Brush-McCoy Pottery**, Huxford $24.95
5034 Collector's Encyclopedia of **California Pottery**, 2nd Ed., Chipman $24.95
2133 Collector's Encyclopedia of **Cookie Jars**, Roerig $24.95
3723 Collector's Encyclopedia of **Cookie Jars**, Book II, Roerig $24.95
4939 Collector's Encyclopedia of **Cookie Jars**, Book III, Roerig $24.95
4638 Collector's Encyclopedia of **Dakota Potteries**, Dommel $24.95
5040 Collector's Encyclopedia of **Fiesta**, 8th Ed., Huxford $19.95
4718 Collector's Encyclopedia of **Figural Planters & Vases**, Newbound $19.95
3961 Collector's Encyclopedia of **Early Noritake**, Alden $24.95
1439 Collector's Encyclopedia of **Flow Blue China**, Gaston $19.95
3812 Collector's Encyclopedia of **Flow Blue China**, 2nd Ed., Gaston $24.95
3813 Collector's Encyclopedia of **Hall China**, 2nd Ed., Whitmyer $24.95
3431 Collector's Encyclopedia of **Homer Laughlin China**, Jasper $24.95
1276 Collector's Encyclopedia of **Hull Pottery**, Roberts $19.95
3962 Collector's Encyclopedia of **Lefton China**, DeLozier $19.95
4855 Collector's Encyclopedia of **Lefton China**, Book II, DeLozier $19.95
2210 Collector's Encyclopedia of **Limoges Porcelain**, 2nd Ed., Gaston $24.95
2334 Collector's Encyclopedia of **Majolica Pottery**, Katz-Marks $19.95
1358 Collector's Encyclopedia of **McCoy Pottery**, Huxford $19.95
3963 Collector's Encyclopedia of **Metlox Potteries**, Gibbs Jr. $24.95
3837 Collector's Encyclopedia of **Nippon Porcelain**, Van Patten $24.95
2089 Collector's Ency. of **Nippon Porcelain**, 2nd Series, Van Patten $24.95
1665 Collector's Ency. of **Nippon Porcelain**, 3rd Series, Van Patten $24.95
4712 Collector's Ency. of **Nippon Porcelain**, 4th Series, Van Patten $24.95
1447 Collector's Encyclopedia of **Noritake**, Van Patten $19.95
1037 Collector's Encyclopedia of **Occupied Japan**, 1st Series, Florence $14.95
1038 Collector's Encyclopedia of **Occupied Japan**, 2nd Series, Florence $14.95
2088 Collector's Encyclopedia of **Occupied Japan**, 3rd Series, Florence $14.95
2019 Collector's Encyclopedia of **Occupied Japan**, 4th Series, Florence $14.95
2335 Collector's Encyclopedia of **Occupied Japan**, 5th Series, Florence $14.95
4951 Collector's Encyclopedia of **Old Ivory China**, Hillman $24.95
3964 Collector's Encyclopedia of **Pickard China**, Reed $24.95
3877 Collector's Encyclopedia of **R.S. Prussia**, 4th Series, Gaston $24.95
1034 Collector's Encyclopedia of **Roseville Pottery**, Huxford $19.95
1035 Collector's Encyclopedia of **Roseville Pottery**, 2nd Ed., Huxford $19.95
4856 Collector's Encyclopedia of **Russel Wright**, 2nd Ed., Kerr $24.95
4713 Collector's Encyclopedia of **Salt Glaze Stoneware**, Taylor/Lowrance $24.95
3314 Collector's Encyclopedia of **Van Briggle** Art Pottery, Sasicki $24.95
4563 Collector's Encyclopedia of **Wall Pockets**, Newbound $19.95
2111 Collector's Encyclopedia of **Weller Pottery**, Huxford $29.95
3876 Collector's Guide to **Lu-Ray Pastels**, Meehan $18.95
3814 Collector's Guide to **Made in Japan** Ceramics, White $18.95
4646 Collector's Guide to **Made in Japan** Ceramics, Book II, White $18.95
2339 Collector's Guide to **Shawnee Pottery**, Vanderbilt $19.95
1425 **Cookie Jars**, Westfall $9.95
3440 **Cookie Jars**, Book II, Westfall $19.95
4924 Figural & Novelty **Salt & Pepper Shakers**, 2nd Series, Davern $24.95
2379 Lehner's Ency. of **U.S. Marks** on Pottery, Porcelain & China $24.95
4722 **McCoy Pottery**, Collector's Reference & Value Guide, Hanson/Nissen $19.95
4726 **Red Wing Art Pottery**, 1920s–1960s, Dollen $19.95
1670 **Red Wing Collectibles**, DePasquale $9.95
1440 **Red Wing Stoneware**, DePasquale $9.95
1632 **Salt & Pepper Shakers**, Guarnaccia $9.95
5091 **Salt & Pepper Shakers** II, Guarnaccia $18.95
2220 **Salt & Pepper Shakers** III, Guarnaccia $14.95
3443 **Salt & Pepper Shakers** IV, Guarnaccia $18.95
3738 **Shawnee Pottery**, Mangus $24.95
4629 Turn of the Century **American Dinnerware**, 1880s–1920s, Jasper $24.95
3327 **Watt Pottery** – Identification & Value Guide, Morris $19.95

OTHER COLLECTIBLES

4704 Antique & Collectible **Buttons**, Wisniewski $19.95
2269 Antique **Brass & Copper** Collectibles, Gaston $16.95
1880 Antique **Iron**, McNerney $9.95
3872 Antique **Tins**, Dodge $24.95
4845 Antique **Typewriters & Office Collectibles**, Rehr $19.95
1714 **Black** Collectibles, Gibbs $19.95
1128 **Bottle** Pricing Guide, 3rd Ed., Cleveland $7.95
4636 **Celluloid Collectibles**, Dunn $14.95
3718 Collectible **Aluminum**, Grist $16.95
4560 Collectible **Cats**, An Identification & Value Guide, Book II, Fyke $19.95
4852 Collectible **Compact Disc** Price Guide 2, Cooper $17.95
2018 Collector's Encyclopedia of **Granite Ware**, Greguire $24.95
3430 Collector's Encyclopedia of **Granite Ware**, Book 2, Greguire $24.95
4705 Collector's Guide to **Antique Radios**, 4th Ed., Bunis $18.95
3880 Collector's Guide to **Cigarette Lighters**, Flanagan $17.95
4637 Collector's Guide to **Cigarette Lighters**, Book II, Flanagan $17.95
4942 Collector's Guide to **Don Winton Designs**, Ellis $19.95
3966 Collector's Guide to **Inkwells**, Identification & Values, Badders $18.95
4947 Collector's Guide to **Inkwells**, Book II, Badders $19.95
4948 Collector's Guide to **Letter Openers**, Grist $19.95
4862 Collector's Guide to **Toasters** & Accessories, Greguire $19.95
4652 Collector's Guide to **Transistor Radios**, 2nd Ed., Bunis $16.95
4864 Collector's Guide to **Wallace Nutting Pictures**, Ivankovich $18.95
1629 **Doorstops**, Identification & Values, Bertoia $9.95
4567 Figural **Napkin Rings**, Gottschalk & Whitson $18.95
4717 Figural **Nodders**, Includes Bobbin' Heads and Swayers, Irtz $19.95
3968 **Fishing Lure** Collectibles, Murphy/Edmisten $24.95
5259 **Flea Market Trader**, 12th Ed., Huxford $9.95
4944 **Flue Covers**, Collector's Value Guide, Meckley $12.95
4945 **G-Men and FBI Toys** and Collectibles, Whitworth $18.95
5263 **Garage Sale & Flea Market Annual**, 7th Ed. $19.95
3819 **General Store Collectibles**, Wilson $24.95
5159 Huxford's Collectible **Advertising**, 4th Ed $24.95
2216 **Kitchen Antiques**, 1790–1940, McNerney $14.95
4950 The **Lone Ranger**, Collector's Reference & Value Guide, Felbinger $18.95
2026 **Railroad** Collectibles, 4th Ed., Baker $14.95
5167 **Schroeder's Antiques Price Guide**, 17th Ed., Huxford $12.95
5007 **Silverplated Flatware**, Revised 4th Edition, Hagan $18.95
1922 Standard **Old Bottle** Price Guide, Sellari $14.95
5154 Summers' Guide to **Coca-Cola**, 2nd Ed. $19.95
4952 Summers' Pocket Guide to **Coca-Cola** Identifications $9.95
3892 **Toy & Miniature Sewing Machines**, Thomas $18.95
4876 **Toy & Miniature Sewing Machines**, Book II, Thomas $24.95
5144 Value Guide to **Advertising Memorabilia**, 2nd Ed., Summers $19.95
3977 Value Guide to **Gas Station** Memorabilia, Summers & Priddy $24.95
4877 Vintage **Bar Ware**, Visakay $24.95
4935 The W.F. Cody **Buffalo Bill** Collector's Guide with Values $24.95
5281 **Wanted to Buy**, 7th Edition $9.95

This is only a partial listing of the books on antiques that are available from Collector Books. All books are well illustrated and contain current values. Most of these books are available from your local bookseller, antique dealer, or public library. If you are unable to locate certain titles in your area, you may order by mail from COLLECTOR BOOKS, P.O. Box 3009, Paducah, KY 42002-3009. Customers with Visa, Discover or MasterCard may phone in orders from 7:00–5:00 CST, Monday–Friday, Toll Free 1-800-626-5420; www.collectorbooks.com. Add $3.00 for postage for the first book ordered and $0.50 for each additional book. Include item number, title, and price when ordering. Allow 14 to 21 days for delivery.